THE ESSENTIAL THEATRE

THE ESSENTIAL THEATRE

Fourth Edition

OSCAR G. BROCKETT

*University of Texas
at Austin*

Holt, Rinehart and Winston, Inc.

*New York   Chicago   San Francisco   Philadelphia
Montreal   Toronto   London   Sydney   Tokyo*

Library of Congress Cataloging-in-Publication Data

Brockett, Oscar Gross, 1923–
  The essential theatre.

  Bibliography: p.
  Includes index.
    1. Theater—History. 2. Drama—History and
criticism. 3. Theater—United States—History—20th
century. I. Title.
PN2101.B72 1988   792'.09   87-294

ISBN 0-03-013012-3

Requests for permission to make copies of any part of the work should be mailed to:
Permissions
Holt, Rinehart and Winston, Inc.
111 Fifth Avenue
New York, NY 10003
PRINTED IN THE UNITED STATES OF AMERICA
8 9 039 9 8 7 6 5 4

Holt, Rinehart and Winston, Inc.
The Dryden Press
Saunders College Publishing

To the Memory of my Wife: Lenyth Brockett

Front Cover Photograph: Steve Sharp
Back Cover Photograph: Henry L. Krantzler

Chapter Opening Photograph Credits

Chapter 1: *The Mystery Plays,* directed by Mary B. Robinson, John Rensenhouse as Adam; Angela Bassett as Eve; Christopher McCann as God. (Courtesy Hartford Stage Company.)

Chapter 2: Arthur Miller's *Death of a Salesman* (1984) starring Dustin Hoffman, Kate Reid, and John Malkovitch. Directed by Michael Rudman. (Photo by Inge Morath/Magnum.)

Chapter 3: Beth Henley's *Crimes of the Heart.* Priscilla Hake Lauris as Lenny; Kamella Tate as Babe; Joan Stuart-Morris as Meg. Directed by James Moll. (Photo by Hank Kranzler. Courtesy Oregon Shakespearean Festival.)

Chapter 4: *Oedipus the King* at the State Theatre, Darmstadt (West Germany). Design by Franz Mertz. (Courtesy German Information Center.)

Chapter 5: A booth stage such as might have been used by traveling players during the Middle Ages. Redrawing of an illustration in a fifteenth-century manuscript. (*L'Ancienne France: Le Théâtre* . . . 1887.)

Chapter 6: Final scene of Shakespeare's *All's Well That Ends Well* at the Oregon Shakespearean Festival, 1985. Directed by Tony Amendola; costumes by Merrily Murray-Walsh; setting by William Bloodgood; lighting by James Sale. (Photo by Hank Kranzler. Courtesy Oregon Shakespearean Festival.)

Chapter 7: Dion Boucicault's melodrama, *The Octoroon,* 1859.

Chapter 8: Ibsen's *The Wild Duck* as performed at the Théâtre Libre, Paris, 1889. Directed by André Antoine.

Chapter 9: Samuel Beckett's *Endgame.* Directed by the author at the Schiller Theater Workshop, West Berlin. (Courtesy German Information Center.)

Chapter 10: Shakespeare's *A Midsummer Night's Dream* as directed by Liviu Ciulei at the Guthrie Theatre, Minneapolis. Production designed by Beni Montresor. (Photo by Joe Giannetti. Courtesy Guthrie Theatre.)

Chapter 11: Ibsen's *Peer Gynt* at the Dusseldorf Schauspielhaus, 1985. Directed by Michael Grüner. (Photo by Lore Bermbach. Courtesy German Information Center.)

Chapter 12: Rehearsal of Arthur Miller's *After the Fall.* At right, Miller; Jason Robards seated on box, with Elia Kazan standing beside him. (Photo by Inge Morath/Magnum.)

Chapter 13: Bill Irwin, as Arlecchino in a *commedia* play, *The Three Cuckolds,* at the La Jolla Playhouse. (Photo by Micha Langer; courtesy La Jolla Playhouse.)

Chapter 14: Ibsen's *Peer Gynt* as produced ta the Thalia Theater, Hamburg. (Photo by Hermann J. Baus. Courtesy German Information Center.)

Chapter 15: *Kabuki Medea,* conceived, directed, and designed by Shozo Sato at the Wisdom Bridge Theatre, Chicago. (Photo by Jennifer Girard. Courtesy Wisdom Bridge Theatre.)

Chapter 16: Karel Capek's *The Insect Comedy.* Design by Josef Svoboda. (Photo by Jaromír Svoboda.)

Appendix: *Big River: The Adventures of Huckleberry Finn,* a musical by William Hauptman and Roger Miller. Ben Halley, Jr. as Jim and Tuck Milligan as Huck Finn. Directed by Des McAnuff. (Photo by Micha Langer. Courtesy La Jolla Playhouse.)

Preface

Behind this edition of *The Essential Theatre* lies almost twenty-five years of publication: the book was published first (in 1976) as an abridged version of *The Theatre: An Introduction*, which appeared originally in 1964. *The Essential Theatre* has now taken on an identity of its own, this being the fourth edition.

Like the earlier versions, this edition is divided into three parts. But within those parts, a number of major changes have been made. The chapter entitled "Performance, Audience, and Critic" has been moved forward (now as the second rather than the final chapter), since many instructors wish students to attend plays and write reviews throughout the course and need this material early rather than at the end of the course. The section on the playwright has also been moved forward and integrated with the chapter on scripts and play analysis. A list of questions designed to assist students in analyzing scripts has also been added to this third chapter.

The greatest number of changes have been made in Part II. The focus in these chapters is now on various types of theatrical experience rather than on a connected account of the theatre's historical development. The chronological arrangement has been maintained, but there is no longer an attempt to provide an overview of the entire history of Western theatre. Furthermore, one Oriental form (Japanese Noh) is examined, not only to familiarize students with that form but also to offer a perspective on Western theatrical conventions. The discussions still consider the historical context, but the major emphasis is now experiential. The number of chapters in Part II has been reduced from nine to seven, but each of the chapters examines in some detail at least two contrasting types of plays and theatrical experiences. One of the chapters is devoted to two major examples of popular theatre: commedia dell'arte and nineteenth-century melodrama.

Part III on contemporary theatrical practices now contains six rather than seven chapters, the material on the producer having been integrated into the chapter on directing and that on the playwright with the chapter on scripts. In all of these chapters, greater attention is paid to the function of each theatre art and the skills and training needed by its practitioners. In all the chapters, additional concrete examples help to clarify the discussions. At the ends of chapters, a number of questions encourage students not merely to attend the theatre but to examine critically what they see there.

Many new illustrations have been added and carefully integrated with the written text throughout. The Appendix, summarizing opportunities open to those who wish to work in the theatre, has been retained, though revised to reflect changes in the profession. The Bibliography, listing books that may be useful in further study or as sources for additional information, has been updated.

In writing this book, I have assumed that students will both read plays and attend theatrical performances. Ideally, students would be able to read a script and then see that script performed. In actuality, this is seldom possible, but reading a play and experiencing a performance, even if not of the same script, illustrate the differences between the text on the printed page and the enacted script on the stage—the differences between drama and theatre.

Recognizing that students have not read a wide range of plays, I have selected most of the examples cited in *The Essential Theatre* from fourteen scripts included in a companion anthology, *Plays for the Theatre* (5th edition), edited by Oscar G. Brockett and published by Holt, Rinehart and Winston in 1988. These scripts also serve as the foundation for discussing varied types of theatrical experience. The plays are: *Oedipus the King, The Menaechmi, The Second Shepherds' Play, The Shrine in the Field* (a Noh drama), *Hamlet, Tartuffe, The Servant of Two Masters, The Wild Duck,* "*The Hairy Ape,*" *The Good Woman of Setzuan, Death of a Salesman, Happy Days, A Raisin in the Sun,* and *Fool for Love.* Those instructors who prefer to have students read a different but parallel set of plays may wish to consider *World Drama,* edited by Oscar G. Brockett and Mark Pape, published by Holt, Rinehart and Winston in 1984. It includes seventeen plays: *Antigone, Iphigeneia at Aulis, Lysistrata, Pseudolus, Everyman, Matsukaze* (a Noh play), *King Lear, The School for Wives, The Recruiting Officer, Uncle Tom's Cabin, A Doll's House, Major Barbara, The Little Foxes, Life of Galileo, Krapp's Last Tape, The Strong Breed* (an African play), *Slave Ship,* and *Buried Child.*

The Essential Theatre is designed to meet the needs of two kinds of courses: introduction to theatre (that is, an overview serving as a unifying foundation for students who expect to major in Theatre—the future theatre makers), and theatre appreciation (that is, an overview providing insight into, and understanding of, theatre for audience members—the future theatregoers). While these two types of courses may cover the same basic subjects, they usually do so from somewhat different angles. Thus, I have assumed that individual instructors will use the material in ways suited to their needs. I have sought to provide a logically organized, comprehensive overview of theatre, but instructors need not rigidly follow my sequence or use all of the material in this book. For example, time or individual preference may keep some instructors from assigning all of Part II, while others may wish to assign Part III prior to Part II. My goal has been to provide helpful discussions of topics pertinent to introductory courses rather than to prescribe how the courses should be organized.

It would be impossible to list all of those to whom I am indebted. The bibliography indicates most of the sources I have used, and captions indicate those persons or organizations who have permitted me to include these illustrations. A few individuals deserve special mention. I want to thank my colleagues for their insightful and useful comments: Doug Cummins, Pan American University; John Ford, Foothill College; Terence Gleeson, Penn State University, Delaware County Campus; James Hawes, Radford University; R. Eugene Jackson, University of South Alabama; Jack McCullough, Trenton State College; Dale Miller, Purdue University; Tice Miller, University of Nebraska at Lincoln; William Shankweiler, Boise State University; Roman Tymchyshyn, University of Illinois at Urbana-Champaign. I also thank those who assisted me in proofreading and indexing: William Stotts, Richard Runkel, Michael Barnes, and Brian Lieske. Finally, I would like to thank my editor at Holt, Rinehart and Winston, Karen Dubno, for her guidance and encouragement, and my senior project manager, Sondra Greenfield, for producing this book.

Oscar G. Brockett

Austin, Texas
October 1987

Contents

Part III
THEATRICAL PRODUCTION   271

11

Theatrical Space and Production Design   273

12

Producing and Directing   291

13

Acting   317

Appendix

Opportunities to Work in the Theatre 408

Part I

FOUNDATIONS

Theatre is a complex art with a recorded history going back at least 2500 years. Understandably, over such a long span of time, it has undergone many changes and followed extremely diverse paths. Its long history invites questions about theatre's fundamental nature—what it is and what its varied manifestations have in common, no matter when or where they have occurred. It also invites questions about the theatre's appeals—why for so long it has continued to attract audiences. In addition, it provokes questions about how we judge theatrical performances—why we think one production is good and another bad.

Let us begin our look at the theatre, then, by examining some basic characteristics of theatre: its nature and function; its relation to other forms of art; criteria for judging performances; the nature of dramatic action; how scripts, the usual starting point of theatrical production, are structured; and other related topics. This exploration should provide a foundation for further study—especially the varieties of theatrical experience and the processes of theatrical production.

The Nature of Theatre

1

Just how and when theatre originated is uncertain, but the earliest records of human activities suggest that by that time people had already developed rituals that used all the elements required for a fully developed theatre: a performance space, performers, masks or makeup, costumes, music, dance, and an audience. The function of these early rites was only incidentally theatrical, however, since they were addressed to supernatural forces thought to control the return of spring, success in hunting or war, or the fertility of human beings and the environment. Although theatre probably had its beginnings in such rites, it undoubtedly stemmed in part from other impulses, such as the love of storytelling and mimicry. From these shadowy origins, the theatre eventually evolved into an activity prized for itself.

Though its origins may be obscure, the theatre has been present in some form throughout human history. At times, it has been highly developed and highly prized; at others, it has been reduced to little more than a skeleton existing on the fringes of respectability. It has as often been denounced as praised, and its value—even its right to exist—has frequently been questioned.

During most of its existence, the theatre has had to contend with contrasting responses: on the one hand, it has been praised as entertaining and insightful; on the other hand, it has been denounced as morally corrupt or as distracting audiences from more important things. This ambivalence has been encouraged in part by theatrical terminology (such as *play, show,* and *acting*) which suggests that theatre is the product of grown-ups who have prolonged their childhood by dressing up and playing games to divert themselves and others. Furthermore, because plays are fictional, they have often been denounced as a form of lying; and because they tend to depict human crises (frequently involving deception or violence), they often have been considered morally suspect (even corrupting). Contrarily, in almost all periods, some segments of society have considered theatre to be not only an acceptable form of entertainment but also one of the most effective means available to human beings in their attempts to understand themselves and their world.

The theatre, then, has had both its detractors and its strong advocates. Nevertheless, those who value it often find themselves on the defensive with those who question whether it has any valid place in a college curriculum or whether a world dominated by film and television would miss theatre were it to disappear altogether.

The Basic Elements of Theatre

One reason for varying responses can be found in the theatre's range and diversity, which are evident in the three basic elements of theatre: what is performed (script, scenario, or plan); the performance (including all the processes involved in its creation and presentation); and the audience (the perceivers). Each is essential, and each affects conceptions of the whole—the theatre.

What is performed may be extremely varied, running the gamut from variety acts to Shakespearean tragedy. A single entertainer may sing a song, play music on an instrument, dance, turn cartwheels, or juggle; or several performers may improvise an event or act out a written script. Any or all of these things may occur in a place we call a theatre. Probably for this reason, we have great difficulty in defining precisely what is meant by *theatre* or in specifying where theatre ceases and some other type of activity begins. Eric Bentley has argued that the various definitions of *theatre* can be reduced to: A performs B for C.

Although variety entertainment is often labeled theatrical, most frequently theatre is thought to involve some degree of storytelling or impersonation. Typically, it utilizes a written text. Nevertheless, theatre does not require a script or dialogue, but even if we restrict theatre to performances in some degree dramatic, we would still be faced with great diversity, for dramatic entertainments may range through improvised scenes, pantomimes, vaudeville sketches, musical plays, and spoken dramas. Furthermore, they may be brief or lengthy; they may deal with the commonplace or the unusual, the comic or the serious. With so much diversity, it is not surprising that attitudes about the theatre very markedly, or that some people think of theatre primarily as popular entertainment whereas others locate the essence of theatre in its capacity to offer penetrating insights into human behavior. If we are to understand

Marcel Marceau, probably the world's best-known mime performer, evolves and performs his own wordless one-character scripts. (Courtesy French Cultural Services.)

the theatre, we must acknowledge its great range and recognize that its potential (like that of most human creations) can be developed in many ways, some desirable and others undesirable.

The second ingredient, *the performance,* is equally complex and diverse. It translates the potential of a script, scenario, or improvised plan into actuality. What the audience sees when it goes to the theatre is a meshing of script or plan with theatrical processes. The performance takes place in a space—which may vary from street, park, or playground to a building intended specifically for theatrical performances. In size, spaces may vary from those accommodating fewer than 100 persons to those (as in ancient Greece) seating 15,000–20,000 persons. Configuration also varies: it may permit spectators to surround the performers, require the audience to sit in rows facing a platform on which the performance occurs, or it may utilize other audience-performer configurations, each of which alters the total theatrical experience. (This subject is explored more fully in Chapter 11.)

A performance normally requires the creative efforts and cooperation of many persons: playwright, director, actors, designers, and technicians. Each component involved in this process may be manipulated to create quite varied effects. All the components may be so skillfully integrated that the spectator is aware only of a single unified impression; or one or more of the components—such as acting or spectacle—may completely overshadow the others. The components may be handled in a way easily understood by almost everyone, or in ways so strange that all but the most sophisticated are puzzled. A performance may therefore seem to one part of the audience clear and entertaining and to another overly obvious and entirely unoriginal; conversely, what to one group may seem strange and incomprehensible may by another be judged insightful and brilliant. Although the possibilities and results of performance may be infinite, the beginning point of the theatrical experience has been reduced to its essentials by Peter Brook in his book *The Empty Space*: "I can take any empty space and call it a bare stage. A man walks across this empty space whilst someone else is watching him, and this is all that is needed for an act of theatre to be engaged."

The third basic ingredient of the theatre is *the audience,* because until material is performed and seen by a public, we usually do not call it theatre. For all the arts, a public is imperative, but for most, this public may be thought of as individuals—the reader of a novel or poem, the viewer of a painting or a piece of sculpture—each of whom may experience the work in isolation. But a theatre audience is assembled as a group at a given time and place to experience a performance.

The audience affects the theatre in many ways, perhaps most importantly through the immediate feedback it provides the performers. The continuous interaction between stage and auditorium is a distinctive characteristic of theatre and a major cause of variations in performances from night to night. Audiences also affect the theatre by giving or withholding support. The members of an audience vary widely in background and taste. Some want merely to be entertained; they want to forget their personal cares and the problems of the world around them; they view the theatre as a form of recreation or escape. Others wish the theatre to provide new insights and provocative perceptions about significant topics, to advocate action about political and social issues, or to increase awareness of, and sensitivity to, others and their surroundings. The latter are apt to support a different kind of performance than are those seeking escapist entertainment. Ultimately, audiences make their opinions known through their attendance or nonattendance. They support what appeals to them and fail to support what they do not understand or like. Thus, audience tastes significantly influence both what is performed and how it is performed.

Audience and performance at the Utah Shakespearean Festival. (Photo by Boyd D. Redington. Courtesy Utah Shakespearean Festival.)

Since there is such diversity in what is performed, in performances, and in audiences, we should acknowledge that not all theatre is likely to appeal to all segments of the public and that responses to theatre are inescapably varied.

Popular Entertainment and Art

Perhaps the reasons for this will become clearer if we divide theatre into two broad (though admittedly oversimplified) categories: *popular entertainment* and *theatre as an art form*. The two may and often do overlap, and what was at one time looked upon as mere popular diversion may later be considered a significant work of art.

As the term implies, popular entertainment seeks primarily to provide diversion for a mass audience. Either consciously or unconsciously, it draws on the dominant attitudes, prejudices, and interests of the day; it usually employs easily recognizable (even stereotyped) characters, situations, and theatrical conventions, while manipulating them with sufficient novelty to be entertaining but usually without offering important new perceptions or raising any disturbing questions that challenge the audience's views. For these reasons, popular entertainment provides important insights into the dominant attitudes and values of its time. But because it seeks primarily to provide diversion, it can easily be grouped with games, sports, and other recreational pastimes. This is not to imply that recreation for large numbers of people is unimportant—to divert audiences from their cares and to offer release from the routine of existence is valuable both psychologically and sociologically. Nor is it meant to suggest that theatre need not be entertaining; if it cannot capture and hold attention, it cannot command a following.

The musical *Cats*, with text by T. S. Eliot and music by Andrew Lloyd-Webber, has become one of the most successful pieces of popular entertainment in recent years. Directed by Trevor Nunn. (Photo by Martha Swope.)

Dramatic performance does share many characteristics with sports and games. All pit one side against another, build suspense, and decide the outcome. Games and theatre also share a dependence on *conventions*—that is, agreed-upon and understood rules, practices, and procedures. In football, the size and shape of the playing field, the number of downs and players, the uniforms, the system of scoring, and the length of the game are conventions that are understood both by players and spectators. (Imagine watching a football game without knowing these conventions.) The theatre depends on conventions, too, although more flexible ones: the stage as a place where fictional events occur; the use of scenery to represent locales; the use in some periods of masks, or of males to play female roles; the singing (rather than speaking) of the text in opera. If we introduce new (or alter old) conventions, we are apt to confuse the spectators, at least at first, although the changes may be accepted once understood. Despite these similarities between games and theatre, we usually do not confuse them, in part because of differences in their conventions, but also because in most scripted drama the outcome is predetermined before the performance begins (Hamlet always avenges the death of his father and dies himself). In addition, the responses of audiences to the characters and their struggles are determined by information revealed during the performance, whereas in games loyalties that existed before the action begins determine which side spectators will root for.

While much of the theatre's appeal lies in its ability to entertain, if it does not offer additional appeals, it may be (and often is) dismissed as insignificant. Therefore, a complete picture of the theatre's potential demands that it also be looked at as one of the arts. But what is *art?* Probably no term has been discussed so frequently or defined so ambiguously. Until the eighteenth century, *art* was used almost always to designate the systematic application of knowledge or skill to achieve some predetermined result. The word is still used in this sense when we speak of the art (or craft) of medicine, politics, or persuasion. During the eighteenth century, it became customary to divide the arts into two groups, "useful" and "fine." Into the latter category were placed literature, painting, sculpture, architecture, music, and dance. At the same time, the idea arose that while the useful arts may easily be taught and mastered, the fine arts, as products of genius, cannot be reduced to rules or principles that, if learned, would equip one to create significant works of art. As a result, since about 1800 art has often been depicted as too complex to be fully understandable. Many critics also have implied that only those with truly superior sensitivity can fully appreciate art and that the average person often mistakes some inferior product (usually some type of popular entertainment) for authentic artistic expression. Thus, those who think of the theatre as an art form are often contemptuous of those who think of it as "show business." (Similarly, in the visual arts, a distinction is usually made betwen works considered worthy of the museum or gallery and those created for advertisements or as illustrations; and in music, a clear line is usually drawn between compositions considered appropriate to a symphony orchestra and those played by a rock band.)

If no definition of art is universally accepted, some of its distinguishing characteristics can be explored by comparing it with other approaches to experience. First and most broadly, art is one way whereby human beings seek to understand their world. In this respect, it may be compared with history, philosophy, or science, each of which strives to discover and record patterns in human experience. All of these approaches recognize that human experience is composed of innumerable happenings that have occurred to an infinite number of people through countless generations, and that each person's life is made up of a series of momentary occurrences, many seemingly coming about wholly by chance. One question they seek to answer is: What significant patterns can be perceived behind the apparent randomness? The methods used to discover truths differ in each field, but they are always directed toward discovering those relationships that reveal order within what would otherwise seem chaotic. As one approach, art shapes perceptions about human experience into forms (or patterned relationships) that help to order our views about humanity and the world in which we live.

There are, however, significant differences in the methods used in various approaches to human experience. Historians, philosophers, and scientists isolate a limited problem, do their research or experiments, and then set down their conclusions in logical, expository prose; they direct their appeal primarily to the intellect. Artists, on the other hand, work primarily from their own perceptions and seek to involve the audience's emotions, imagination, and intellect directly. A play consequently shows events as though occurring at that moment before our eyes; we absorb them in the way we absorb life itself—through their direct operation on our senses. Art differs from life by stripping away irrelevant details and organizing events so that they compose a connected pattern. Thus, a play illuminates and comments (though sometimes indirectly) on human experience even as it creates it. Nevertheless, a play often is not perceived to be a way of knowing and understanding because we are aware that it is fiction.

How, then, can imagined stories be ways of knowing and understanding? The key is probably the one offered by Shakespeare in *As You Like It* (II, 7): "All the world's a stage, /And all the men and women merely players." Not only does this speech state that we may think of the world as a stage upon which each person plays a role, but conversely, that the stage is a symbolization of the world where we can see reflected the fundamental patterns of human behavior. What we see onstage may not be factually real, but rather distillations of types of human beings, situations, motivations, and actions. Thus, though fictional, plays may provide insights about humans that are more "truthful" than those obtained from the statistical study of actual human beings.

As spectators, our responses to a play differ from those to an actual event. Just as we do not mistake a statue for a real person, we do not mistake stage action for reality. Rather, we usually view a play with what Samuel Taylor Coleridge called a "willing suspension of disbelief." By this he meant that, while we know the events of a play are not real, we agree for the moment not to disbelieve their reality. We are nevertheless not moved to immediate action by what we see on the stage as we might be by real-life events. We watch one man seemingly kill another, but make no attempt to rescue the victim or to call the police. We are aware that we are watching actors impersonate characters, but we acquiesce in granting them temporary reality. This state in which we are sufficiently detached to view an artistic event semiobjectively is sometimes called *esthetic distance*. At the same time, the distance must not be so great as to induce indifference. Therefore, while a degree of detachment is necessary, involvement is of equal importance. This feeling of kinship is sometimes called *empathy*. Thus, we watch a play with a double sense of concern and detachment. It is both a removed and an intensified reaction of a kind seldom possible outside esthetic experience. Another way of putting this is that art lifts us above the everyday fray and gives us something like a "god's-eye" view of experience.

Some attributes of art, then, are these: art is one method of discovering and presenting patterns that provide insights, perceptions, and understanding about ourselves and our world; art is one form of knowledge. In addition, it is an imaginative reshaping of experience that operates directly on our senses in a way that involves us both esthetically and empathically, allowing us to be simultaneously at a distance from and involved in the experience so that we participate in it emotionally even as we gain insights from it. Art lays claim, then, to being serious (in the sense of having something important to communicate), but because its methods are so indirect (it presents experience but does not attempt to explain all of its ramifications), it is often ambiguous, only partially understood, and open to alternative interpretations.

Special Qualities of Theatre

Even within the fine arts, theatre holds a special place as the art that comes closest to life as it is lived from day to day. As Shakespeare has Hamlet say (III, 2), "the purpose of playing . . . is to hold . . . the mirror up to nature; to show virtue her own feature, scorn her own image, and the very age and body of the time his form and pressure." Not only is human experience and action its subject, theatre uses live human beings (actors) as its primary means of communicating with an audience. Quite often the speech of the performers approximates that heard in real life, and the actors may wear costumes that might be seen on the street; they may perform in settings that recall actual places. Not all theatre attempts to be so realistic, and at times it may even approximate other arts (such as dance, music, or visual arts), but it remains the art most capable of recreating typical human experience.

Such *lifelikeness* is also one of the reasons theatre is often insufficiently valued: a play, a setting, and the acting may so resemble what is familiar to spectators that they fail to recognize how difficult it is to produce this lifelikeness skillfully. To a certain degree all people are actors; they vary the roles they play (almost moment by moment) according to the people they encounter and their relationship to them (parent, priest, friend, lover, enemy, etc.). In doing so, they utilize the same tools as the actor— voice, speech, movement, gesture, psychological motivation, and the like. Consequently, most persons do not fully recognize the problems faced by a skilled actor.

The theatre further resembles life in being *ephemeral.* As in life, each episode is experienced and then immediately becomes part of the past. When the performance ends, its essence can never be fully recaptured, since—unlike a film, novel, painting, or statue, each of which remains relatively unchanged—a theatrical production when it ends lives only in the play script, program, pictures, reviews, and memories of those who were present.

Theatre resembles life also in being the most *objective* of the arts, since characteristically it presents both outer and inner experience through speech and action. As in life, it is through listening and watching that we come to know characters both externally and internally. What we learn about their minds, personalities, and motivations comes from what they say and do and from what others tell us about them. Thus, we absorb a theatrical performance the way we do a scene from real life.

Additionally, the theatre can be said to resemble life because of the *complexity of its means,* for like a scene from life itself it is made up of intermingled sound, movement, place, dress, lighting, and so on. Another way of putting this is to say that theatre draws on all the other arts: literature in its script; painting, architecture, and sculpture (and sometimes dance) in its spectacle; and speech and music in its audible aspects. In some ways, then, theatre encompasses all the other arts.

Furthermore, theatre is psychologically the most *immediate* of the arts. Several contemporary critics have argued that the essence of the theatre (what distinguishes it from other dramatic media such as television and

Shakespeare's *King Lear* is usually considered one of the world's greatest works of art. Shown here is the storm scene on the heath with the Fool, Lear, and Edgar. Directed by Karl Rempelfort at the Rührfestspiele, Recklinghausen. (Courtesy German Information Center.)

film) lies in the simultaneous presence of live actors and spectators in the same room.

On the surface, theatre may seem to have several drawbacks compared with other dramatic media. For example, more people often see a filmed or televised show on a single evening than attend the live theatre during an entire year. In fact, the theatre may be likened to a handcrafted product in an age of mass production, for it must be recreated at each performance and for a relatively small group of spectators. Contrarily, thousands of copies of a film may be printed and shown throughout the world simultaneously and year after year, and a televised program may be videotaped and repeated at will. These media, too, may make performers world-famous almost overnight, whereas the actor who works only in the theatre may build up an international reputation only gradually and over a considerable period of time.

Nevertheless, the theatre has important attributes that television and film cannot duplicate. The most significant of these are the three-dimensionality of the theatrical experience and the interrelationship between performers and spectators. In film and television, the camera is used to select what the audience can see and to ensure that it will see nothing more; the camera can frame the picture so as to restrict our view to a facial expression, the twitch of a hand, or a small object. In the theatre, the director uses various means to focus the audience's attention on a specific character or object, but, because the full acting area remains visible and close-ups are impossible, the audience may choose to watch something else. Perhaps most important, during a live performance there is continuous interaction between performer and spectator; the pacing of a scene, for example, affects how the audience responds, and in turn the audience response may stimulate the actors to alter the pace. Because of such interaction, each performance differs in many details. Thus, the audience plays a far more active role in the theatre than it does in film or television. Ultimately, there is a fundamental difference in the psychological responses aroused by electronic media and theatre, because the former present pictures of events whereas the latter performs the actual events in what amounts to the same space as that occupied by the audience. This difference results in one unique characteristic of the theatre: the simultaneous presence of live actors and audience.

These special qualities—lifelikeness, ephemerality, objectivity, complexity, and immediacy—explain many of the theatre's weaknesses and strengths.

The Problem of Value in Art

Despite all that one can say about its nature and value, art is still not widely understood by the general public. In a society preoccupied with material success, as ours has been, art does not appear to be very useful, since it does not produce such obvious benefits as those of medicine or engineering. Even artists (including performers) who are widely known and accepted are usually admired more for their commercial success than for their artistic talents, having shown that they can command high salaries or sell their works for large sums. Most artists never achieve financial security; consequently, parents typically try to discourage their children from seeking a career in the arts. By the time they reach adulthood, most Americans have suppressed the artistic inclinations they may have had. Thus, far too many adults are cut off from, or are only partly aware of, one of people's primary ways of knowing the world and understanding themselves.

Still, it is difficult to defend art on the basis of its immediate utility. Art ultimately must be valued because of its capacity to improve the quality of life—by increasing our sensitivity to others and our surroundings, by sharpening our perceptions, by reshaping our values so that moral and societal concerns take precedence over materialistic goals. Of all the arts, theatre has perhaps the greatest potential as a humanizing force, for at its best it asks us to enter imaginatively into the lives of others so we may understand their aspirations and motivations. Through role-playing (either in daily life or in the theatre), we come to understand who and what we are and to see ourselves in relation to others. Perhaps most important, in a world given increasingly to violence, the value of being able to understand and feel for others as human beings cannot be overestimated, because violence depends on dehumanizing others so that we no longer think of their hopes, aims, and sufferings but treat them as objects to be manipulated or on whom to vent our frustrations. To know (emotionally, imaginatively, and intellectually) what it means to be human in the broadest sense ought to be one of the primary goals of both education and life; and for reaching this goal, no approach has greater potential than theatre, since humanity is its subject and human beings its primary medium.

But the theatre's great potential is not always or automatically fulfilled. Those working in theatre often are preoccupied with the immediate process or with egotistical goals, while audiences often concentrate only on surface qualities. Furthermore, the skill and content of theatrical performances are not always of high quality.

Unfortunately, quality—unlike quantity—is not measurable except subjectively. And subjectivity takes us into the realm of taste, judgment, and a host of variables about which agreement is seldom possible. There are many tastes, many degrees of complexity, and a wide range of quality. But if we cannot expect ever to achieve complete agreement, we each can sharpen our own perceptions of the theatre and its processes. To do this, we need first to understand the theatre and how it works. Second, we need to develop some approach through which we can judge the relative merits of what is performed and how it is performed. Then, we should work to encourage the theatrical values that seem important to us.

Sound judgment about the theatre usually depends on knowledge about, and experience with, plays and performances. This book is designed to assist in this process by providing an overview of the theatre in its various aspects: how plays are structured; the varieties of theatre experience, both past and present; how the theatre functions today; and how each theatre artist makes use of available materials and techniques. Taken all together, these discussions should provide a foundation for intelligent and sensitive reactions to the theatre.

Performance, Audience, and Critic

2

When a play is performed on stage, the production represents a specific visualization of the script. If this visualization is effective, it frees the spectators from the necessity of imagining everything for themselves, for the demands and implications of the script have been given concrete form. Bringing to life all the details (the actions of the characters, how they are dressed, the appearance of the setting, the stage business, the lighting, and so on) leaves the spectators free to experience the developing action, the relationships among the characters, the rhythms, and the overall meaning of the drama. The spectators are allowed to absorb the play as they would a scene from real life—through watching and listening—rather than, as in reading, seeking inwardly both to see and to hear everything.

Nevertheless, performance has its drawbacks. The spectators must allow themselves to be carried along at whatever pace the performers set, and spectators who miss a line or piece of business cannot go back and recover it. In the theatre there are no instant replays. Readers may proceed at their own pace, turn back, or look ahead. Additionally, readers may decide that there are several valid (or possible) interpretations of a line or scene, whereas the director must choose one version and ignore the others. Nevertheless, a performance, because it is much more complex than a script, is, when all goes well, far more rewarding than a reading.

Not all productions go well. The director may have had to cast actors not wholly suited to their roles; the designers may not have captured sought-after qualities; the performance space may make hearing and seeing difficult. Because of the numbers of persons involved, the precise coordination required to integrate all the elements moment by moment, and the unpredictability of personnel and equipment, it is extremely difficult to keep productions free of errors. Consequently, a production differs somewhat at each performance. Often audiences are unaware of mistakes, but even if they are aware, they usually do not let minor flaws seriously affect their response to the total performance. It is the challenge of trying to control the artistic medium and audience response—even as one acknowledges the unpredictability of audiences, performers, and equipment, both from moment to moment and from performance to performance—that makes the task of the director so challenging.

Watching a Performance

There are no rules about how to watch a performance. Watching intelligently is primarily a matter of being willing to give one's full attention to what is happening on the stage moment by moment and noting meaningful patterns as they emerge.

Attending a play differs in several ways from going to a film. A live performance has more of a sense of special occasion. Except in large cities, live performances are not always readily available. One must usually buy tickets in advance and go to the theatre at a specified time, since performances are not continuous. Because tickets for a live performance usually prescribe the seat in which one is to sit, much more attention is paid than at movies to such matters as ushering spectators to their seats. At live performances, spectators are also usually provided with programs that give information about the cast, production staff, and the play. Since today the stage is seldom hidden by a curtain, the spectator can usually examine the stage and scenery and gain some idea of the production approach before the performance begins. Frequently, music is used to get the audience into the appropriate mood. Most live performances have one or more intermissions, which permit audience members to leave their seats, mingle, and discuss what they have seen or what is to come.

As a performance unfolds, many questions raised when a play is read are answered automatically (at least for this production of the play): What is the appearance of the stage setting? How are the characters dressed? At what tempo does the action proceed? How do the characters move and relate to each other? Unlike a film, in which the setting is usually realistic (often photographed actual places), a live performance may use little scenery. Therefore, the spectator may still need to imagine much that is merely suggested by a few set pieces, projected images, lighting, or dialogue; the same basic setting may be used to represent different locales. Costumes may be realistic, or the actors may wear ordinary street dress while the audience must imagine them to be biblical or historical personages. Often the audience is asked to project itself into visual styles that vary considerably from ordinary modes of perception. These and other conventions may make great demands on the spectator's imagination.

In addition to using imagination, the spectators must be able to concentrate. Unless they watch intently, letting their eyes and ears be carried along by the production, the spectators may fail to comprehend what is significant in the complex stage picture, all of which remains visible since directors cannot use close-ups, directional shots, and other filmic devices to force the audience to see only what they wish it to.

The Audience and Critical Perspective

Each time we see a performance, no matter how simple or complex it may be, we pass some kind of judgment on it, however subjective or fleeting. Most playgoers probably restrict themselves to generalized responses such as "I really enjoyed it" or "I thought the actors did a good job with a weak play." More sophisticated responses require an analytical approach to each element that has gone into the production (the script, the directing, acting, scenery, costumes, lighting) as well as appropriate criteria for judging both the individual elements and the overall achievement. In other words, thoughtful criticism is required.

Although every member of the audience is in some sense a critic, this title is usually reserved for those who formulate their judgments for publication. These critics should have considerable theatregoing experience (an inexperienced theatre critic is comparable to a sports columnist who has never seen a baseball game); they also need to understand what goes into a production (the potentials and limitations of the various theatre arts), so they can assess the contributions of each element to a production. Critics need to be aware of the audience they are writing for, so that they can express themselves in terms comprehensible to it.

Usually, the critic has a particular type of reader in mind. The reviews of plays published in daily newspapers are addressed to a general public that may have no extensive knowledge of theatre; the critical articles written for literary quarterlies or scholarly journals are addressed to a more restricted and demanding audience. Consequently, a single piece of criticism seldom serves the needs of all readers.

Critics who write reviews for newspapers often think of themselves as consumer guides, alerting readers to which productions are worth their time and money, and which are not. It is often charged that an adverse

Scene from the original production of *Death of a Salesman*, 1949. On the lower level, Lee J. Cobb as Willy and Mildred Dunnock as Linda; on the upper level, Arthur Kennedy as Biff and Cameron Mitchell as Happy. Designed by Jo Mielziner; directed by Elia Kazan. (Photograph by Eileen Darby.)

review in *The New York Times* is sufficient to close a Broadway production, unless the play has substantial advance sales. In recent years, many television stations have also begun reviewing plays (usually in short spots of two to five minutes); these reviews have had substantial impact on ticket sales (understandably, now that on Broadway a single ticket may cost as much as fifty dollars).

In this chapter, there are four examples of reviews, all of Arthur Miller's *Death of a Salesman*. If you have not read Arthur Miller's *Death of a Salesman,* you should do so, as it will contribute greatly to your understanding of this chapter. If you cannot read the play, you will find a discussion of it on pages 220–223.

Three of the reviews concern the original Broadway production in 1949. One is by Brooks Atkinson, the highly respected critic for *The New York Times* for some forty years. The second was written by Joseph Wood Krutch, professor at Columbia University and critic for the weekly magazine *The Nation.* Krutch was known especially for his contention that it is impossible to write tragedy in the twentieth century because we consider humans too petty and selfish to rise to the nobility of motive, thought, and action required for tragic drama. A third review was written by Eric Bentley, since the 1940s one of America's major critics of drama and a professor who has taught at several leading universities. Atkinson's review was written immediately after seeing the production; Krutch's was written some three weeks after the opening; and Bentley's was written still later and eventually published in a volume of theatrical criticism intended for a relatively sophisticated audience. The fourth review was written by Frank Rich, the present reviewer for *The New York Times,* when Miller's play was revived in 1984, thirty-five years after the original production and by which time the play had been accorded the status of an "American classic."

These selections can help us understand criticism and the reviewing of theatrical productions. To many persons, criticism always means adverse response, but the true meaning of the word is "the act of making judgments." Therefore, the most complete criticism concerns both excellence and shortcomings. Not all critics provide balanced discussions, either for lack of space or because they believe that a play or a production is so good or inadequate that there is nothing of importance to be said on the other side. Atkinson's review is entirely favorable; Krutch is most concerned with voicing his reservations about Miller's play and with showing that it is not nearly so good as other critics have suggested; Bentley, while predominantly favoring both the play and the production, points out what he considers significant problems; Rich also acknowledges some flaws in the play but dismisses them as unimportant in the face of its great strengths and concentrates on the interpretation of the script, especially as embodied in Dustin Hoffman's Willy. In each of these selections, the critic establishes a point of view and seeks to validate it by citing evidence drawn from the script or from other sources thought to be relevant.

Review by Brooks Atkinson of the original production of *Death of a Salesman* written immediately after the opening night performance.

Arthur Miller has written a superb drama. From every point of view "Death of a Salesman," which was acted at the Morosco last evening, is rich and memorable drama. It is so simple in style and so inevitable in theme that it scarcely seems like a thing that has been written and acted. For Mr. Miller has looked with compassion into the hearts of some ordinary Americans and quietly transferred their hope and anguish to the theatre. Under Elia Kazan's masterly direction, Lee J. Cobb gives a heroic performance, and every member of the cast plays like a person inspired.

Two seasons ago Mr. Miller's "All My Sons" looked like the work of an honest and able playwright. In comparison with the new drama, that seems like a contrived play now. For "Death of a Salesman" has the flow and spontaneity of a suburban epic that may not be intended as poetry but becomes poetry in spite of itself because Mr. Miller has drawn it out of so many intangible sources.

The Cast

DEATH OF A SALESMAN a play by Arthur Miller. Staged by Elia Kazan; scenery and lighting by Jo Mielziner, incidental music by Alex North; costumes by Julia Sze; produced by Kermit Bloomgarden and Walter Fried. At the Morosco Theatre

Willy Loman . . . . Lee J. Cobb
Linda . . . . Mildred Dunnock
Happy . . . . Cameron Mitchell
Biff . . . . Arthur Kennedy
Bernard . . . . Don Keefer
The Woman . . . . Winnifred Cushing
Charley . . . . Howard Smith
Uncle Ben . . . . Thomas Chalmers
Howard Wagner . . . . Alan Hewitt
Jenny . . . . Ann Driscoll
Stanley . . . . .Tom Pedi
Miss Forsythe . . . . Constance Ford
Letta . . . . Hope Cameron

It is the story of an aging salesman who has reached the end of his usefulness on the road. There has always been something unsubstantial about his work. But suddenly the unsubstantial aspects of it overwhelm him completely. When he was young, he looked dashing; he enjoyed the comradeship of other people—the humor, the kidding, the business.

In his early sixties he knows his business as well as he ever did. But the unsubstantial things have become decisive; the spring has gone from his step, the smile from his face and the heartiness from his personality. He is through. The phantom of his life has caught up with him. As literally as Mr. Miller can say it, dust returns to dust. Suddenly there is nothing.

This is only a little of what Mr. Miller is saying. For he conveys this elusive tragedy in terms of simple things—the loyalty and understanding of his wife, the careless selfishness of his two sons, the sympathetic devotion of a neighbor, the coldness of his former boss' son—the bills, the car, the tinkering around the house. And most of all: the illusions by which he has lived—opportunities missed, wrong formulas for success, fatal misconceptions about his place in the scheme of things.

Writing like a man who understands people, Mr. Miller has no moral precepts to offer and no solutions of the salesman's problems. He is full of pity, but he brings no piety to it. Chronicler of one frowsy corner of the American scene, he evokes a wraithlike tragedy out of it that spins through the many scenes of his play and gradually envelops the audience.

As theatre "Death of a Salesman" is no less original than it is as literature. Jo Mielziner, always equal to an occasion, has designed a skeletonized set that captures the mood of the play and serves the actors brilliantly. Although Mr. Miller's text may be diffuse in form, Mr. Kazan has pulled it together into a deeply moving performance.

Mr. Cobb's tragic portrait of the defeated salesman is acting of the first rank. Although it is familiar and folksy in the details, it has something of the grand manner in the big size and the deep tone. Mildred Dunnock gives the performance of her career as the wife and mother—plain of speech but indomitable in spirit. The parts of the thoughtless sons are extremely well played by Arthur Kennedy and Cameron Mitchell, who are all youth, brag and bewilderment.

Other parts are well played by Howard Smith, Thomas Chalmers, Don Keefer, Alan Hewitt and Tom Pedi. If there were time, this report would gratefully include all the actors and fabricators of illusion. For they all realize that for once in their lives they are participating in a rare event in the theatre. Mr. Miller's elegy in a Brooklyn sidestreet is superb.

Review by Joseph Wood Krutch written some three weeks after the opening night performance for a weekly journal directed to a well-informed public.

It has been a good many years since any serious play has provoked enthusiasm as unqualified and as nearly universal as that which greeted Arthur Miller's "Death of a Salesman" (Morosco Theater). That it is powerful, veracious, and theatrically effective can hardly be denied; but perhaps a reviewer who has the privilege of making a delayed report may be forgiven if he undertakes to suggest that, like every work of art, it is good only in its own particular way and that there are virtues which it does not exhibit.

The action recounts the last few days in the life of a traveling salesman who has outlived his usefulness and is discharged by the firm for which he has worked all his life. Behind him lie the memories of a drab and unsuccessful existence which was sustained by a shabby illusion of his own importance and by a belief in what I suppose it would now be fashionable to call his "myth"—that is to say, in a philosophy of life which assumes that "self-confidence" and "influence" are the instruments and "being well liked" the outward sign of success. His wife is exhausted by years of attempting to meet installment payments, and his two sons, whom he has encouraged to believe that importance on the high-school football team will open all doors, are flashy fakers. Now that he can no longer believe that he has "influence" or that he is "well liked," nothing lies before him except confession of failure. He chooses therefore to commit suicide in order that the wife may at least have his insurance money to live on.

This being 1949, one naturally assumes that such a story is most likely to be told in order to expose the evils of our social system. No doubt in some very general way "The Death of a Salesman" may be taken to do just that. But I was unable to perceive anything in the slightest degree doctrinaire, and at least as much stress seems to be laid on the intellectual and moral weakness of the central character as upon any outward necessity determining his fate. The moral can be taken to be merely "Know Thyself," since the only positive suggestion seems to be that the hero would have been a good deal better off if he had realized that what he calls "success" is not for such as he and that he could have been humbly happy cultivating the soil or working with a carpenter's tools—two things he actually enjoys doing. Like the central character in "The Ice Man Cometh" Mr. Miller's salesman dies when he loses his illusions, but "Death of a Salesman" is without the mystical suggestions of O'Neill's play and is actually in theme and effect a good deal closer to Elmer Rice's "The Adding Machine," which, indeed, it seems to me to resemble more closely than has so far been recognized.

Like "The Adding Machine" it has as hero a Mr. Zero, and it employs nonrepresentational techniques. Thus the admirable set designed by Jo Mielziner is multiple like the same designer's set for "Summer and Smoke," and the action involves many flash-backs presented as recalled in the memory of the principal personage. But—still more consistently than in "The Adding Machine"—the material is strictly naturalistic, and it is this fact which limits its effect upon this one spectator at least. All the action and all the characterizations are recognizably true to life, but almost every feature of either is both familiar and without other than literal meaning. To me there is about the whole something prosy and pedestrian; a notable absence of new insight, fresh imagination, or individual sensibility. The dialogue serves its purpose as well as the dialogue of a Dreiser novel, but it is also almost as undistinguished, as unpoetic, as unmemorable and as unquotable. Among the performances that of Mildred Dunnock seems to me the best, while that of Lee Cobb, though hailed with unbounded enthusiasm by the audience, struck me as being—necessarily perhaps—as convincing but also as heavy-footed as the dialogue itself.

Since Tennessee Williams is the only other recently emerged playwright who has awakened even remotely similar enthusiasm, certain comparisons will inevitably be made between them. Against Williams it will be said that he is eccentric and neurotic and that he has so far dealt exclusively with abnormal people, whereas "Death of a Salesman" involves characters and situations true to life as everyone has observed it and presented with an objectivity which everyone can recognize. But to me it seems equally evident that in Mr. Williams's work there are unique qualities which are absent from Mr. Miller's earlier "All My Sons" and from his present play, both of which, by the way, turn so closely around a father-son relationship as to permit almost as strongly as in the case of the Williams plays the objection that the author is obsessed with one theme. Almost hysterical though "A Streetcar Named Desire" may sometimes seem, it offers moments of new insight, and it reveals, as "Death of a Salesman" does not, a unique sensibility as well as a gift for language, sometimes misused and precious, but increasingly effective as it is increasingly purified. That Mr. Miller's new play is extremely good in its own way I have already said, and that it will appeal to an even larger audience than was attracted to either "A Streetcar" or "Summer and Smoke" seems probable. But to me at least it seems, nevertheless, relatively old-fashioned.

The Nation 168 (March 5, 1949), 283–84. Reprinted by permission of The Nation Magazine/Nation Associate, Inc.

Commentary by Eric Bentley on *Death of a Salesman* written considerably after its opening and intended for a culturally sophisticated audience.

To my mind, [*Death of a*] *Salesman* is first and foremost an occasion, a signal event in New York theatrical life. In the second place, it is one man's performance, a rock of a performance, strong enough to hold up any play. I mean Lee Cobb's rendering—or creation?—of Willy Loman.

If American actors give very poor renditions of Frenchmen and Englishmen, they often give a marvelously nuanced account of their own countrymen, and none more brilliantly—with more body and bounce—than those who worked with Clurman and Odets in the Group Theatre. This theater, it might be said, undertook the study of American life on its lower social levels to see what could be taken over into stage performance. Lee Cobb's work in *Salesman* is presumably the most triumphant application of this patient research. He brings to it a knowledge of the salesman's character (as expressed in his limbs, the hunch of his shoulders, vocal intonation, facial expression) which is not provided in the script. Coming to this performance straight from Paris, I was struck with the completeness of its Americanism. What an idiom expresses in language, Lee Cobb can express in stance or movement or vocal color.

I suppose the performance is also a

triumph of the Stanislavsky approach to a role. Cobb is deeply sunk in the role (though not so deeply that he can't place a witticism in the lap of the audience). Each small movement seems to come welling up from the weary, hurt soul. According to the pattern, Cobb strongly identifies himself with the role; and the audience identifies itself with Cobb. Thus the attempt is made at what Miller himself has called the tragedy of the common man. We all find that we are Willy, and Willy is us; we live and die together; but when Willy falls never to rise again, we go home feeling purged of (or by) pity and terror.

Meanwhile, what has become of the attack on "the American way"? Has it been successfully subsumed under the larger heading "the human way"? This is what Arthur Miller's admirers tell us. Are they right? The impression I had was not of the small purpose being included within the large, but of the two blurring each other. The "tragedy" destroys the social drama; the social drama keeps the "tragedy" from having a fully tragic stature. By this last remark I mean that the theme of this social drama, as of most others, is *the little man as victim.* Such a theme arouses pity, but no terror. Man is here too little and too passive to play the tragic hero.

More important even than this, the tragedy and the social drama actually conflict. The tragic catharsis reconciles us to, or persuades us to disregard, precisely those material conditions which the social drama calls our attention to and protests against. Political antagonists of Miller have suggested that he is a Marxist who, consciously or unconsciously, lacks the courage of his convictions—or is it that "Stalinism" today welcomes a sentimental haze? Certainly, had *Salesman* been written a dozen years earlier, it would have ended with a call to revolt, and would thus have had more coherence than the play Miller has written. Or is Miller a "tragic" artist who, without knowing it, has been confused by Marxism? There is no need to make of any criticism of the play a special accusation against its author, for its confusions are those of a whole class, a whole generation.

It is interesting that critics who have never shown any love for poetry praise *Salesman* as a great poetic drama. The poetry they like is bad poetry, the kind that sounds big and sad and soul-searing when heard for the first time and spoken very quickly within a situation that has already generated a good deal of emotion. I think it was Paul Muni who made the classic comment that in *Salesman* you can't tell where the prose leaves off and the poetry begins. You can tell, though, that the prose is often relatively satisfactory and that the poetry is ham. Mere rhetorical phrasing—as witness any of the longer speeches. What is relevant here is that this kind of poetry contributes very liberally to that blurring of outlines which enables Miller to write a social drama and a tragedy at the same time and thus please all.

Absolutely everything in the production contributes too; and thus Elia Kazan and Jo Mielziner please all. The great vice of Miller's style is a false rhetorical mode of speech heard only on Broadway and in political speeches. There is an equivalent of this rhetoric in Kazan's directing and Mielziner's designing and lighting. Things move fast in a Kazan show. So fast you can't see them. If anything is wrong, you don't notice. If a false note is struck, its sound is at once covered by others. One has no time to think. "Drama isn't time to think," the director seems to be saying, "it's action that sweeps you off your feet." The Mielziner staging reinforces the effect. It is above all murky. It reveals—or hints at—a half-world of shadows and missing walls and little spotlights that dimly illuminate the corridors of time. As to this last point, Mielziner is of course staying close to the form of the play Miller gave him, a play in which the chief formal device is the flashback. Now, there is no reason why time in a play shouldn't go backward instead of forward. The thing is that the device of going back has always up to the present been used to create one sort of emotional state: that of nostalgia, mystery, phantasmagoria. . . . In fact the flashback has become primarily a way of rendering these moods, and there is usually something portentous and false about it. We never know where we are. "Light," the designer seems to be saying, "makes of the stage a magic carpet, carrying us wherever we wish." But where *do* we wish? Mielziner helps Miller to be vague.

If it is too much to ask that Miller know which of two feasible plays he wanted to write, one can ask that he clear aside rhetorical and directorial bric-a-brac and look more closely at his people. Has he given us a suitable language for his tarts (in the whoring sequence)? Are the sons of Willy *seen* with the eye or just constructed from the idea that the present generation is "lost"? Is the Alaskan uncle more than a sentimental motif? After all that Mildred Dunnock does for the wife's part, is Willy's marriage *there* for us to inspect and understand down to its depths? It would be unfair to push these questions as far as Willy himself, for he could not be a satisfactory character while the central contradiction of the play stands unresolved. Is his littleness the product of the capitalist system? Or is it Human Nature? What attitude are we to have to it? Pity? Anger? Or just a lovely mishmash?

Arthur Miller seems to be a serious writer. He is therefore, among playwrights, a man in a thousand. He knows what the other playwrights know: how to shape up a story for actors. But he wants to write truly. He knows that there is more drama in the actual facts than in the facts as modified by threadbare rhetoric and directorial legerdemain. If he can in the future act more resolutely on this knowledge, *Salesman* will *not* be the great American drama of the midcentury.

Eric Bentley, excerpted from review of Arthur Miller's *Death of a Salesman* in *In Search of Theater*. Copyright 1953 Eric Russell Bentley; copyright renewed © 1981 Eric Bentley. Reprinted with the permission of Atheneum Publishers, Inc.

Review by Frank Rich of the revival of *Death of a Salesman* in 1984.

The Cast

DEATH OF A SALESMAN, by Arthur Miller; directed by Michael Rudman; scenery by Ben Edwards; costumes by Ruth Morley; music composed by Alex North; lighting by Thomas Skelton; makeup by Ann Belsky; hair design by Alan D'Angerio; production associate, Doris Blum; production stage manager, Thomas A. Kelly; casting, Terry Fay. Presented by Robert Whitehead and Roger L. Stevens. At the Broadhurst Theater, 235 West 44th Street.

Willy Loman	Dustin Hoffman
Linda	Kate Reid
Happy	Stephen Lang
Biff	John Malkovich
Bernard	David Chandler
Women from Boston	Kathy Rossetter
Charley	David Huddleston
Uncle Ben	Louis Zorich
Howard Wagner	Jon Polito
Jenny	Patricia Fay
Stanley	Tom Signoreli
Miss Forsythe	Linda Kozlowski
Letta	Karen Needle
Walter	Michael Quinlan

As Willy Loman in Arthur Miller's "Death of a Salesman," Dustin Hoffman doesn't trudge heavily to the grave—he sprints. His fist is raised and his face is cocked defiantly upwards, so that his rimless spectacles glint in the Brooklyn moonlight. But how does one square that feisty image with what will come after his final exit—and with what has come before? Earlier, Mr. Hoffman's Willy has collapsed to the floor of a Broadway steakhouse, mewling and shrieking like an abandoned baby. That moment had led to the spectacle of the actor sitting in the straightback chair of his kitchen, crying out in rage to his elder son, Biff. "I'm not a dime a dozen!," Mr. Hoffman rants, looking and sounding so small that we fear the price quoted by Biff may, if anything, be too high.

To reconcile these sides of Willy—the brave

fighter and the whipped child—you really have no choice but to see what Mr. Hoffman is up to at the Broadhurst. In undertaking one of our theater's classic roles, this daring actor has pursued his own brilliant conception of the character. Mr. Hoffman is not playing a larger-than-life protagonist but the small man described in the script—the "little boat looking for a harbor," the eternally adolescent American male who goes to the grave without ever learning who he is. And by staking no claim to the stature of a tragic hero, Mr. Hoffman's Willy becomes a harrowing American everyman. His bouncy final exit is the death of a salesman, all right. Willy rides to suicide, as he rode through life, on the foolish, empty pride of "a smile and a shoeshine."

Even when Mr. Hoffman's follow-through falls short of his characterization—it takes a good while to accept him as 63 years old—we're riveted by the wasted vitality of his small Willy, a man full of fight for all the wrong battles. What's more, the star has not turned "Death of a Salesman" into a vehicle. Under the balanced direction of Michael Rudman, this revival is an exceptional ensemble effort, strongly cast throughout. John Malkovich, who plays the lost Biff, gives a performance of such spellbinding effect that he becomes the evening's anchor. When Biff finally forgives Willy and nestles his head lovingly on his father's chest, the whole audience leans forward to be folded into the embrace: we know we're watching the salesman arrive, however temporarily, at the only safe harbor he'll ever know.

But as much as we marvel at the acting in this "Death of a Salesman," we also marvel at the play. Mr. Miller's masterwork has been picked to death by critics over the last 35 years, and its reputation has been clouded by the author's subsequent career. We know its flaws by heart—the big secret withheld from the audience until Act II, and the symbolic old brother Ben (Louis Zorich), forever championing the American dream in literary prose. Yet how small and academic these quibbles

look when set against the fact of the thunderous thing itself.

In "Death of a Salesman," Mr. Miller wrote with a fierce, liberating urgency. Even as his play marches steadily onward to its preordained conclusion, it roams about through time and space, connecting present miseries with past traumas and drawing blood almost everywhere it goes. Though the author's condemnation of the American success ethic is stated baldly, it is also woven, at times humorously, into the action. When Willy proudly speaks of owning a refrigerator that's promoted with the "biggest ads," we see that the pathological credo of being "well liked" requires that he consume products that have the aura of popularity, too.

Still, Mr. Rudman and his cast don't make the mistake of presenting the play as a monument of social thought: the author's themes can take care of themselves. Like most of Mr. Miller's work, "Death of a Salesman" is most of all about fathers and sons. There are many father-son relationships in the play—not just those enmeshing Willy's neighbors and employer. The drama's tidal pull comes from the sons' tortured attempts to reconcile themselves to their fathers' dreams. It's not Willy's pointless death that moves us; it's Biff's decision to go on living. Biff, the princely high school football hero turned drifter, must find the courage both to love his father and leave him forever behind.

Mr. Hoffman's Willy takes flight late in Act I, when he first alludes to his relationship with his own father. Recalling how his father left when he was still a child, Willy says, "I never had a chance to talk to him, and I still feel—kind of temporary about myself." As Mr. Hoffman's voice breaks on the word "temporary," his spirit cracks into aged defeat. From then on, it's a merciless drop to the bottom of his "strange thoughts"—the hallucinatory memory sequences that send him careening in and out of a lifetime of anxiety. Mr. Rudman stages these apparitional flashbacks with bruising force; we see why Biff says that Willy is spewing out "vomit from his mind." As Mr. Hoffman stumbles through the shadowy recollections of his past, trying both to deny and transmute the awful truth of an impoverished existence, he lurches and bobs like a strand of broken straw tossed by a mean wind.

As we expect from this star, he has affected a new physical and vocal presence for Willy: a baldish, silver-maned head, a shuffling walk; a brash, Brooklyn-tinged voice that well serves the character's comic penchant for contradicting himself in nearly every sentence. But what's most poignant about the getup may be the costume (designed by Ruth Morley). Mr. Hoffman's Willy is a total break with the mountainous Lee J. Cobb image. He's a trim, immaculately outfitted go-getter in a three-piece suit—replete with bright matching tie and handkerchief. Is there anything sadder than a nobody dressed for success, or an old man masquerading as his younger self? The star seems to wilt within the self-parodistic costume throughout the evening. "You can't eat the orange and throw away the peel!," Willy pleads to the callow young boss (Jon Polito) who fires him—and, looking at the wizened and spent Mr. Hoffman, we realize that he is indeed the peel, tossed into the gutter.

Mr. Malkovich, hulking and unsmiling, is an inversion of Mr. Hoffman's father; he's what Willy might be if he'd ever stopped lying to himself. Anyone who saw this remarkable young actor as the rambunctious rascal of "True West" may find his transformation here as astonishing as the star's. His Biff is soft and tentative, with sullen eyes and a slow, distant voice that seems entombed with his aborted teen-age promise; his big hands flop around diffidently as he tries to convey his anguish to his roguish brother Happy (Stephen Lang). Once Biff accepts who he is—and who his father is—the catharic recognition seems to break through Mr. Malkovich (and the theater) like a raging fever. "Help him!" he yells as his father collapses at the restaurant—only to melt instantly into a blurry, tearful plea of "Help me! Help me!"

In the problematic role of the mother, Kate Reid is miraculously convincing. Whether she's professing her love for Willy or damning Happy as a "philandering bum," she somehow melds affection with pure steel. Mr. Lang captures the vulgarity and desperate narcissism of the younger brother, and David Chandler takes the goo out of the model boy next door. As Mr. Chandler's father—and Willy's only friend—David Huddleston radiates a quiet benevolence as expansive as his considerable girth. One must also applaud Thomas Skelton, whose lighting imaginatively meets every shift in time and mood, and the set designer Ben Edwards, who surrounds the shabby Loman house with malevolent apartment towers poised to swallow Willy up.

But it's Mr. Hoffman and Mr. Malkovich who demand that our attention be paid anew to "Death of a Salesman." When their performances meet in a great, binding passion, we see the transcendant sum of two of the American theater's most lowly, yet enduring parts.

The New York Times, March 30, 1984. Copyright © 1984 by the New York Times Company. Reprinted by permission.

While these reviews of *Death of a Salesman* are representative of critical approaches, they do not exhaust the possibilities. Some commentaries may be almost wholly descriptive. A writer might explain how Miller's (or some other) play is constructed or how the director has approached the script. Or a reviewer might provide information about certain aspects of the production (the visual appearance of the scenery or costumes, how the production differs from previous ones of the same play, and so on) without passing judgment on these features. Such descriptive pieces can perform a valuable function. For productions of little-known or difficult plays or for productions focused on controversial directorial concepts or utilizing unfamiliar conventions, such writing can help an audience to appreciate a production or play it might otherwise find baffling.

The selections reprinted here also do not illustrate another tendency among many reviewers to be flippant or condescending. Famous examples of flippancy are Dorothy Parker's remark that Katherine Hepburn ran the gamut of emotion from A to B (in a Broadway production in 1933) and John Mason Brown's statement, "Tallulah Bankhead barged down the Nile last night and sank" (in his review of her performance in Shakespeare's *Antony and Cleopatra*). Examples of condescension are John Simon's remarks on Grotowski's *The Constant Prince.* "I was so dumbfounded by the infantilism and coarseness of the proceedings that sheer amazement kept me from even trying [to take notes]," and George Jean Nathan's about a production of Shakespeare's *Richard III.* "To the multiplicity of the play's murders, Mr. Coulouris and his company added another: that of the play itself." While such quips may be amusing, they can be infuriating and discouraging to theatre workers whose efforts are dismissed out of hand, often rather callously. Such reviews contribute significantly to the antipathy that often exists between theatre artists and critics.

The Basic Problems of Criticism

The critic is concerned with three basic problems: understanding, effectiveness, and ultimate worth. Or, put another way, What were the playwright, director, and other theatre artists trying to do? How well did they do it? Was it worth doing?

In attempting to deal with the first question, critics may follow several paths to increased understanding. If the script is available, they may study it carefully and analyze it prior to attending the production. They may seek to find out more about the author's life and other works and about what other critics have said about the playwright's plays. They may wish to refresh their memory of previous work by the director and production team, or of previous productions of the same play. Note in the reviews reprinted here the references to previous work by the playwright, director, and designer, and, in Rich's review, comparisons with earlier interpretations of the roles. Some reviewers deliberately avoid any preparation for viewing a production on the grounds that they wish to attend a production much as any other spectator might, so that they may react without any preconceptions about the play or how it should be performed.

By choice or necessity, many reviewers write about plays they have not read and which they know only from a single performance. Under these circumstances, reviewers may restrict themselves to reporting their impressions and avoid any attempt at analysis; nevertheless, reviewers are often guilty of damning a play rather than its inadequate production, or a performance rather than its inadequate script, because of the great difficulty in sorting out the sources of strengths and weaknesses after a single viewing.

In dealing with the second question (How successful were the playwright, director, and other theatre artists in accomplishing what they set out to do?), the critic may choose to focus on the playwright's intention or the director's concept. Rarely does a playwright state intentions directly. Rather, they are indicated by the way conflicts, characters, and ideas are handled, and by the look and sound of the production. Evidence of the director's concept usually comes entirely from what the critic sees and hears during the performance, although sometimes the director explains this concept in notes printed in the program, in interviews prior to the opening, or in publicity releases. The director may seek to embody the author's intentions as faithfully as possible, or (increasingly nowadays) may choose a concept at variance with them. The critic may assess how the director's concept is related to, or differs from, the dramatist's intentions. But the critic who is concerned with the production as such (rather than as an attempt to embody a script faithfully) must concentrate on how well the director has used the acting, scenery, costumes, and lighting to realize whatever concept he has chosen. Although the critic may believe that the director is misguided in the choice of concept, this belief is irrelevant in the critic's assessment of whether the concept has been realized.

In assessing a production's effectiveness, critics may take into account audience response. They need to recognize, however, that while such response may be an accurate measure of the audience's enjoyment, it does not necessarily give a true indication of a play's potential power. (For example, the director may have sought to impose an inappropriate concept on the script, one or more actors may have failed to project their characters' inner feelings, and so on.) Other factors—such as unfamiliar dramatic or theatrical conventions or complex ideas—may be responsible for an audience's failure to appreciate a play's power. The fault does not necessarily lie with the play; it may indicate shortcomings in the audience. But if the play has been adequately performed and has been understood by the spectators, audience response may reinforce the critic's assessment.

Even though a play or production is understood and judged successful in carrying out its intention, it may still be found unsatisfactory in relation to some larger system of values. Consequently, before passing final judgment, the critic may wish to ask whether the accomplishments are sufficiently significant to merit the highest commendation. Making this final judgment is the critic's greatest problem, for there are no universally accepted standards of worth, and none can be proven incontestably better than another.

To judge a play or performance, it must be surrounded by some context that places it in perspective. When a production, or any aspect of it, is judged to be good, bad, effective, ineffective, successful, unsuccessful, adequate, or inadequate, a reasonable question is: In relation to what? Often we are puzzled by judgments because we do not know what standards have gone into making them. Why does a friend detest a play or movie that we have greatly admired? If we discuss our differing responses, we often find that we are looking at the same work from differing perspectives. We may praise a production's comic inventiveness, while a friend may acknowledge the qualities we praise but find the work's treatment of women (or some other element) so appalling that nothing can compensate for this shortcoming. Like most disagreements about worth, this one stems from differences about appropriate contexts.

The contexts used for judging plays are numerous and varied. Some critics find the only meaningful context to be other plays of the same type. Krutch, in his review of *Death of a Salesman,* places considerable emphasis on how Miller's play relates to other American plays about somewhat similar subjects. Other critics may value a production for its emotional power, its relevance to contemporary issues, its insights into human behavior, its innovations, its embodiment of the script, or its entertainment. Conversely, critics may damn productions for failing to satisfy criteria appropriate to the context they have chosen but perhaps inappropriate to another context. Critics do not necessarily remain within a single context in making their judgments. Examine carefully the reviews of *Death of a Salesman* and note the stated or implied criteria that underlie the various value judgments expressed by the four critics.

Most of us are probably not aware of the preconceptions and prejudices that underlie our judgments. We would each do well to ask ourselves what makes us find a production satisfying or unsatisfying. Many people believe that the most satisfying production is one that so fully absorbs their attention that they completely forget themselves. Others have argued that to enter so empathetically into a production makes it impossible to watch critically or to be aware of the ideology that undergirds the action.

In assessing your own critical stance, here are some questions that may be helpful: Are you open to unfamiliar subjects, ideas, or conventions? In the theatre, are you uncomfortable with moral stances that differ from your own? Are there subjects that you think should not be treated on the stage? If so, which? What standards do you think should be used in judging a play or performance? Why? Other questions could be posed, but all would relate to understanding one's own convictions and biases, since these enter significantly into one's critical judgments.

Critical responses, whether those of the casual spectator or the professional critic, ultimately involve the major questions already posed: What was attempted? How fully was it accomplished? Was it worth doing? An informed and perceptive reviewer usually deals with elaborations on the following major questions:

1. What play was performed? Who is the author? Is it a significant work? What information about the author or script is important to the production?
2. Where and when did the performance take place? Will there be additional performances?
3. Who was involved in the production—producer, director, actors, designers? Not everyone need be named, and comments about those who are may be scattered throughout the reviews.
4. How effectively was the script performed (directed, acted, designed)?
5. Should others see it? Why?

As is clearly demonstrated by the reviews of *Death of a Salesman* a critic may not deal with all of these questions or in this order, and answers to each question may vary in length and complexity.

Qualities Needed by the Critic

Because the theatre is a composite art and because each of us is subject to many influences, it is difficult to become a good theatre critic. A reliable critic usually has had years of theatregoing on which to draw, as well as a firm foundation of study and reading about the theatre and its processes.

Some of the qualities for which the critic should strive are these: to be sensitive to feelings, images, and ideas; to become as well acquainted as possible with the theatre of all periods and of all types; to be willing to explore plays and production processes; to be tolerant of innovation; to be aware of one's own prejudices and values; to be articulate and clear in expressing judgments and their bases. Perhaps most important, the critic must avoid becoming dogmatic or unwilling to consider alternative views. The theatre is constantly changing, and critics must be willing to reassess their standards in light of innovations even as they seek to evaluate the changes.

The Script and the Playwright

3

The play script is the typical starting point for a theatrical production. It is also the most common residue of production, since the script usually remains intact after its performance ends. Because the same script may serve as a basis for many different productions, it has greater permanence than its theatrical representations and therefore may come to be considered a literary work. Consequently, drama is often taught quite apart from theatre, and many people who read plays have never seen a live dramatic performance. Probably the majority of students get their first glimpse of theatre through reading plays in literature classes. But a script may seem unsatisfactory or puzzling, for it is essentially a blueprint that demands from both reader and performer the imaginative recreation of much that is only implied on the printed page. Therefore, learning how to read, understand, and fill out the script (either in the mind or on the stage) is essential if the power of a play is to be fully realized.

On Reading a Play

There are no rules about how one should read a play. Nevertheless, some observations may be helpful to those for whom play reading is a new experience. First, one must accept that the ability to read imaginatively and perceptively is a basic skill needed by all persons who seek to become educated, for without it much of human experience is forever lost, and intellectually we remain children suffering from historical and cultural amnesia.

Since all writers do not express themselves in the same form, all written works cannot be read in the same way. Each form has its own characteristics, and each makes distinctive demands on the reader. Thus, we cannot read a play in the same way we read an historical treatise, an essay, a biography, a novel, or a poem. To read a play adequately, we must first adjust our minds to the dramatic form so that its contents may be perceived. A play is distinctive in part because it is a form made up primarily of dialogue that must be constructed with great care in order to convey its intentions precisely while at the same time creating the sense of being the spontaneous oral utterances of characters involved in a developing action. Thus, it is at once a highly formal structure and a simulated spontaneous reflection of human experience.

Drama requires the reader to contribute more than most other forms of fiction do. Not only must the reader see and understand what is explicitly said and done, but one must also be aware of all that is implied or left unsaid. The dramatist may use stage directions to clarify setting, situation, or tone, but for the most part conveys intentions through dialogue. Therefore, in reading a play, we should assume that what is written is precisely what the writer wishes to say. But because the dramatist must convey intentions through a likeness of conversation, we must be sensitive—as in real life—to the implications, unspoken feelings, and even deliberate deceptions typical of human interaction. Therefore, the reader must be alert to the nuances and shadings of each word and phrase. Although inwardly and imaginatively seeing and hearing a script is not a simple undertaking, it can be done adequately if we cultivate the imagination and develop the understanding appropriate to the task. Perhaps the best place to begin is with a look at how plays are constructed.

Dramatic Action

Broadly speaking, a play is, as the Greek philosopher Aristotle wrote in his *Poetics,* a representation of human beings "in action." But by "action" he did not mean mere physical movement; he included within that term the psychological motivations that lie behind visible behavior. Thus, he was concerned not only with what characters in a play do but also with why they do it. The *dramatic action* of almost any play, therefore, can be summed up in a brief statement about the focus of the events around a goal and the purpose of that goal. Thus, we might state the dramatic action of Sophocles' *Oedipus the King* as "to find and expel the murderer of Laius in order to cleanse the city." Or we might state the dramatic action of *Death of a Salesman* as "to recover the past in order to validate Willy's life." Either of these statements of dramatic action might be restated or refined, so long as they incorporate what is actively done and the purpose for which it is done. Francis Fergusson has argued that the dramatic action of a serious play involves three phases: purpose, passion, and perception. By *purpose* he means awareness of some desire or goal; by *passion* he means the suffering or anguish that a character undergoes in seeking to fulfill that goal; and by *perception* he means the understanding that eventually comes out of the suffering. In *Death of a Salesman*, we see Willy searching for some explanation for his failure, we see the increasing anguish into which his search leads him and which forces him to face the truth about himself and Biff, and we see his eventual attempt to make amends, although we may question whether he ever achieves full understanding of the inadequacy of the values he has accepted and forced on his sons.

The range of human motivation and behavior is so great that a single play can depict only a small part of the totality. Furthermore, each playwright's vision differs from that of others, and consequently each drama is in some respects unique. Still, plays are sufficiently similar that we may draw some general conclusions about the characteristics of effective dramatic action. Aristotle stated that a dramatic action should have a beginning, middle, and end. On the surface, this statement seems obvious, but it summarizes a fundamental principle: a dramatic action should be *complete and self-contained* (that is, everything necessary for understanding it should be included within the play). If this principle is not observed, the action will probably seem confused or unsatisfying. Effective dramatic action is *deliberately shaped* or organized to reveal its purpose and goal and to evoke from the audience specific emotional responses (pity, fear, laughter, thoughtful contemplation). Effective dramatic action, in addition to having a definite purpose, must also have *variety* (in story, characterization, idea, mood, spectacle) to avoid sameness and monotony. Effective dramatic action *engages and maintains interest*. The situation must be sufficiently compelling to arouse curiosity, the characters must excite interest, the issues be vital enough to provoke concern, or the spectacle and sound be novel enough to attract attention. Effective dramatic action is *probable*—that is, all of the elements are logically consistent. Even if the events might be impossible in real life, they should be consistent with the particular logic (or rules of the game) created in the opening section of the play. It is probability (internal consistency) that leads us to accept the events as believable.

Methods of Organizing Dramatic Action

A play is composed of incidents organized to accomplish some purpose. Organization is primarily a matter of directing attention to relationships that create a unified, meaningful pattern. In analyzing a play, it is helpful to pinpoint the source of unity; otherwise, the play may appear to be a collection of unrelated happenings rather than a whole. The most common sources of unity are: cause-to-effect arrangement of events; character; and thought. (To understand the following discussion most fully, the reader should be familiar with Arthur Miller's *Death of a Salesman* and Samuel Beckett's *Happy Days*. A discussion of the latter play can be found on pages 227–230.)

The majority of plays from the past are organized around the *cause-to-effect arrangement of events*. This is the primary organizational principle in *Death of a Salesman*. Using this method, the playwright sets up in the opening scenes the necessary conditions—the situation, the desires and motivations of the characters—out of which later events develop. The goals of one character come into conflict with those of another, or two conflicting desires within the same character may lead to a crisis. Attempts to surmount the obstacles make up the substance of the play, each scene growing logically out of those that precede it. Any organizational pattern other than cause-to-effect is apt to seem loose, often giving the effect of randomness.

Less often, a dramatist uses a *character* as the source of unity. Such a play is held together primarily because all the events focus on one person. Few plays are unified predominantly through character, however, because, to create a sense of purpose, more is required than that all the incidents involve one person. In addition, plays must either tell a connected story or embody some theme. Beckett's *Happy Days* is unified in

Samuel Beckett's *Happy Days* at Stage West (Springfield, MA) in 1986. Ellen Laurie as Winnie. Directed by Gregory Boyd. (Photo by Peter Gould.)

40

part because Winnie creates the action, but ultimately the play's primary unity comes from thought. *Death of a Salesman* also gains much of its sense of purpose from Willy Loman, but the play is organized primarily through the structure of its incidents. Plays with primary emphasis on character are usually biographical, as is Robert Sherwood's *Abe Lincoln in Illinois*.

Many twentieth-century dramatists have organized plays around *thought,* with scenes linked primarily because they are connected through a central theme. Beckett's *Happy Days* is organized somewhat like a musical composition, in which a theme or motif is introduced and then elaborated on in a series of variations; ultimately, these variations fuse to create a vision of human existence as an attempt to make the best of the senseless universe in which we are trapped. Beckett does not tell a story so much as embroider upon a central idea.

Although a play usually has one major source of unity, it also uses secondary sources, since every script involves a sequence of incidents, uses characters, and implies some theme or set of ideas. Other lesser sources of unity include a dominant mood, visual style, or distinctive language. All contribute to the sense of oneness or wholeness.

The organization of dramatic action may also be approached through the parts of drama, which, in Aristotle's terms, are six: *plot, character, thought, diction, music,* and *spectacle.*

Plot

Plot is often considered merely the summary of a play's incidents, but—though it includes the story line—it also refers to the organization of all the elements into a meaningful pattern. Plot is thus the overall structure of a play.

The Beginning   The beginning of a play establishes some or all of these: the place, the occasion, the characters, the mood, the theme, and the type of probability. A play is somewhat like coming upon previously unknown places and persons. Initially, the novelty may excite interest, but as the facts about the place and people are established, interest either wanes or increases. The playwright is faced with a double problem: to give essential information and at the same time make the audience want to stay and see more.

The beginning of a play thus involves *exposition,* or the setting forth of information—about earlier events, the identity and relationship of the characters, and the present situation. While exposition is an unavoidable part of the opening scenes, it is not confined to them, for in most plays information about the past is only gradually revealed.

The amount of exposition required is partly determined by the *point of attack,* the moment at which the story is taken up. Shakespeare typically uses an early point of attack (that is, he begins the play near the beginning of the story and tells it chronologically). Thus, he needs relatively little exposition. Greek tragic dramatists, on the other hand, use later points, which require that many previous events be summarized for the audience's benefit. Thus, they actually show only the final parts of their stories. *Death of a Salesman* is unusual in having a late point of attack but in using flashbacks to show earlier events rather than merely talking about them. The point of attack in *Happy Days* can be called middle, since Winnie's situation in Act I has long existed but in Act II is far more advanced; the point is that her situation would be similar no matter what the point in time.

Playwrights motivate exposition in many ways. Ibsen most frequently introduces a character who has returned after a long absence. Answers to questions about happenings while the character was away supply the needed background information. On the other hand, many of Euripides' tragedies open with a monologue-prologue summarizing past events. In a musical play exposition may be given in song and dance. Miller uses Willy's disturbed state of mind to motivate hallucinations that take us back into the past.

In most plays, attention is usually focused early on a question, potential conflict, or theme. The beginning of such plays therefore includes what may be called an *inciting incident,* an occurrence that sets the main action in motion. In Sophocles' *Oedipus the King,* a plague is destroying the city of Thebes; the oracle at Delphi declares that the murderer of King Laius must be found and punished before the plague can end. This is the event (introduced in the prologue) that sets the action in motion.

The inciting incident usually leads directly to a *major dramatic question* around which the play is organized, although this question may change as the play progresses. For example, the question first raised in *Oedipus the King* is: Will the murderer of Laius be found and the city saved? Later, this question changes as interest shifts to Oedipus' involvement in the crime. In *Death of a Salesman,* Willy relentlessly asks, Where did I go wrong?

Not all plays include inciting incidents or clearly identifiable major dramatic questions. All have focal points, nevertheless, frequently a theme or controlling idea around which the action is centered. *Happy Days* is a good example of this alternative pattern.

The Middle   The middle of a play is normally composed of a series of complications. A *complication* is any new element that changes the direction of the action—the discovery of new information, for example, or the arrival of a character. The substance of most complications is *discovery* (any occurrence of sufficient importance to alter the direction of action). Discoveries may involve objects (a wife discovers in her husband's pocket a weapon of the kind used in a murder), persons (a young man discovers that his rival in love is his brother), facts (a young man about to leave home discovers that his mother has cancer), values (a woman discovers that self-esteem is more important than marriage), or self (a man discovers that he has been acting from purely selfish motives when he thought he was acting out of love for his children). Each complication normally has a beginning, middle, and end—its own development, climax, and resolution—just as does the play as a whole.

Means other than discoveries may be used to precipitate complications. Natural disasters (earthquakes, storms, shipwrecks, automobile accidents) are sometimes used. These are apt to seem especially contrived if they resolve the problem (for example, if the villain is killed in an automobile accident and as a result the struggle automatically ends).

Oedipus. the King by Sophocles is one of the oldest and most admired of all tragedies. Oedipus (at center), the Old Shepherd (kneeling), and two guards. Design by Desmond Heeley. (Courtesy Guthrie Theatre, Minneapolis.)

Plot   **43**

The series of complications culminates in the *crisis,* or turning point of the action. For example, in *Oedipus the King* Oedipus sets out to discover the murderer of Laius; the crisis comes when Oedipus realizes that he himself is the guilty person. In *Death of a Salesman,* the crisis comes in the final scene between Willy and Biff.

Not all plays have a clear-cut series of complications leading to a crisis. *Happy Days,* for example, is less concerned with a progressing action than with a static condition. Nevertheless, interest is maintained by the frequent introduction of new elements and an ongoing pattern of tension and relaxation.

The End The final portion of a play, often called the *resolution* or *dénouement* (unraveling or untying), extends from the crisis to the final curtain. It varies in length, but in each instance it ties off the various strands of action and answers the questions raised earlier. It brings the situation back to a state of balance and satisfies audience expectations.

Character and Characterization

Character is the primary material from which plots are created, for incidents are developed through the speech and behavior of dramatic personages. *Characterization* is the playwright's means of differentiating one personage from another. It may be divided into four levels.

The first level of characterization is *physical* and concerns such basic facts as sex, age, size, and coloration. Sometimes a dramatist does not supply all of this information, but it is present whenever the play is produced, since actors necessarily give concrete form to the characters.

The second level is *social.* It includes a character's economic status, profession or trade, religion, family relationships—all the factors that place a character in a particular environment.

The third level is *psychological.* It reveals a character's habitual responses, desires, motivations, likes, and dislikes—the inner workings of the mind. Since drama most often arises from conflicting desires, the psychological is the most essential level of characterization.

The fourth level is *moral.* It is most fully developed in serious plays. It reveals what characters are willing to do to get what they want. It also shows what characters actually do when faced with making a difficult choice (as opposed to what they have said they or others should do in such situations). Moral decisions differentiate characters more fully than any other type, since such decisions cause characters to examine their own motives, in the process of which their true natures are revealed both to themselves and to the audience. (Analyzing Willy and Winnie in terms of the four levels will tell much both about these characters and the plays in which they appear.)

A playwright can emphasize one or more of these levels and may assign many or few traits, depending on *how the character functions in the play.* For example, the audience needs to know very little about a maid who appears only to announce dinner. The principal characters, on the other hand, need to be drawn in considerable depth.

A character is revealed in several ways: through *descriptions in stage directions, prefaces, or other explanatory material* not part of the dialogue; through *what the character says;* through *what others in the play say about the character;* and, most important, through *what the character does.*

Dramatic characters are usually both *typified* and *individualized.* On the one hand, spectators would be unable to understand a character who was totally unlike any person they had ever known. Therefore, characters can usually be placed in one of several large categories or types of persons. On the other hand, the audience might be dissatisfied unless the playwright goes beyond this typification and gives characters individualizing traits. The most satisfactory dramatic characters are usually easily recognizable types with some unusual or complex qualities.

A playwright may be concerned with making characters *sympathetic* or *unsympathetic.* Normally, sympathetic characters are given major virtues and lesser foibles, while the reverse is true of unsympathetic characters. A character who is made either completely good or bad is apt to be unacceptable as a truthful reflection of human behavior. Acceptability varies, however, with the type of play. Melodrama, for example, oversimplifies human psychology and clearly divides characters into good or evil. Tragedy, on the other hand, normally depicts more complex forces at work both within and without characters and requires greater depth of characterization.

Thought

The third basic element of a play is *thought.* It includes the themes, arguments, and overall meaning of the action. It is present in all plays, even the most lighthearted farce: a playwright cannot avoid expressing some ideas, since events and characterization always imply some view of human behavior. Thought may also be used to unify a play's dramatic action.

Meaning in drama is usually implied rather than stated directly. It is suggested by the relationships among characters; the ideas associated with unsympathetic and sympathetic characters; the conflicts and their resolution; and such devices as spectacle, music, and song. Sometimes the author's intention is clearly stated in the script, as when characters advocate a certain line of action, point of view, or specific social reform.

Dramatists in different periods have used various devices to project ideas. Greek playwrights made extensive use of the *chorus,* just as those of later periods employed such devices as *soliloquies, asides,* and other forms of *direct statement.* Other tools for projecting meaning are *allegory* and *symbol.* In allegory, characters are personifications of abstract qualities (mercy, greed, and so on), as in the medieval play *Everyman.* A symbol is a concrete object or event that, while meaningful in itself, also suggests a concept or set of relationships. In *Happy Days,* the mound in which Winnie is trapped and which progressively rises around her serves as a symbol of the human condition and visually sums up the play's thought.

Just because plays imply or state meaning we should not conclude that there is a single correct interpretation for each play. Most plays permit multiple interpretations, as different productions of, and critical essays about, the same play clearly indicate. Nevertheless, evidence to support any interpretation should be discoverable in the script.

Diction

Plot, character, and thought are the basic ingredients of drama. To convey these to an audience, playwrights have at their disposal only two means—sound and spectacle. Sound includes language, music, and other aural effects; spectacle refers to all the visual elements of a production (the physical appearance and movement of performers, the costumes, scenery, properties, and lighting).

Language is the playwright's primary means of expression. When a play is performed, other expressive means (primarily music, sound effects, and spectacle) may be added; but to convey intentions to others, the dramatist depends almost entirely on dialogue and stage directions. Thus, language (diction) is the playwright's primary tool.

Diction serves many purposes. It is used to *impart information,* to *characterize,* to *direct attention* to important plot elements, to *reveal the themes and ideas* of a play, to *establish tone or mood and level of probability,* and to *establish tempo and rhythm.*

The diction of every play, no matter how realistic, is more abstract and formal than that of normal conversation. A dramatist always selects, arranges, and heightens language more than anyone does in spontaneous speech. In a realistic play, although the dialogue is modeled after everyday usage and may retain its rhythms and basic vocabulary, the characters are usually more articulate and state their ideas and feelings more precisely than would their real-life counterparts. (Reread the reviews by Krutch and Bentley for comments on the diction in *Death of a Salesman.*)

The dialogue of nonrealistic plays (such as Greek and Shakespearean tragedies) deviates markedly from everyday speech. It employs a larger vocabulary, abandons the rhythms of conversation, and makes considerable use of imagery and meter. Other types of nonrealistic plays may emphasize the clichés and repetitiveness of conversation as a way of commenting on the mechanical quality and meaninglessness of exchanges that pass for communication.

The basic criterion for judging diction is its *appropriateness* to the characters, the situation, the level of probability, and the type of play.

Music

Music, as we ordinarily understand the term, does not occur in every play. But if the term is extended to include all patterned sound, it is an important ingredient in every production, except those wholly silent.

Language has been described as the playwright's principal means of expression. But a written script, like a musical score, is not fully realized until the performers—through the elements of pitch, stress, volume, tempo, duration, and quality—transform print into sound. It is through these elements that meaning is conveyed. For example, though the words of a sentence may remain constant, its meaning can be varied by manipulating emphasis or tone ("You say *he* told her?" as contrasted with "You say he told *her?*" or the differences that result if the tone is shifted from joy to sarcasm). Because written language is not always precise in emphasis or tone, actor and director may unintentionally interpret a passage differently than the playwright intended.

The spoken aspect of language varies considerably in its formal qualities. In some plays, among them *Death of a Salesman,* it simulates the loose rhythms of everyday speech; in others, such as Shakespeare's *Hamlet,* it is shaped into formalized metrical patterns.

In addition to the sound of the actors' voices, a play may also use music in the form of incidental songs and background music, or—as in musical comedy and opera—it may utilize song and instrumental accompaniment as integral structural means. Music (especially in combination with lyrics) may serve many functions. It may *establish mood,* it may *char-*

acterize, it may *suggest ideas,* it may *compress* characterization or exposition (by presenting information, feelings, or motivations in a song), it may *lend variety,* and it is *pleasurable* in itself.

Spectacle

Spectacle encompasses all the visual elements of a production: the movement and spatial relations of characters, the lighting, settings, costumes, and properties. Since others normally supply these elements, the playwright does not have full control over them; and because the script seldom describes the spectacle precisely, the other theatre artists must discover the playwright's intentions through a careful analysis of the play's text. Similarly, the reader of a script must try to envision the spectacle in order to grasp a play's full power. The visual picture of Winnie embedded in the mound is essential to *Happy Days,* as is a setting flexible enough to permit instantaneous shifts in time and space in *Death of a Salesman.*

Some scripts give the reader more help than others. Many older plays contain almost no stage directions, and all clues must be sought in the dialogue. Beginning in the nineteenth century, when the visual elements were given added prominence, stage directions became usual. Since that time, the printed texts of plays have typically included many aids designed to help the reader visualize the action. Spectacle, like the other elements of a play, should be *appropriate* and *distinctive.* (The process of transferring the written script to the stage is treated more fully in later chapters.)

Analyzing Scripts

The structure of drama can best be understood by analyzing specific plays. Following is a list of questions useful in play analysis. Applying them to *Death of a Salesman* and *Happy Days* should further clarify the preceding discussion of dramatic structure.

1. How is the dramatic action unified? through cause-to-effect relationship of incidents? character? theme/motif/idea?
2. What are the given circumstances? (geographical location? period? time of day? socioeconomic environment? attitudes and

relationships of characters at the beginning of the play? previous action?) How is this exposition conveyed?

3. At what point in the total story does the play begin (that is, where is the point of attack)? What sets the dramatic action in motion (the inciting incident)?

4. What is the major conflict, dramatic question, or unifying theme? What is the climactic scene? How is the action resolved?

5. Are there subplots? If so, how is each related to the main plot?

6. For each character, list the physical, social, psychological, and moral traits indicated in the script. Which traits of each character are most important to the dramatic action? What is each character willing to do to achieve his/her desires?

7. What are the major ideas/themes/implications of the dramatic action? Is there a clear-cut message? If not, how is significance conveyed? Are there a number of possible interpretations of the play? If so, which seems most defensible based on the play's action, characterizations, and other elements in the script?

8. To what extent do the vocabulary, rhythm, and tempo of speeches follow or deviate from everyday colloquial usage?

9. What information is given or implied in the script about settings? costumes and makeup? lighting? Is this information significant to the dramatic action? If so, how?

10. For what kind of theatrical space was the play written? What characteristics of the script are explained by the theatrical or dramatic conventions in use at the time the play was written?

Not all of these questions need be answered for each script. Contrarily, additional questions may be needed for some scripts or for specialized interests (to meet the needs of actors, designers, and others) or for atypical scripts.

Form in Drama

Scripts are frequently classified according to form: tragedy, comedy, tragicomedy, melodrama, farce, and so on. Considerable emphasis used to be placed on understanding the essential qualities of each dramatic form and the proper classification of each script. *Death of a Salesman,* for example, provoked a lengthy controversy over whether it was a true tragedy. Since the 1960s, concern over dramatic form has lessened considerably, in part because much recent drama defies formal classification.

Nevertheless, one cannot read very much about drama without encountering formal labels. Consequently, some information about dramatic form is helpful.

Basically, *form* means the shape or configuration given something for a particular purpose. A sentence is a form created by words arranged in a particular order so as to convey a complete thought. Similarly, a play is a form created by arranging incidents in a particular order so as to create a dramatic action. All plays have in common certain formal elements that permit us to recognize them as plays rather than as novels, epic poems, or essays. Still, those works that we recognize as plays are not all alike. In fact, critics have divided them into a number of groupings (or dramatic forms) on the basis of certain characteristics, the most important of which are type of action, overall tone, and basic emotional appeals. Throughout much of history, *tragedy* and *comedy* have been considered the two basic forms.

Tragedy   The oldest known form of drama, tragedy, presents a genuinely serious action and maintains a serious tone throughout, although there may be moments of comic relief. It raises significant issues about the nature of human existence, morality, or human relationships. The protagonist, or leading character, of tragedy is usually a person who arouses our sympathy and admiration but who encounters disaster through the pursuit of some goal, worthy in itself, that conflicts with another goal or principle. The emotional effect of tragedy is the arousal of a strongly empathetic response for those who strive for integrity and dignity. Tragedy is a form associated above all with ancient Greece and Elizabethan England. (In later chapters, two of the world's greatest tragedies, Sophocles' *Oedipus the King* and Shakespeare's *Hamlet,* will be discussed in detail.) Few plays in the twentieth century have been called tragedies, perhaps because, as some critics have argued, we no longer consider human beings capable of the kind of heroic and unselfish action associated with the great tragic heroes.

Comedy   A dramatic form that had its origins in ancient Greece, comedy is based on some deviation from normality in action, character, or thought. It must not pose a serious threat and an "in-fun" tone is usually maintained. Comedy also demands that an audience view the situation objectively. Henri Bergson argues that comedy requires "an anesthesia of the heart," since it is often difficult to laugh at anything about which we feel deeply. We may find it funny to see someone slip on a banana peel, but if we discover that it is a friend who is just recovering from a serious operation, our concern will destroy the laughter. Similarly, we may dislike some things so intensely that we cannot see their ridiculous qualities. Nevertheless, any subject, however trivial or important, can become the subject of comedy if we place it in the right framework and if we distance ourselves sufficiently from its serious implications. Comedy arouses emotions ranging between joy and scorn, with laughter as their common feature.

Other Forms   Not all plays are wholly serious or comic. The two are often intermingled to create seriocomic effects. Perhaps the best known of the mixed types is *melodrama,* the favorite form of the nineteenth century and still the dominant form among television dramas dealing with crime and danger. A melodrama develops a temporarily serious action that is initiated and kept in motion by the malicious designs of a villain; a happy resolution is made possible by destroying the villain's power. Melodrama depicts a world in which good and evil are sharply differentiated; there is seldom any question where the audience's sympathies should lie. The appeals are strong and basic, creating a strong desire to see the "good guys" triumph and the "bad guys" punished. This desire is usually met in a double ending, one kind for the good and another for the bad. Melodrama is related to tragedy through its serious action and to comedy through its happy ending. It is a popular form, perhaps because it assures audiences that good triumphs over evil.

During the twentieth century, concern for giving formal labels to plays has greatly diminished, probably because we no longer consider it possible to categorize situations and people precisely. Boundaries have come to seem so fluid that a single event may be viewed almost simultaneously as serious, comic, threatening, or grotesque. Thus, tone may shift rapidly; elements that in the past were associated with tragedy or comedy may appear and disappear or be transformed into their opposites. As a result, the old formal categories have lost their significance. Since World War II, plays have been labeled "tragic farce," "anti-play," "tragedy for the music hall," and a variety of other names that suggest the intermingling of elements from earlier categories.

Despite all the changes, we need to recognize that each play has a form; otherwise, we would not be able to read or comprehend the script. It is perhaps best to remember that the form of each play is in some respects unique—no two plays are exactly alike—but that there are sufficient similarities among certain plays to group them into a common category. Whether or not we have precise notions about tragedy, comedy, or other formal labels for plays, we are aware of distinctions between the serious and the funny, and most of us freely use "tragic," "comic," and "melodramatic" to describe events in the world around us. Basic awareness of dramatic form will be helpful in many of the subsequent discussions in this book.

Style in Drama

Even plays of the same form vary considerably. One reason for this variety is *style*. Like *form*, the word *style* is difficult to define because it has been used to designate many things. Basically, however, style is a characteristic that results from a distinctive mode of expression or method of presentation. For example, style may stem from traits attributable to a period, a nation, a movement, or an author. In most periods, the drama of all Western nations has certain common qualities caused by prevailing religious, philosophical, and psychological concepts and by current theatrical conventions. Thus, we may speak of an eighteenth-century style. Within a period, national differences permit us to distinguish a French from an English style. Furthermore, the dramas written by neoclassicists have qualities that distinguish them from those written by romantics, expressionists, or absurdists. Finally, the plays of individual authors have distinctive qualities that set them off from the work of all other writers. Thus, we may speak of Shakespeare's or Sophocles' style.

Style in theatre results from three basic influences. First, it is grounded upon assumptions about truth and reality. Dramatists of all movements or periods have sought to convey truthful pictures of humanity, but they have differed widely in their answers to the following questions: What is ultimate truth? Where is it to be found? How can we perceive reality? Some have argued that surface appearances only disguise reality, which is to be found in some inner or spiritual realm. Others have maintained that truth can be discovered only by objective study of things that can be felt, tasted, seen, heard, or smelled. To advocates of the latter view, observable details hold the key to truth; to advocates of the former view, the same details only hide the truth. Although all writers attempt to depict the truth as they see it, the individual playwright's conception of truth is determined by basic temperament and talents and by the philosophical, social, and psychological influences that have shaped him.

Second, style results from the manner in which a playwright manipulates the means of expression. All dramatists have at their disposal the same means—sound and spectacle. Nevertheless, the work of each playwright is distinctive, for each perceives the human condition from a somewhat different point of view, and these perceptions are reflected in situations, characters, and ideas, in manipulation of language, and in suggestions for the use of spectacle. In the process of writing, playwrights set their distinctive stamps (or style) on their plays.

Third, style results from the manner in which the play is presented in the theatre. The directing, acting, scenery, costumes, and lighting used to translate the play from the written script to the stage may each be manipulated in many ways; the distinctive way in which these elements are handled in a production characterize its style. Because so many people are involved in producing a play, it is not unusual to find conflicting or inconsistent styles in a single production. Typically, unity of style is a primary artistic goal. Each theatre artist usually seeks to create qualities analogous to those found in the written text, and the director then coordinates all of the parts into a unified whole. Ultimately, style results from the way in which means are adapted to ends. Style contributes significantly to a sense of unity and wholeness, which is one mark of effective drama and performance.

The Playwright

So far we have been looking at plays as texts already in existence. But plays are created by dramatists, and thus, how playwrights work is of some interest, at least broadly speaking.

There is no standard approach. Each writer tends to have a point of view or a range of interests that make some subjects more attractive than others. Samuel Beckett* is preoccupied with the human predicament in an unknowable universe, whereas Arthur Miller* is concerned with personal and social morality. While both are concerned with writing truthfully, their interests draw them to widely differing subjects, just as their personal perceptions about human beings and the human condition cause them to treat their subjects distinctively.

The inspiration for a play may come from an actual event, a personal experience, an anecdote, an unusual character, an idea, or almost any other source, since the possibilities for drama are ever present, and almost anything can stimulate a dramatist's imagination.

Approaches to actual writing are equally varied. Bertolt Brecht* began with a story outline and then elaborated on it. Victorien Sardou (probably the most successful of nineteenth-century playwrights) wrote the climactic scene first and then worked backward from it. Henrik Ibsen* made numerous notes about situations and characters, often over a period of years, before actually beginning a play. Sam Shepard* has said that he begins with a visual image and starts writing without knowing where it will lead. Since the 1960s, several plays have been written with

*These playwrights, among the world's best-known dramatists, are discussed at length later in this book. A play by each is also included in the companion anthology, *Plays for the Theatre* (5th edition).

Variations in visual style in different productions of the same script can be seen in the illustrations of scenes from Ibsen's *Peer Gynt*.

Peter Stein's production of Ibsen's *Peer Gynt*. This scene shows the insane asylum at the foot of the Sphinx in Egypt. The audience seating is beyond the board wall at center left. Theater at the Halleschen Ufer, West Berlin. (Courtesy German Information Center.)

Ibsen's *Peer Gynt* at the Dusseldorf Schauspielhaus, 1985. The stage floor is divided into sections, each mounted on an elevator that permits it to be lowered or raised. Here Peer, standing in a trench, is separated from Solveig both by levels and lighting. Directed by Michael Grüner. (Photo by Lore Bermbach. Courtesy German Information Center.)

Painted background of a ship at sea with openings for characters supposedly on the ship, thus deliberately undercutting any realistic effect created by the picture. Ibsen's *Peer Gynt* as produced at the Thalia Theater, Hamburg. It required two evenings to perform and used two actors in the leading role, one for the young Peer, another for the old Peer. (Photo by Hermann J. Baus. Courtesy German Information Center.)

Ibsen's *Peer Gynt* at the Guthrie Theatre, Minneapolis. Note the spotlights in the upper left corner and the grouped candles on the floor at lower right. Note also the mirrored wall at the rear, which provides another view of the scene. Directed by Liviu Ciulei. Designed by Santo Loquasto. (Photo by Joe Giannetti. Courtesy Guthrie Theatre.)

the aid of group improvisations on an outline, situation, or idea; as situation, movement, and dialogue evolve, the dramatist selects and shapes what seems most effective.

Similarly, the mechanics of writing vary widely from one writer to another. Beckett does most of his writing by hand in bound notebooks. Some writers compose at the typewriter or at word processors, others try out dialogue by speaking lines into tape recorders and then listening to it. Through these or other methods, a text gradually takes shape. Seldom does a playwright arrive at the final version of a script on the first try. It is sometimes said that plays are not written but rewritten. The goal is to shape the many elements of a script into a compelling dramatic action that can command and hold attention and that will be effective on the stage and not merely on the page. Some writers spend years refining a script. On the other hand, Sam Shepard long refused to revise at all on the grounds that to do so would be like cheating, because it changed the way the play had come out originally.

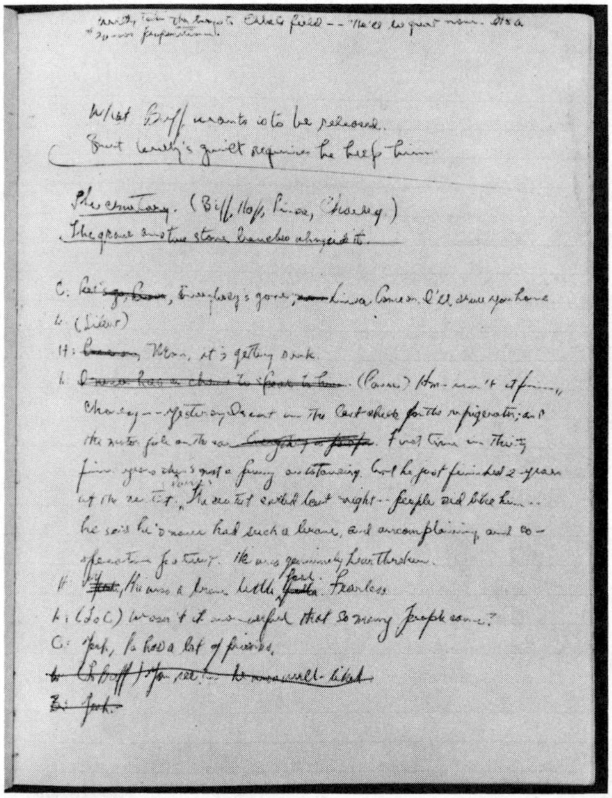

Page from a bound notebook in which Arthur Miller wrote parts of *Death of a Salesman*. Shown here is the beginning of the Requiem (the final) scene of the play. (Courtesy Mr. Miller and the Harry Ransom Humanities Research Center, University of Texas at Austin.)

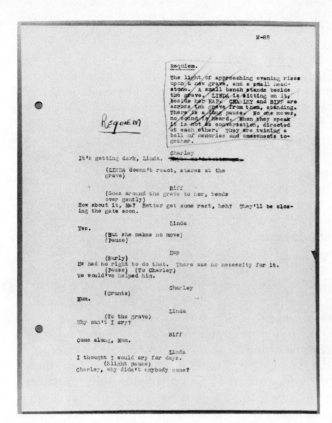

Page from the typescript of the next-to-final version of *Death of a Salesman*. Differences among the handwritten, typed, and printed versions of this scene reveal much about the process of rewriting. (Courtesy of Mr. Miller and the Harry Ransom Humanities Research Center, University of Texas at Austin.)

Because plays are intended for the stage, most writers need to see their work performed before they can be sure they have accomplished what they intended. Lines that read well may seem contrived when spoken; additionally, a writer needs to be certain that the dialogue positions the emphasis of a speech at just the right point, that the rhythms are effective when spoken aloud, that speeches make their intended points, and that the speech patterns are those appropriate to each character. The writer must also make sure that the dramatic action is clear, that revelations create the intended effect, that tension mounts and relaxes as it should. In other words, the dramatist seeks to write a play that is completely stageworthy.

In the past, many playwrights were intimately involved with production. Greek playwrights usually staged their own works. Shakespeare wrote his plays for the company in which he acted—apparently, he knew in advance who would play each role—and he was undoubtedly involved in staging his own plays. Molière was head of his own company as well as it principal playwright and actor. Although not all playwrights of earlier times had close connections with the theatre, many more did than in modern times. Since the nineteenth century, playwrights have most usually worked in isolation, not knowing who will perform their plays or if they will find someone willing to produce their scripts. Only a few playwrights today have close ties to theatre organizations. Thus, although their work is essential to the theatre, contemporary playwrights are usually the theatre artists most removed from the actual processes of play production.

When today's dramatists wish to see their plays performed professionally, they must find a producer. They frequently send copies of their plays to the various resident theatre companies now located in major cities. Sometimes this gains the desired result, but the problems involved in finding a producer and in making contractual arrangements are so complex that most writers prefer to work through an agent, who understands the legal and financial aspects of production and can devote time to placing a play. (For these services the agent usually receives ten percent of the client's earnings.) Most playwrights also belong to the Dramatists Guild, whose purpose it is to protect authors.

A producer who is interested in a play may take an option on it by securing rights to perform it within a specified time limit. If the producer then decides to present the play, the dramatist is given a contract, most frequently one with the standard provisions specified by the Dramatists Guild. The playwright seldom relinquishes the television, film, amateur, or foreign rights to the producer. The contract usually specifies that the writer must be available for consultation and to make revisions throughout the rehearsal period, conditions that most writers are eager to meet.

Although a script is considered essential, playwrights usually find that almost everyone believes that he or she can improve their work. Even before a producer sees a play, the writer's agent may suggest alterations. A producer may express a desire to consider a play again after certain changes have been made. Sometimes, although much more rarely now than formerly, well-known actors indicate an interest in a play if it can be rewritten to show off their talent to greater advantage. But the most meaningful requests are usually those made by the director prior to or during rehearsals, for it is the director who stages the play and who has the most direct working relationship with the dramatist. Some directors content themselves with helping the writer achieve more precision in the script; others assume the role of coauthor and demand that changes be made to suit their own ideas of effectiveness. When *Cat on a Hot Tin Roof* was being rehearsed for Broadway, Tennessee Williams was cajoled by his director Elia Kazan into rewriting the final act. Williams so dis-

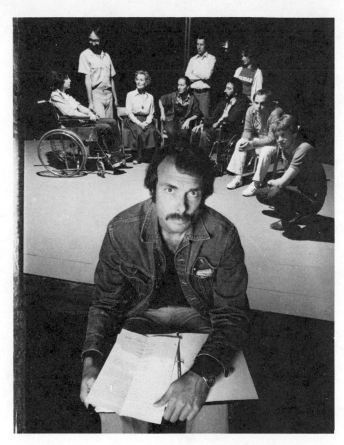

The playwright Arthur Kopit with the cast of his play *Wings*. (Photo by Jack Mitchell.)

approved of the result that when he published the text, he included both his preferred ending and the ending he had written to please Kazan.

Often the playwright revises the text right up to opening night. Formerly, plays destined for Broadway were given a series of out-of-town tryouts; after each performance, audience responses and critical notices were carefully studied, and revisions intended to overcome problems were made and tested. Sometimes a play was almost completely rewritten during this process. Nowadays, most of the plays seen on Broadway have been presented first in resident companies outside of New York or in Off-Off Broadway theatres, or have been imported from abroad. Most playwrights prefer the present situation because they usually can retain greater control over their scripts when they work in non-Broadway theatres. A playwright may continue to work on a script even after its initial production is over. Tennessee Williams wrote and published multiple versions of several of his plays.

Several organizations now attempt to assist young playwrights to develop their talents. The Eugene O'Neill Foundation in Waterford, Connecticut, selects a few playwrights each summer to come there and work with a director, critic, actors, and audience to improve their scripts. The Actors Theatre in Louisville stages a festival of new short plays each fall and one of new full-length plays in the spring each year; critics and producers from both the United States and abroad now look forward to this major showcase of new talent. These are only two of several schemes to develop new dramatists.

The health of playwriting is of vital concern, since the script has been the usual starting point for production since the beginning of theatre. Thus, in the chapters that follow we will return often to the playwright and to scripts as we examine the varied forms the theatre has taken and the various functions it has served, both past and present.

Part II

VARIETIES OF THEATRICAL EXPERIENCE

Some form of theatrical activity has probably existed since the very earliest times, although surviving records only permit us to trace it back with any certainty for about 2500 years. That span of time is sufficient, as one might expect, to show us that the theatre has not always been the way it is now and that it has been shaped into many different modes serving a number of different functions in human society. When we look at today's theatre, we see only a small part of what the theatre is capable of, and we are given all too few clues about what it has been or might be. If we are to understand the theatre, we need to be aware of its multiple possibilities and some of the transformations it has undergone. This is true not for the sake of knowing the theatre's history but because awareness of differing kinds of theatrical expression can stimulate the imagination to reshape theatrical elements in previously untried ways. Creative artists do not merely repeat old forms, they also reshape them, usually stimulated by awareness of alternative possibilities.

In the theatre, awareness of the past is important for other reasons. Many plays from the past still form a significant part of the repertory. Each of these plays was written with a particular kind of theatre structure, set of theatrical conventions, and audience in mind. Although plays may transcend the conditions of time and place—otherwise they would not communicate with us today—we can understand them most fully in the context within which they originated. They are among the best indicators we have of the society from which they sprang. Thus, they are simultaneously specific to a particular context and universal in their ability to speak to us in the much broader context of human experience in general.

The Greek and Roman Theatre Experiences

4

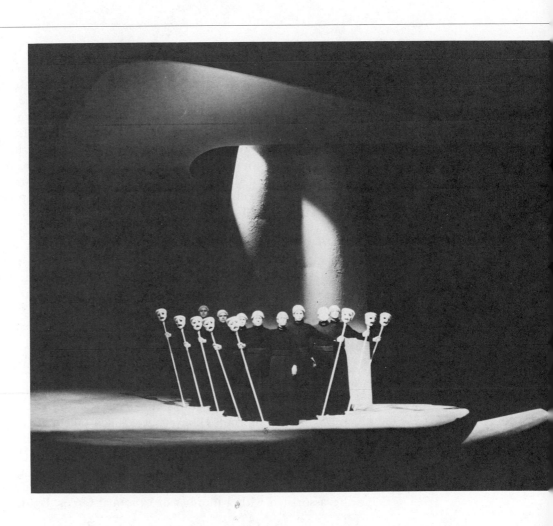

Theatre in the Western World can be traced back to ancient Greece. Our first definite record of a theatrical event is found in 534 B.C., when a contest was initiated for the best tragedy. The winner of this contest was Thespis, the earliest playwright and actor whose name has come down to us. It is from him that we derive the term *thespian,* still used to refer to performers.

From the beginning, Greek drama was presented exclusively at festivals honoring Dionysus, one of the many gods worshiped by the Greeks, who conceived of their gods essentially as superior immortal humans. The gods were numerous, and consequently each had power over only a limited sphere of activity. Like humans, these gods had many failings: they were jealous of each other; bickered among themselves; were vindictive when they considered themselves to have been slighted by humans; took sides in both human and divine quarrels; indulged frequently in adulterous affairs; and in general made human existence unpredictable. Perhaps because there were so many gods, the Greeks did not observe a holy day comparable to the Sabbath. Rather, they had a series of religious festivals scattered throughout the year, one or more of which were dedicated to each god.

Dionysus, the god in whose honor plays were presented, was the god of wine (one of the principal products of Greece) and fertility. Thus, his blessing was sought in order to ensure fertility of both human beings and the land. Supposedly the son of Zeus (the greatest of Greek gods) and Semele (a mortal), Dionysus was killed (allegedly at the behest of Zeus' jealous wife), dismembered, resurrected, and deified. The myths associated with him were closely related to the life cycle and seasonal changes: birth, growth, decay, death, and rebirth; spring, summer, fall, winter, and the return of spring. As the god of wine and revelry, he was also associated with a number of irrational forces. By the fifth century

B.C., Athens held four festivals in honor of Dionysus each year, at three of which theatrical performances were offered. Plays were not presented at the festivals held for any other god.

The major Dionysian festival in Athens was the City Dionysia. Extending over several days near the end of March, it was one of the most important civic occasions of each year and a major showcase for Athenian wealth and power. By the mid-fifth century Athens had become head of a confederation of small states for which it provided leadership and protection in return for sizable financial tributes. It was this arrangement that permitted Athens to build the Parthenon—a temple dedicated to Athena, the city's patron goddess—and other major structures, including the Theatre of Dionysus. The City Dionysia was open to the whole Greek world, and during the festival, the tribute paid by Athens' satellite states was exhibited in the theatre. Thus, the festival was both a religious and civic celebration, and was under the direct supervision of the principal state official. Theatrical performances, therefore, were viewed in a radically different light than they are today. They were offerings of the city to a god. At the same time, they were expressions of civic pride—indications of the cultural superiority of Athens over the other Greek states, which only later developed their own theatres.

Athens was also the originator of the dramatic form we call tragedy. Throughout the fifth century, three tragic dramatists competed at each

Greek vase painting of the late fifth century B.C., depicting actors of a satyr play. Some of the actors hold their masks in their hands. The embroidered robes resemble those thought to have been worn by tragic actors. Note at bottom center the flute player, who provided the musical accompaniment for dramatic performances. (From Baumeister, *Denkmaler des Klassischens Altertums*, 1888.)

City Dionysia, each writer presenting a group of four plays—three tragedies and one satyr play (a short play of comic or satiric tone, poking fun at some Greek myth, using a chorus of satyrs, and played following the tragedies, perhaps as a way of sending the audience home in a happy frame of mind). Thus, nine tragedies were produced at each City Dionysia, a total of 900 during the fifth century. Of these, only thirty-two have survived, all written by three dramatists—Aeschylus (523-456 B.C.), Sophocles (496-406 B.C.), and Euripides (480-406 B.C.), who are still ranked among the world's great playwrights.

Of the surviving tragedies, *Oedipus the King* by Sophocles is often said to be the finest. Performed about 430 B.C.—approximately 100 years after the establishment of the contest for tragedy—it continues to be produced frequently. Before we look more closely at this play and its performance, let us examine some features of the Greek theatre building and the conventions that affected staging.

The Theatre of Dionysus

Plays were performed in the Theatre of Dionysus, laid out on the slope of the hill just beneath the Acropolis, a fortified area that included the Parthenon, the city treasury, and other buildings considered essential to the city's survival. The theatre was located within a compound that included a temple and a large outdoor altar dedicated to the worship of Dionysus. Originally, the slope (without any seating) served as the *theatron* ("seeing place," the origin of our word *theatre*). A flat terrace below the slope served as the *orchestra* (dancing place), in the middle of which was placed an altar (*thymele*) dedicated to Dionysus.

This arrangement was gradually formalized and converted into a stone structure. The auditorium became a semicircle of stadiumlike stone seats extending up the hill to the retaining walls of the Acropolis. When completed, it held at least 14,000 persons and perhaps as many as 17,000. This seating curved partway around a circular orchestra measuring about 65 feet in diameter and used as performance space, especially for the chorus. On the side of the orchestra facing the seats was the *skene* ("hut" or "tent," probably indicative of the original structure that was used as a place to which the actors could retire or where they could change costumes, and the origin of our word *scene*). Once its possibilities as a background for the action was recognized, the *skene* was elaborated into a structure some 75–100 feet long and probably two stories high. It is usually thought that this scene house had three doors— a large central doorway flanked on either side by somewhat smaller

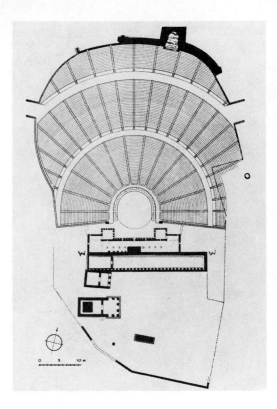

Plan of the precinct devoted to the worship of Dionysus, showing the temple and altar at the bottom and the theatre at top. Note the scene house below the circular orchestra and the *paradoi* (passageways) between the ends of the scene house and the auditorium. (From Dörpfeld-Reisch, *Das Griechische Theater,* 1896.)

doors—all opening onto the acting area, but the exact number is unknown. The roof of this structure could also be used as an acting area to represent high places or for the appearance of gods. The scene house was not architecturally joined to the auditorium; the spaces (called *paradoi*) at either side between the *skene* and the auditorium were used as entrances and exits for performers (especially the chorus) and by spectators before and after performances. Since the original scene house has long since disappeared, no one knows exactly how it looked. Some possibilities are shown in the illustrations on page 69.

The scene house probably served as a formalized background for all plays, even those set in woods, on seashores, or before caves (as would be true later in Shakespeare's theatre). This convention meant that locale was established by the dialogue and not by representational scenery. The action in Greek plays usually took place out-of-doors, but occasionally the outcome of events that occurred indoors was shown. Most of these scenes involved the corpses of characters slain offstage but required by the dramatic action to be shown onstage. For this purpose, the large central doorway seems to have been opened and a wheeled platform

The best preserved of all ancient Greek theatres is that at Epidaurus, which is still used for festival performances. The scene house, at left, is a temporary structure erected on the ruins of the original. A tragic chorus, composed of fifteen persons, is seen in the orchestra. This picture conveys a sense of the auditorium's size and the audience-performer relationship. Another version is shown in the color photos following page 112. (Courtesy Embassy of Greece.)

(the *eccyclema*) pushed out. Another common occurrence in Greek plays was the appearance of a god. Sometimes the roof was used, but in many plays the god had to descend to ground level or be lifted from the orchestra to roof level. For this purpose, a cranelike device (the *machina*) was used. (The overuse of gods to resolve difficult dramatic situations led to any contrived ending being labeled a *deus ex machina*—god from the machine—ending.) Probably nothing better illustrates the nonrepresentational conventions of the Greek theatre than the machine, for its fulcrum arm, ropes, and pulleys were visible to the entire audience. It was not intended to fool anyone; rather, it was used to suggest the *idea* of flying, a power possessed by the gods and denied to humans.

From our standpoint, one of the most remarkable things about the Theatre of Dionysus is its size. Today, a theatre with an audience ca-

Four versions of how the scene house of the Theatre of Dionysus may have looked in the fifth century B.C. (From Ernst Fiechter. *Antike Griechische Theaterbauten*. Courtesy Verlag W. Kohlhammer GmbH, Stuttgart, and Dr. Charlotte Fiechter.)

pacity of even 3000 persons is considered to be almost unusable for drama because of the difficulty of seeing and hearing. We expect realistic visual effects and acting, and we feel cheated if we cannot see every detail as we do on the movie or television screen. Obviously, the Greeks had different expectations, as is clear from the conventions they developed and accepted. The structures today that most resemble Greek theatres are sports arenas, and keeping in mind the scale of such structures will help us understand many other conventions of the Greek theatre.

The Performers

The performers in the Greek theatre may be divided into four categories: actors, chorus, supernumeraries, and musicians. All were male.

The rules of the Athenian drama contests restricted the number of speaking actors to three for each author. This did not mean that the roles were restricted to three; rather, all speaking parts had to be assumed by three actors. This often meant that the same actor had to play several roles, and that the same three actors appeared in all three of the tragedies presented by a competing dramatist. Supernumeraries (extras) could be used, but they were not permitted to speak lines. This convention probably developed because the state supplied and paid the actors for each contest. A principal actor was assigned each playwright by lot. (The playwright usually staged his own plays.) The playwright and this leading actor then probably chose the other two. A prize was offered for the best tragic actor at each festival, but only the leading actors were eligible to win.

The chorus was composed of fifteen men. A playwright wishing to present his plays at the City Dionysia had to apply to the principal government official for a chorus. We do not know how this official decided which playwrights would be granted choruses, but it is clear that being granted a chorus was the mark of acceptance. This official also paired the dramatist with a *choregus*, a wealthy citizen who bore the expense of training and costuming that dramatist's choruses and also paid the musicians needed to accompany the choruses during their training and during performances. The well-to-do citizens of Athens were required to take turns serving as *choregoi*, and most seem to have done so willingly. (Thus, the financing of productions was undertaken entirely by the state and a few wealthy citizens.) The prize awarded for the best group of plays was shared by the playwright and his *choregus*.

Choruses were awarded some eleven months prior to the next festival. Just how much of the available time was spent in training is unknown, but apparently the routine was not unlike that applied today in training athletes. Exercises and diets were controlled, and the chorus worked under the strict and strenuous supervision of a trainer. A great deal of emphasis was placed on both singing and dancing, since the fifteen members both sang and danced the choral passages. Thus, much of their training resembled that of opera singers and of dancers. Usually they performed in unison, but at times they were divided into semichoruses of seven members, which performed in turn or exchanged speeches. The chorus leader sometimes had solo lines, but the rest of the chorus usually responded as a group or as two subgroups that performed and responded alternately to each other.

The chorus was one of the distinctive conventions of the Greek theatre. It usually made its entrance following the prologue and was present thereafer until the end of the play. The choral odes between episodes divided the action into segments something like the acts of a modern play. The chorus served several functions in Greek drama. First, it was treated as a group character who expressed opinions, gave advice, and occasionally threatened to interfere in the action. Second, it often seemed to express the author's point of view and established a standard against which the actions of the characters could be judged. Third, it frequently served as the ideal spectator, reacting to events and characters as the author would like the audience to react. Fourth, it helped to establish mood and heighten dramatic effects. Fifth, it added color, movement, and spectacle as it sang and danced the choral interludes.

The principal musical accompaniment in Greek tragedy was provided by the flute player, who preceded the chorus as it made its entrance and then (like the chorus) remained onstage throughout. Thus, the source of the musical accompaniment was visible to the audience and not kept offstage, as in most modern productions. The flute player wore a sandal with a metal clapper on its sole with which he marked time. Both percussionist and flutist, he also seems to have composed the music he played.

Although there was a large amount of music in a Greek theatrical performance, almost none of it has survived, and the texts of Greek plays do little to make us aware that we should be hearing certain passages sung or recited to musical accompaniment. (It was out of experiments intended to unite music and text as they had been in Greek tragedy that opera originated in Italy in the late sixteenth and early seventeenth centuries.) Greek music had a great variety of musical modes, each with a particular tonal quality thought appropriate to cer-

Statuette of a tragic actor showing mask, headdress, and long robe. This figure is from a period later than fifth century B.C., and is more exaggerated in appearance than would have been typical in Sophocles' time. The projections below the statuette are pegs that were used to attach it to a base, now missing. (From *Monumenti Inediti*, II [1879].)

tain kinds of subjects or emotions. It probably more nearly approximated the sounds of present-day music of the Near East than that of Western Europe or America. As used in the Greek theatre, it may have had much in common with film music, which is intended to enhance the mood and emotion of the action it accompanies.

All of the performers with the exception of the musician wore masks made of lightweight wood, cork, or linen. This is another of the Greek theatre's distinctive conventions and one that served several purposes: it facilitated the rapid change of roles required when three actors had to play all the parts; it made it easier for male performers to embody female roles; it helped the actor in assuming roles that differed widely in age or character type; and it assisted communication in the large theatres by capturing and emphasizing the essential qualities of each character. Each mask covered the entire head and included the appropriate hair and headdress. Thus, the actor's appearance could be changed instantaneously with a change of mask.

A variety of clothing was used for stage purposes. A long-sleeved, heavily embroidered tunic was worn by some characters, but since there are references in the plays to characters in rags, in mourning, and in Greek or in foreign dress, it seems unlikely that all characters were dressed alike. The selection of costume was probably determined by its appropriateness to the role. The sleeved, embroidered tunic, which was not worn in Greek daily life, may have been reserved for supernatural or non-Greek characters, while native dress was used for others. The usual dress in Greece was an ankle-length or knee-length garment called a *chiton*. On his feet the tragic actor wore a soft, flexible, high-topped boot in common use at that time.

All of these conventions suggest that performance in the Greek theatre was highly formalized. When we remember that the same actor played several roles, that men played both male and female roles, that the performers wore masks, that much of the text was sung and danced, and that the scale of the theatre prevented small details from being seen, we are faced with a performance mode quite different from that of the present day. That this mode was extremely pleasing to the Greeks emphasizes a simple truth: what any group accepts as effective theatrical performance depends to a great extent upon the group's familiarity with, and acceptance of, a particular set of conventions and upon the skill with which those conventions are handled.

Oedipus the King and Its Performance

Among the many events at the City Dionysia was the re-enactment of Dionysus' arrival in Athens. This involved a procession that included the major officials of Athens, the actors and others associated with the performances to be presented, and many citizens who carried gifts for the god. This procession wound through much of Athens, stopped for dances and ceremonies at various altars, and ended at the precinct dedicated to Dionysus, where a bull was sacrificed on the main altar. Subsequently, there were five days of performances that, in addition to the tragedies, included comedies and dithyrambs (hymns to Dionysus sung and danced by groups of fifty men or boys). At the end of the festival, prizes were awarded. Thus, the performance of *Oedipus the King* was embedded within the much larger festival framework.

Everyone was encouraged to attend the performances. Prisoners were even released during the festival. A public fund was established to provide tickets for those who could not afford the very low price of admission. Seats at the front of the auditorium were reserved for public officials and special guests, and the center seat in the front row was reserved for the head priest of the Dionysian cult. The audience was composed of men, women, boys, and even slaves. Officials were responsible for keeping order, and violence in the theatre was punishable by death. It is usually assumed that performances lasted all day, since a number of plays were presented without intermission. If so, there must have been considerable coming and going and much eating and drinking in the theatre. The audience expressed itself noisily and at times hissed actors off the stage. The atmosphere must have resembled a mixture of religious festival and athletic event.

Performances seem to have begun at dawn. There was no artificial lighting in the theatre, no proscenium arch or curtain. The auditorium rose rather sharply up the hill, so that most of the spectators looked down on the acting areas and could see over the stage house across a plain to the sea. The total visual context was immense.

The beginning of *Oedipus the King* was signaled by the entrance through one of the *paradoi* of a group of people of all ages carrying branches, the symbol of the suppliant. Oedipus, masked and in full-length *chiton,* appeared through the central doorway of the stage house (which in this play represented a palace) to hear their petition; then Creon, returning from Delphi with his news, arrived through the other *parados*. After the suppliants left, the chorus of fifteen elderly Thebans, all as nearly identical in appearance as possible and preceded by the flute player, marched into the orchestra and sang the first choral song while moving in stately patterns. Thus, the play proceeded, although space does not permit us to follow it moment by moment. Instead, let us stop and look more closely at the script.

The Script

The skill with which *Oedipus the King* is constructed can be appreciated if we compare the complex story (which actually begins with a prophecy prior to the birth of Oedipus) with Sophocles' ordering of the events. In the play, there is a simultaneous movement backward and forward in time as the revelation of the past moves Oedipus ever nearer to his doom in the present.

The division of the play into a prologue and five episodes separated by choral passages is typical of Greek tragedy. The prologue is devoted principally to exposition: a plague is destroying the city of Thebes; Creon returns from Delphi with a command from the oracle to find and punish the murderer of Laius; Ocdipus promises to obey the command. All of the necessary information is given in a very brief scene, and the first important question—Who is the murderer of Laius?—is raised. The prologue is followed by the *parodos,* or entry of the chorus, and the first choral song, which offers prayers to the gods for deliverance.

The first episode begins with Oedipus' proclamation and his curse upon the murderer. This proclamation has great dramatic power because Oedipus is unknowingly pronouncing a curse upon himself. Then Tiresias, the seer, enters. His refusal to answer questions provokes Oedipus' anger, the first display of a response that is developed forcefully throughout the first four episodes. Oedipus' quick temper, we later discover, has caused him to kill Laius. By the time Tiresias has been driven to answer, Oedipus suspects some trickery. The scene ends in a stalemate of accusations.

It is interesting to note that while the first four episodes move forward in the present, they go successively further backward in time. This first episode reveals only that part of the past immediately preceding Oedipus' arrival at Thebes. The choral passage that follows the first episode reflects upon the previous scene, stating the confusion that Sophocles wishes the audience to feel.

The second episode builds logically upon the first. Creon comes to defend himself against the accusations of conspiracy with Tiresias. Queen Jocasta is drawn to the scene by the quarrel, and she and the chorus persuade Oedipus to abate his anger. This quarrel illustrates Oedipus' complete faith in his own righteousness. In spite of Tiresias' accusation, no suspicion of his own guilt has entered Oedipus' mind. Ironically, Jocasta's attempt to placate Oedipus leads to his first suspicion about himself. She tells him that oracles are not to be believed and as evidence points to Laius' death, which did not come in the manner prophesied. But her description recalls to Oedipus the circumstances under which he has killed a man. He insists that Jocasta send for the one survivor of Laius' party. This scene continues the backward exploration of the past, for Oedipus tells of his life in Corinth, his visit to the oracle of Delphi, and the murder of the man who is later discovered to have been Laius. The choral song that follows is concerned with the questions Jocasta has raised about oracles. The chorus concludes that if oracles are proven untrue, then the gods themselves are to be doubted.

Though Jocasta has called oracles into question, she obviously does not disbelieve in the gods, for at the beginning of the third episode she makes offerings to them. She is interrupted by the entrance of the Messenger from Corinth, who brings news of the death of Oedipus' supposed father, Polybus. But this news, rather than arousing grief, as one would expect, is greeted with rejoicing, for it seems to disprove the oracle's prediction that Oedipus would kill his father. This seeming reversal only serves to heighten the effect of the following events. Oedipus still fears returning to Corinth because the oracle also has prophesied that he will marry his own mother. Thinking that he will set Oedipus' mind at ease, the Messenger reveals that he himself brought Oedipus as an infant to Polybus. The circumstances under which the Messenger acquired the child bring home the truth to Jocasta. This discovery leads to a complete reversal for Jocasta, for the oracles she has cast doubt upon in the preceding scene have suddenly been vindicated. She strives to stop Oedipus from making further inquiries, but he interprets her entreaties as fear that he may be of humble birth. Joscasta goes into the palace; it is the last we see of her.

This scene not only has revealed the truth to Jocasta, it has also diverted attention from the murder of Laius to the birth of Oedipus. The scene goes backward in time to the infancy of Oedipus. The choral song that follows is filled with romantic hopes, as the chorus speculates on Oedipus' parentage and suggests such possibilities as Apollo and the nymphs. The truth is deliberately kept at a distance here in order to make the following scene more powerful.

This choral song is followed by the entry of the Herdsman (the sole survivor of Laius' party at the time of the murder and the person from whom the Corinthian Messenger had acquired the infant Oedipus). The Herdsman does not wish to speak, but he is tortured by Oedipus' servants into doing so. In this very rapid scene, everything that has gone before is brought to a climax. We are taken back to the beginning of the story (Oedipus' birth), we learn the secret of his parentage, we find out who murdered Laius, we discover that Oedipus is married to his mother. The climax is reached in Oedipus' cry of despair and disgust as he rushes into the palace. The brief choral song that follows comments upon the fickleness of fate and points to Oedipus' life as an example.

The final episode is divided into two parts. A Messenger enters and describes what has happened offstage. The "messenger scene" is a standard part of Greek drama, since Greek sensibilities dictated that scenes of extreme violence take place offstage, although the results of the violence (the bodies of the dead, or in this case Oedipus' blindness) might be shown. Following the messenger scene, Oedipus returns to the stage and seeks to prepare himself for the future.

Oedipus the King is structurally unusual, for the resolution scene is the longest in the play. Obviously, Sophocles was not solely concerned with discovering the murderer of Laius, for the interest in this lengthy final scene shifts to the question: What will Oedipus do now that he knows the truth?

Up to this scene, the play has concentrated upon Oedipus as the ruler

Oedipus the King at the Stratford Shakespearean Festival (Canada). Oedipus is at center; in the background at left are Jocasta and Creon; the Chorus surrounds Oedipus. Directed by Tyrone Guthrie; designed by Tanya Moiseiwitsch. Two costumes and masks for this production may be seen in the color photographs following page 112. (Photo by Donald McKague. Courtesy Stratford Shakespearean Festival Foundation of Canada.)

of Thebes, but in the resolution, Oedipus as a man and a father becomes the center of interest. By this point, he has ceased to be the ruler of Thebes and has become the lowest of its citizens, and much of the intense pathos is the result of this change. An audience may feel for Oedipus the outcast as it never could feel for the self-righteous ruler shown in the prologue.

Oedipus' act of blinding himself grows believably out of his character, for his very uprightness and deep sense of moral outrage cause him to punish himself so terribly. Although he is innocent of intentional sin, he considers the deeds themselves (murder of a blood relative and incest) to be so horrible that ignorance cannot wipe away the moral stigma. Part of the play's power resides in the revulsion with which people in all ages have viewed patricide and incest. That they are committed by an essentially good man only makes them more terrible.

In drawing his characters, Sophocles pays little attention to the physiological level. The principal characters—Oedipus, Creon, and Jocasta—are mature persons, but Sophocles says almost nothing about their age or appearance. One factor that is apt to distract modern readers—the relative ages of Jocasta and Oedipus—is not even mentioned by Sophocles. When Oedipus answered the riddle of the Spinx, his reward, being made king, carried the stipulation that he marry the queen, Jocasta. Sophocles never questions the suitability of the marriage on the grounds of disparity in age.

Sophocles does give brief indications of age for other roles. The Priest of the prologue is spoken of as being old; the chorus is made up of Theban elders; Tiresias is old and blind; the Herdsman is an old man. In almost every case, age is associated with wisdom and experience. On the other hand, there are a number of young characters, none of whom speaks: the band of suppliants in the prologue includes children, and Antigone and Ismene are very young. Here the innocence of childhood is used to arouse pity.

On the sociological level of characterization, Sophocles again indicates little. Oedipus, Creon, and Jocasta hold joint authority in Thebes, although the power has been delegated to Oedipus. Vocational designations—priest, seer, herdsman, servants—are used for some of the characters.

Sophocles is principally concerned with psychological and ethical characteristics. For example, Oedipus' moral uprightness, his reputation for wisdom, his quick temper, his insistence on discovering truth, his suspicion, his love for his children, his strength in the face of disaster, are emphasized. These qualities make us understand Oedipus. But even here, a very limited number of traits is shown.

Creon is given even fewer characteristics. He has been Oedipus' trusted friend and brother-in-law. He is quick to defend his honor and is a man of common sense and uprightness who acts as honorably and compassionately as he can when the truth is discovered. Jocasta is similarly restricted. She strives to make life run smoothly for Oedipus, she tries to comfort him, to mediate between him and Creon, to stop Oedipus in his quest; she commits suicide when the truth becomes clear. We know nothing of her as a mother, and the existence of the children is not mentioned until after her death.

Unlike a modern play, then, in which characterization is usually built out of numerous realistic details, here the characterization is drawn with a few bold strokes; the most important traits are psychological and moral, but even they are few in number. Everything is pared down to its essentials and then somewhat enlarged and formalized, in part because of the scale of the theatre, but also to emphasize the seemingly inevitable fate that overwhelms the characters.

All of the speaking roles had to be played by three actors. Discovering which of the actors played which set of roles and how many lines elapse between an actor's exit and his next entrance as another character can be very revealing.

In addition to the three speaking actors, a great many supernumeraries are required, many of whom no doubt appeared in more than one scene. For example, the band of suppliants in the prologue includes children, two of whom could later appear as Antigone and Ismeme. Some who portrayed suppliants probably also later appeared as servants and attendants. To the actors must be added the chorus of fifteen members. Therefore, the total number in the cast of *Oedipus the King* was probably not less than thirty-five.

In reading the play, it is sometimes difficult to keep in mind that there were so many participants and that the visual and aural appeals were so numerous and continuous. The power of the play and of the production was so great that *Oedipus the King* became one of the most admired plays in ancient Greece. Aristotle (384-322 B.C.), author of the *Poetics*, the oldest surviving treatise on drama, thought it the finest of all Greek tragedies, and his opinion has been echoed by others down to the present day. It is still among the most frequently performed Greek plays. Today, productions of *Oedipus the King* inevitably deviate markedly from the original because the occasions, theatre structures, conventions, and audiences are quite unlike those of classical Greece. A director now must search the text for those features that remain vital despite the passage of 2400 years. As some of the illustrations included in this chapter indicate, Greek conventions (especially masks and treatments of the chorus) may be used, but they are almost always adapted so as make them acceptable to modern sensibilities.

But why has *Oedipus the King* continued to attract audiences? We have already looked at its skillful construction and its concern with moral taboos (incest and patricide) that touch us deeply. In addition, it develops several themes that have universal relevance. First, the fall of Oedipus from the place of highest honor to that of an outcast demonstrates the uncertainty of human destiny. A second theme is humanity's limitation in controlling fate. Oedipus has done what he considers necessary

Setting by John Ezell for *Oedipus Rex*, a modern version of the Greek myth by Jean Cocteau and Igor Stravinsky. Note the exits embedded in oversized creatures who seem to dominate (or control) the human figures below them. The overall effect is one of human beings at the mercy of Fate. (Courtesy Mr. Ezell.)

to avoid the terrible fate predicted by the oracle (that he will kill his father and marry his mother). But he cannot foresee what is in store for him. The contrast, then, between man seeking to control his destiny and the external forces shaping destiny is clearly depicted.

It is significant that no attempt is made to explain why destruction comes to Oedipus. It is implied that a man must submit to fate and that in struggling to avoid it, he only becomes more entangled. An irrational, or at least an unknowable, force is thus at work. No one asks who or what has determined Oedipus' fate. The truth of the oracle is established, but the purpose is unclear. The Greek concept of the gods did not assume that all the gods were benevolent—all supernatural forces were deified, whether good or evil.

It is possible to interpret this play as suggesting that the gods, rather than having decreed the characters' fates, have merely foreseen and foretold what will happen. Such an interpretation shifts the emphasis, but it does not contradict the picture of humanity as a victim of forces beyond its control, no matter by what name we call them.

Another motif—blindness versus sight—is emphasized in poetic images and in various comparisons. A contrast is repeatedly drawn between physical sight and the inner sight of understanding. For example, Tiresias, though blind, can see the truth that escapes Oedipus, while Oedipus, who has penetrated the riddle of the Sphinx, cannot solve the puzzle of his own life. When it is revealed to him, he blinds himself in an act of retribution.

Another theme, which may not have been a conscious one with Sophocles, is that of Oedipus as scapegoat. The city of Thebes will be saved if the one guilty man can be found and punished. In a sense, then, Oedipus takes the troubles of the city upon himself, and in his punishment lies the salvation of others.

Greek Comedy

In addition to tragedy and satyr plays, Athens developed a distinctive comic drama. Comedy became an official part of the Dionysian festivals some fifty years later than did tragedy. Although comedy was performed at the City Dionysia alongside the tragedies, it eventually found its most sympathetic home at the Lenaia, a festival observed during the winter, when few outsiders were present and at which the playwrights were allowed to ridicule Athenian events more pointedly.

Five comic dramatists competed each year at the Lenaia, but each presented only one play. The conventions of comedy also differed sig-

A figure from Old Comedy. (From Robert, *Die Masken der Neueren Attischen Komoedie* [1911].)

nificantly from those of tragedy. Greek comedy was usually concerned with contemporary matters of politics or art, with questions of war and peace, or with persons or practices disliked by the author. Occasionally, playwrights used mythological material as a framework for satire, but usually they invented their own plots. Comedy used a chorus of twenty-four members, often nonhuman (birds, wasps, frogs, clouds) and not always identical in appearance or all of the same sex. Many of the male characters wore a very tight, too-short *chiton* over flesh-colored tights, creating a ludicrous effect of partial nakedness. This effect was further emphasized by an enormous *phallus* attached to the costumes of most male characters. This was not only a source of humor but was also a constant reminder of the purpose of the Dionysian festival: the encouragement of fertility. Masks also contributed to the ridiculous appearance of the characters.

Numerous authors wrote Old Comedy, as the plays written prior to 400 B.C. are called, but works by only one—Aristophanes (448-380 B.C.)—have survived. His plays mingle slapstick, fantasy, beautiful lyric poetry, personal abuse, literary and musical parody, and serious commentary on contemporary affairs. The plot of an Old Comedy revolves around a "happy idea" and the results of putting it into practice. For example, in *Lysistrata,* probably the best known of all Greek comedies, the women of Greece successfully use a sex strike to end a war. Old Comedy has several typical features: a *prologue,* during which the happy idea is introduced; a *parados,* or entry of the chorus; an *agon,* or debate over the merits of the happy idea, ending in its adoption; a *parabasis,* or choral passage addressed to the audience, most frequently filled with advice on civic or other contemporary problems; a series of *episodes* showing the happy idea in practice; and a *komos,* or exit to feasting and revelry. The unity of Old Comedy is found in its ruling idea rather than in a series of causally related events. Sometimes days or weeks are assumed to have passed during one or two speeches, and place may change often. Furthermore, stage illusion is broken frequently as characters make comments about or to the audience.

After the fifth century, Greek drama declined markedly in quality, although not in quantity. During the fourth century B.C., the theatre spread throughout the eastern Mediterranean areas and eventually was no longer performed entirely at Dionysian festivals. Comedy also changed markedly during this period, becoming primarily concerned with the intrigues of everyday domestic life. This New Comedy was adapted and expanded by the Romans, who had gradually gained domination over the Mediterranean basin.

The Roman Theatre Experience

Rome became a major power some 200 years after the first performance of *Oedipus the King.* It eventually gained control of Greece as well as of the entire eastern Mediterranean and most of western Europe and North Africa. For some 600 years, the Romans reigned over an extensive empire.

The Romans were great assimilators, accepting, borrowing, or changing those things that seemed useful or desirable. When they encountered Greek drama in the mid-third century B.C., they imported a Greek writer, Livius Andronicus, to adapt Greek drama to Roman tastes. The first of his plays were produced in 240 B.C., and soon native Romans began to write plays. But the taste for this Greek-style drama seems to have peaked quickly, since the major period of such Roman drama was over by about 150 B.C.

This does not mean that the interest in theatrical performance ended, merely that the taste for full-length scripted drama sharply declined after the mid-second century B.C. The demand for theatrical entertainment actually increased steadily, but Roman taste favored variety entertainment: short comic plays of various sorts, dancing, singing, juggling, tightrope-walking, acrobatics, trained animals, gladiatorial contests, animal baiting, water ballets, mock sea fights, and a host of other events. From one day given over to theatrical entertainments in 240 B.C. the number had grown to 101 by A.D. 354 with another seventy-four days devoted to chariot races and gladiatorial combats. Roman taste favored novelty and variety. When Greek-style plays were introduced in 240 B.C., they were novelties to be elaborated and exploited. When their appeal faded, they were displaced in the theatre by other kinds of entertainment, although they did not disappear altogether for some time.

Because play scripts survive and artifacts relating to other kinds of theatrical entertainment most often do not, accounts of theatrical activity usually emphasize performances based on full-length written scripts. This is true of accounts of Roman theatre, which typically concentrate on theatrical production between 205 and 159 B.C., the time span covered by twenty-six comedies by two authors—Plautus (c.254–184 B.C.) and Terence (195–159 B.C.)—the only surviving Roman plays intended for performance. Nine tragedies by Seneca (5 B.C.–65 A.D.), written in the first century A.D., have also survived, but they apparently were not intended for public performance. Let us look then at the theatrical experience in the age of Plautus and Terence.

The Roman Theatrical Context

The Roman theatre in many ways resembled that of Greece, but it also differed in significant ways. As in Greece, theatrical performances were part of religious festivals, but in Rome they might be for any of several gods. It is perhaps significant also that the Roman term for these festivals was *ludi* (games). At the *ludi*, in addition to religious ceremonies and sacrifices, many other activities were offered for the pleasure of the god being honored—as well as for the diversion of the Roman people. The activities (other than the ceremonies and sacrifices) varied from festival to festival and from year to year, but all involved tests of skills, frequently with prizes for the most skillful or popular performers. The theatrical company that won the greatest favor with the audience received extra payments, just as did the winners of chariot races, horse races, animal baitings, acrobatic feats, and other activities. The Romans seemingly placed their theatrical performances in much the same category as sports and other forms of diversion and skill.

The Romans were always ambivalent about anything derived from Greece, which they considered to be decadent. This ambivalence about drama is probably reflected in Roman comedy, all surviving examples of which are adapted from Greek plays. In these adaptations, the setting and characters remain Greek, even though, as many critics have pointed out, the manners and customs depicted in the plays are far more Roman than Greek. In the period when the Roman comedies were written, Rome placed great emphasis on "gravity" (seriousness of purpose) in its citizens, and historians have suggested that the Greek setting was retained in the comedies so as not to offend the Roman authorities who controlled the festivals and their contents.

The Romans seem to have been much more legalistic (or superstitious) in their religious observances than were the Greeks. They believed that the religious ceremonies had to be performed precisely or else they would be ineffective, and they repeated an entire ceremony if any mistake was made. They worshiped their own versions of the Greek gods but also accepted many others. They even erected a temple to the unknown god in case they had missed one. The nonreligious portions of the festivals were looked upon as offerings to the gods, whose tastes were considered to coincide with those of the Roman populace. Such attitudes led increasingly to theatrical offerings that appealed to the greatest common denominator.

As in Greece, the expenses of theatrical production were assumed by the state. The government made an appropriation for each festival as a whole, and the officials in charge, usually wealthy citizens who often used the occasion to curry favor with the Roman populace, frequently contributed additional funds. Rather than choosing the plays, as seems to have been the rule in Greece, these officials contracted with the heads of theatrical companies for productions. The officials probably viewed the productions before they were presented, more for the sake of guarding against unacceptable material than for judging artistic merit.

In addition to underwriting production expenses, the Roman state also supplied the theatre in which the plays were presented. In the time of Plautus and Terence, the theatre was a temporary structure (no permanent theatre was built in Rome until 55 B.C.). We cannot be completely certain about the appearance of these temporary structures, but it is usually assumed that they were somewhat less elaborate versions of the one depicted in the illustration on page 86. Tiered seating for several thousand people apparently surrounded a semicircular orchestra (half of the Greek orchestra). A long stage (probably more than 100 feet long and 20 or more feet deep) rose some 5 feet above the orchestra and was enclosed at either end and across the back by a facade (*scaenae frons*).

Theatre at Ostia, near Rome. A conjectural reconstruction of one of the oldest permanent Roman theatres, built between 30 and 12 B.C. (D'Espouy, *Fragments d'Architecture Antique*. I [1901].)

This facade had three doors in the back wall and one at either end. In comedy, it was treated as a street, with the doors in the back wall serving as entrances to houses fronting on the street, and the doors at the ends serving as continuations of the street. The facade also had windows and a second story that could be used as demanded by the action. All Roman comedies take place out-of-doors, most frequently in a street in front of one or more houses. The orchestra seems never to have been used in the comedies, which did not include a chorus. The scale of the Roman theatre, then, was comparable to that of the Greek. It, too, was an outdoor structure, but the stage house and the auditorium were joined and of the same height, and consequently the audience could not see over the stage house. The individual performer was also much more prominent because of the raised stage and the absence of a chorus.

Admission to this theatre was free, seats were not reserved, and audiences were often unruly. Guards were present to enforce some order, but since a series of plays were presented each day, coming and going was frequent. The plays also had to compete with other attractions, and consequently the actors had to provide entertainment that would satisfy a mass audience. Terence states in the prologue to one of his plays that it is the third attempt to present the play; the earlier two attempts had been abandoned because once the audience left to see rope dancers and another time to see gladiators. The total context of attractions had something in common with the multiple channels on our television sets, which permit us to move from one attraction to another, seeking the most entertaining.

By the time of Plautus and Terence, there seem to have been a number of professional theatre companies. We do not know what they did when they were not performing at the festivals, but probably they traveled about or gave private performances for wealthy Romans. In any case, more than one company was hired to give performances at the festivals. Once hired, they were responsible for all details of production: finding scripts, providing the actors, costumes, musicians, and so on. Each company was assured a certain payment, but special incentives were offered in the form of prizes to those companies receiving the most favorable response from the audiences.

The actors wore Greek costumes similar to those of daily life, although there may have been some exaggeration for comic purposes. Since most of the characters were "types," certain colors came to be associated with particular groups, such as red with slaves and yellow with courtesans. This conventional use of color extended to wigs as well. All of the performers were male and wore masks.

Roman comedy does not deal with political or social issues but with everyday domestic affairs. Almost invariably, the plots turn on misunderstandings of one sort of another: mistaken identity (frequently involving long-lost children), misunderstood motives, or deliberate deception. They show the well-to-do middle class (the older man concerned with his wealth or children; the young man who rebels against authority) and those around them (the slaves, parasites, courtesans, the slave dealers, the cowardly soldier). Of all the characters, the most famous is perhaps the "clever slave," who, to help his master, devises all sorts of schemes, most of which go awry and lead to further complications. Very few respectable women appear in Roman plays, and while love affairs may be the source of a play's intrigues, the women involved seldom appear onstage.

In reading a Roman play, one should try to remember the musical element. In Plautus' plays, about two-thirds of the lines were accompanied by the flute. Thus, a Roman comedy closely resembles a modern musical. The flute player remained on stage throughout the play, although his presence was ignored by the actors. There were also a number of songs by the characters (rather than by the chorus, as had been the practice in Greek drama).

The Menaechmi

Of all Roman comedies, Plautus' *The Menaechmi* has perhaps been the most popular. It served as the basis for Shakespeare's *Comedy of Errors* as well as for a number of other plays.

As in most of Plautus' plays, *The Menaechmi* begins with a prologue that tells much about the audience and the performance situation. It lays out the background of the action very carefully and goes over important points more than once. The prologue also makes abundant use of humorous commentary on the events and characters in order to keep the audience's attention, explaining that the stage today represents a street in Epidamnus but that in another play it will represent a different city and the houses of other characters. Both the actor who delivers the prologue and several of the characters in the play sometimes talk directly to the audience (a convention usually referred to as "breaking the illusion"), thus calling attention to the theatrical medium.

By the time the play actually begins, the audience has been given a summary of the prior action, leaving the introductory scenes to establish the present conditions out of which the comedy will grow: the dispute between Menaechmus I and his wife; the visit of Menaechmus I to the courtesan Erotium, his gift to her of a dress stolen from his wife, their plans for a banquet later in the day, and the departure of Menaechmus I to the Forum; the entrance of Menaechmus II and his slave, Messenio. The remainder of the play presents a series of scenes in which the two Menaechmi are in turn mistaken for each other and accused of acts about which they know nothing. Eventually they meet, and the complications are resolved.

Plautus subordinates everything to his main purpose—to entertain— and develops his material with great economy. Not only has he eliminated everything that does not contribute to his principal aim, he also has made effective use of such devices as the stolen dress. This item becomes a source of unity as it passes through the hands of practically all the characters before being used as evidence to support almost all the charges brought against the two Menaechmi.

Although Plautus' comic sense is everywhere evident, it may be seen at work especially in the reunion, which might have concluded the play on a sentimental note. Instead, the final lines give the story a twist in

Plautus' *The Menaechmi*. Directed by Harrold Shiffler, designed by Richard Baschky. (Courtesy University of Iowa Theatres.)

keeping with the sophisticated tone of earlier scenes: Menaechmus I offers all of his goods for sale—including his wife, if anyone is foolish enough to buy her.

The characters of *The Menaechmi* are motivated principally by selfish and material interests. With the possible exceptions of Messenio and the father, none of the characters may be considered admirable. Plautus has little interest in social satire. He concentrates on the ridiculous situation without exploring its significance. Consequently, when his characters indulge in adultery, stealing, or deception, they merely contribute to the overall tone of good-humored cynicism.

As in most Roman comedy, the characters in *The Menaechmi* are types rather than individuals. Some roles are summed up in their names: Peniculus (or "Brush") suggests the parasite's ability to sweep the table clean; the cook is called Cylindrus (or "Roller"); and the courtesan is named Erotium (or "Lovey"). Each character has a restricted number of motivations: the twins wish to satisfy their physical desires; the wife wants to reform her husband; the father desires to keep peace in the family; and the quack doctor is seeking a patient upon whom he can practice a lengthy and costly treatment. In spite of the restricted number of traits, however, all characters are sufficiently delineated for their functions in the play.

Shakespeare's *Comedy of Errors* (adapted from *The Menaechmi*) as performed at Stratford (England). Note the mingling of Elizabethan and nineteenth-century clothing. Directed and designed by Theodor Komisarzhevsky. (Courtesy Shakespeare Birthplace Trust.)

The ten speaking roles of *The Menaechmi* could easily be performed by a company of six. Doubling was common in the Roman theatre, and all of the actors had the advantage of masks and conventionalized costumes and colors of garments and wigs to assist in changing roles. The play does not require actors who are skilled in the subtle portrayal of a wide range of emotions; rather, they must have that highly developed comic technique that produces precision in the timing of business and dialogue. The scenes of quarreling, drunkenness, and madness indicate that physical nimbleness is essential. Most of the actors also must be skilled singers, since the main characters have "entering songs" and sometimes additional songs.

The musical accompaniment was played on a flute, although not of the type used today. It had two pipes, each about 20 inches long. Sometimes it was bound to the player's head so as to free his hands for working the stops.

Comic scene. At left are two older men, at right a young man and a slave, and at center the flute player. Note the masks and costumes. (Pougin, *Dictionnaire . . . du Théâtre*, 1885.)

Some sense of the overall stage conventions can be derived from the illustration above, although it does not give an adequate sense of the size of the stage.

Other Roman Drama and Theatre

In addition to comedy, the Romans also wrote tragedy. The only surviving examples are by Seneca, who wrote in the first century A.D., although probably not for production. Like Greek tragedies, his are based on mythological subjects, including the Oedipus story, but they are filled with exaggerated emotions and onstage violence, features that centuries later were to appeal to the tragic writers of Shakespeare's age.

As indicated earlier, the Romans preferred variety entertainment and short plays, and from the first century B.C. onward, these forms virtually drove regular comedy and tragedy from the stage. The favorite form in late Rome was the *mime,* a short, topical, usually comic, often improvised playlet. (It was not silent, as today's mime is.) In the mime, the female roles were played by women (the first form in which female performers appeared), and none of the actors apparently wore masks. Especially in late Rome mimes often centered around adultery and used obscene language. As Christianity grew, its sacraments and beliefs became topics of ridicule in the mimes. In turn, the Christian church came to think of the mimes and theatre as synonymous, and consequently it is not surprising that the church became a principal opponent of the theatre— not only for its subject matter but also because it was associated with the worship of pagan gods.

In addition to the mimes, late Rome increasingly emphasized "blood sports," among them gladiatorial contests, in which opponents engaged in hand-to-hand armed combat until at least one was decisively defeated and usually killed, and the pitting of human beings against man-eating wild animals. It was to accommodate such "sports" that the Colosseum (holding some 45,000 persons) was built. And it was there that Christians were "thrown to the lions" during the time when the Roman state sought to stamp out Christianity. The mimes, other variety entertainment, and blood sports were considered appropriate parts of religious festivals. Thus, it is not surprising that in later times Christians often opposed the theatre (except when it specifically upheld Christian doctrine).

The Greek and Roman theatre experiences, then, were alike in some ways and quite unlike in others. Both were occasional (that is, performances were given on special occasions and not on a continuing basis as today), ceremonial (parts of religious festivals and considered offerings to a god), financed by the state and wealthy citizens, and open to all. The Greeks and Romans also used many similar conventions: male performers only (except in mimes), masks, musical accompaniment, extremely large theatres, and formalized scenic backgrounds.

Along with these similarities there were many differences. The chorus, while not absent from some Roman forms, played a much larger role in Greek theatre, as did dance. In Roman theatre, the musical element was more equally distributed throughout the play and was associated with the actors more than with the chorus. The theatre structures also differed somewhat. But the most important differences were those that reflected basic values. The Greeks seem to have placed great stress on profundity, whereas the Romans were more concerned with popular entertainment. Probably that is why *Oedipus the King,* despite many features that connect it with the time and place of its origins, still moves audiences deeply today, for embedded in the myth and formal conventions are basic human experiences that transcend time and place. On

A Funny Thing Happened on the Way to the Forum, a musical adaptation of Roman Comedy, by Burt Shevelove, Larry Gelbart, and Stephen Sondheim. Trinity Repertory Theatre (Providence, RI) production, directed by Tony Giordano. (Photo by Mark Morelli. Courtesy Trinity Repertory Theatre.)

the other hand, *The Menaechmi* is concerned with a story that seems not unlike those of a television situation comedy, while its conventions tend to distance it from us. Perhaps that is why Roman comedy seems to have fared best in our theatre in such musical adaptations as *A Funny Thing Happened on the Way to the Forum* and *The Boys from Syracuse*, for while the story remains much the same, the conventions have been updated to our own. Whatever explanation we offer, it should be clear that these theatrical experiences depended in large part upon the total cultural context within which they functioned and which they helped define.

The Theatre Experiences of Medieval England and Japan

5

Around A.D. 500, the Roman Empire disintegrated. One consequence was the loss of the official and financial support that had sustained the theatre for some 1000 years. For almost 500 years thereafter, the theatre in Western Europe was carried on only by small bands of players or by individuals who performed wherever they could. These performers were often denounced by the Christian church (by then the dominant and most stable institution) and denied its sacraments. It is ironic, therefore, that the return of theatrical strength owes most to the church's discovery that the dramatization of Biblical episodes was an effective means of bringing home Christian teachings.

The earliest known example of a liturgical play (that is, one incorporated into the church service, or liturgy) dates from about A.D. 970. It dramatized the arrival of women at the tomb of Christ, the announcement by an angel that Christ had risen, and the subsequent rejoicing. This short play (only four lines of sung dialogue) was performed during the Easter service. Subsequently, many other Biblical episodes were dramatized, but all remained short so as not to interfere with the regular services. They were written in Latin (the language of the church throughout Western Europe), were chanted or sung, and were performed by choirboys or members of the clergy.

Around A.D. 1200, some religious plays began to be performed outside the church, and by around 1375, a religious drama had developed quite independent of the liturgy. Plays of this new type were performed throughout most of Western Europe until the late sixteenth century, when controversy over religious doctrine (exemplified in the Protestant secessions from the Roman Catholic church) led to the suppression of the plays almost everywhere. But for about 200 years, these religious plays had been the major theatrical expression of Western Europe. They differed from liturgical drama in being written in the vernacular language of the region rather than in Latin, in being spoken rather than chanted or sung, and in being acted primarily by laymen rather than the clergy. They also were financed by the community rather than by the church.

This medieval religious theatre in some ways resembled that of Greece and Rome. Like those earlier theatres, it was a religious occasion in which the entire community was invited to participate. Still, no one would confuse a Greek or Roman festival with a medieval festival: Though similar in purpose they differed markedly in their conditions, details, and conventions.

Trade Guilds and the Corpus Christi Festival

The production of the outdoor religious dramas was made possible in part by the rise of trade guilds around the thirteenth century. The return of relative stability after centuries of warfare and general uncertainty had by that time encouraged increased trade among various parts of Europe, and this in turn encouraged increased manufacture. Eventually, the need to regulate working conditions, wages, the quality of products, and other matters led craftsmen in various trades—bakers, brewers, goldsmiths, tailors, and so on—to establish guilds, which promoted the common good of those in each trade. These guilds were organized hierarchically: each was governed by a council of masters (those who owned their shops and supervised the work of others); under each master were a number of journeymen (those skilled in the trade but who worked for wages) and apprentices (boys or young men who received room and board while learning a trade, usually over a period of seven years). The forces that gave rise to the guilds also encouraged the growth of towns. And as the towns and guilds grew, power came to rest primarily with the guilds, since they usually elected the mayor and the council from among their members.

This increased prominence of secular concerns seems also to have been at least partially responsible for the church's desire to incorporate ordinary people more fully into its activities. One result was the creation of a new feast day: Corpus Christi. This festival was officially approved in 1311 and was being observed throughout Europe by about 1350. It celebrates the redemptive power of the sacraments of bread and wine (the body and blood of Christ), the mystery that, to the medieval mind, gave meaning to existence—the union of the human and divine in the person of Christ and the promise of redemption through his sacrifice.

Thus, all biblical events could be related to it, and eventually Corpus Christi became the occasion on which dramas encompassing everything from the Creation to the Last Judgment could be performed without anachronism. (Previously, plays about the birth of Christ had been done at Christmas, about his resurrection at Easter, and so on according to the supposed calendar dates of the biblical events.) Corpus Christi, observed sixty days following Easter, could vary from May 23 to June 24. Coming during warm weather and when the days were near their longest, it was favorable to outdoor performance.

The central feature of the Corpus Christi festival was a procession through the town with the consecrated bread and wine. The church sought to involve everyone in the festival by including representatives from every rank and profession (churchmen, nobles, merchants, craftsmen). It is often suggested that this cooperative venture marked the beginning of an association that would eventually lead to the guilds assuming a dominant role in the staging of outdoor religious plays. This procession may also be the forerunner of the type of staging eventually adopted in several English towns: mounting plays on wagons and performing them at various stops—a combination of procession and performance.

In the British Isles, plays were produced by about 125 different towns at some time during the Middle Ages. Nevertheless, only a few plays have survived, and most of these are parts of cycles (a number of short plays that taken together dramatize the Bible from Creation to Doomsday) and come from four towns: York (48 plays), Chester (24 plays), Wakefield (32 plays), and an unidentifiable town (42 plays). All of these date originally from about 1375 and were performed at intervals (that is, regularly but not every year) over the next two centuries. During that time, the cycles underwent many changes as individual plays were rewritten, new ones added, others dropped. The surviving texts show the cycles as they existed near the end of their active production life. All of the plays dealt with the same basic subject: God's ordering of existence as revealed in the Bible. Consequently, regardless of where they were written, they have many common characteristics and make use of shared conventions.

Conventions of Medieval Theatre

One major convention of medieval drama involves the handling of time. In the Middle Ages, humanity was thought to participate in two kinds of time, eternal and earthly. God, Satan, and human souls exist in eternity—which, unlike physical being, has neither beginning nor end. Thus, earthly existence is a short interlude in the ultimate reality, eternity, and human beings must choose which path to take. Medieval staging often made the human dilemma visible by using a stage that depicted Heaven at one end and Hell at the other (see the illustration shown below). The plays illustrated this situation as well, especially in the Doomsday (or Last Judgment) play. Because earthly time and place were relatively unimportant, the historical period or geographical location of an event was insignificant. Consequently, there was little sense of historicity in the plays: ancient Israelites were dressed in medieval garments, and Old Testament characters referred to Christian saints.

The fluidity of time is also reflected in the structure of the cycles. Rather than treating one of many myths or a restricted story (as the Greeks and Romans did), the medieval cycles encompass the total range of existence. Seldom was any causal relationship established among the various plays of a cycle or even among the incidents of a single play. Events were thought to happen simply because God willed them. Both time and place were telescoped or expanded as needed by an incident rather than according to realistic standards.

Staging also involved a number of conventions. There were no permanent theatres, so theatrical spaces were improvised. The principal

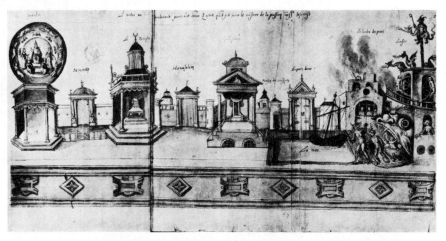

Outdoor stage used for a religious drama at Valenciennes (France). At the extreme left is the mansion representing Heaven, while at extreme right is the Hell mansion (including a "hell mouth" entrance). The mansions between Heaven and Hell represented various locations on earth. This play required twenty-five days to perform. Various scenes from the play are depicted in the color photos following page 112. (Courtesy Bibliothèque Nationale, Paris.)

requirement was that there be sufficient open space to accommodate a large crowd.

The stages might be either fixed or movable. Fixed stages were most typically set against buildings on one side of a town square or large courtyard, but they might extend down the middle of a square (and be viewed from two or three sides) or be set up in the ruins of a Roman amphitheatre or other circular space (and be viewed in the round). The movable stage was essentially a wagon that could be moved from one location to another.

Portion of a painting by Denis van Alsloot of a celebration held in Brussels in honor of a visiting ruler in 1615. The pageant wagon shown here depicts the Nativity. Mary, Joseph, and the Christ child are seen between the two columns at center. Although they apparently carried fixed tableaus rather than plays, these wagons exemplify one type of medieval movable stage. (Courtesy Victoria and Albert Museum, London.)

Regardless of the type of stage or location, the basic staging conventions were the same everywhere. There were two parts to the stage space: *mansions* and *platea*. Mansions, used to represent locales, were small scenic structures, sufficient to indicate place but not meant to do so in its entirety. A single play might require more than one mansion, and an entire cycle might require as many as seventy. The *platea* was undifferentiated stage space. Once the location of the action was established by relating it to a mansion, the actors could move out and use as much of the stage space as the action required; this space then was considered to be part of the place represented by the mansion. Thus, the same stage space might change its identity merely by associating it with a different mansion. Place, then, was almost as fluid as time. There was no proscenium arch or other framing device. The overall setting ultimately symbolized (as the total cycle indicates) the entire universe: human and earthly existence framed by Heaven and Hell.

Costumes were used to distinguish among the inhabitants of Earth, Heaven, and Hell. Secular, earthly characters (no matter the period or place of the action) wore contemporary medieval garments appropriate to their rank or profession, since no attempt was made to achieve historical accuracy. God, the angels, the saints, and certain biblical characters wore church garments, usually differentiated by adding accessories. For example, angels wore church robes with wings attached, while God was dressed as a high church dignitary and often had his face gilded. Many saints and biblical personages were associated with specific symbols. For example, St. Peter carried the "keys to the Kingdom of Heaven," and the Archangel Michael wielded a flaming sword. Because such visual symbolism was common and well understood in the Middle Ages, it quickly identified characters for the audience. The greatest design imagination went into the costumes of devils, who were fancifully conceived with wings, claws, beaks, horns, or tails. The devils also often wore masks to emphasize their deformities.

There were frequently a number of realistic special effects. Hell with its horrors was depicted with great care so as to make it as repulsive as possible. The entrance to Hell was often represented as the mouth of a fire-breathing monster (the "hell mouth"). Many miracles described in the Bible also were staged as convincingly as possible so as to reinforce faith. But realism was not the typical goal, since several widely separated places were usually juxtaposed within a limited stage space and represented by fragmentary scenery. Thus, medieval staging ranged between realistic and symbolic devices. Overall, the conventions permitted rapid switches from rather broad outline to specific detail, and asked the audience to use its eyes in a way somewhat analogous to present-day cinematography—focusing in, pulling back, cutting from one locale to another. Much in medieval staging may now seem naive, but in its own time it made efficient use of conventions that evoked the human condition as the medieval mind understood it.

The Wakefield Cycle

Let us look at the English cycle staged at Wakefield, a town in central England. The surviving manuscript of this cycle contains thirty-two plays, beginning with the Creation and extending through the Judgment. As with all the cycles, the authors (there appear to have been several) are anonymous. Most medieval artists did not strive for individual glory and recognition, but contented themselves with serving God, the church, and the community. Some of the Wakefield plays are borrowed from other cycles, while others have qualities that suggest varied origins. Five of the plays are by the same unknown author, usually referred to as "the Wakefield Master." His plays are noted for their details of everyday life and their comic scenes. One of these, *The Second Shepherds' Play*, will be examined in some detail later.

The production of the Wakefield cycle was a community effort that involved the town council, the church, and the guilds. The council decided if the plays were to be given in a particular year, but the church had to accede to this decision, since the plays were part of a church festival. The church also had to approve the play texts to ensure that they did not distort church doctrine. There was an official copy of the cycle, which had to be adhered to in performance. The usual rationale for presenting the plays was "to honor God, to edify man, and to glorify the city." Most of the actual work of production was undertaken by the guilds.

The decision to perform the plays apparently was made several months prior to Corpus Christi. One official document is dated September 29, thus permitting some nine months of preparation time, although it is not certain how much of this time was actually devoted to preparation. Individual plays apparently were assigned according to some perceived relationship between the guild's specialty and the events of a play. The assignments at Wakefield have not survived, but we know that at other places the Shipwrights, Fishers, or Mariners were assigned the plays dealing with Noah (building the ark and the Flood), while the Goldsmiths were usually given the play in which the Three Kings bring gifts to the Christ child. Sometimes the connections are not immediately apparent. At Chester, the Shepherds' play was assigned to the Painters, while at York it was assigned to the Candlemakers (perhaps because they used tallow from sheep in making candles). Each guild was expected to assume the costs of producing its play, and the council levied fines against those who failed to fulfill their obligations adequately.

At Wakefield, processional staging apparently was used. Each play was mounted on a pageant wagon (somewhat like a modern float) that was drawn through the streets from one playing place to another and in the order indicated in the script. No reliable description of a pageant wagon has survived. They were probably as large as the narrow streets would accommodate and were probably designed to meet the requirements of specific plays. Since the same guild produced the same play at each festival, its pageant wagon and scenery could be designed and built to meet the specific requirements of its play. The wagons could also be stored and refurbished as needed for subsequent festivals. Each vehicle usually had to carry one or more mansions and might require some machinery for special effects. It seems probable that at each playing place the wagon was drawn up alongside a stationary platform that served as the *platea*. The actors also sometimes performed scenes in the street. (See the illustrations on page 103 and below for conjectures about how the performance space was arranged.)

In addition to providing the pageant wagon and its equipment, each guild had to supply performers and someone to oversee the production. All of the personnel involved in production were essentially amateurs,

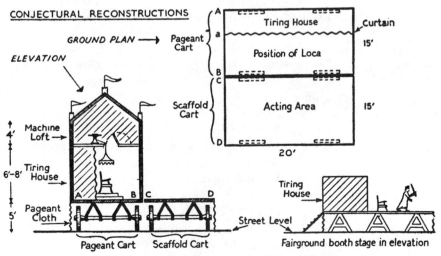

Possible arrangement for performances of English cycle plays mounted on pageant wagons. A wagon with scenery is pulled up alongside another which served as acting area. (Glynne Wickham, *Early English Stages,* vol. 1. Reprinted by permission of Columbia University Press.)

Reconstruction of a performance on a pageant wagon accommodating not only the scenery but the acting area as well. (Sharp, *A Dissertation on the Pageants or Dramatic Mysteries . . . at . . . Coventry. . . . 1825.*)

but as time went by, some became quite skilled and seem to have approached the status of professionals. One actor was often paid so much more than the others that it seems likely he was in charge of the total production (that is, served as director). Some guilds put the same person under contract for several years to stage their part of the cycle. Actors were recruited from the local populace and were not restricted to members of the guild producing that play. We do not know how many rehearsals were held, but the plays were relatively short, and often the same actor played the same role at many different festivals. All of the actors were male, the female roles being played by boys or young men.

Costumes for the most part were clothing in common use in medieval England and were usually supplied by the actors or borrowed. Church robes, the starting point for ecclesiastical and angelic costumes, could be borrowed or rented from the church, but the costumes of devils usually had to be made.

Each guild rehearsed and prepared its play separately from all the others. No dress rehearsal of the entire cycle was needed, since coordinating the individual plays merely required that the pageant wagons be lined up in the correct order.

The council specified the places at which the plays would be performed; at Wakefield there probably were two or three. The actors were required to be in their pageants by 5 A.M., presumably the starting time. When all was ready, the first pageant wagon moved to the first performance place, where the actors performed the play, and then moved on to the next. Thus, all of the plays were performed in the prescribed order at each of the designated places.

On the day of performances, all normal work was suspended. A large percentage of the town's residents must have crowded into the places designated for the performances. Furthermore, word about the performances was usually sent to neighboring towns, and a large number of spectators probably came from outside Wakefield. Provisions for the audience seem not to have been extensive, other than choosing sites that permitted a crowd to assemble. The majority of spectators stood, but some seating may have been erected. The windows and roofs of houses overlooking the place were in great demand and probably were rented. The council's proclamation provided that sizable fines were to be levied against anyone who disturbed the plays or hindered their procession; carrying weapons also was forbidden. Even if the performances began at 5 A.M., they probably required all the daylight hours (at that time of the year in central England until around 10 P.M.) to complete the full cycle at all the prescribed stops. That would have made for a very long day, but this seems not to have bothered people of the time. Spectators were as mobile as the wagons and could move from one viewing place to another, watch only some of the plays, move forward or back along the route, choose how long they wanted to stay. The atmosphere must have been as festive as it was reverential. It was both a holiday and a holy day.

It is impossible here to examine in detail a performance of the entire Wakefield cycle. Therefore, one play, considered by many to be the best of all the English cycle plays, has been chosen. It is the thirteenth play, *The Second Shepherds' Play* (so called because another Shepherds' play appears in the manuscript of this cycle and presumably was performed at this point before it was replaced by this second version).

The Second Shepherds' Play

Before the spectators saw *The Second Shepherds' Play*, they had already viewed several others beginning with *The Creation* and moving through events foreshadowing the birth of Christ. Thus, this play comes approximately one-third of the way into the cycle. The majority of *The*

Second Shepherds' Play is an elaboration of a single sentence from the New Testament (Luke 2:8): "And there were in the same country shepherds abiding in the field, keeping watch over their flock by night." The number of shepherds is not specified in the Bible, but three are used in the play, probably to suggest a parallel with the three Wise Men.

The play introduces in leisurely fashion the characters and situation as each shepherd in turn complains about a different problem. The opening is made even more casual by the inclusion of a song. This simple beginning serves several purposes that may not be readily apparent. First, through the various complaints, it depicts a world in need of Christ's coming. Second, it relates the biblical story to the contemporary scene and thereby to the audience. Third, the introduction prepares for an unusual occurrence by the third Shepherd's recital of abnormal conditions. Nevertheless, by today's standards this opening section seems overly long, since there is little forward movement of the action until the character Mak appears.

The section from the entrance of Mak until the appearance of the angel makes up a relatively complete short comic play, probably the most

The opening scene of *The Second Shepherds' Play*, one part of *The Mystery Plays* as performed by the Hartford [CT] Stage Company, 1985. Adaptation by John Russell Brown; directed by Mary B. Robinson. (Photo by Lanny Nagler. Courtesy Hartford Stage Company.)

enjoyable part for many of the spectators. Modern readers sometimes find it strange to encounter such farcical sections in religious plays, perhaps especially one about the birth of Christ. But during the Middle Ages, the church permitted many satirical elements in its festivals. The Feast of Fools, for example, was a New Year's celebration during which the minor clergy ridiculed the Mass and their superiors. But in the plays, comic elements were restricted to scenes about devils, amoral or evil persons, or lower-class characters.

Mak's reputation as a trickster is established immediately by the Shepherds' concern for their sheep. Soon, however, they all lie down for the night. When the Shepherds are safely asleep, Mak steals a sheep and carries it home to his wife, Gill. As a precaution against discovery, she suggests that they place the sheep in a cradle and pretend that it is a newborn baby. Mak then goes back to the fields and lies down as before.

The Shepherds awake and, with difficulty, arouse Mak, who has been feigning sleep. After Mak takes his leave, the Shepherds discover that a sheep is missing, and they immediately suspect Mak. While the Shepherds search his house, Mak protests his innocence and Gill counterfeits postchildbirth pains. As they are leaving, one of the Shepherds remembers the child and insists upon presenting a gift to it; the sheep is discovered, and Mak is tossed in a blanket as punishment.

After recovering their sheep, the Shepherds return to the field. A marked change now takes place as the tone of the play becomes serious and devotional. In contrast with what has gone before, the play now becomes stiff and formal. An Angel appears and announces the birth of Christ; the Shepherds go to Bethlehem, worship the child, and present their gifts. Christ has appeared within a familiar scene; his promise is not to some forgotten past, but to the immediate present.

The Second Shepherds' Play has frequently been viewed as a work composed of two unrelated stories of sharply contrasting tone. Nevertheless, it is unified through its themes and ideas. There are many parallels between the two stories. In both there is a father, mother, and child; the child is in a cradle; one "child" is a lamb, and the other is Christ, the "Lamb of God"; the Shepherds present gifts to both. The difference between the two stories is to be found in the significance of the events: one shows a world in need of Christ, the other portrays his arrival.

There are seven roles—not counting the infant. All performers were male; the same actor could have played both Gill and Mary. Little is indicated about the physical appearance of the characters. All are adults of unspecified age except the third Shepherd—a boy—and the Christ child—probably represented by a doll. The sociological traits are also limited. The Shepherds, Mak, and Gill are peasants; it is implied that Mak lives by stealing.

The final scene of *The Second Shepherds' Play,* Hartford Stage Company, 1985.
(Photo by Lanny Nagler. Courtesy Hartford Stage Company.)

Psychological characterization is slight but effectively drawn. The three Shepherds are differentiated primarily through their opening monologues. All are generous, as may be seen from their reactions to the supposed child of Gill and to the Christ child, and from their decision not to prosecute Mak. (In medieval times, stealing was a hanging offense.) A good impulse, the desire to give the "child" a gift, leads to the uncovering of Mak's guilt. Mak is a clever knave who is somewhat henpecked and cowardly. Gill is shrewish and clever; it is her idea to put the lamb in the cradle and pass it off as a child.

There is a considerable amount of physical action in the play, and with the exception of the Angel's appearance, all of it is reasonably realistic. Transitional action, however, is indicated only sketchily. For example, the Shepherds lie down and appear to fall asleep instantly. The actors therefore probably supplied many details, or else these transitions could have seemed very abrupt. Because they each have only one speech, Mary and the Angel are characterized least and seem especially stiff and formal compared to the other characters.

Most of the actors must sing. The Shepherds have a song in the introductory scene and another at the end of the play. Mak sings a lullaby to his stolen sheep, and the Angel sings *Gloria in excelsis.*

The Second Shepherds' Play calls for three locales—the fields, Mak's house, and the stable at Bethlehem. One mansion might have been sufficient, however, since the fields really require no background, and the other two are so similar in scenic demands that the same mansion could be used in both.

No doubt the mansion used for Mak's house and the stable was equipped with a curtain that could be drawn to reveal the interior. Mak's house requires a door (at which he knocks), a cradle, and a bed. All of these would be appropriate items for the stable (the bed for Mak's house need only be made of straw). The mansion or mansions were mounted on the wagon, which was probably pulled up alongside a platform at each playing place; this platform then would have served as the open fields and as the *platea* for the two other locations.

The costume demands for the play are simple: for the Shepherds, Mak, and Gill, the everyday contemporary dress of the lower classes; for the Angel, an ecclesiastical garment with wings added; for Mary, an upper-class medieval garment (the traditional way of representing her in art by this time) and the symbols associated with her.

Since the spectators crowded around the performance space, the actors were seen at very close range by many, and the total configuration of the playing places meant that the performance was viewed from a variety of angles. Thus, the spatial relationship between audience and performer and the overall scale differed markedly from those of the Greek and Roman theatres. In addition, the degree of formalization apparently was less than in the classical theatres, for most elements of performance in *The Second Shepherds' Play,* though perhaps altered and somewhat exaggerated, were variations on things familiar to the audience.

As the play ended, the wagon moved on to another site and was replaced by the next wagon, bearing a play about the Three Kings. Twenty more plays would have to be performed before the day ended.

Other Medieval Theatre and Drama

In addition to religious plays, several other dramatic types were popular during the Middle Ages, among them *moralities*, *farces*, and *interludes*. *Morality* plays flourished between 1400 and 1550. Unlike the religious plays, which treated biblical or saintly characters, the morality treated the spiritual trials of ordinary persons. It was an allegory about the moral temptations that beset all human beings. The protagonist (often called Everyman or Mankind) was advised and cajoled by personifications of good and evil; most frequently he succumbed to temptation but was eventually recalled to the path of righteousness by a character called Faith or Mercy or by the grace of God. The most famous morality play is *Everyman,* in which God orders Death to summon the title character. Everyman seeks someone among his companions (Kindred, Knowledge, Five Wits, Beauty, Strength) to accompany him on his journey, but once his destination is known, all except Good Deeds refuse to go with him. Through this search, Everyman comes to understand the relationship of his earthly life to salvation. During the sixteenth century, the morality play was gradually secularized, as its original subjects were replaced by such new ones as the ideal training of rulers and the content of a proper education. Then, when religious controversies erupted, moralities were used to attack one's opponents, either the Protestants or Catholics being associated with good or evil, depending on one's position. Such changes moved the morality play increasingly toward a wholly secular drama, and thus it served as a transition between the medieval religious drama and the secular drama of Shakespeare's time.

A comic secular drama, *farce* appeared around the thirteenth century, but since the form was not officially encouraged, it remained a minor though highly entertaining type, emphasizing as it did the ridiculous and comically depraved aspects of human behavior. One of the best examples is *Pierre Patelin,* an anonymous French farce of the fifteenth century. It is the story of an impoverished lawyer who buys a piece of cloth from a merchant, whom he invites to dinner to receive his payment. When the merchant arrives, Patelin is in bed and his wife swears he has not been out of the house. Patelin pretends madness, beats the merchant, and drives him away without payment for the cloth. This story is loosely joined to a second in which Patelin agrees to defend a shepherd against a charge of stealing sheep. He counsels the shepherd that during the trial he should only answer "Baa" no matter what anyone says to him. The accuser turns out to be the merchant, who creates total confusion during the proceedings by his alternating charges against the shepherd and Patelin. In view of this confusion and the shepherd's seeming feeblemindedness, the judge dismisses the case, but when Patelin tries to collect his fee, the shepherd runs away, calling "Baa." Like many farces, *Pierre Patelin* shows clever knaves outwitting each other, but it adds another comic twist by having the seemingly stupid shepherd outwit the experienced lawyer.

The *interlude* was a nonreligious serious or comic play. It was probably called an interlude because it was performed between the parts of a celebration (such as the courses of a banquet). It was also associated with the rise of professional performers, who developed their art in the specialized entertainments held in the households of kings and nobles. Eventually, these servants were permitted, when not needed at home,

An interlude performance during a medieval banquet. The scene being performed involved St. George and the Dragon, but almost any kind of play (farce, morality, interlude) might be presented. The ruler's table is at upper center. Note also the spectators in a gallery at upper left. (Pougin. *Dictionnaire . . . du Théâtre*, 1885.)

to travel about and perform for pay. Thus, the interlude is also associated with the rise of the professional actor and the professional theatre.

In addition to those discussed here, many other celebrations also utilized theatrical elements, for the Middle Ages was a time when ceremony, both religious and secular, played an important role in people's lives. But, amidst all the diversity, the religious drama was the most important and characteristic. More than any other type, it appealed to (and actively involved) the largest cross section of the populace and most fully embodied those concerns that the age idealized—the biblical vision of human history and destiny.

Medieval Japan

At about the time the religious cycles were flourishing in Europe, a drastically different kind of theatrical experience was available halfway round the world in Japan. There, Noh theatre was perfected and codified so thoroughly that it is still performed today much as it was 500 years ago. It came into being in complete isolation from Western theatre, and thus represents a wholly distinct theatrical tradition.

To understand Noh theatre, we need to look at the political and cultural context out of which it developed. During the sixth century A.D., the Buddhist religion arrived in Japan and with it a written language and many non-native arts and crafts. Then, in the seventh century, an emperor was able to to gain power over Japan and to take ownership of all land. For some 400 years, Japan flourished under this system, but by the twelfth century the emperor had lost most of his political power. Finally, in 1192, he ceded his secular authority to a *shogun* (military dictator), although he retained his status as a near-god in the religious realm. The shogunate became hereditary, although new families won possession of the title from time to time. Japan was ruled in this manner until 1867, when American intervention led to the downfall of the shogunate and the return of power to the emperor.

Under the shogunate Japan developed a strict social hierarchy. The highest class was the *samurai* (warriors), with the *shogun* at their head. Below them were merchants, artists and craftsmen, and farmers and peasants. Each rank had its specified code of behavior and mode of dress. Codes were sufficiently strict that Japanese life became highly structured and formalized.

In 1338, the Ashikaga family gained control of the shogunate and retained it for the next 250 years. One of its goals was to eliminate foreign cultural influences and develop native art forms. Of the native forms, Noh was to enjoy special favor. Noh had originated much earlier and had come to be used by Buddhist priests as a teaching medium. In this respect, Noh resembled Western religious drama, although its content, form, and conventions were quite unlike those of the European plays.

Noh Theatre

The most significant developments in Noh theatre began around 1375, when the *shogun* took the Noh performer and dramatist Kiyotsugu Kan'ami (1333–1384) and his son Zeami Motokiyo (1363–1444) under his patronage and granted them high status in his court. Working within this rather refined atmosphere, these two men gave Noh its characteristic form. Zeami is considered the greatest of Noh dramatists. He wrote more than 100 of the 240 plays that still make up the active Noh repertory. He also defined the Noh's goals and conventions. No play written during the past 400 years holds a place in the present Noh repertory, and the plays are still performed today much as they were when written. Thus, Noh is essentially a product of the fourteenth, fifteenth, and sixteenth centuries.

The major influence on Noh's view of the world was Zen Buddhism, which teaches that ultimate peace comes through union with all being, that individual desire must be overcome, and that nothing in earthly life is permanent. Noh plays typically have as protagonists ghosts, demons, or obsessed human beings whose souls cannot find rest because in life they were devoted to worldly honor, love, or other goals that keep drawing them back to the physical world and its imperfections.

Noh dramas are classified into five types: god plays, warrior plays, women plays, madness plays, and demon plays. Traditionally, a program is made up of one play of each type performed in the order listed above. These make up a pattern that shows, first, the innocence and peace of the world of the gods; then man's fall, repentance, and possibility of

Noh performance of *The Lady Aoi* by Zeami Motokiyo. This play has the same protagonist as *Nonomiya*, but here she is depicted as a demon (at left in demon mask). Kneeling at right is the *waki* character; standing center is a commoner (performed by a *kyogen* actor). The musicians (drummers and flute player) are at the rear of the stage. (Courtesy Kokusai Bunka Shinkokai.)

The ancient Greek theatre at
Epidaurus. The stage house is
temporary, erected on the ruins of
the original. A modern-day
performance is shown.
(Constantine Manos/Magnum.)

Masks and costumes for Jocasta (left) and Oedipus by Tanya Moiseiwitsch for a production of Sophocles' *Oedipus the King* at the Stratford (Ontario) Festival. (Photo by David Behl.)

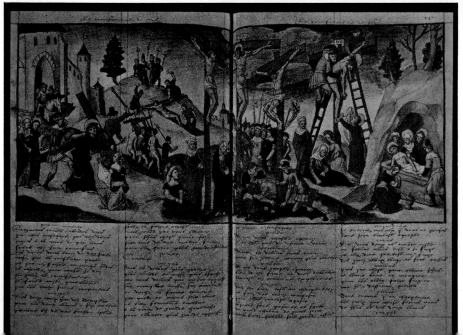

A double page from the manuscript of the medieval outdoor religious drama staged at Valenciennes (France) in 1547. At bottom, the text of the play; above, simultaneous drawings of several scenes. At left, Christ carrying the cross; top left, Christ being nailed to the cross; center, the crucifixion; right center, the descent from the cross; and right, the entombment. (Courtesy Bibliothèque Nationale, Paris.)

A painting entitled *Les Délices du Genre Humain*, showing major French actors and popular stage characters of the seventeenth century. Molière is seen at extreme left. Harlequin is at center front; Pantalone and Brighella are at right. (Courtesy Comédie Française, Paris.)

A commedia dell'arte troupe. Harlequin is seen at upper left. An anonymous painting. (Museo del Burkardo, Rome; Photo Researchers.)

Interior of the Theatre Royal, Turin (Italy), in 1740. The proscenium arch is so deep that it contains a box for spectators on each of five levels. Note the actors' costumes, the vendors of fruit and drink, and the soldier posted to keep order. The scenery is by Guiseppe Bibiena, noted for his monumental painted settings. Despite its apparent realism, all of the details of the setting are painted on wings, drops, and borders. Painting by Pietro Domenico. (Courtesy Civic Museum, Turin.)

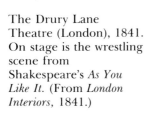

The Drury Lane Theatre (London), 1841. On stage is the wrestling scene from Shakespeare's *As You Like It*. (From *London Interiors*, 1841.)

redemption; and, finally, the glory of defeating the forces that stand in the way of peace and harmony.

Each Noh script is very short (often shorter than a Western one-act play). It does not emphasize storytelling. The dialogue serves primarily to outline the circumstances that lead up to, and culminate in, a dance. Above all, Noh is a musical dance-drama that evokes an emotional state and mood. Most of the lines (written partly in verse and partly in prose) are sung or intoned. Even the brief spoken passages are recited in a stylized manner. Ordinary speech is used only when a player comes on stage between the parts of a two-part piece to summarize the first part.

The performers can be divided into three main groups: actors, chorus, and musicians. The actors are trained from childhood and expect to devote twenty or more years to perfecting their craft. There are five hereditary schools of Noh performance, all of which have handed down their traditions and conventions since the fifteenth century. There are two main divisions of actors: those who play the secondary character, the *waki*, and his followers (whose function it is to introduce the drama and lead the main character toward the climactic moment); and those who play the *shite*, the main character, and his followers. There are also *kyogen*, actors whose primary skill is in performing the short comic pieces that accompany the Noh plays but who appear in Noh in the role of commoners, peasants, and narrators, and *kokata*, child actors who as students play child or minor roles.

The chorus is composed of from six to ten members, depending upon the play. They sit at one side of the stage throughout and sing or recite many of the actor's lines (especially while he is dancing) or narrate events. The musicians include two or three drummers, as specified by the play, and one flute player. The drummers also punctuate the performance with a variety of vocal sounds. In addition to the performers, there are two stage attendants, whom the audience is supposed to ignore. One assists the musicians. The other assists the actors in changing or adjusting costumes or masks, and he sets or removes stage properties as needed. All of the performers and assistants are male.

The *shite* and his companions wear masks of painted wood, many of them passed down for generations. Costumes are rich in color and design, based on the official dress of the fourteenth and fifteenth centuries but adapted to give an air of grandeur and to increase the performer's stature. Most are made of elaborately embroidered silk. Several garments are usually worn one over the other and can be added to, removed, or changed onstage during the performance. Each character has his traditional costume, headdress, hand properties, and positions onstage. The chorus, musicians, and attendants wear stiff shoulder boards and divided skirts, the traditional dress of the *samurai*.

Hand properties are few and conventionalized. The fan is most important since it can be used to suggest such varied things as the wind, the ripple of water, the rising moon, falling rain, and many emotional responses. Swords and spears are also common.

The Noh stage has been standardized for almost 400 years. It is raised about three feet. The two principal areas, the stage proper *(butai)* and bridge *(hashigakari)*, are both roofed like the shrines from which they are descended. The roof of the *butai* is supported by four columns, each with its own name and use. By the upstage right pillar *(shitebashira*, or principal character's pillar), the actor pauses when he enters and announces his name and where he comes from. While reciting this speech, he faces the downstage right pillar *(metsukabashira*, or gazing pillar). The

A Noh stage. At left is the bridge; at center rear can be seen the pine tree painted on the back wall and the bamboo on the side wall. The *waki-za* (position of chorus) is in the background on the right. The main acting area is outlined by the four upright posts. Note also the temple roof above the stage. (Courtesy Kokusai Bunka Shinkokai.)

downstage left pillar *(wakibashira)* marks the place where the *waki* sits when he is not directly involved in the action. The upstage left pillar *(fuebashira,* flute pillar) marks the flute player's position.

The stage is divided into three principal areas, although none is marked off architecturally except by the pillars (see the diagram shown below). The largest area, the main stage, is enclosed by the four pillars and is about 18 feet square. Back of the upstage pillars is the rear stage *(atoza),* where the musicians and attendants sit. To stage left of the main stage is the *waki-za,* where the chorus sits cross-legged on the floor in two rows. There are two entrances to the stage. The principal one, the bridge *(hashigakari),* is a railed gangway about 6 feet wide and 40 feet long leading from the mirror room, where the actors prepare for their entrances. In front of the bridge are three live pine trees symbolizing heaven, earth, and man. The bridge is used as an entrance for the musicians and for all important characters. The other entrance, the "slit" or "cut-through" door, located upstage left, is only about 3 feet high and is used by the chorus and stage assistants. The rear walls of the stage and bridge are made of wood. Painted on the wall behind the orchestra is a pine tree and on the stage left wall is bamboo, perhaps reminders of the natural scenery that formed the background in the earliest years of Noh. There is no other scenery as such in the Noh theatre. A few stage properties are used, but these are usually miniature skeletal outlines of boats, huts, shrines, etc., typically made of bamboo. These are set in place and removed as needed by the stage attendant.

The audience views the performance from two sides: in front of the main stage and alongside the bridge. The theatres used today hold 300 to 500 persons. Although they are now indoor structures, they retain

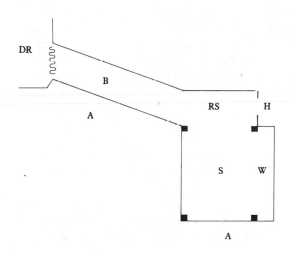

Plan of a Noh stage. A—audience; B—bridge *(hashigakari)*; DR—dressing room (or mirror room); H—"slit" or "cut-through" door; RS—rear stage *(atoza)*; S—main stage *(butai)*; W—side stage for chorus *(wakiza)*. (Drawing by Douglas Hubbell.)

Noh Theatre   115

many outdoor features; the shrinelike roof of the stage is complete under the ceiling of the auditorium, and lighting simulates the even distribution of outdoor light. Noh was never intended to appeal to a mass audience, as were the theatres of Greece, Rome, and medieval Europe. In medieval Japan, Noh was, with few exceptions, reserved for the samurai class and was seen only on special occasions. Today, it is presented for the general public, and while it has a considerable following, its appeal is to a relatively small audience, probably because of the special demands it makes on the spectators.

Noh theatre, then, differs markedly from Western theatre. Every element of performance is strictly controlled by conventions that have been established for centuries. Rather than encouraging innovation, Noh seeks to perfect and preserve an art form. In many ways, therefore, it resembles religious ritual in its repetitive use of accepted patterns. Let us look more closely at a Noh play.

The Shrine in the Fields (Nonomiya)

The Shrine in the Fields (Nonomiya) is usually attributed to Zeami, although his authorship cannot be established beyond question. It belongs to the third category, a "woman" play, and is based on episodes from one of the most famous of Japanese novels, *The Tale of Genji.* In the novel, Lord Genji is the lover of Lady Rokujo (the *shite* of *The Shrine in the Fields,* in which she is called Miyasudokoro), but after a time neglects her. During a festival, attendants on Lord Genji's wife publicly humiliate Lady Rokujo when they push her carriage out of the procession and disable it. She decides to leave the capital and go to Nonomiya, where her daughter is being prepared to become the priestess of Ise, the sun goddess. While at Nonomiya, Lady Rokujo is visited by Lord Genji, who brings her a branch of *sakaki* (a sacred evergreen tree) as a sign of his trustworthiness, and begs her to return with him. Although she does not, she is forever after haunted by her humiliation and sense of loss. Lord Genji's visit and Lady Rokujo's response to it provide the emotional focus of *The Shrine in the Field.* In this play, Lady Rokujo is treated sympathetically, though in other plays she is depicted as a vengeful demon who causes the deaths of others. In the Noh drama *Aoi no Ue,* her spirit torments Lady Genji on her sickbed and then, transformed into a horned demon, fights with a priest.

Each Noh play is set in a specific season of the year, named early in the drama, and the mood and imagery of the entire play must be in keeping with that season. In *The Shrine in the Field,* the date is specific:

late autumn, the seventh day of the ninth month, the day on which Lord Genji visits Lady Rokujo at Nonomiya. The mood throughout is one of melancholy and bittersweet longing.

As is typical in Noh drama, the introductory scene compresses time and place: an itinerant priest (the *waki* or secondary character) travels almost instantaneously from the capital to Nonomiya, where his curiosity is aroused by the seeming perfect preservation of the shrine, although it has long been abandoned. When the ghost of Miyasudokoro (the *shite*) appears in the guise of a village girl, he questions her about the shrine and herself, and gradually it becomes apparent that there is something mysterious about both her and the place. This first portion of the play occurs at dusk, and when the moon (a symbol of Buddha) appears, she

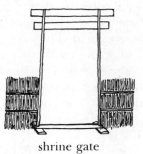

Noh stage properties: shrine gate with hedge fence; straw hut; retreat; grave mound; large board hut; well curb with *susuki* grass; plum tree stand; carriage. (From Kunio Komparu, *The Noh Theater: Principles and Perspectives*. Courtesy John Weatherhill, Inc., Tokyo.)

shrine gate

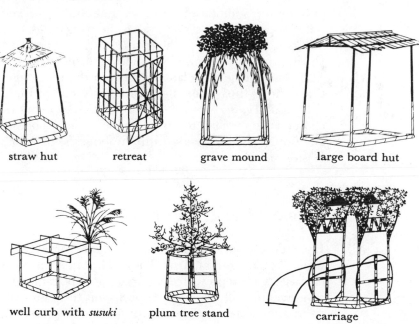

straw hut   retreat   grave mound   large board hut

well curb with *susuki*   plum tree stand   carriage

vanishes and then returns (having changed both mask and costume) as the Miyasudokoro of long ago. As she recalls the festival at which she was publicly disgraced, her emotion builds, and she prays that the attachments that forever draw her back to this place will leave her.

As in all Noh plays, the climactic moment is expressed in dance. The script does little to indicate the length of the dance, which continues in performance for twenty or more minutes. In this final portion of the play, the pulls between this world and the next are symbolized in the passing back and forth through the gate of the shrine. At the end, the freeing of her soul is indicated by her departure from the "burning house," an image for the world. In Buddhist teaching, enlightened persons are counseled to leave the world as willingly as they would flee a burning building.

In Noh, a number of devices distance the spectator from the play. The language is stylized throughout; most of the passages are intoned or sung; and the lines of dialogue are divided in ways that differ markedly from the practices typical of Western drama, so that a single thought may be divided between the *shite* and *waki* or between a character and the chorus; the *shite* sometimes speaks of herself in the third person; and the chorus frequently speaks the lines of both the *waki* and the *shite*. In addition, numerous quotations from, or allusions to, earlier literary works are embedded in the text.

For *The Shrine in the Fields,* the basic appearance of the stage is altered only by the addition of a stylized gate and brushwood fence, and the only property of any significance is the sprig of *sakaki* that Miyasudokoro brings on and places at the shrine gate (as Lord Genji had long ago). During the performance, the chorus (seated at stage left), and the musicians and stage attendants (seated on the rear stage) were also visible throughout, thus becoming part of the visual picture.

Overall, *The Shrine in the Fields* does not seek to tell a story or to develop character so much as to capture a particular mood, to distill a powerful emotion, and to express an attitude about the physical world and human existence.

Other Japanese Theatre Forms

Japan developed two other traditional theatrical forms: doll theatre (now usually called Bunraku) and Kabuki. The doll theatre, in which the characters are represented by large puppets, came to prominence in the seventeenth century. The puppets went through many changes. Originally, they were only heads with drapery representing the body; later,

A doll (or puppet) theatre performance. Puppets and their handlers are seen at center and at left. In the background right are the musicians and narrator. Note also the painted scenery at center left and overhead. (Courtesy Kokusai Bunka Shinkokai.)

hands and feet, and then movable eyes, movable eyebrows, and jointed and movable fingers, were added. Eventually the puppets were also doubled in size—to their present 3 or 4 feet tall—and elaborately costumed.

Each puppet is operated by three handlers, all visible to the audience. One handler manipulates the head and right arm, a second the left arm, and a third the feet. A narrator tells the story, speaks the dialogue, and expresses the feelings of each puppet. He is accompanied by a *samisen* (a three-stringed instrument with a skin-covered base that is simultaneously struck and plucked) and other instruments of lesser importance. The stage itself is long and narrow. Unlike Noh, Bunraku represents all locales scenically, and the scenery is changed as the action requires. Bunraku is probably the most complex puppet performance in the world.

Kabuki also first appeared in the seventeenth century. It has long been the most popular of the traditional forms and has also been the one most open to change. It has borrowed many of its plays and conventions from Noh or Bunraku, but it has adapted them to its own needs. Originally, Kabuki was performed on a stage resembling that used for Noh. But as time passed, it underwent many changes and today bears little resemblance to the Noh stage. The Kabuki stage is now very wide—about 90 feet—but only about 20 feet high. The auditorium is correspondingly wide and shallow, with all seats facing the stage. A raised gangway (the *hanamichi*) connects the stage to the back of the auditorium. Most important entrances and exists are made along it, and some major scenes are also played there. Thus, much of the action occurs in the auditorium in the midst of the audience.

Unlike Noh, Kabuki uses a great deal of scenery, although the settings are not meant to be wholly illusionistic. White mats are used to represent snow, blue mats to indicate water, and gray mats for the ground. Relatively realistic buildings are depicted frequently, but the entry gates to houses are often removed by stage assistants when no longer needed. These and other conventions constantly call attention to the fictional nature of the performance. Sets are changed in full view of the audience by stage attendants (although by Japanese stage convention these stage attendants are considered to be invisible).

Most Kabuki plays are divided into several acts made up of loosely connected episodes emphasizing strong, highly emotional incidents. The climactic moment in many scenes is reached in a pose struck and held

A Kabuki performance. Note the painted scenery in the background and the practical scenic elements at center and overhead. Note also the facial makeup of the characters and the makeup lines on the legs and chest (to emphasize musculature) on the actor at left. (Courtesy Kokusai Bunka Shinkokai.)

Lion dance from *Pacific Overtures*, an American musical by Stephen Sondheim, which borrowed many conventions from Japanese theatre, especially Kabuki. This musical concerns how Japan was forcibly opened to Western trade in the mid-nineteenth century. (Photo by Martha Swope.)

(a *mie*) by the principal character. Actors in heroic or villainous roles are offered numerous opportunities to demonstrate their skill through these *mie*s, which are greatly admired by Japanese audiences. The most popular of all Kabuki plays is Takedo Izumo's *Chushingura* (1748), the eleven acts of which require a full day to perform. A play of honor and revenge, it tells how forty-seven faithful samurai avenge the wrongs done to their master.

Song and narration are important in Kabuki. Those plays adapted from Noh or Bunraku retain many conventions of the original forms. Therefore, in some plays a narrator or chorus performs some passages. Since the Kabuki actor never sings, passages that must be sung also require a chorus. Much of Kabuki action is accompanied by an orchestra, the composition of which varies according to the origin of the play. It often includes flutes, drums, bells, gongs, cymbals, and strings, although the most essential instrument is the *samisen*.

Kabuki acting is a combination of stylized speaking and dancing. Almost all its movement borders on dance, distilling the essence of real emotions and deeds into stylized postures, gestures, and movements. Similarly, the spoken lines follow conventionalized patterns of intonation. Roles are divided into a small number of types: loyal, good, courageous mature men; villains; young men; comic roles (including comic villains); children; and women. All types are played by males, and all require many years of training. Most leading actors come from a few families for whom acting is a hereditary profession. Each family has an elaborate system of stage names, some of them so honored that they are awarded (in elaborate public ceremonies) only to those considered undisputed masters of their art.

Kabuki actors do not wear masks, but some roles use boldly patterned makeup to exaggerate the musculature of face or body. The makeup of each role typifies the character. Each role also has its traditional costumes, some so heavy (up to 50 pounds) that stage attendants must assist the actors in keeping them properly arranged.

Although Kabuki is highly conventionalized, it includes many elements that resemble those typical of Western theatre. Consequently, Kabuki is the Japanese form that appeals most to Westerners, and in recent years many European and American directors have borrowed Kabuki conventions (some of which Westerners have become familiar with through their use in Japanese films), especially for productions of Greek and Shakespearean tragedies. Nevertheless, Westerners usually understand Japanese conventions only in a very general way. The conventions of Noh drama remain the least understood. But even though we do not comprehend Japanese plays fully, they remind us that theatrical conventions and theatrical experiences vary widely from one culture to another. They force us to recognize that the kinds of theatre with which we are most familiar do not exhaust the possibilities inherent in the theatrical form.

The Theatre Experiences of Elizabethan England and Seventeenth-Century France

6

The European theatrical experiences we have examined up to this point all had a number of common characteristics. They were parts of festivals sponsored by governmental and religious authorities, performed on special occasions for the entire community, financed by the state or wealthy citizens, and considered to be offerings of the community to some god. But a significant change occurred during the sixteenth century, and by the mid-seventeenth century, the role of the theatre within society had largely been redefined.

The forces that brought the changes had been underway for some time. Among these was a growing secularization of thought as people devoted increased attention to life here and now rather than being preoccupied with the life hereafter. This enlargement of concerns led to a revival of learning in many fields. Thus, the period is often referred to as the Renaissance (or rebirth). In pursuing these new interests, people turned once more to Greece and Rome for guidance, and they became increasingly interested in classical plays and theatrical practices, even though their understanding of them was often severely flawed. Nevertheless, educated people began to perceive alternatives to medieval drama, and gradually playwrights began to write plays that imitated or adapted classical subjects and forms or that amalgamated medieval and classical elements.

The spirit of inquiry generated by the Renaissance was also felt in religion, and during the sixteenth century disputes over church doctrine and practices led to secessions from the Roman Catholic church and the formation of several Protestant sects. The various factions soon found theatrical performance a good propaganda medium (especially since the majority of the audience could not read), and they exploited it in plays that ridiculed their opponents and upheld their own views. The disputes often erupted into violence, even wars. The plays sometimes attacked rulers, who usually had to choose sides in the religious controversies. In England, the state-sanctioned church changed four times during the sixteenth century, and each time numerous persons were executed because of their opposition.

Under these circumstances, it is not surprising that by 1550 both church and state had begun to look for ways to reduce disturbances. Shortly after Elizabeth I succeeded to the English throne in 1558, she decreed that no plays dealing with religious or political subjects were to be performed. This, in effect, was the death knell for the cycle plays. By 1600, they had all but disappeared, not only in England but throughout Europe, where similar circumstances and prohibitions occurred. Thus, a type of theatrical experience that had enjoyed enormous popularity for 200 years was wiped out by the institutions (church and state) that had encouraged it.

Forbidden to perform plays on religious or political subjects, the theatre had no alternative but to turn to secular material, and it found its richest sources in classical literature, historical chronicles, and medieval tales. In other words, a new kind of drama was born in part out of necessity. Perhaps more important, an alternative kind of theatre had to be exploited. Since the state, church, and wealthy individuals had withdrawn their patronage, other kinds of support had to be found. The theatre, in effect, was forced to become a commercial enterprise. Rather than remaining occasional, celebratory, officially supported, and free to the public, it became continuous, self-supporting, and sufficiently attractive to keep a paying public coming back.

Somewhat surprisingly, those who had been the most enthusiastic supporters of the religious cycles were the most vehement opponents of a professional theatre. To them, the presentation of plays for the glory of God, the honor of the city, and the edification of man seemed worthy goals, but devoting one's life to performing plays for money was considered wasteful and sinful. The guilds that had produced many of the cycle plays in England sought to have the professional theatre banned on the grounds that it took people away from work, encouraged sinful behavior, spread diseases, and offered cover for seditious activities. Thus, the guilds saw the professional theatre in a quite different light than they had seen the largely amateur theatre of the Middle Ages.

To survive, the professional groups had to be able to play often, had to have a repertory of plays sufficiently large and varied to keep the limited available audience coming back, had to have a performance space large enough to accommodate a sizable number of spectators and contained enough to permit the company to control access and collect entrance fees. They also had to own or control their own costumes, scenery, and other production elements, and had to assemble a company of actors and production personnel that would devote full time to theatrical production and performance.

Accomplishing these tasks was difficult because in the sixteenth century acting was not an accepted profession, and therefore it did not fit into the then-dominant trade-guild scheme under which there was a clear-cut hierarchy of responsibility and authority. Actors were considered to be "masterless men," meaning that no one was responsible for them; thus, they fell into the category of vagrants who, because of their threat to the social order, were subject to arrest and punishment. To get around this difficulty, acting companies found noblemen to serve as their patrons; technically, then, the actors became servants of these patrons and therefore were no longer masterless. In Shakespeare's time, the acting companies had such titles as the Lord Admiral's Men, the Lord Chamberlain's Men, and the King's Men as indications of legal status. Without the patronage of rulers and noblemen, the professional theatre would have had difficulty surviving. Nevertheless, patronage brought little financial support.

If the rulers helped to protect the companies, they also imposed some restrictions by insisting that every company have a license from the crown and that every play be approved before being performed. Such licensing made it possible for the ruler to ensure that the companies did not perform plays that might stir up political or religious controversy. Nevertheless, despite the legal status of acting companies, the London city council (made up of guild members) did all it could to discourage performances within the city. Consequently, when permanent theatres were built, they were erected outside the city limits.

Though the problems were many, by 1600 the English acting companies had overcome most of them and were in the midst of what many consider the greatest theatrical era the world has known.

Shakespeare and the Globe Theatre

The reputation of the Elizabethan theatre rests above all on the work of William Shakespeare (1564–1616), perhaps the greatest playwright of all time, and the company of which he was a member (the Lord Chamberlain's Men, later the King's Men). Of course, Shakespeare was only one of many significant dramatists of that time. Others included Thomas Kyd, Christopher Marlowe, Ben Jonson, John Fletcher, and John Webster.

Theatrical conditions favored the development of playwriting. From the 1580s until 1642, there were always at least two (and sometimes as many as four) companies playing in London. Since they performed six times a week (every day except Sunday) in the afternoon (beginning around 2 P.M.) during normal working hours, and since London was still a relatively small city of around 200,000, the companies were in strong competition for audiences. They could not rely on long runs; normally, they changed the bill every day. A new play was performed once and then at intervals from time to time until it lost its appeal. In the 1590s, a London company produced a new play about every seventeen days. The average life of a play was ten performances (that is, the total number of times played—spread over one or more seasons—before it was dropped from the repertory). New plays were in constant demand, a situation obviously favorable to playwrights.

Playwrights had other incentives to be prolific. Once a company had paid the dramatist for his play, it belonged to the company and he received no further income from it. A writer who depended entirely on his plays for a living had to sell four or five a year. Shakespeare seems to have written about two a year, but he was also an actor and a major shareholder in his company (that is, he was a part owner of the com-

The Swan Theatre, London, 1596. This is the only surviving drawing made of an English public theatre during Shakespeare's lifetime. It shows three levels of seating in the galleries; a stage jutting to the middle of an unroofed yard; a roof canopy over part of the stage; and two doors at the rear of the stage (but no "discovery space" between the doors). (Bapst, *Essai sur l'Histoire du Théâtre*, 1893.)

pany's assets and involved in the running of the company) and a part owner of the Globe theatre, in which the company performed. Thus, he was involved in almost every aspect of the theatre and became far wealthier than most of his fellow dramatists.

In addition to a steady supply of new plays, a company needed a performance space. Once the professional theatre began to establish a foothold, buildings intended specifically for theatrical performances began to be erected in Europe for the first time since the fall of Rome. In England, the first was probably built in 1576 and was called simply The Theatre. Others soon followed. While the English public theatres varied in details, all had similar features that drew on medieval conventions but transformed them.

Let us look at the Globe, the theatre used by Shakespeare's company after 1599 and of which Shakespeare was part owner. Basically round with an exterior diameter of approximately 100 feet, the Globe had three levels of roofed galleries, each about 15½ feet deep, which enclosed an unroofed open space (the yard) approximately 69 feet in diameter. The stage extended to the middle of the yard. Approximately 41 feet 6 inches wide and 27 feet 8 inches deep and raised 5–6 feet above the yard, the stage was viewed from three sides by spectators seated in the galleries or standing in the yard. It was sheltered by a roof ("the heavens" or "the shadow") supported by two posts near the front of the stage platform. At the back of the stage platform was a multilevel facade. On the stage level, two large doors, one at either side, served as exits and entrances or as openings through which stage properties could be moved on and off the stage. These doors were the most essential part of the background. Changes of locale were often indicated by the exit of characters through one door, followed by the entrance of different characters through the other door. Usually, the doors remained unlocalized, but at times they were used to represent houses, city gates, castles, or other places. There may have been another opening between these two doors that could be used for "discoveries"—revealing objects or persons that are hidden until some crucial moment—common occurrences in the plays of Shakespeare and other dramatists of the time. Some people believe that the stage doors were used for this purpose, but others argue that there was something like a small inner stage that could be concealed or revealed by a curtain. The second level of the facade included an acting space used to represent balconies (as in *Romeo and Juliet*), windows, battlements, or other high places. There may have been a playing area on the third level as well, but this has not been verified.

Overall, then, this stage was an adaptation of medieval conventions. The facade served the function of mansions in the medieval stage, while the stage platform served as platea. Stage properties, such as tables,

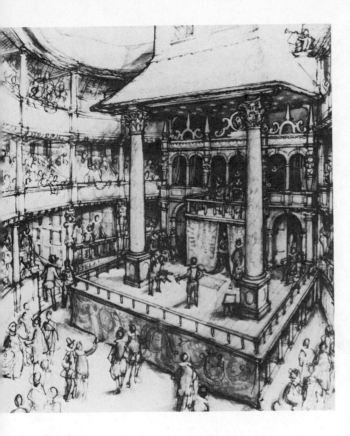

Conjectural reconstruction of the interior of the Globe. Drawing by C. Walter Hodges. (*The Third Globe: Symposium for the Reconstruction of the Globe Playhouse*. Courtesy Wayne State University Press.)

thrones, tents, beds, altars, and scaffolds, were sometimes brought onto the stage, usually because the action demanded them rather than to localize a scene. This stage also had some things in common with those of Greece, Rome, and Japanese Noh, since the background for all scenes was the formalized facade, and the specific location of a scene was established primarily through dialogue. When place was important, the characters named it or described it. This conventional way of establishing the setting is sometimes called "spoken decor." Overall, the Elizabethan structure and the conventions that governed its use greatly facilitated staging, since one scene could flow into another without pauses for changing scenery. Thus, the playwright had almost unlimited freedom in handling time and place.

The conventions that governed costuming and lighting also resembled those of the medieval theatre. Most characters, regardless of the historical era of the action, were clothed in Elizabethan garments appropriate to their rank, age, and profession. Other kinds of costumes were used

The stage of the Stratford (Canada) Shakespearean Festival Theatre, an adaptation of the Elizabethan public stage. (Photo by David Cooper. Courtesy Stratford Shakespearean Festival Foundation of Canada.)

sparingly: Greek and Roman characters were often identified by drapery superimposed on Elizabethan dress; fanciful garments (corresponding to accepted ideas of the appearance of such creatures) were used for ghosts, witches, fairies, and allegorical figures; and sometimes racial or national stereotypes (Turks, Indians, Jews, Moors) were indicated by dress. Costumes and banners accounted for much of the color and pageantry of Elizabethan theatre, since there were many processions, battles, and celebrations. Maintaining an adequate wardrobe was one of a company's greatest expenses. Since performances took place out-of-doors during daylight hours, lighting was no problem, except in scenes supposedly occurring at night or in the dark. Darkness was indicated either through the dialogue or by characters carrying torches, lanterns, or candles.

Most important was the acting company itself. It was made up of about twenty-five persons, of whom about half were shareholders in the company, who made all important decisions and shared any profit. There were a number of hired men who acted, served as prompters, musicians,

Sketch (supposedly made in 1595) showing characters from Shakespeare's *Titus Andronicus*. Note the variety in costumes. The character standing at center wears drapery suggesting Roman times; the character at extreme right also has some features suggesting the classical era. The others wear Elizabethan costumes. Some scholars consider this drawing to be a forgery. (Reproduced by permission of the Marquess of Bath, Longleat House, Warminster, Wiltshire, England)

stagehands, and wardrobe-keepers, and were paid a weekly wage. There were also four to six apprentices, boys who played female roles. All members of the company were male. (There were no English actresses until 1661.) Since a company usually performed a different play each day, there was much double-casting, and each actor was responsible for a large number of roles. Although the overall performance style was probably not realistic in the modern sense, it was considerably closer to everyday behavior and appearance than a Greek or Noh performance. Elizabethan actors did not wear masks (except as disguises), all lines were spoken, and behavior was based on that familiar to the audience. The conventions that most removed the performances from realism were the verse in which much of the dialogue was written, the use of males to play female roles, and the formalized background.

There was a considerable musical element. Trumpets sounded flourishes to mark the entrances of kings, to call attention to important announcements, and to serve as signals in the numerous battles. Music also accompanied songs and dances in many plays; most performances concluded with a jig, a short music-and-dance piece.

Taken altogether, then, Elizabethan acting companies learned quickly how to make the theatre fully professional and sufficiently attractive and remunerative to support a fairly large number of persons. The other important ingredient was the paying audience, among which backgrounds and tastes varied considerably. Therefore, the plays usually included something for everyone. Shakespeare's plays have plots as complex as a modern soap opera and often have as much violence as a television police series, but they also use poetic language and other devices that direct attention to the significance of events and provide insights into human behavior so profound that the plays have retained their appeal down to the present day.

When the audience arrived at the theatre, everyone paid the same small general-admission fee. This covered standing room in the yard. If one wished to sit, one had to pay another, larger free for admission to the galleries. There were also a few private boxes in the galleries ("lords' rooms"), entry to which required another and still larger fee. Altogether, the Globe probably held about 3000 people, although seldom did that many attend. There were no intermissions, and wine, beer, ale, nuts, and playing cards were sold in the theatres by vendors who circulated during performances. The atmosphere must have been somewhat like

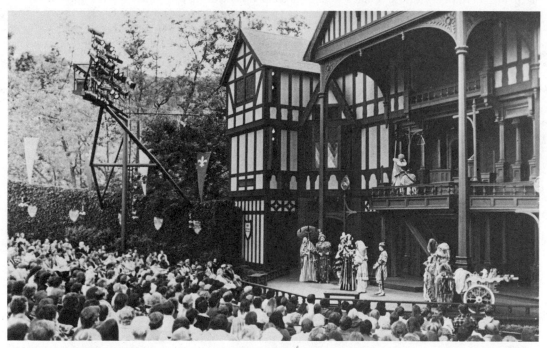

The [Ashland] Oregon Shakespearean Festival stage and auditorium during a performance of *The Comedy of Errors* in 1982. (Photo by Hank Kranzler. Courtesy Oregon Shakespearean Festival.)

a modern sports event. Keeping the audience quiet and attentive depended on the power of the play and the skill of the performers.

Let us look at one of the thirty-eight plays by Shakespeare that have come down to us. It is both representative of Elizabethan drama in its story, structure, and conventions, and superior to most plays of the time in being one of the world's great tragedies. The theatrical experiences summed up in *Oedipus the King* and *Hamlet* epitomize the differences between the Greek and the Elizabethan theatre experiences.

Hamlet

Like *Oedipus the King*, *Hamlet* concerns a man charged with the duty of punishing the murderer of a king. But Shakespeare uses a much broader canvas than Sophocles does and includes within his drama more facets of the story, more characters, and a wider sweep of time and place.

Shakespeare organizes his action with great skill. The opening scene, in which the Ghost appears at midnight on the castle ramparts, quickly captures the spectators' attention and establishes a mood of mystery and expectation of revelations to come. The remainder of Act I introduces the main characters and establishes the dramatic situation—the murder and the demand that Hamlet revenge his father's death. In Act II, Hamlet's strange behavior causes Claudius and others to seek the reason for it. This phase of the action reaches its climax in Act III, Scene 2, when Claudius' response to a play confirms his guilt. But this scene also reveals to Claudius that Hamlet is aware of Claudius' guilt; consequently, Hamlet—who until this point has been the pursuer—now becomes the pursued. The remainder of the play shows Claudius intriguing to have Hamlet killed in ways that will not draw suspicion to himself.

Shakespeare's skill is also shown in the way he interweaves this main plot with the subplot concerning Polonius and his family. The two strands of action are related through Hamlet's love for Ophelia, Polonius' relation to the King, and Laertes' wish to revenge his father's death (just as Hamlet has sought to revenge his). The final scene, during which Claudius' plan to have Hamlet killed ends not only in Hamlet's death but also in that of Gertrude, Laertes, and Claudius, resolves both main and subplot.

All of Shakespeare's main characters are drawn from the nobility or aristocracy. He does not tell us the age of his characters or reveal much about their physical appearance. Nevertheless, age and contrast are important. The young and innocent—Hamlet, Ophelia, and Laertes—suffer most.

Aidan Quinn as Hamlet and Lisa Dodson as Ophelia in a present-day setting of the play. The "To be or not to be" soliloquy was spray-painted on the set, rather than spoken, by Hamlet. Directed by Robert Falls at the Wisdom Bridge Theatre, Chicago, 1985–86. (Courtesy Wisdom Bridge Theatre.)

Many people consider Hamlet to be among the most demanding roles ever written for a tragic actor, in part because the actor must project one set of attitudes and responses to the characters and another to the audience. So carefully balanced are the demands that an ongoing controversy has developed over whether Hamlet feigns madness or whether for a time he is actually mad. Another controversy concerns whether Hamlet procrastinates unduly. Some critics have argued that Hamlet is so sensitive that he cannot at first bring himself to kill Claudius; others argue that it is not Hamlet's sensitivity, but his desire to be certain of Claudius' guilt, that causes him to delay, and that he acts as quickly as circumstances permit. Hamlet is a sensitive young man who, faced with a series of disillusioning revelations, reveals his nature in the complexity of his feelings and thoughts until the final scenes, when—recognizing Claudius' villainy not only against the dead king but against others—he acts decisively. The actor playing this role is faced with a range of complex emotional responses, ambiguous speech and action, and with showing energy kept under great restraint until the final scenes, when it bursts forth.

Like Hamlet, Ophelia is sensitive; having little knowledge of the world, she is easily led by her father, Polonius. Hamlet's seeming rejection of her and his killing of her father come as such shocks to her that she goes mad—rather than feigning madness, as Hamlet apparently does. Her brother, Laertes, who is near Hamlet in age, rushes into action, rather than hesitating, when faced with a situation comparable to that with which Hamlet must deal. Claudius, playing on Laertes' impulsiveness, is able to talk him into a deception that is contrary to his nature. One may well conclude that, while Claudius, Gertrude, and Polonius get what they deserve, the young people are victims of their elders' weaknesses.

Claudius apparently is a suave and charming man, since otherwise it would be difficult to understand how he is able to deceive so many people. He has the support of the court, he had seduced Gertrude (who apparently is unaware that he has murdered her husband), and he easily takes in Laertes. Not until the final scene do most of the characters perceive Claudius' villainy. Claudius' surface respectability also provides one explanation as to why Hamlet cannot act hastily or openly, since Hamlet probably would not have been believed had he accused Claudius of murder.

Hamlet's mother, Gertrude, is still relatively young (she need not be more than forty); she is a weak and sensuous woman who has been seduced by Claudius and has married him hastily following her husband's death, perhaps to prove to herself that she has sinned out of love. Polonius is a pompous, self-important, and verbose politician who gives unsolicited advice and reaches unwarranted conclusions. He is often played as a buffoon, but there is danger in exaggerating his ridiculousness, as this tends to diminish the obstacles that must be overcome by Hamlet.

Shakespeare's dramatic poetry is generally recognized as the finest in the English language. The basic medium is blank verse, which retains much of the flexibility of ordinary speech while elevating and formalizing it. Still, there are also many passages in prose, especially those involving such lower-class characters as the gravediggers and the actors.

Probably the most important element in Shakespeare's dialogue is figurative language. The principal purpose of a figure of speech in dramatic poetry is to set up either direct or indirect comparisons. Shakespeare's superiority over other writers of dramatic poetry lies in his use of comparisons that enlarge the significance without distracting attention from the dramatic situation. His poetic devices partially fulfill the same function as the visual representation of Heaven and Hell on the medieval stage: they relate human actions to the divine and demonic forces of the universe and treat human affairs as significant to all creation.

Shakespeare's language makes special demands on the actor. Figures of speech are apt to seem contrived and bombastic if the actor does not appear to be experiencing feelings strong enough to call forth such language spontaneously. Shakespeare's plays may be damaged in performance if actors do not rise to the emotional demands of the poetry. Therefore, the very richness of expression can be a stumbling block for both performer and reader.

The action of *Hamlet* occurs in a large number of places, but Shakespeare envisioned them all in terms of stage properties, costumes, and the movement of the actors. But, though scenery was not important, the change of place was. The main stage, discovery space, and upper stage facilitated the flow of one scene into the next. The relatively bare stage was constantly being varied by such scenes as the sentry patrols and the appearance of the Ghost, the elaborate procession and court ceremony in Act I, the play-within-the-play, the burial of Ophelia and the fight between Hamlet and Laertes in her open grave, the duel and the stage littered with dead bodies.

Costumes added to the visual effect. Though most of the characters were probably dressed in the garments of Shakespeare's own time, Hamlet was set off from the others by his black mourning clothes amid the bright clothes the others wear to celebrate the marriage of Claudius and Gertrude.

Sounds also added to the overall effect. They include trumpet flourishes, cannons, and the offstage crowd. But most important was the sound of the actors' voices speaking Shakespeare's poetry.

Hamlet is rich in implications, of which the most important concern the shock of betrayal, especially by those one has most trusted. The betrayals are pervasive—brother of brother, wife of husband, parent of child, friend of friend. After an apparently uneventful youth, Hamlet is suddenly faced with a series of shocking revelations: his father has been murdered by his uncle; his mother has been unfaithful to his father; his mother has accepted his uncle's usurpation of the throne that should rightfully have been Hamlet's; and his supposed friends have become his uncle's spies. It is not surprising that these discoveries make Hamlet suspicious of almost everyone, even of Ophelia, the woman he loves. Considering the nature of the betrayals and the rapidity with which they come, it also is not surprising that both Hamlet and others wonder if he has gone mad.

A second theme is the opposing demands made on Hamlet—to right the wrongs occasioned by his father's death (seemingly requiring him to murder his uncle) and to adhere to Christian teaching (under which the murder of his uncle would be a deadly sin). Since Hamlet is not certain that the Ghost who has demanded revenge has not been sent by the

The final scene of *Hamlet* as directed by B. Iden Payne on a simulated Elizabethan stage. Note the upper stage at top and the stage post at left. (Courtesy Department of Drama, University of Texas at Austin.)

Devil to tempt him to a deed that will damn his soul, Hamlet feels that he must verify the accusation before he acts.

A third theme concerns the way one crime sets off a chain of evil as the wrongdoer tries to conceal the crime. Everything in *Hamlet* can be traced back to Claudius' murder of his brother and the series of deceptions he devises to hide it. It is this deed that leads to the total destruction of two families.

Another set of implications concerns the nature of kingship and the need to rule oneself before attempting to rule others. This motif is seen especially in the conduct of Claudius and is suggested through the contrast between Claudius and his dead brother and with Hamlet and Fortinbras (who is left to return order to the state). There are many other implications, for a play as rich as *Hamlet* cannot be wholly exhausted. Perhaps for that reason, the play has been able to transcend the time and place of its origins to appeal to all succeeding generations. It is one of the few plays that has never been out of the active performance repertory.

The Theatre Experience in Seventeenth-Century France

Another of the theatre's great eras occurred in France during the seventeenth century. Although it flourished only shortly after Shakespeare's death, it represents a different kind of experience based on conventions that would displace those of Shakespeare's theatre and dominate European practices until the nineteenth century. This tradition, rather than building on medieval practices, descended from conventions developed and exploited in Italy in the sixteenth century. Let us look briefly at this Italian background.

The Italian Background   The reawakened interest in Greek and Roman thought, literature, and art had led by the late fifteenth century to occasional performances of Roman comedies at the courts of the many small states into which Italy was divided at that time. In the early sixteenth century, plays imitating classical forms began to be written in Italian. To present such plays was considered a mark of a ruler's cultural enlightenment, and soon theatrical entertainments became standard features of the court festivals given to celebrate betrothals, weddings, births of royal children, visits of emissaries from other states, and similar events. Thus, theatre played a role somewhat like that in Greece and Rome, although the occasions were secular and were intended to reflect glory on the ruler. The subject matter of plays and the themes developed in the many events of a festival were most usually drawn from classical mythology.

In mounting these festivals, the Italians also drew on classical sources, especially *De Architectura* by Vitruvius (a Roman architect of the first century B.C.), which described how a theatre is laid out and the types of locales appropriate to three kinds of plays—tragedy, comedy, and pastoral. Italian artists sought to recreate what they found in Vitruvius' treatise, but in doing so they transformed it radically. Eventually, they arrived at the kinds of theatre structures and scenic practices that were to dominate the European theatre until modern times.

Since they had no permanent theatres, the Italians created temporary performance spaces, usually in large halls of state (something like the large ballrooms of modern hotels). In 1545, Sebastiano Serlio published *Architettura*, in which he showed how to erect a theatre within an existing room. He also included drawings showing his version of Vitruvius' tragic, comic, and pastoral settings (see the illustrations on page 139). These drawings fuse classical theatre architecture and Renaissance perspective painting.

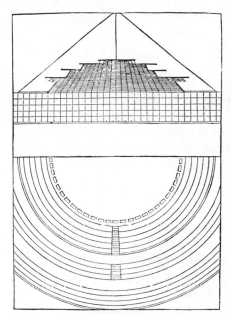

Serlio's plans for setting up theatres within existing halls. Left, floor plan of the seating (bottom) and the stage (top). Right, Serlio's design for the comic scene. The squares on the raked stage, diminishing in size from front to back, helped to create apparent depth, as did the downward slope of the upper portions of buildings. (Serlio, *Architettura*, 1545.)

The principles of perspective had been developed during the fifteenth century. It is difficult today to appreciate the Renaissance excitement over perspective, which was sometimes viewed almost as a form of magic, since with it the artist seemed to create space and distance where they did not exist. Given this enthusiasm, it is not surprising that by the sixteenth century perspective had been adapted to stage use.

The acceptance of perspective scenery is of profound importance, for it signaled a movement away from the formal and architectural stage to the representational and pictorial stage. The Greek, Roman, Noh, and Elizabethan stages all had in common a formalized architectural facade as the basic background for all plays; in these theatres, the facade could be modified by the addition of small elements, but no stage property or pictorial element could ever disguise the fixed facade. Any added elements merely identified (rather than represented realistically) a scene's locale. The mansions of the medieval theatre lay somewhere between the formal and pictorial traditions, since semirepresentational structures were often used to represent two or more places simultaneously. Still, no place was represented in its entirety, and the gaps between places were telescoped. With the coming of perspective, each place was represented in its entirety as seen from a fixed eyepoint. If more than one place was involved, they were shown sequentially, not simultaneously. During the course of the seventeenth century, pictorial representation of place would become the standard for stage scenery throughout Europe, remaining so until the twentieth century.

How to transform a two-dimensional drawing into a stage setting that occupies three-dimensional space was a problem that the Renaissance artists had to solve. The solution eventually accepted everywhere was to break up the picture and paint the parts on one of three scenic elements: side wings, backdrops, and overhead borders. Everything painted on the wings, drops, and borders was drawn as seen from a fixed eyepoint located somewhere in the auditorium (originally the seat of the ruler). The floor of the stage raked upward toward the back, thus giving us our terms "upstage" and "downstage," and the height of the side wings diminished as they receded from the audience; both of these features helped perspective achieve greater apparent depth within the restricted space. The goal was to create a complete and convincing picture.

A pictorialized setting demanded a frame, since otherwise spectators would see around or over the setting, and the apparent scale would be negated. Out of this need came the proscenium arch, used to frame the stage opening (the "picture-frame stage"). Originally, the frame was a temporary structure like the scenery itself, but eventually the advantage of a permanent architectural frame was recognized. The oldest surviving theatre with a permanent proscenium arch is the Teatro Farnese, built in 1618 in Parma, Italy. Soon thereafter, the proscenium arch became a standard feature of theatres and remained so until recently; even now, the picture-frame stage is the most common type.

A setting that depicted a single place in its entirety created another problem: how to move from one locale to another. The solution required that two-dimensional wings be set up parallel to the front of the stage and in a series from front to back. At each wing position, as many different flats were used (one immediately back of another) as there were scenes to be depicted during the performance. To change from one set to the next, the visible wings were pulled offstage, revealing others that represented the next scene. The set was enclosed at the back by painted flats, which met at the center of the stage. Several back-scenes could be set up and shifted in the same way as the side wings. (Eventually, drops that could be lowered and raised replaced the back-scenes.) Borders (two-dimensional cloths, most often representing clouds or the sky) hung above each set of wings and enclosed the scene overhead. Until the mid-nineteenth century, scene changes were usually made in full view of the

Teatro Farnese, Parma (Italy), built in 1618. This is the oldest surviving permanent proscenium-arch theatre. (Streit, *Das Theater*, 1903.)

audience. The front curtain was raised at the beginning of a performance and not lowered again until the end. Thus, scene shifts were parts of the overall visual experience.

The desire to shift scenery was inspired by the love of spectacle and special effects, which the Italians exploited primarily in *intermezzi* (or interludes) between the acts of regular plays (which usually did not require any changes of place or special effects). Intermezzi were essentially elaborate compliments that suggested parallels between some mythological hero and the person in whose honor the festival was being given; usually, the hero routed the forces of chaos through magical feats involving elaborate special effects. Music and dance were also major features. More effort usually went into the staging of intermezzi than the plays they accompanied.

The appeals of intermezzi were eventually absorbed into *opera*, a new form that originated in the 1590s out of attempts to recreate the relationship between music and speech found in Greek tragedy. Opera soon became a popular form, combining drama, music, dance, spectacle, and special effects. Opera also became the primary medium for popularizing perspective scenery and the picture-frame stage, both of which had developed in the rarefied atmosphere of the Italian courts, where performances were not open to the general public. In 1637, a public opera house in Venice made the pleasures of the court theatres available to the general public for the first time. It was so successful that soon there were four opera houses in Venice.

These Venetian opera houses were in many ways the prototypes of those that came after, for not only did they incorporate the proscenium

Set by Giacomo Torelli for *Bellerophon* at one of Venice's public opera houses, 1642. Note the sea creatures in the water and the figure in the cloud. Such elaborate special effects were regular features of opera. Torelli, who went to France around 1645, greatly influenced French theatrical practices. (Courtesy French Cultural Services.)

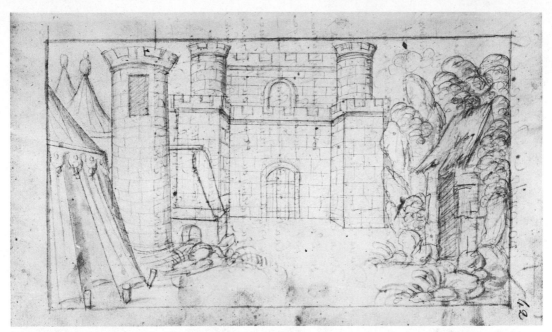

A design by Laurent Mahelot for *La Prise de Marsilly* in the 1630s. Note the simultaneous locales. (Courtesy Bibliothèque Nationale, Paris.)

arch and perspective scenery, they also had auditoriums divided and arranged as would be typical until the late nineteenth century. The divisions (into box, pit, and gallery) reflected the class structure of Europe; they permitted every class to attend the theatre without having to mingle with persons of another class. The auditorium was surrounded by two or more levels of boxes (which permitted well-to-do or snobbish spectators to be more or less private while in a crowded place), the most expensive seats; on the ground floor was the pit (today's orchestra), less expensive than the boxes and favored by those unconcerned about reputation; at the top of the theatre was the gallery, the least desirable and cheapest seats, usually inhabited by working-class patrons. The popularity of opera, which burgeoned during the seventeenth century, spread the Italian scenic and architectural conventions throughout Europe. They were to be major influences on French theatre in the seventeenth century.

The French Background   The development of the French theatre had been interrupted by the civil wars that grew out of religious controversy in the sixteenth century and that recurred in the seventeenth century. Stability did not return until around 1630, by which time Cardinal

Theatre built by Cardinal Richelieu in his palace in 1641. Seated in the foreground (from right to left) are Richelieu, Louis XIII, and the Queen. After Richelieu's death, the theatre was called the Palais Royal. It was used by Moliere's company from 1660 until his death in 1673. (A contemporary engraving.)

Richelieu, Louis XIII's prime minister, having secured absolute power for the king, set out to make France the cultural center of Europe. Up to that time, France's theatre had remained under medieval influence. Although religious plays were outlawed in Paris in 1548, the theatre had continued to use simultaneous settings for its plays, most of which were sprawling pieces with multiple plots requiring numerous locales. (See the illustration on page 143 for a typical stage setting around 1630.) Richelieu believed that the French stage needed drastic reform, and he looked to Italy for guidance. He advocated adoption of the Italian stage and scenic practices and a drama that would adhere to theoretical principles that had been articulated in Italy during the sixteenth century. These principles make up what came to be called the neoclassical ideal.

The neoclassicists recognized only two legitimate forms of drama, tragedy and comedy, and argued that the two should never be mixed. To them, tragedy could only be written about kings and nobles, while comedy should deal with the middle or lower classes. They also thought that all plays should be written in five acts, that they should observe the unities of time (all the action should occur within twenty-four hours), place (all the action should occur in the same place), and action (there should be only one plot), that the endings of plays should uphold "poetic justice" (that is, punish the wicked and reward the good). There were other demands, but these were the most important.

Although Richelieu and others favored them, these rules were not widely known or accepted in France until 1636, when *The Cid* by Pierre Corneille (1606–1684) became the most popular play yet written in France. Despite its popularity, the play was viciously attacked because it failed to adhere to the neoclassical rules. As the controversy dragged on, awareness of the rules became widespread for the first time. Richelieu asked the French Academy (made up of the forty supposedly most eminent literary figures of the day) to deliver a verdict on the play. The Academy praised the play for many of its qualities, but faulted it wherever it deviated from the rules. This controversy is a watershed event in French theatre, for it effectively legitimized the neoclassical view. After 1640, Corneille adopted the new mode, and it was later perfected by Jean Racine (1639–1699). The tragedies of Corneille and Racine were to set the standard for serious playwriting throughout Europe until the nineteenth century.

But the transition to the new ideal also required that the theatre be altered. To set an example, Richelieu in 1641 had the first theatre in France with a proscenium arch erected in his own palace. By 1650, all the Parisian public and court theatres had been transformed into picture-frame stages of the Italian type. Thus, by the mid-seventeenth century, the Italian order had replaced the medieval heritage almost completely.

Molière and Seventeenth-Century French Theatre Practice

Just as Corneille and Racine set the standard for tragedy, Molière (1622–1673) set the standard for comedy. Like Shakespeare, he was involved in every aspect of the theatre. He was head of his own company, its principal actor, and its principal playwright. He was not part owner of a theatre, however, since his company performed in the one Richelieu had built, which had become the property of the crown upon the cardinal's death. Usually referred to as the Palais Royal, this theatre had a picture-frame stage and a box, pit, and gallery auditorium. Thus, Molière performed for the general public in a theatre owned by the king.

Despite the many differences between the Elizabethan and French stages, their acting companies had many features in common. The French companies, like the English, were organized on the sharing plan. They usually included from ten to fifteen sharing members, but other persons were employed on salary as actors, musicians, stage assistants, and so on. A major difference was that the French companies included women, who had equal rights with the men and received comparable pay. At the end of each performance, the costs of production were deducted from the receipts, and the remainder was divided among the shareholders. All the leading companies in Paris (usully four or five) received a subsidy from the crown, but the sum was not sufficient to guarantee them against loss.

Plays were selected by a vote of the shareholders after hearing a reading of the play. A play might be bought outright, but the more usual method of payment was to give the author a percentage of the receipts for a limited number of performances, after which the play belonged to the company. An acting company usually had in its active repertory fifty or more plays which were alternated in order to keep the audience coming back.

Casting was simplified because each actor played a limited range of roles. Eventually, actors were hired according to "lines of business" (that is, according to the type of characters they played); most actors remained in the same line throughout their careers. A new actor in the company usually learned roles from the person he or she was understudying or replacing, and thus many roles came to be played in a traditional manner that was handed down from one generation to the next. Such practices continued well into the nineteenth century, not just in France but everywhere.

In France, actors were expected to furnish their own costumes; maintaining a wardrobe was one of an actor's major expenses. Fortunately, as on the Elizabethan stage, most costumes were contemporary garments, although there were exceptions, especially for Near Eastern, Indian, Moorish, and classical characters. The typical dress for classical heroes was the *habit à la romaine* (Roman costume), an adaptation of Roman armor, tunic, and boots, which by the late seventeenth century had become highly stylized. (See the illustration on page 147.)

The scenic demands of regular comedy and tragedy were simple. Ordinarily, in compliance with the neoclassical rules, such plays were set in one place and required no scene changes. (Opera and other "irreg-

The *habit à la romaine,* the costume for heroes of tragedies set in ancient Greece and Rome. Originally based on Roman armor, it became increasingly stylized and ornate, as in this drawing. An engraving based on a painting by Watteau. (Gillaumont, *Costumes de la Comédie Française,* 1884.)

ular" forms were permitted many scene changes and elaborate effects.) Most settings were so general in their features (appropriate to a particular kind of play but without individualizing details) that the same set was used for several different plays. The setting was also removed from detailed specificity by the practice of using only those stage properties (chairs, tables, beds, etc.) absolutely demanded by the action. Thus, the stage was largely bare. This emphasis on the general served as well to keep down the costs of both scenery and costumes.

Since the theatre was now indoors, lighting was also a concern. The available illuminants were candles and oil lamps. Usually, the auditorium was lighted by chandeliers; those hung just forward of the stage were of special importance, since they, along with a row of footlights at the forward edge of the stage, were the primary lighting sources for the actors, who usually played near the front of the stage. Thus, audiences as well as actors were lighted throughout performances, thereby promoting considerable interaction between auditorium and stage. Sometimes, chandeliers were also hung above the stage, but more often the onstage lighting sources were concealed by overhead or side masking. Along the sides, behind the proscenium and each wing position, were vertical poles on which oil lamps were mounted, one lamp above the other. Lamps were also mounted on horizontal pipes above the proscenium and behind the overhead borders. Reflectors were sometimes used to increase the amount of light that reached the stage. At least three methods were used to darken the stage: lights were extinguished (although this was awkward if they had to brighten again), open cylinders were suspended above the lamps and lowered over them to darken the stage, then raised to brighten it; or the lamps were mounted on rotating poles that could be turned either toward or away from the visible portions of the stage. Since the intensity of lamps and candles was so limited, providing an adequate level of illumination took precedence over all other functions of stage lighting.

These were the prevailing practices during the years 1658–1673, when Molière performed in Paris. With them in mind, let us look more closely at one of his most popular plays, *Tartuffe*.

Tartuffe

Tartuffe is concerned with religious hypocrisy. The most likely target of Molière's satire is the Company of the Holy Sacrament, a secret society of the time, one of whose purposes was the improvement of morals through "spiritual police" who spied on the private lives of others. Molière read *Tartuffe* to several persons before it was first produced in 1664, and the Company immediately organized an attack upon it. The controversy became so heated that Louis XIV forbade further performances. Molière revised the play in 1667, only to have it withdrawn again. But by 1669, the opposition was largely gone.

Whether or not Molière had the Company in mind, it is clear that he was thinking of groups like the Company, which feel that they alone can tell true piety from false, thus creating conditions under which hypocrites can flourish.

As in all of Molière's works, the balanced view of life is upheld in *Tartuffe*. To Molière, true piety demands not the abandonment of pleasure but the right use of it. The truly devout try to reform the world by actions that set a good example, rather than by pious speeches.

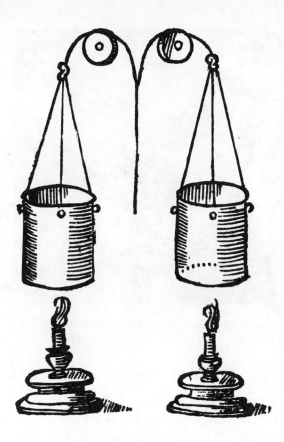

Device for dimming candles. The hollow pipe was lowered to obscure the light or raised to brighten it. (Sabbattini, *Manual for Constructing Theatrical Scenes and Machines,* 1638.)

The plot of *Tartuffe* can be divided into five stages: the demonstration of Tartuffe's complete hold over Orgon; the unmasking of Tartuffe; Tartuffe's attempted revenge; the foiling of Tartuffe's plan; and the happy resolution. There are three important reversals. The first (the unmasking of Tartuffe) brings all of the characters to an awareness of the true situation. The resulting happiness is quickly dispelled, however, when Orgon is shown to be at the mercy of Tartuffe.

The first two reversals (turning the tables on Tartuffe, Tartuffe turning the tables on Orgon) have been carefully foreshadowed, but the final one and the play's resolution have not. The contrived ending (in which Tartuffe is discovered to be a notorious criminal) is emotionally satisfying in the sense that justice triumphs, but the contrivance has little foundation in the preceding dramatic action.

To prevent any confusion about Tartuffe's true nature, Molière uses two acts to prepare for his entrance. The first act also includes a lengthy argument by Cleante, the character who apparently represents Molière's point of view, in which true piety is distinguished from false.

Tartuffe as performed at the Circle in the Square, New York, 1977. Tartuffe at front center; Orgon and Elmire at right. Directed by Stephen Porter. (Photo by Martha Swope.)

The structure of *Tartuffe* may also be clarified by examining the use made of various characters. Cleante appears in Act I, where he performs his principal function—to present the commonsense point of view. He does not appear again until Act IV; in that act and in Act V, he merely reinforces the ideas he set forth in Act I. Cleante does not influence the action, he clarifies the theme.

While Dorine, the maid, appears in each act, her role is virtually completed after the beginning of Act III, even though she has been a major character up to that point. Her frankness and openness are used as a foil to show off Orgon's credulity, the lovers' petulance, and Tartuffe's false piety. Her wit and common sense set their exaggerated behavior in proper perspective.

Even Tartuffe is given rather strange treatment when he finally makes his appearance after two acts of preparation. Most of his time on stage is given over to his two "love scenes" with Elmire. Molière seems to take it for granted that the audience will accept the picture of Tartuffe painted by the other characters and that the play need only emphasize one aspect of his hypocrisy.

Tartuffe displays another side of his character when he is denounced by Damis. Rather than defend himself, he appears to accept the accusations with humility. This scene, more than any other, shows why Orgon has been taken in by Tartuffe.

The lovers, Valère and Mariane, first appear in Act II and are unimportant thereafter. They serve merely to show how far Orgon has been influenced by Tartuffe, since Orgon is planning to marry his daughter Mariane to Tartuffe. The lovers' quarrel is a source of amusement largely unrelated to the rest of the play.

Elmire appears in Act III (in which Tartuffe tries to seduce her), but she has only a few lines, and most of these treat Tartuffe's suggestions with an air of frivolity. Most of her lines come in Act IV, where she serves as the instrument for unmasking Tartuffe. This uneven distribution of the role has led some critics to argue that Elmire's moral character is questionable. It seems clear, however, that Molière had in mind a reasonably worldly but upright woman.

Orgon's role is the one most evenly distributed throughout the play. While the Tartuffes of the world are dangerous, they can exist only because of the Orgons, since the success of the wicked depends on the gullibility of the foolish. Just as Molière emphasizes Tartuffe's calculated piety, so too he emphasizes Orgon's impulsiveness and stubbornness. Orgon errs largely because he acts without considering sufficient aspects of a question. When Tartuffe is finally unmasked, Orgon's character remains consistent; failing to see the difference between hypocrisy and piety, he says: "I'm through with pious men: Henceforth I'll hate the whole false brotherhood." Thus, instead of returning to middle ground, he assumes an equally exaggerated, though opposite, position.

Little indication is given of the age or physical appearance of the characters. Since Molière wrote with his own company in mind and directed the play, he did not need to specify every detail in his script. The role of Tartuffe was written for DuCroisy, a large man with a ruddy complexion. No doubt this was one of the sources of humor. All of Tartuffe's talk about scourges and fasting was contradicted by his obvious plumpness and lecherousness. Orgon was played by Molière, noted for his expressive face and body; Elmire was acted by Molière's wife, who was twenty-seven in 1669. As was often the case with comic old women, Mme. Pernelle was played by a man. Thus, the character was no doubt intended to be seen as ridiculous in her denunciation of pleasure. All of the characters are drawn from the middle or lower classes (in accordance with neoclassical theories of comedy).

In *Tartuffe*, Molière uses the verse form which by that time had become standard in tragedy—the alexandrine (twelve-syllable lines, with each pair of adjacent lines rhyming). The nearest equivalent in English is the rhymed couplet, although this form seems far more unnatural than the French alexandrine because English verse, unlike French, uses repeated

A radically different interpretation of *Tartuffe*, directed by the Romanian director Lucian Pintilie at the Guthrie Theatre (Minneapolis) in 1984. In this production, the action progresses through various periods. In the final scene, the rescuers arrive in an automobile. Set by Radu Boruzescu, costumes by Marina Boruzescu, lighting by Beverly Emmons. (Photo by Joe Giannetti. Courtesy Guthrie Theatre.)

heavy stress patterns within lines, and these, in combination with rhymed line endings, encourage a singsong quality. In French verse, in which these stress patterns are absent, rhymed endings are far less intrusive. Critics agree that Richard Wilbur's translations of Molière's plays are the most satisfactory, both for accuracy of sense and for versification. Wilbur also retains Molière's scene divisions. Molière, like most French dramatists down to modern times, started a new scene each time a character entered or exited, in order to indicate an alteration in motivations or focus created by the change of characters on stage. Thus, though the action may be continuous, the printed text is divided into numerous scenes. Such divisions are usually referred to as "French scenes."

The unities of time and place are strictly observed. Only a single room is required, and even that need have only a table, under which Orgon can be concealed, and a closet, in which Damis can hide; no specific use is made of the setting except in these two instances. The action is continuous, or nearly so, and occurs in a single day. All of the episodes, with the possible exception of the lovers' quarrel, are directly related to the main theme of the play. *Tartuffe* is clearly within the neoclassical tradition. It has remained in the repertory almost continuously and has been performed more often than any other play by Molière.

The Elizabethan and French Traditions

Although Shakespeare and Molière are among the world's great dramatists and were separated in time by only a few years, they worked within different theatrical traditions. Shakespeare's offered greater flexibility, but before the end of the seventeenth century, it had been replaced by Molière's, probably because the tide of taste was moving steadily toward a preference for representationalism. When the English theatres reopened in 1660, after having been closed for eighteen years because of another civil war growing partially out of religious controversy, they adopted the picture-frame stage, perspective scenery, and the neoclassical vision (although, largely because of Shakespeare's influence, never so completely as elsewhere in Europe).

This period in English theatre, usually referred to as the Restoration, was noted principally for its comedy of manners, which focused on the amoral behavior and witty verbal exchanges of the rich and idle upper class. Restoration theatre was concerned above all with sexual conquests, advantageous marriages (in which love played little part), the latest fashions, and a seeming determination to be shocked at nothing. The butts of ridicule included the fop, the old man who marries a young wife, the old woman who tries to appear young, the pretender at wit and sophistication, and the self-deceived. The moral tone of these plays has made them controversial ever since they were written. Restoration comedy originated with such works as Sir George Etherege's *The Man of Mode* (1676) and *She Would if She Could* (1668) and reached its peak in the plays of William Congreve, especially *Love for Love* (1695) and *The Way of the World* (1700).

By 1700, while there were still obvious differences among the theatres of various European countries, they shared the same basic conventions. The theatre had made the transition from festival offering to secular entertainment. While it could still offer profound insights into human behavior, as Shakespeare and Molière show, its role within society had altered markedly.

Popular Theatre Experiences: Commedia dell'Arte and Melodrama

7

When studying the arts, it has been typical to concentrate on "high art" (that is, on only the best as determined by elitist taste) and to ignore what the general public ("popular taste") favored and supported. But, in almost every period, there has been a considerable gap between elitist and popular taste, and to deny significance to the cultural experiences of the majority is to deny the importance of the arts, whatever form they take, to the lives of ordinary people. Popular culture may be as sound a key as elitist art to understanding a society. Today, television is the dominant medium of popular culture and, as with similar media in the past, is more often condemned than praised by those who want to impose elitist artistic and moral codes on it.

Prior to the twentieth century, the theatre was the readiest medium of popular culture, since as yet there was no radio, film, or television, and since there were virtually no professional spectator sports (which today draw away many who formerly looked to the theatre for diversion). A partially literary medium when based on scripted drama, the theatre nevertheless does not require a literate public, since the actors "read" the script to the audience. Thus, the theatre has probably served as popular entertainment more often than as provider of profound insights into human behavior, though, at its best, it has done both simultaneously.

Two of the most popular theatrical experiences of the past were based on *commedia dell'arte* (from around 1575 until the eighteenth century) and melodrama (especially during the nineteenth century). Today, commedia is often romanticized as a vanished theatrical form, while nineteenth-century melodrama is usually derided as the naive entertainment of an unsophisticated audience and therefore left unread. What made these forms so popular in their own day? And why did commedia disappear and melodrama change? Let us look more closely at these two types of popular theatre.

Commedia dell'Arte

Commedia dell'arte emerged in Italy between 1550 and 1575, a time when rulers of the many small Italian states were mounting festivals to glorify themselves. To demonstrate their cultural superiority, these rulers invested large sums of money in building picture-frame stages, where plays based on classical models were performed in perspective settings. The plays were usually written by court poets, the stages and scenery were the work of court architects and painters, and the performers were court musicians and courtiers. Thus, despite the high visual quality of the productions and their influence on later theatrical practice, these were essentially amateur performances given for very restricted audiences. At the same time, however, a wholly professional Italian theatre was coming into being through the work of the commedia dell'arte troupes.

Commedia dell'arte (comedy of professional players) and commedia all'improviso (improvised comedy) are terms used to distinguish the plays performed by professional troupes from those presented by the amateur actors at court (*commedia erudita,* or learned drama). No one knows precisely how or when commedia dell'arte came into being. Some try to trace it back to the mimes and other entertainers of Roman times, whose traditions were supposedly continued by small wandering troupes until conditions became more favorable in the Renaissance. Others see the form as evolving out of improvisations based on the plays of Plautus and Terence. There are still other theories, but none can be proven right or wrong. Whatever its origin, commedia dell'arte first became clearly evident in the 1560s. If it was new at that time, it grew rapidly, for by 1600 companies were playing not only throughout Italy but in France, Spain, and other European countries. Wherever they went, they found ready audiences both among the common people and the ruling classes.

The actor was the heart of commedia dell'arte and almost the only essential element. The commedia companies could play almost anywhere: in town squares or at court; indoors or out; on improvised stages or in permanent theatres. If elaborate scenery was available, they used it, but they could function as well with a curtain (with slits for entrances and exits) as background. Adaptability was one of their major assets.

The script was a scenario that merely summarized the situations, complications, and outcome. The actors improvised the dialogue and fleshed out the action. Therefore, although the broad outlines of a script were always the same, the details differed at each performance, depending on the inspiration of the moment and the response of the audience. Several hundred scenarios have survived. A few are tragic, melodramatic, or musical, but by far the greatest number are comic, revolving around love affairs, intrigues, disguises, and cross-purposes.

Improvisation, a distinguishing feature of commedia, was facilitated by the use of the same characters in all the plays performed by the same troupe, and by the same actor always playing the same role with its fixed attributes and costume. Over the years, the actors must have developed surefire dialogue and stage business that they could call on as needed. Some pieces of comic business *(lazzi)* became sufficiently standardized to be indicated in the plot outlines, as lazzi of fear, hat lazzi, food lazzi, and so on. In addition, the actors who played the fashionable young men and women were encouraged to keep notebooks in which to record appropriate sentiments from poetry and popular literature. Therefore, many lines and actions were probably repeated in various plays. Nevertheless, performances undoubtedly created the impression of spontaneity because no actor could be certain what the others would say or do, and thus each had to concentrate moment by moment on the unfolding action and respond appropriately.

The stock characters, commedia's best known feature, can be divided into three categories: lovers, masters, and servants. The lovers' roles were the most realistic. Young and handsome, they did not wear masks and were usually dressed in the latest fashions. Each company had at least one pair of lovers, and most had two. The lovers were often the children of those characters who fell into the category of masters, and their love affairs were typically opposed by their fathers and aided by their servants.

Three masters recurred most often: Pantalone, Dottore, and Capitano. Pantalone was an elderly Venetian merchant, often the father of one of the young lovers or a would-be lover himself. His costume consisted of a tight-fitting red vest, red breeches and stockings, soft slippers, a black ankle-length coat, a soft brimless cap with trailing wisps of hair, a brown mask with a large hooked nose, and straggling gray beard. Dottore was usually Pantalone's friend or rival. He was a lawyer or doctor who loved to show off his spurious learning in speeches filled with Latin (often ludicrously incorrect). Despite his supposed wisdom, he was extremely credulous and easily tricked. His dress was the academic cap and gown of the time. Originally, the Capitano was one of the lovers, but eventually he was transformed into a braggart and coward who

The young lover and Scapin (or *Zanni*) of commedia dell'arte. Etchings by Jacques Callot, 1618-19.

boasted of his great prowess in love and war, only to be discredited in both. He usually wore cape, sword, and feathered headdress, often greatly exaggerated to indicate his braggadocio. He typically was an unwelcome suitor to one of the young women.

The most varied of the commedia types were the servants (the *zanni*—the origin of the English word *zany*). Most companies included at least two, one clever and one stupid, but there might be as many as four. They figured prominently in the action; their machinations kept the plots moving as they sought to help or thwart their masters. Most of the servants were male, but there might be one or more maids *(fantesca)* who served the young women. Typically young, coarsely witty, and ready for intrigue, they carried on their own love affairs with the male servants while helping their mistresses. Occasionally, one was older and served as hostess of an inn, wife to a servant, or the object of the older men's affections.

Pantalone, Capitano, and Arlechinno of commedia dell'arte. (Maurice Sand, *Masques et Bouffons*, 1859.)

Of the *zanni*, Arlecchino (Harlequin) eventually became the most popular. A mixture of cunning and stupidity and an accomplished acrobat and dancer, he was usually at the center of any intrigue. His costume, which began as a suit with irregularly placed multicolored patches, evolved into one with a diamond-shaped red, green, and blue pattern. He wore a rakish hat above a black mask and carried a wooden sword, a "slapstick," so called because it was slit down the middle so it would make a sharp sound when struck against someone, and the source of our term "slapstick comedy." The slapstick figured prominently in the many fights and beatings. While each company had a Harlequin-like character, not every company used that name for the character. Name variations included Truffaldino and Trivellino.

Harlequin's most frequent companion was a cynically witty, libidinous, and sometimes cruel servant. His mask had a hooked nose and moustache, and his jacket and trousers were ornamented with green braid. He was called variously Brighella, Scapino, Mezzetino, and Flautino. Another character, Pulcinello, was always a Neopolitan, but his function in the scripts varied. Sometimes he was a servant, but he also might be the host of an inn or a merchant. He had an enormous hooked nose, a humped back, and wore a pointed cap. He was the ancestor of the

English puppet character, Punch. There were many variations, both in name and attributes, on these *zanni,* since each company tended to develop its own version of these types.

A commedia troupe averaged ten to twelve members (seven or eight men and three or four women). Most companies were organized on the sharing plan, although some of the younger actors and assistants may have been salaried. Most troupes traveled frequently, but some were able to settle down in one place for considerable periods of time. For example, Molière shared his theatre in Paris with a commedia troupe and alternated days of performance with it. (Molière—like many other dramatists of his day—learned much of his comic technique from commedia, and a number of his plays incorporate commedia characters and situations.)

Scene from the commedia play *The Fairies, or the Tales of Mother Goose.* Harlequin is seen at center among the female characters of the play. (Ghérardi, *Le Théâtre Italien.* 1741.)

Commedia was most vigorous and popular in the years between 1575 and 1650, but it continued into the last half of the eighteenth century. Its last stronghold was Venice, where two playwrights sought to reform and preserve it but contributed to its destruction. Carlo Goldoni (1707–1793), Italy's most famous comic dramatist, began writing scenarios for commedia companies in Venice around 1734. Because he believed the situations in commedia had become hackneyed and vulgar, he refined and sentimentalized the characters and situations. He also thought the usual level of improvisation was inadequate, and he was able to persuade companies to accept scripts with practically all dialogue written out. In addition, he campaigned for the abandonment of masks because he thought they handicapped the actors by preventing variety of facial expression. Goldoni wrote a number of plays (many of them still performed) using commedia characters, but the changes he championed, if implemented, would have done away with most of the basic conventions of commedia. He was bitterly opposed by another dramatist, Carlo Gozzi (1720–1806), who emphasized fantasy and improvisation in his scripts. Their battle for a time aroused new interest in commedia,

Carlo Gozzi's *King Stag* as performed at the American Repertory Theatre (Cambridge, MA) in 1984. Directed by Andrei Serban; sets by Michael Yeargan, costumes by Julie Taymor, lighting by Jennifer Tipton. (Photo by Richard Feldman.)

but by about 1775, this theatrical mode had largely ceased to be a living form, perhaps because of overfamiliarity after 200 years or because its rather broad, often coarse, farcical humor had lost its appeal in the more refined atmosphere of the eighteenth century.

Although numerous scenarios have survived from the period when commedia was at its peak, they are too bare in outline to convey the flavor of a commedia performance. Goldoni's *The Servant of Two Masters,* though it comes from the last days of commedia and lacks most of the improvisational element, probably brings us as near to the commedia experience as we can come today. Therefore, let us look more closely at this play.

The Servant of Two Masters

The Servant of Two Masters was written by Goldoni in 1745 for a Venetian commedia dell'arte troupe that permitted him to write out all the dialogue. While this eliminated much of the improvisational element, it did not do away with it altogether, for the actors were left free to improvise much comic business. The script also incorporates others of Goldoni's reforms, including taking away the more exaggerated qualities of certain characters. For example, Goldoni's Pantalone has none of the miserly traits typical of the character in early scenarios, and Brighella has been deprived of his libidinous and cruel traits. In fact, both have become solid citizens with virtually no ridiculous aspects. As in Goldoni's non-commedia scripts, in *The Servant of Two Masters* middle-class characters are treated with considerable respect, and the women are far more sensible than the men. (Smeraldina's comments on society's double standard for men and women reflect similar ideas found in other Goldoni plays.) Goldoni has also avoided the rather coarse, often smutty humor and sexual double entendre of earlier commedia.

Nevertheless, the cast of characters (and the basic traits of each) clearly belong to commedia. There are two pairs of lovers (Clarice and Silvio, Beatrice and Florindo), two masters (Pantalone and Dottore), and three servant types (Truffaldino, Brighella, and Smeraldina), although Brighella has been elevated in position to innkeeper. Silvio has also been given some traits (his exaggerated threats and his easy defeat in the fight with Beatrice) that relate him to the Capitano of other scripts. There are four minor roles (two porters and two waiters), but two actors could easily play the four roles. Thus, the total company size is probably eleven or twelve—typical for a commedia troupe.

Goldoni's *The Servant of Two Masters*. At center, Truffaldino; at right, Florindo; at left, the Porter. Engraving from an early-nineteenth-century edition of Goldoni's plays.

By far the most important character is Truffaldino, who has all the charcteristics of Arlecchino—a person of both cleverness and stupidity who is outfitted with black mask, particolored costume, and slapstick. Though the story line concerns the lovers, it is Truffaldino's stupidity that creates many of the difficulties and his cleverness that often resolves them. He is the principal source of humor and is onstage far more than any other character. He is also offered the greatest number of opportunities to improvise lazzi. These opportunities include dealing with the porters who carry the trunks; sealing the letter with chewed bread; tearing up the bill of exchange to illustrate how to arrange a table; unpacking and mixing up the contents of the trunks; showing Smeraldina her suitor; and, above all, serving dinner to two masters at once. Opportunities to improvise comic business are also offered other characters, including the argument between Pantalone and Dottore (a traditional feature of commedia); the fight between Beatrice and Silvio; the suicide attempts of Beatrice and Florindo; the reconciliation of Silvio and Clarice; and the beatings of Truffaldino by Beatrice and Florindo.

Goldoni is a master of plot development. Everything is neatly set up in the opening scene, and each complication is carefully prepared for and clarified for the audience, even as the play's characters become more confused. Goldoni further demonstrates his skill by making many complications grow out of the characters: Pantalone's haste in arranging another marriage for Clarice is the source of one chain of complications; Beatrice's decision to adopt a disguise delays the achievement of her goals; Truffaldino's invention of the imaginary Pasquale eventually trips him up; Silvio's and Dottore's habit of leaping to conclusions increases rather than solves their problems. Coincidence is an equally important ingredient: Beatrice arrives at Pantalone's just as the betrothal is concluded; Beatrice and Florindo take up residence at the same inn and employ the same servant; Truffaldino mixes up precisely those contents of the trunks that are most important to his masters.

Goldoni wrote for a company that performed in a public theatre of the kind then typical: box, pit, and gallery arrangement of the auditorium, and picture-frame stage with wing-and-drop, perspective scenery. *The Servant of Two Masters* is divided into three acts with a total of ten

Smeraldina and Truffaldino in *The Servant of Two Masters* as performed at the San Jose [CA] Repertory Company in 1985. Directed by Julian Lopez-Morillas. Costumes by Marcia Frederick. (Photo by Sharon Hall. Courtesy San Jose Repertory Company.)

scenes, although it requires only five settings: a room in Pantalone's house; the courtyard of Pantalone's house; the street in front of Brighella's inn; a room in Brighella's inn; and a street. None of these has any great specificity. No furniture is mentioned for Pantalone's house (and probably none was present); a sign identifying it and an entrance to Brighella's inn are the only important requirements of that set; four doors are the only practical features of the room in the inn; and neither the courtyard nor the street state any specific details. Except for the inn's sign, all of the scenic requirements could easily have been met from the stock scenery of any theatre of the period. Lighting would have differed little from what had been available for *Tartuffe* almost a century earlier.

The Servant of Two Masters does not achieve the level of characterization and social commentary found in many of Molière's comedies, but Goldoni was not seeking profundity. He was concerned primarily with providing entertainment for a popular audience by reworking the conventions of a long-familiar form. That he achieved his goal is indicated by the popularity of his play, which has continued to the present day.

The Emergence of Melodrama

Shortly after commedia dell'arte ceased to be a vital form, melodrama began to attain the level of popularity once enjoyed by commedia. The term "melodrama" first came into regular use in France around 1800, and was soon adopted almost everywhere as a label for a form of drama that amalgamated elements from many sources that had evolved during the eighteenth century.

The popularity of melodrama was in part a reaction against the neoclassical rules that had dominated dramatic writing since the mid-seventeenth century. These rules, although not always followed, had attempted to restrict the action of each drama to a time span of twenty-four hours, to one place (additional places were permitted so long as they could be reached without stretching the twenty-four-hour limit), and to one plot (subplots were tolerated only if they were clearly offshoots of the main plot). Neoclassicism also sought to rule out fantasy and supernatural elements. And, because it believed that human nature is the same in all times and places, it sought to depict universal (rather than historically accurate or individualized) traits, behavior, and visual elements. As indicated earlier, settings were so generalized that they could be used in many different productions. For example, if the place of action was a prison, the goal was to depict the essence of a prison rather than any particular prison; therefore, the same set could be used for any prison scene. Similarly, characters were usually dressed in clothing of the period of the performance no matter what the historical period of the action, since to place characters in a specific historical milieu might suggest that the play's depiction of human behavior was true only for that earlier time and place. Therefore, in the eighteenth century, Hamlet wore the fashionable dress of that century, and Macbeth was dressed in the uniform of a British general.

Most of the strictures of neoclassicism were applied only to "regular" drama (that is, comedy and tragedy written in five acts). Perhaps for this reason a number of "irregular" forms emerged and gained considerble popularity during the eighteenth century. Many were probably influenced by opera, which had never been subjected to the rules and included numerous special effects, changes of scene, music, dance, and other appeals denied regular drama. But opera had become an elitist entertainment in most of Europe because of high ticket prices. Consequently, many of its features, in modified form, were brought into the

David Garrick (one of England's greatest actors) and Mrs. Pritchard as Macbeth and Lady Macbeth. Macbeth is dressed as a British general, and Lady Macbeth wears the fashionable dress of the late eighteenth century. (*English Illustrated Magazine*, 1776.)

popular theatres through new types of musical drama. England developed the ballad opera, which incorporated in an otherwise spoken drama numerous lyrics set to the tunes of well-known popular songs or ballads. The most famous example is John Gay's *The Beggar's Opera* (1728). In France, comparable pieces were called *opéra comique* and in Germany *Singspiele* (of which Mozart's *The Magic Flute* is the best known example, though it is now performed as an opera). Another popular form was pantomime, in which Harlequin was usually the main character. Through some strange occurrence, Harlequin's slapstick became a magic wand, thereby motivating a number of spectacular transformations of persons and places; the action was accompanied throughout by music, and there were usually several dances. Thus, "irregular" pieces overcame the restrictions imposed by the neoclassical rules, although they were always considered inferior to the "regular" dramas.

Toward the end of the eighteenth century, the attitudes that had supported neoclassicism began to change, and by the early nineteenth century, they had undergone almost complete reversal. Perhaps the

Gay's *The Beggar's Opera*. Polly and Lucy are pleading for Macheath's life. As was typical at this time, some spectators are seated on either side of the stage. Engraving by William Blake based on William Hogarth's painting of 1729.

changes are best illustrated in critical attitudes about Shakespeare. Although Shakespeare had always been popular in England, and many of his plays continued to hold a firm place in its repertory, they were not performed in any other European country until the late eighteenth century. Except in England, Shakespeare was considered barbarous, since his plays were at complete odds with the then-accepted neoclassical rules. Even in England, many of the plays were subjected to rewriting intended to bring them more nearly into accord with neoclassical demands. English critics tried to explain Shakespeare's appeal by labeling him a "natural genius" who, despite his ignorance of the rules, had managed to write effective though flawed dramas. Nevertheless, they implied, he would have been more successful had he known and followed the rules.

During the last quarter of the eighteenth century, Shakespeare's plays began to be translated into other European languages and staged, although at first only in heavily adapted versions. As Shakespeare's reputation grew, the plays were altered less and less, and by the early nineteenth century, his works were becoming the standard against which plays were judged throughout Europe. During the nineteenth century, Shakespeare achieved the reputation he has been accorded ever since as the greatest dramatist of all time. Since he had written without regard to the neoclassical rules, he became an argument for ignoring them, and the unities of time, place, and action gave way to actions occurring over many years, in numerous places, and through a tangle of plots. Variety often took precedence over unity. The mysterious and supernatural, which had been deplored by the neoclassicists, became common occurrences in the new drama, as did concern for the characteristic features of specific times and places. Historical accuracy in settings and costumes began to be sought, although it was not fully obtained until around 1850. In sum, the theatre underwent major alterations during the early nineteenth century. In this new climate, melodrama flourished. It was to popular audiences what Shakespeare was to elitist audiences (although Shakespeare was not without appeal to the masses) and the theatrical popular-culture manifestation of a movement in the arts that dominated the first half of the nineteenth century: romanticism.

Melodrama emphasized clear and suspenseful plots in which a virtuous protagonist was hounded by a villain and rescued from seemingly insurmountable difficulties only after undergoing a series of threats to life, reputation, or happiness. All important events occurred on stage; typically, there was at least one elaborate spectacle (earthquake, burning building, explosion, etc.) and/or scene of local color (festival, dance, picturesque customs or conditions of a specific country or city). Typical plot devices included concealed or mistaken identity, abductions, strange coincidences, and hidden documents. Comic relief was often provided by a servant, ally, or companion of one of the principal characters. Perhaps most important, strict poetic justice was meted out: the evil people were punished, and the good were rewarded. The villain might keep things going his way until the final scene, but ultimately he was unmasked and defeated.

Melodrama also had a large musical element, as suggested by its name, which literally means "music drama." Originally, there were a number of songs in each play, but more important, the action was accompanied by a musical score (every theatre in the nineteenth century employed an orchestra) that enhanced the action and the emotional tone of each scene. With its simple, powerful stories, unequivocal moral tone, elaborate spectacle, and music, melodrama offered compelling and popular entertainment to the mass audiences of the nineteenth century. It was the originator of many features taken over by film in the twentieth century.

The popularity of melodrama in the nineteenth century is explained in part by fundamental changes in social and economic conditions stemming from the Industrial Revolution. As inventions such as the steam engine, power loom, steamship, and locomotive were exploited, the factory system of mass production gradually replaced the system of individual craftsmen that had persisted since medieval times. Since workers had to live near the factories, urbanization accelerated rapidly; this increased concentration of population created large potential audiences for theatrical entertainment. The largest city in Europe, London, had supported only two or three theatres during the eighteenth century, but between 1800 and 1850, its population doubled and the number of its theatres reached more than twenty. Both its population and number of theatres continued to grow through the remainder of the century. As in television programming today, the theatres sought to attract the largest possible audiences. Melodrama and variety entertainment proved to be the answer. Many critics argue that catering to mass taste led to rapid decline in the quality of theatrical offerings. As the population continued to grow, theatre managers eventually discovered that they did not have to appeal to everyone, and during the last half of the nineteenth century, each theatre began to aim its programming at a specific segment of the population or a particular taste.

Since the basic pattern of melodrama is always much the same (good persecuted by evil, with the eventual triumph of good), variety was gained through such novelties as exotic locales, ever-more spectacular effects, increased realism, incorporation into the action of the latest inventions, and dramatizations of popular novels or notorious crimes. A few melodrama theatres even incorporated facilities for horseback riding and featured plays with spectacular feats of horsemanship and last-min-

Astley's Amphitheatre, London, 1815. In addition to a stage, it included a riding ring so that melodramas involving daring horsemanship could be presented. (Wilkinson, *Londina Illustrata*, 1825.)

ute rescues by mounted riders. Others installed water tanks under their stages to accommodate "aquatic" melodramas. The first important writer of melodramas, Guilbert de Pixérécourt, resolved one of his plays by having the villain destroyed as lava from a volcanic eruption inundated the stage. Dion Boucicault, one of the most popular playwrights of the English-speaking stage between 1840 and 1900, used the newly invented camera in 1859 to reveal the identity of a murderer in *The Octoroon;* and Augustin Daly, an American playwright, in *Under the Gaslight* (1867) was the first to use a character tied to a railroad track in the path of a thundering locomotive and rescued at the last possible moment.

After electricity became common in the 1880s, electric motors were coupled with treadmills to stage horse or chariot races. To make the races seem realistic, moving panoramas (long cloths on which a continuous scene was painted) were suspended in overhead tracks and run around upright spools on either side of the stage. The movement of these panoramas was synchronized with that of the treadmills so that the horses were kept onstage by the treadmills while the scene painted on the panorama behind them rushed by, creating the effect that the horses were racing around a track. (See the illustration shown below.) The trend was toward ever more realistic effects. By the end of the nineteenth century, the potential of the stage for this kind of production had been more or less exhausted. In the early twentieth century, film inherited this tradition and thereafter continued to exploit it. Once the potential of film was established, the theatre largely abandoned such productions.

Realistic spectacle, thrilling effects, novelty, suspense, and the vindication of virtue were the major appeals of melodrama. They encouraged the development of realism in the visual aspects of theatre while clinging to recognizable and comforting stereotypes of characterization and morality. About this theatrical experience David Grimsted (in *Melodrama Unveiled: American Theatre and Culture, 1800–1850*) has written: "[Melodrama's] conventions were false, its language stilted and commonplace, its characters sterotypes, and its morality and theology gross simplifications. Yet its appeal was great and understandable . . . its moral parable

A horse race on stage at the Union Square Theatre, New York, 1889, using a moving panorama and treadmills run by electric motors, the speed of which was controlled by the man at upper right. (*Scientific American*, 1889.)

struggled to reconcile social fears and life's awesomeness with the period's confidence in absolute moral standards, man's upward progress, and a benevolent providence that insured the triumph of the pure."

Let us look more closely at an example of nineteenth-century melodrama.

Monte Cristo

Monte Cristo is a dramatization of Alexandre Dumas *père*'s *The Count of Monte Cristo* (1845), one of the world's most popular novels. Dumas himself made a dramatization of the work in 1848, but it was in twenty acts and required two evenings to perform. Several other dramatizations were made, but the one that eventually held the stage was by Charles Fechter, a French actor who had a long and distinguished career on the stages of France, England, and America. In 1885, the rights to this version were purchased by James O'Neill (1847–1920), who subsequently made numerous revisions. Thus, the text as it now stands is the work of several persons. It is indelibly associated with O'Neill, who became so identified with the role of Edmund Dantès that the public would go to see him in no other play; he toured the United States for some thirty years in essentially the same production. His plight resembled that of numerous actors of recent times who have become so identified with their roles in television series that they have no subsequent careers. O'Neill's sense of being trapped by the role is forcefully stated in *Long Day's Journey into Night,* written by his son, Eugene O'Neill, often considered the greatest dramatist America has produced.

Reducing Dumas' novel of several hundred pages to a play that could be performed in two or three hours was a formidable task, but not unusual in the nineteenth century, since popular novels were typically dramatized quickly following their publication. Almost all of Charles Dickens' novels were adapted for the stage, and *Uncle Tom's Cabin,* adapted from Harriet Beecher Stowe's novel, became the most popular play of the nineteenth century. Film and television have continued this practice in the twentieth century.

The sweep of *Monte Cristo* is nearer to that of Shakespeare's plays than to those of Sophocles, Molière, or Goldoni. The incidents are numerous, though the basic pattern is relatively simple. The hero, a ship's officer named Edmund Dantès, returns from a voyage prepared to marry his fiancée, Mercedes. He quickly runs afoul of three villains—Danglars (the ship's cargo officer), Fernand (who loves Mercedes), and Villefort (a government prosecutor who fears that his brother, Noirtier, will ruin

Final act of *Uncle Tom's Cabin,* the most popular melodrama of the nineteenth century. Simon Legree is punishing Uncle Tom because he will not betray his fellow slaves. (Courtesy Theatre and Music Collection, Museum of the City of New York.)

his career if he obtains a letter Edmund is bringing from the deposed emperor Napoleon). These three arrange for Dantès' arrest as a traitor, and he is subsequently imprisoned on the notorious penal island, the Chateau d'If. Edmund remains in prison for eighteen years, but during that time an elderly prisoner, Faria, befriends him and reveals the location of his family's vast fortune—the island of Monte Cristo. When Faria dies, Edmund takes the corpse's place in the sack which—in the prison's burial practice—will be thrown into the sea. Through this ruse, Edmund escapes, recovers the Faria fortune, and sets out to punish those who have wronged him. While Edmund has been in prison, his betrayers have prospered: Villefort has become Minister of Justice, Danglars a major financier, and Fernand a general, a peer of France, and Mercedes' husband (though only after she had been persuaded that

Edmund is dead). As the Count of Monte Cristo, Edmund relentlessly tracks down his persecutors and punishes each in turn. By the story's end, all the villains have been publicly disgraced and are dead.

Like other melodramas, *Monte Cristo* shows goodness victimized and evil triumphant for a time, but ultimately evil is exposed and punished and goodness is vindicated. It differs from most melodramas in rescuing the hero early from danger (at the end of Act II) and in the great amount of time devoted to punishing the villains. By actual time, of course, the hero languishes in prison for eighteen years, but in the play, those years are passed over in the interval between Acts I and II. Edmund is actually seen in prison in only one scene (whereas the novel devotes many chapters to his sufferings). The play also omits showing Edmund's recovery of Faria's treasure and his intricate preparations for revenge. Furthermore, many of the events (especially the way in which Villefort is punished) and character relationships (most importantly in making Albert the son of Edmund and Mercedes rather than of Fernand and Mercedes) differ from those in the novel.

The overall result of the omissions and alterations is to impose an almost symmetrical pattern on the action. The potential for happiness and harmony in the opening scenes is thwarted by a series of betrayers (Danglars, Fernand, and Villefort), who then prosper from Edmund's downfall. The turning point, Edmund's escape, has a miraculous quality both in the event itself and in Faria's legacy of enormous wealth, which makes Edmund's revenge possible. In this scene, Edmund also proclaims himself to be an instrument of revenge. Reading the script fails to convey the effect created in performance by Edmund rising from the sea, climbing onto a rock, and proclaiming, "The world is mine." This became one of the best-loved moments of the nineteenth-century theatre. Following this powerful scene, the villains are punished in the reverse order of their betrayals (Villefort first, then Fernand, and finally Danglars). As each is punished, Edmund announces the score—"One," "Two," "Three"—an accounting so satisfying to O'Neill's audiences that they often counted aloud with him. At the end, the play achieves additional symmetry by implying the possibility of achieving the happiness promised in the opening scene. Though the plot may be intricate, the underlying pattern is simple—and deeply reassuring in its inexorable meting out of just rewards and punishments.

Characterization is far simpler than plot in *Monte Cristo*. The characters may be divided into three basic categories: good (Edmund, Mercedes, Noirtier, Albert), evil (Danglars, Fernand, Villefort), and functional (sailors, fishermen, policemen, servants). A drunken and henpecked innkeeper, Caderousse, has a special place as the source of comic relief. The main characters are primarily types with minimal indivi-

Final scene of James O'Neill's production of *Monte Cristo*. The set's apparent depth was created by using cut drops—portions of each drop cut away so another can be seen through the openings. The acting area is very shallow. (Albert Davis Collection, Hoblitzelle Theatre Arts Library, Harry Ransom Humanities Research Center, University of Texas at Austin.)

dualizing traits. Edmund seems almost entirely good. He has only one moment of doubt: when he discovers that Albert, whom he has intended to kill, is his son and not Fernand's as he had thought. Most of the characters are at some point torn briefly between truth and self-interest, but the bad always choose self-interest, and the good, truth. Melodrama seldom suggests that moral choices are determined by environmental forces; rather, awareness of good and evil are innate, and each character is free to choose right or wrong. Values are viewed as absolute rather than relative, as they are in most twentieth-century drama.

From our perspective, language is one of nineteenth-century melodrama's greatest weaknesses. In *Monte Cristo*, it seems stilted and self-conscious, at times archaic (especially in its use of such words as "thee," "thou," "hadst," "knowest," and similar outdated forms). The characters are always wholly conscious of their motives and feelings and state them to the audience. To prevent any misperception, they use "asides" to inform the audience (or another character) of reactions they do not wish to share with all those onstage. (The aside, a convention almost as old as drama itself, came under attack in the late nineteenth century as unrealistic and was eventually abandoned except in self-consciously non-realistic plays.)

Next to suspenseful and morally satisfying plots, melodrama owed its appeal most to spectacle. By the 1880s, when O'Neill achieved his triumph in *Monte Cristo,* producers, unlike those of the seventeenth and eighteenth centuries, were priding themselves on the realism and authenticity of their costumes and settings. The first act of *Monte Cristo* takes place in 1815 (when Napoleon was in exile on Elba), while the other acts occur around 1833. Therefore, costumes would have played a major role in marking both passage of time and alteration in the economic and social status of the characters. Much of the "local color" of time and place would have been created through the dress of sailors, policemen, tavern patrons, and partygoers. Disguises are also important to both Noirtier and Edmund.

Monte Cristo requires eight sets, two of which were probably simple and very shallow, permitting more complex sets to be erected back of them while a scene was in progress. The shallow scenes are those for Villefort's office and a room in Fernand's house. These occur in the only acts (I and II) with multiple scenes. The scene in Villefort's office takes place between two others set in taverns overlooking the harbor. Thus, both tavern sets probably shared a number of elements, and the necessary alterations and changes could easily have been made during the scene in Villefort's office. The Act II scene in Fernand's house involves only a few characters and no unusual physical action. It was probably set up in front of the Chateau d'If setting, the most elaborate of the play, involving as it does two levels, one of which sinks, thereby concealing the prisoners' cells and revealing the water into which Edmund's body is thrown and the rock onto which he climbs triumphantly.

The demands of the Chateau d'If scene illustrate well the changes that had occurred in scenic practices by the late nineteenth century. O'Neill first played his version of *Monte Cristo* at Booth's Theatre in New York. This theatre, opened in 1869, had been built by one of America's greatest actors, Edwin Booth, and apparently was the first theatre in modern times to have a flat floor and to do away with the traditional arrangement of wings. Its stage embodied a recognition that new ways of handling scenery were required by the growing emphasis on three-dimensional, practicable pieces and on including furniture and other details found in

The stage at Booth's Theatre, New York, where James O'Neill first performed his version of *Monte Cristo*. Note the hydraulic lift used to raise and lower properties and scenic pieces. This was one of the first stages in modern times to have a flat floor and to dispense with grooves. At left, stage braces are being used to support scenery now that grooves are no longer available. (*Appleton's Journal*, May 28, 1870.)

real-life places. Wings had become increasingly unsatisfactory because they were two-dimensional, parallel to the front of the stage, and arranged in symmetrical pairs from front to back. In combination with the raked stage floor, wings also made it difficult to move large three-dimensional pieces on and off the stage. The flat floor and the absence of wing positions in Booth's Theatre permitted scenery to be erected wherever desired and to be moved on and off without hindrance. This theatre also had a number of elevator traps that raised and lowered sections of the floor hydraulically.

By the late nineteenth century, the stage floor in most theatres was divided into sections a few feet wide, any of which could be removed to create an opening ("bridge") extending completely across the stage. In the second act of *Monte Cristo*, the sinking of one part of the setting undoubtedly utilized one or more bridges. Upstage (and probably partially to one side) was the sea and the rock, both of which became visible as the cells sank. The sea was represented by a painted cloth moved up and down rhythmically by ropes attached to the underneath side. The sack (containing a dummy) was thrown into the water (no doubt with accompanying splash), and then, after a time, a soaked Edmund rose, probably through a trapdoor, climbed onto the rock, and uttered his triumphant "The world is mine." Such complex spectacle was typical of melodrama. The sets for the final three acts, though elaborate, could be changed in the intervals between acts. Considered all together, the settings provided great variety. They had to be designed and constructed with considerable care, for O'Neill toured this production throughout the country beginning in the 1880s and continuing for the next thirty years.

Touring such complex productions was made possible by the development of dependable transportation, which became a reality with the spread of railroads. The first transcontinental line in the United States was completed in the 1860s; by the late 1870s, it was possible to reach almost any area of the country by rail, and numerous theatrical productions were touring with set, costumes, properties, and actors. Such companies soon became the major purveyors of theatrical entertainment in most of America and remained so until displaced by sound motion pictures in the 1930s.

Richard Thomas in *The Count of Monte Cristo*, a revival of James O'Neill's version, by the American National Theatre at the Kennedy Center in Washington, D. C., 1985. Directed by Peter Sellars. (Photo by Joan Marcus. Courtesy Peter Sellars.)

Melodrama's visual appeal was further enhanced by lighting, the potential of which had increased greatly after gas replaced candles and oil during the first half of the nineteenth century. For the first time, the stage could be lighted as brightly as desired. Equally important, control over intensity became possible through a "gas table," a central location from which all the gas lines ran and from which the supply of gas to any part of the theatre could be controlled. Thus, lights could be dimmed or brightened as desired by one person situated at the gas table. It was now possible to darken the auditorium and light it again when needed. These improvements encouraged greatly increased concern for atmosphere and mood in stage lighting. Gas also made possible the development and exploitation of the "limelight," a type of spotlight (from which we get our expression "being in the limelight"). The limelight was made by placing a column of calcium (lime) inside a hood equipped with reflector and lens; onto the lime were directed compressed hydrogen and oxygen along with a gas flame; the lime was thus heated to incandescence until it gave off an extremely bright light used to create such atmospheric effects as rays of moonlight or sunlight or to focus attention on a character or object. At the end of Act II in *Monte Cristo,* the stage direction reads: "The moon breaks out, lighting up a projecting rock. Edmund rises from the sea, he is dripping, a knife in his hand, some shreds of sack adhering to it." The effectiveness of this scene depended on the limelight.

O'Neill's production of *Monte Cristo* calls attention to still another change then underway: long runs of single plays were replacing a repertory of plays performed in rotation by a company (the system that had prevailed since Shakespeare's day). The theatre had begun to adopt those practices that have been typical since the late nineteenth century.

With melodrama, the theatre in the late nineteenth and early twentieth centuries achieved its greatest mass appeal. It developed the audience and many of the conventions taken over by film, which displaced it as the prime medium of popular entertainment, especially after sound was added around 1930. And through film this legacy was subsequently passed on to television. Film forced theatre to reassess what it could do most effectively, and as a result it largely abandoned attempts to create the kind of realistic spectacle seen in *Monte Cristo*, which can be done much more convincingly by film. With their capacity to replicate their products endlessly, film and television were analogous in their effects on theatre to those of factories on individual craftsmen in the nineteenth century. They have made theatre into the equivalent of a handcrafted product and, consequently, one that has difficulty competing in a world attuned to mass production. Theatre had tried to meet the nineteenth-century demand for mass production by mounting elaborate productions and sending them throughout the country by the most efficient means of transportation then available. But theatre ultimately is not a medium adapted to mass production. Film is. The popular entertainment of the late nineteenth and early twentieth centuries, especially as represented by melodrama, was the common meeting ground of theatre and film and crucial in the subsequent history of both.

The Modernist Temperament

8

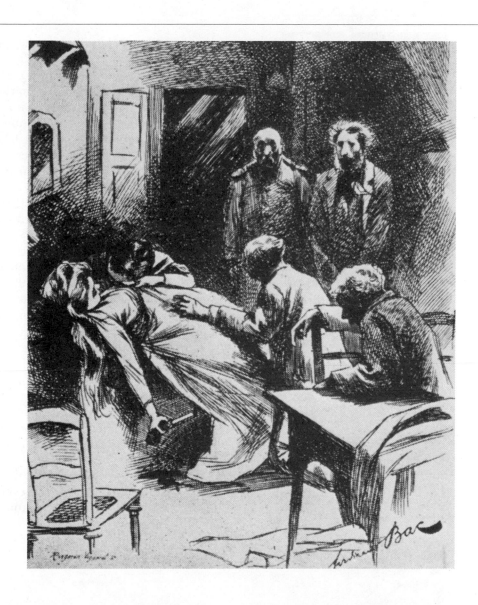

Even as James O'Neill was achieving his great popular success in *Monte Cristo,* various attitudes quite different from those undergirding melodrama were blending to create *modernism,* a complex set of theories and beliefs that marked a shift from absolute to relative values and proved to be a major influence on most subsequent artistic expression. While complete unanimity of belief was never an actuality, Western civilization throughout the Christian era had looked to the Bible as the ultimate authority on values and moral principles. Furthermore, the biblical version of creation and subsequent events was often accepted literally. Thus, in the nineteenth century, the earth was thought to be only about 6000 years old, the date of the Creation having been calculated by counting back through the generations that, according to the Bible, had preceded the birth of Christ.

In the late nineteenth century, a number of intellectual and scientific developments called some biblical passages into question. One came with the development of new fields of learning, among them geology and anthropology. When geologists began to suggest that the earth is millions (or even billions) of years old, and when anthropologists began to discover animal and human remains thousands of years older than the supposed date of the world's creation, heated controversies resulted. But by far the greatest controversy was provoked by Charles Darwin's *Origin of Species* (1859), in which he argued (1) that all forms of life have developed gradually from a common ancestry, and (2) that this evolution of species can be explained by the "survival of the fittest"—those most capable of adapting to specific environmental conditions. This theory was, and remains, anathema to those who interpret literally the biblical account of the Creation.

Darwin's theories have many implications. First, they suggest that heredity and environment are the primary causes of everything human beings are or do. Second, they suggest that, since human beings have no control over their individual heredity (it is fixed at birth) and little control over their environment (especially during the early years, when an individual's personality and values are being formed), people cannot be held fully responsible for what they do; if blame is to be assigned, it must be shared by the society that has countenanced undesirable hereditary and environmental forces. (Indecisiveness over how blame is to be apportioned is the primary source of contemporary arguments over such issues as the leniency or harshness of court decisions.) Third, Darwin's theories strengthened the idea of progress, since if humanity evolved from an atom of being to its present complexity, improvement appears to be inevitable. (Many of Darwin's contemporaries believed that progress, even though inevitable, could be hastened with the help of science and technology.) Fourth, Darwin's theories tended to absorb humanity into nature. Until that time, humanity had always been set apart from the rest of nature and considered superior to it.

These implications were crucial in the development of the modern temperament, for they suggested that change (rather than fixity) is the norm. They challenged the biblical account, which indicates that humanity was a deliberate creation and implies that human beings have been the same (at least biologically) since the time of Adam. Furthermore, Darwinism implied that heredity and environment determine human behavior, thereby contradicting the conventional explanation for the superiority of humanity to the rest of nature: human awareness of right and wrong. Most persons in the nineteenth century believed that conscience is innate—that human beings instinctively know the difference between right and wrong. (Melodrama is built on this premise.) Late-nineteenth-century thought, on the other hand, tended increasingly to support the belief that moral standards are relative to each culture and that concepts of right and wrong vary widely from one society to another.

The new ideas about human conscience received their most influential statement in the writings of Sigmund Freud (1856–1939), the most pervasive influence on psychology in the twentieth century. Freud argued that the only human instincts are aggression and sexuality—self-preservation and procreation. Left alone, humans would seek to satisfy their instincts without regard for others; if they are to become members of a community, they must undergo socialization. Through rewards and punishments, they learn what is acceptable and what is unacceptable, and each develops a superego (censor or judge)—what had previously been called the conscience. This sense of right and wrong is not absolute and does not come from God; it is relative to the society and specific environment in which it develops. Freud further argues that the process of socialization causes us to suppress many desires and urges (bury them in the unconscious mind) and find socially acceptable substitutes that the conscious mind can openly acknowledge. Overall, Freud's view of human psychology implies not only that we can never fully understand others but also that we can never be certain of our own motives. To assess people and situations, in addition to noting what is consciously said and done, we must also be aware of the subtext—what is not being openly stated or done. According to this view, then, not only are moral values relative, but also language and behavior are only partially reliable indicators of a person's state of mind.

Relativity affected every area of thought and action. It entered the theatre through the first modernist movements, *realism* and *naturalism*.

Realism and Naturalism

Realism was first recognized during the 1850s, and naturalism (essentially a more extreme version of realism), during the 1870s. In the theatre, these movements seemed in some ways mere extensions of practices already in common use, especially in the area of spectacle. Since around 1800, emphasis on visual accuracy in scenery and costumes had steadily increased. Therefore, one type of realism had already been achieved. Nevertheless, this realism, as is demonstrated by *Monte Cristo,* was exploited primarily as spectacular or picturesque background. In contrast to all preceding movements, realism and naturalism believed that character is determined in part by environment, and thus required settings to play an enlarged role—as representations of societal forces that shape character and (consequently) action. In other words, setting was conceived as environment and not merely as appropriate or impressive background. One consequence was the conclusion that each play's scenic needs are unique, since each play's environment is unlike that of any other. Perhaps more important, this approach to setting implies that what a character is and does is relative to specific environmental forces. Thus, though in their visual elements realistic theatrical productions might seem mere variations on melodrama (or even Shakespearean) productions, their underlying premises were quite different.

The basic views of realists and naturalists were grounded in the scientific outlook. They emphasized the need to understand human behavior in terms of natural cause and effect rather than notions of Providence or other unverifiable influences. Therefore, they restricted their pursuit of truth to knowledge that can be verified through the five senses. They further argued that since we can know the real world only through direct observation, playwrights should write about the society around them and should do so as objectively as possible. Given these premises, it was only logical that realists and naturalists would introduce subjects and behavior not previously seen on the stage. Conservative critics charged that the theatre had become little better than a sewer, but the realists replied that since they were depicting conditions truthfully, they were acting morally because truth is the highest morality. Furthermore, the realists argued, their critics wanted them to distort reality so as to make it conform to a vision of what it should be; instead, they declared, if audiences do not like the life portrayed on stage, they should change the society that furnished the models rather than denounce the playwrights who have had the courage to present life truthfully. The real issue was the relationship of art to morality and social norms: whether, like melodrama, it should always show good triumphant; or whether, if art shows deviations from accepted morality and behavior, it should reaffirm the validity of certain values even if they do not triumph; or whether, as the realists and naturalists argued, the playwright should follow truth wherever it leads without concern for conformity to the social codes and moral values of society. Ultimately, it was a controversy over absolute and relative values.

The issues were brought into sharp focus about 1880 through the plays of Henrik Ibsen (1828–1906), a Norwegian often called the founder of modern drama. Ibsen had begun his playwriting career around 1850 with verse dramas about Scandinavian legends, but in the 1870s he abandoned verse and turned exclusively to contemporary subjects. *A Doll's House* (1879) stirred a worldwide controversy because its heroine, Nora, realizing that she has always been treated as a plaything by her father and husband and is so uninformed that she has no basis for making decisions of any significance, leaves her husband and children so that she may learn to think and act for herself. This play was viewed by many as an attack on marriage and family, the foundations of society. Ibsen's next play, *Ghosts* (1881), showed the destruction of a family by hereditary and environmental forces, among them syphilis and the societal demands that a woman continue in a marriage even with a depraved husband. *Ghosts* created an even greater storm than *A Doll's House* and was denied production almost everywhere by people who found it immoral and corruptive. Nevertheless, these plays were widely read and discussed, and were the first dramas to make a significant impression on the public through questioning of moral values and social norms long considered absolute. Let us look more closely at one of Ibsen's plays.

Ibsen's *A Doll's House*, Marianne Owens as Nora and Barrie Ingham as Torvald. Directed by Michael Kahn. (Courtesy Department of Drama, University of Texas at Austin.)

The Wild Duck

In *The Wild Duck* (1884), Gregers Werle returns home after an absence of fifteen years, decides that the lives of all his acquaintances are based on lies, and determines to make them face the truth. His efforts lead to catastrophe. Probably no play better illustrates the dangers of trying to make everyone conform to an idealized conception of truth.

The principal characters are Old Werle (Gregers' father), Hjalmar Ekdal (Gregers' childhood friend), and Old Ekdal, Gina, and Hedwig (Hjalmar's father, wife, and daughter). Old Werle is prosperous, while the Ekdals live in comparative poverty. Years ago, however, Werle and Ekdal were business partners before Ekdal was sent to prison for illegal dealings. Gregers suspects that his father let Ekdal accept blame that was partially his, and that Old Werle arranged Hjalmar's marriage to Gina, a former maid in the Werle household, because Gina was pregnant by Werle. Thus, he thinks that Hedwig is not Hjalmar's child.

Gregers takes a room at the Ekdals, over Gina's protest, and through insinuation and leading questions gradually brings his "truth" into the open. After Hjalmar rejects Hedwig because Gregers has convinced him that she is not his biological daughter, she decides, with a child's simplicity of reasoning, that only some great sacrifice can prove her love for Hjalmar; consequently, she kills herself.

Essentially, *The Wild Duck* is a play about alternative truths. Dr. Relling, another tenant in the Ekdal house, says that most persons need "a saving lie" to help them retain a degree of self-respect. All the characters reshape reality to fit their own needs. The most polarized views are held by Relling, who believes that everyone needs to create illusions, and Gregers, who believes that truth is absolute and that happiness depends on facing it.

Ibsen has strengthened his theme through the symbol of the wild duck. First, the duck, happy and carefree, lives in a wild state. Then it is wounded by a hunter, survives, is placed in an artificial environment, and, though crippled, appears to be as happy as in its wild state. Ibsen

The Wild Duck, Act III. From left to right, Hedwig, Hjalmar, Relling, Gina, Molvig, and Gregers. (Courtesy Norwegian Embassy Information Service.)

seems to suggest that the wild duck's experiences parallel those of human beings, who, wounded by circumstances, construct a new reality that permits them to regain a sense of purpose.

The Ekdal family is reflected in the wild duck, since all in a sense are victims of Old Werle (the hunter). Old Ekdal has lived in an illusory state so long that it has become part of his nature. Since his release from prison, he has constructed a make-believe life around the attic, which he treats as a "forest," complete with "wildlife" (the duck and the rabbits).

Ibsen draws interesting parallels and contrasts between Old Werle and Hedwig. It is possible that Hedwig is the daughter of Old Werle (this is never clarified); both have weak eyesight, and both try to make amends to others. But Old Werle has treated life as though it were the sport of hunting, and when he wounds, he makes amends through such material compensations as money and arranged marriages. On the other hand, Hedwig responds to life with her whole being; rather than wound others, she kills herself. Old Werle faces up to his shortcomings at the end of the play, but he still believes that material gifts can atone for the wounds he has inflicted on others.

Ibsen's principal effort goes into the roles of Hjalmar and Gregers. Hjalmar's speeches proclaim his sensitivity, ambition, and idealism, but his actions show that he is insensitive, lazy, and self-centered. Gina runs the photographic studio; she and Hedwig sacrifice every comfort for him. To Hjalmar, Old Ekdal's disgrace is an excuse for easy sentiment, just as Hedwig's death will be in the future. But Hjalmar is perfectly happy in his illusions, for he can indulge himself and, at the same time, find excuses for being ineffectual. That Gregers accepts Hjalmar as a hero demonstrates his own lack of experience. He has hidden away from the world for fifteen years and has avoided becoming involved in life. Although he never attempts to change his own life, he feels free to meddle in the affairs of others.

Relling is used as a foil for Gregers. A doctor, he ministers to the psychic wounds of the characters by providing for them "saving lies," while Gregers destroys the illusions that have made life tolerable.

In spite of the obvious use of characters to illustrate ideas, Ibsen employs realistic techniques in creating roles. Every important characteristic is shown through action. Furthermore, each character's traits are brought out through well-motivated and lifelike speech or action. Ibsen is careful to fill in the sociological backgrounds of his characters, and each attitude and trait is grounded in particular social circumstances. All are creations (and victims) of heredity and environment. All are complex personalities with good and bad traits. There are no villains and no heroes, merely human beings.

As in most of his plays, Ibsen uses a late point of attack. In *The Wild Duck*, Gregers, because of his long absence, can believably inquire about the past and realistically motivate the complex exposition. Many of Ibsen's plays are written in four acts, but *The Wild Duck* has five, in part because two are required to establish the situation. The need for two acts of preparation is also illustrated by the use of two settings to contrast Old Werle's and the Ekdals' living conditions. By the end of the second act, both situation and characters have been clarified, the symbolism of the wild duck has been introduced, and Gregers has indicated his intention of rectifying the errors of the past. The final three acts grow logically out of the first two.

There are no extraneous scenes, and almost nothing could be removed without destroying clarity. At the same time, there is no feeling of haste, for each event seems to develop as it might in real life. Nevertheless, each act is built through a series of complications leading to a high point of suspense near the end of the act, while the play as a whole builds to

The Wild Duck directed by Lucian Pintilie at the Arena Stage, (Washington, DC), 1986. From left to right, Hedwig, Hjalmar, and Gina. (Photo by Joan Marcus. Courtesy Arena Stage.)

the climactic scene of Hedwig's death. Ibsen thus achieves great dramatic power while giving the effect of naturalness.

The Wild Duck used *box sets* (that is, sets that fully enclosed the acting space on three sides like the walls of a room, complete with ceiling, or, as suggested by the name, like a box with one side removed). Box sets permitted far more realistic representations of indoor spaces than could be achieved with wings and drop. The realistic effect was further enhanced by the addition of those furnishings, pictures, drapes, rugs, and bric-a-brac typical of the place being depicted. Furthermore, instead of standing throughout on a stage largely devoid of furnishings, as had been typical prior to the nineteenth century, actors now sought to behave as they would in real rooms, rather than letting the sets serve merely as visual identification of place. In *The Wild Duck,* the characters seem to live in the settings. In the Ekdals' studio they eat, retouch photographs, entertain friends, and carry on their daily existence. Action, character, and environment are interdependent.

Zola and Naturalism

Naturalism, unlike realism, had little success in the theatre, probably because it was too extreme in its demands. Its chief advocate, Emile Zola (1840–1902), thought many realists were more concerned with theatrical effectiveness (building complications, crises, and resolutions) than with truth to life. One of Zola's followers suggested that these temptations could be overcome by thinking of a play merely as *a slice of life*—a segment of reality transferred to the stage. The naturalists, thus, were far more rigorous than realists in their demands for truth in art and for a drama that demonstrated the inevitable laws of heredity and environment. In practice, naturalism tended to emphasize the deprivations and degradations of the lower classes, a subject little treated in earlier drama. It was the first artistic movement to present working-class characters with the same seriousness as the upper classes. (Prior to naturalism, lower-class characters in drama were assigned comic, minor, or eccentric roles; their economic and social status was considered evidence of unworthiness for serious concern.) Zola was fond of comparing naturalistic art with medicine, and he believed that the dramatist, like the medical pathologist, should examine and depict social ills so that their causes could be discovered and removed. With such rigorous (and often unattainable) goals, it is not surprising that naturalism had a short life and was soon absorbed into realism. Taken together, realism and naturalism struck major blows against rigid social codes and absolute values. They laid the foundations on which modernists built.

A naturalistic production of a play adapted from Zola's novel, *The Earth*, as directed by André Antoine at the Theatre Antoine, Paris, 1902. Note the many naturalistic details, including the hayloft in the background and the live chickens in the foreground. (*Le Théâtre*, 1902.)

The Emergence of the Director

Throughout history, someone has had to assume responsibility for staging plays. In the Greek theatre, the playwright usually staged his own plays; in subsequent periods, the heads of companies (or someone appointed by them) had that responsibility. Nevertheless, the director of today—the person who assumes responsibility for overall interpretation of the script and has the authority to approve and coordinate all the elements that make up a production—is primarily a product of the modernist movement. Why did the modern director appear then? The reasons are several.

The need for someone to coordinate and unify all the elements of a production became increasingly evident as the nineteenth century progressed. From the Renaissance to the nineteenth century, the elements of production, though representational, were so generalized as to require little attention. Each theatre had a stock of sets (prison, palace, street, country landscape, etc.) that was used over and over. To achieve some variety, prosperous theatres acquired two or more sets for each general type of scene. Costumes were typically clothing worn in contemporary life, usually chosen or supplied by the actors; some categories of characters (such as classical or Near Eastern) appeared in noncontemporary dress, but these costumes were so formalized that the same ones could be used for all characters in the same category.

Acting was also formalized during the period, in that actors were hired according to lines of business and always played the same limited range of roles. Additionally, the actors usually stood near the front of the stage (in part for visibility in the low-intensity lighting) and directed their lines as much to the audience as to the other characters (the auditorium, like the stage, was lighted). Since there was seldom any furniture on stage, the actors used a pattern of movement that gave downstage center to whichever character had an important speech at that point; when the speech was over, the actor moved away from center stage so the next actor could have that position. Thus, there were frequent changes of place determined by a pattern so well understood that the actors did not need to be told when and where to move. Consequently, rehearsals were restricted largely to establishing where entrances and exits were to be made and to such complex action as duels. The person in charge of staging had little to do other than to make sure that all the elements were assembled and to settle any disputes that arose. Rehearsals usually numbered no more than seven to ten.

As the nineteenth century progressed and the theatre became much more complex, the number and specificity of sets and costumes increased, especially as elaborate spectacle and special effects multiplied. Much of the effect of melodrama depended on split-second timing and precise stage business, and the introduction of box sets with furniture altered the movement patterns typical of earlier times. All these changes required increased supervision, coordination, and rehearsal. Nevertheless, each area of theatrical production tended to work in isolation— scene painters did the sets, seamstresses and tailors the costumes, and so on—with little consultation. Even within an area, the work was often parceled out to several persons (for example, each set for a five-set production might be done by a different scene painter, each according to what he thought appropriate). By the mid-nineteenth century, the need for greater unity and more control was becoming evident.

The acceptance of the modern director owes most to two influences: the theory of Wagner and the practice of Saxe-Meiningen. Richard Wagner (1813–1883), now known primarily as a composer of operas, sought to create a "master artwork" through a fusion of all the arts. Opposed to realism, he chose his stories primarily from German myth and set his dramas to music, not only to avoid the realistic mode but also to control how the text was performed. He argued that spoken drama is at the mercy of the actor, who is free to speak the lines however he chooses, whereas the singer is forced to follow the tempo, pitch, and duration dictated by the musical score. He also wished through his music-dramas to create a theatrical experience so overpoweringly empathetic that the audience would be drawn out of its everyday, mundane existence into an idealized, communal, near-religious experience.

To realize his goal, Wagner erected a new kind of theatre building, opened at Bayreuth in 1876. This theatre was the first in the West to do away with the box, pit, and gallery arrangement in favor of a "democratic" configuration, with seating laid out in a fan-shaped pattern that supposedly created equally good seeing and hearing conditions for all. This theatre was also one of the first in which the auditorium was always darkened during performances so as to distinguish between the everyday world (the auditorium) and the ideal realm (the stage), into which the

Auditorium and stage of Wagner's Bayreuth Festival Theatre. Note the absence of boxes or center aisle. The setting on stage is for Wagner's opera *Parsifal*. (*Le Théâtre*, 1899.)

performance sought to pull the audience. Wagner's contribution to the development of the director came primarily from his strong demand for complete "unity of production"—that is, for productions in which everything has been filtered through a single consciousness so as to achieve a unified artistic effect. This theoretical position has undergirded the twentieth-century idea of the director.

Georg II, Duke of Saxe-Meiningen (1826–1914), is now usually considered to have been the first director in the modern sense. Ruler of a small German state, Saxe-Meiningen gained international renown between 1874 and 1890 with his company's tours throughout Europe. The fame of the company did not stem from a new repertory, innovative design, or outstanding acting, but from its directorial practices. Saxe-Meiningen exerted complete control over every aspect of production. He designed the scenery, costumes, and properties himself and insisted that they be constructed to his precise specifications both in materials and appearance. Unable to afford well-known actors, he depended on long rehearsal periods (sometimes extending over several months) to achieve the effects he sought. His company was known especially for its crowd scenes, which (unlike those in other companies) were staged with

Saxe-Meiningen's production of Shakespeare's *Julius Caesar*. Seen here in Marc Antony's oration over Caesar's corpse. (*Die Gartenlaube*, 1879.)

great precision, variety, and emotional power. In Saxe-Meiningen's productions, the total stage picture was worked out carefully moment by moment, and the superior results came to be seen as convincing arguments for a strong director who can impose his authority and implement his vision. The Meiningen company validated many of Wagner's views, and the need for unified production (achieved through the director) soon became a basic tenet of theatrical production.

The Independent Theatre Movement

By the 1880s, innovative plays by realists and naturalists had appeared, but censorship had kept most of their plays from production. Similarly, Wagner and Saxe-Meiningen had established the importance of the director, but Wagner had devoted his attention to opera, and Saxe-Meiningen's company was staging mostly poetic drama (by Shakespeare or nineteenth-century playwrights). Therefore, the new drama and the new staging had remained isolated from each other. They were finally to meet in the "independent" theatres.

Throughout most of Europe, plays could not be performed for public audiences until they had been approved by a censor. Most of Ibsen's prose plays were not performed in the 1880s because censors would not license them. On the other hand, "private" performances (those done by a group for its members only) were not subject to censorship. Beginning in the late 1880s, this loophole was exploited by a number of small, "independent" theatres, which were open only to subscribing members and therefore were not subject to censorship. Consequently, these theatres were able to accomplish what more established theatres had not: the uniting of the new drama with the new staging techniques.

The first independent theatre was the Théâtre Libre, founded in Paris in 1887 by André Antoine. An enthusiastic follower of Zola and Ibsen, Antoine produced their plays and those of similar writers in settings that reproduced every detail of an environment (in one instance, he hung carcasses of real beef in a butcher-shop set). Like Saxe-Meiningen, he exerted control over every element of production.

Antoine's was only the first of numerous independent theatres. In 1889, the Freie Bühne was founded in Berlin, and in 1891, the Independent Theatre was inaugurated in London. The London group is especially important for having induced George Bernard Shaw, who was to be among the most important dramatists of the twentieth century, to begin writing plays. Not only did these independent theatres meet an important need, they also provided a permanent lesson, for since that time, whenever established theatres have become insufficiently responsive to innovation, small companies (variously called "art" theatres, "little" theatres, Off Broadway, Off-Off Broadway, or "alternative" theatres) have been formed to meet the need.

Another organization that emerged from the independent theatre movement—the Moscow Art Theatre—was to be of special importance. Founded in 1898 by Constantin Stanislavsky (1863–1938) and Vladimir Nemerovich-Danchenko (1859–1943), it achieved its first great success with the plays of Anton Chekhov. His *The Sea Gull, Uncle Vanya, The Three Sisters,* and *The Cherry Orchard* mingled the comic, serious, pathetic, and ironic so thoroughly that to assign them meaningful formal labels is impossible. Chekhov does not pass judgment on his characters; rather, he treats all with tolerance and compassion. Complexity of tone, along with characters who do not understand their own feelings and who seek to conceal as much as to reveal their responses, makes these plays excellent examples of the modernist temperament.

The Moscow Art Theatre eventually made its greatest impact through Stanislavsky's system of acting, which, disseminated through his books (*My Life in Art; An Actor Prepares; Building a Character;* and *Creating a*

Chekhov's *The Three Sisters* (the final act) as performed by the Moscow Art Theatre. (Photo by Fred Fehl. Courtesy Hoblitzelle Theatre Arts Collection, Harry Ransom Humanities Research Center, University of Texas at Austin.)

Role), has been the most pervasive influence on acting during the twentieth century. Stanislavsky's basic premises are five in number: (1) The actor's body and voice must be thoroughly trained and flexible so that they can respond to all demands. (2) To act truthfully, the actor must be a skilled observer of human behavior. (3) If an actor is not merely to play himself, he must thoroughly understand the script, the character's motivation and goal in each scene and in the play as a whole, and the character's relationship to all the other roles and to the total dramatic action. (4) Actors must project themselves into the world of the play and may learn to do so through the "magic if" (that is, by inducing belief and understanding by imagining how one would feel or act *if* one were this specific character in this specific situation). Actors may also employ "emotion memory" (recalling one's own emotional responses in situations comparable to those in the script). (5) Onstage, the actor should concentrate moment by moment, as if the events were happening spontaneously and for the first time. Overall, Stanislavsky sought to deal with all aspects of acting. What he wrote has been interpreted variously, but it continues to be the best-known attempt to describe what is involved in effective acting.

Although realism and naturalism marked the first phases in the development of modernism, they were soon followed by other movements of equal importance. In some respects, realism and naturalism are the logical culmination of developments that began in the Renaissance, when the picture-frame stage and perspective scenery were introduced. At that time, the stage became essentially representational, and subsequent trends were toward ever-more-convincing pictures. Acting had also moved toward realism by accepting women in female roles and by doing away with masks (except in commedia dell'arte). Thus, though the theatrical conventions of the seventeenth and eighteenth centuries were far more formal than those of the nineteenth century, naturalism can be viewed as the culmination of the trend toward actualism.

Symbolism

By around 1890, attempts to counteract the influence of realism and naturalism were making an impact. The first of these nonrealistic movements was symbolism. It denied the claims made by realists that ultimate truth is to be discovered in evidence gained through the five senses, arguing instead that truth can only be intuited and therefore cannot be expressed directly or through wholly rational means; truth can only be suggested through symbols that evoke feelings and states of mind corresponding imprecisely to our intuitions. Maurice Maeterlinck, the best-known of the symbolist playwrights, wrote about drama:

> Great drama . . . is made up of three principal elements: first, verbal beauty; then the contemplation and passionate portrayal of what actually exists about us and within us . . . and, finally enveloping the whole work and creating the atmosphere proper to it, the idea which the poet forms of the unknown in which float about the beings and things which he evokes, the mystery which dominates them. . . . I have no doubt that this last is the most important element.

Unlike the realists, the symbolists chose their subjects from the past or the realm of fancy and avoided any attempt to deal with social problems or environmental forces. They aimed to suggest a universal truth independent of time and place that cannot be logically defined or rationally expressed. Thus, their drama tended to be vague and mysterious.

Established theatres, finding symbolist drama incomprehensible, were even less inclined to produce it than the works of Ibsen and Zola. Consequently, the symbolists, like the realists and naturalists, established independent theatres to perform their plays. The most important was the Théâtre de l'Oeuvre, founded in Paris in 1892 and headed by Aurelien-Marie Lugné-Poë. The symbolists believed that the most important aspect of a production is mood or atmosphere. They used little scenery, and even that was vague in form and devoid of historical detail. They often placed a gauze curtain just back of the proscenium so the action would appear to be taking place in a mist or timeless void. Color was chosen for its mood value rather than for representational accuracy. The actors chanted their lines and used unnatural gestures. The goal was to remove the action from the everyday world. One can scarcely conceive of productions more unlike those of the naturalists. They so differed from what audiences had become accustomed to that many spectators were baffled. As a movement in the theatre, symbolism soon lost its appeal, and by 1900 had largely ceased. Nevertheless, symbolism is important as the first of the nonrealistic movements that would proliferate in the twentieth century.

Symbolism is also important because it disrupted a pattern that had persisted since the beginning of theatre. In each period, the same conventions and approach to production had been used for all plays during that period. There had been transitions from one approach or set of conventions to another (as is seen in England with the shifts from medieval to Elizabethan and then to the picture-frame stage), but transitions were gradual; once established, the same conventions were used for all plays. This is the primary reason why no need was felt for a director in the modern sense—the conventions and working methods were so well understood that detailed supervision and control were unnecessary. The various settings for the same play could be assigned to different scene painters because the visual style, theatrical conventions, and audience expectations were sufficiently clear that detailed instructions or close supervision would have been considered a lack of trust in the artist. Common stylistic goals, and faith that each production area was capable of achieving those goals, characterized theatre until the late nineteenth century. Then, as we have seen in examining the emergence of the director, the increased complexity of production (greater number of sets, more realistic special effects, more detailed stage movement and business, etc.) had led by 1875 to recognition that greater control and better coordination from a central authority was desirable. Nevertheless, even then, stage conventions remained much the same; only production processes were being refined.

But when symbolism challenged realism and naturalism, two radically different sets of conventions came into conflict. The implications of this conflict are crucial to understanding modernism and its domination of twentieth-century art. Prior to the twentieth century, artistic movements occurred linearly (that is, one succeeded another chronologically), whereas in the twentieth century, several have existed simultaneously. For example, between 1910 and 1920 movements called expressionism, futurism, dadaism, cubism, and a number of others (including realism) coexisted. Each was based on a separate set of premises about the nature of truth and the world in which we live, and consequently each required a different set of conventions to embody its vision. With such fragmentation, there was no longer a unified view based on absolute values; rather there were multiple views, each based on values a group accepted as true but that were perhaps considered false by others. Thus, the transition had been made from the absolute to the relative—the most characteristic feature of the modernist temperament.

Modernism influenced all of the arts. From the Renaissance to the twentieth century, the visual arts (including theatrical scenery) had depicted everything in relation to a fixed eyepoint. In the early twentieth century, however, the visual arts no longer always depicted all details of the same picture as seen from one eyepoint. The best-known examples are works by Picasso in which various parts of the same subject are painted as though seen from different eyepoints. Attention also shifted from content to the elements of art forms. In painting, representational subjects were sometimes abandoned altogether, resulting in wholly abstract works. Such painting had to be judged by formal criteria (effectiveness in manipulating line, color, and composition) rather than by representational accuracy. Similar developments in music displaced melody, so that a composition could be valued not for its tune but for its handling of time and atonal relationships.

Appia, Craig, and Reinhardt

During the early twentieth century, two theorists—Appia and Craig—were especially successful in reshaping ideas about the visual elements of the theatre and in establishing the need for designers rather than mere scene painters. Adolphe Appia (1862–1928) began with the idea that artistic unity in theatre is fundamental but difficult to achieve because of conflicting elements: the moving actor, the horizontal floor, and the vertical scenery. He sought to replace flat, painted scenery (and all decorative detail) with three-dimensional structures as the only proper environment for three-dimensional actors. Instead of a flat stage floor, he used steps, levels, and ramps to provide transitions from horizontal to vertical planes and to encourage variety in composition and movement.

Appia was also a major theoretician of stage lighting. To reveal the shape and dimensionality of the setting and actor, Appia advocated the

Adolphe Appia's design for the entrance to the underworld in Gluck's opera, *Orpheus and Eurydice.* (Courtesy Adolphe Appia Fondation, Schweizerische Theatersammlung, Geneva.)

use of light from various directions and angles. He considered light the most flexible of all theatrical elements because, like music, it can change moment by moment to reflect shifts in mood and emotion and because it blends and unifies all the other elements through its intensity, color, direction, and movement. Appia's views on lighting came at a crucial time—just as the technology needed to implement his theories was becoming available. The incandescent light bulb was invented in 1879, and as the first medium that did not use an open flame, it gained acceptance rapidly because of its safety. But initially, the wattage of electric lamps was very small, and not until 1911 were lamps available with a concentrated filament of sufficiently high wattage to permit the development of spotlights. By around 1915, most of the technology (electric lamps, spotlights, color filters, and dimmers) needed to implement Appia's theories was available and in use.

Gordon Craig (1872–1966) was far more militant than Appia, and his combativeness kept him and his ideas about theatre in the public eye. Craig denied that the theatre is a fusion of other arts; rather, he saw it as a wholly autonomous art whose basic elements—action, language, line, color, and rhythm—are fused by a master artist. He once suggested that actors should be replaced by large marionettes, because they, unlike actors, would not impose their own personalities on a production and undermine the master artist's intentions. Like Appia, Craig advocated a simplicity in scenery, costumes, and lighting that depended on line, mass, and color rather than on decorative detail. Both men sought to

A design by Gordon Craig. Note the emphasis on verticality and the absence of decorative detail. (*Stage Yearbook,* 1914.)

replace the representational approach to visual elements with one concerned only with the line, mass, color, texture, and mood appropriate to the dramatic action. Appia and Craig also promoted the concept of the director as the supreme theatre artist.

The influence of Appia and Craig reinforced that of Max Reinhardt, who was then amending earlier conceptions of the director. During the late nineteenth century, Wagner, Saxe-Meiningen, Antoine, Lugné-Poë, and others had won acceptance for the director, but each of these men still used basically the same approach in every production. As new artistic movements appeared, each was faced with the need to establish a theatre specializing in its distinctive style, since each existing theatre was devoted to a single approach in theatrical production. A breakthrough was achieved aorund 1900, when the German director Max Reinhardt (1872–1943) began to treat each production as a new challenge demanding its own unique stylistic solution. Using this approach, the plays of all movements and periods could be accommodated in the same theatre. For the first time, theatre history became important to directing, for Reinhardt built each production around elements significant to the theatrical context in which the play originally appeared. Often he tried to recreate the audience-performer spatial relationship. (As examples, he remodeled a circus building to accommodate Greek plays; for a medieval play he transformed a theatre into a cathedral; and he presented many eighteenth-century plays in a hall of state in an eighteenth-century palace.) He unified some productions around dominant visual motifs and others around theatrical conventions typical of the period when the play was written. Thus, knowledge of the theatre's past was crucial in many of his productions.

Reinhardt's method further enhanced the role of the director. Since the stylistic approach to be used in any production was flexible, the choice was the director's to make; as the originator of the vision undergirding each production, the director was also the arbiter of all choices made by those who worked to implement this approach. Nevertheless, although Reinhardt considered the director's the primary artistic consciousness, he did not, as many of his successors were to do, alter the time or place of a play's action. He believed that the production should serve the script (rather than the script the production, as has become common in more recent times). His productions, viewed from today's perspective, do not seem stylistically as varied as they did to his contemporaries, for most were still partially representational. Nevertheless, Reinhardt established eclecticism as the dominant directorial approach. Once accepted, eclecticism was (and continues to be) elaborated and extended by others, frequently in ways never envisioned by Reinhardt. With Reinhardt, relativism triumphed in directing (as it already had in

Reinhardt's production of *Oedipus the King* in the Circus Schumann, Berlin, 1910. (*Le Théâtre*, 1911.)

many other areas), for now instead of applying the same approach to all plays (the absolutist's way), the approach was altered to suit each play (the relativist's way).

Expressionism

The artistic movements of the early twentieth century are far too numerous to explore individually. Therefore, let us choose one—expressionism—to examine more closely. Expressionism, which emerged around 1910 in Germany, sought to counter materialism and industrialism, which it saw as the principal perverters of the human spirit. It charged that the industrial age had effectively turned human beings into machines with conditioned responses and shriveled souls trapped in materialistic values. It wished to change the world to accord with what is best in the human spirit. Expressionists envisioned "the regeneration of man" and the emergence of "the new man."

Most expressionist drama shows how the human spirit has been distorted by false values. Therefore, it is message-centered and usually involves a search (for truth, fulfillment, or a means to change the world). Many of the conventions reflect the protagonist's internal state—almost always warped by the callousness of materialism—causing us to see the external world through his distorted vision. Therefore, buildings or the walls of rooms may lean in threateningly, color may reflect emotion (for example, the protagonist's jealousy may make the sky green rather than blue), movement and speech may be robotlike, or a number of persons or objects may be identical in appearance. Expressionism most typically presents a nightmarish vision of the human situation.

The plays of August Strindberg (1849–1912) are often seen as forerunners of expressionism. In the preface to his *A Dream Play* (1902), Strindberg wrote:

> The writer has tried to imitate the disconnected but seemingly logical form of the dream. Anything may happen; everything is possible and probable. Time and space do not exist. On an insignificant background of reality, imagination designs and embroiders novel patterns: a medley of memories, experiences, free fancies, absurdities, and improvisations.

In other words, Strindberg was seeking to destroy the limitations of time, place, logical sequence, and appearance by adopting the viewpoint of the dreamer. One event flows into another without logical transition, characters dissolve or are transformed into others, and widely separated places and times blend to tell a story of tortured and alienated mankind. It was from Strindberg that the expressionists borrowed many of their techniques.

Expressionist drama flourished in Germany, especially immediately after World War I, when optimism over the establishment of Germany's first democratic government made the realization of expressionist goals seem possible. But by the mid-1920s, disillusionment had replaced optimism, and the popularity of expressionism faded rapidly. Nevertheless, expressionism had attracted a number of writers in various countries. In the United States, noteworthy expressionist plays were written. Of these, the best known are Elmer Rice's *The Adding Machine* (whose accountant-protagonist is little more than an adding machine himself) and Eugene O'Neill's *"The Hairy Ape."* O'Neill (1888–1953), son of James O'Neill and the first American dramatist to win international recognition, is often considered the greatest playwright America has produced. His plays, ranging through practically every style, are major expressions of the modernist temperament. Let us look more closely at *"The Hairy Ape"* as an example of expressionist drama and O'Neill's plays.

Strindberg's *A Dream Play* at the Royal Dramatic Theatre, Stockholm, 1970. Max von Sydow is seen at left. Note how the realistic elements are contradicted by slicing through the window and by the character peering over the wall of the room. Directed by Ingmar Bergman. (Courtesy Swedish Information Service.)

"The Hairy Ape"

"The Hairy Ape" derives its unity from its central theme: humanity's frustrated search for identity in a hostile environment. When the play begins, the protagonist, Yank, is confident that he and his fellow stokers are the only ones who "belong" because they make the ship go (and, by extension, the factories and machines of the modern, industrialized society). Yank represents for his fellow workers "a self-expression . . . their most highly developed individual." They do not recognize that their quarters resemble "the steel framework of a cage" or that they themselves resemble Neanderthal men.

The second scene introduces Mildred Douglas, the wealthy shipowner's daughter. Seen against the natural beauty of the sea, she appears "inert and disharmonious," completely lacking in purpose. In Scene 3, she insists on visiting the stokehole to watch the men shovel the coal that makes the ship's engines run. When she sees Yank, "the hairy ape," she is so horrified that she faints and must be carried away. This is the catalytic moment for Yank, since Mildred's revulsion makes him begin to question all of his beliefs. According to O'Neill, from the fourth scene onward, Yank "enters into a masked world; even the familiar faces of his mates in the forecastle have become strange and alien."

In Scene 5, seeking to reestablish his sense of belonging, Yank goes to Fifth Avenue, where the shops that cater to the rich and powerful display "magnificence cheapened and made grotesque by commercialism." The people, dressed identically, look like "gaudy marionettes." When Yank tries to get their attention, they ignore him; resorting to force, he strikes the men, but they remain oblivious to his existence and give their full attention to a monkey-fur coat in the shop window.

In Scene 6, Yank is in jail (called "the zoo"), where the cages run on "numberless, into infinity." He decides that he will get his revenge by

Scene 1 of O'Neill's *The Hairy Ape* in its first production (1922), Provincetown Playhouse, New York. Directed by James Light; designed by Robert Edmond Jones and Cleon Throckmorton. (Photo by Vandamm. Courtesy Performing Arts Research Center, The New York Public Library at Lincoln Center.)

destroying the steel and machinery over which he originally thought he had power. Learning that the IWW (International Workers of the World) opposes the owners of factories and ships, Yank, upon being released from jail, goes to an IWW office (described as "cheap, banal and commonplace") and offers to blow up the IWW's enemies. His offer is greeted with contempt, and he is thrown into the street. In the final scene, Yank arrives at the zoo, where he finds a gorilla that seems to understand him, but when he frees the gorilla, it crushes him and throws him into the cage. Yank dies without achieving the sense of belonging that he has so desperately sought.

Yank is symbolic of modern humanity in an industrialized society—cut off from a past when human beings were an integral part of the natural environment and trapped in an existence where they are little better than cogs in the industrial machine. In a speech to the gorilla, Yank sums up his feelings of alienation: "I ain't got no past to tink in, nor nothin' dat's comin', on'y what's now—and dat don't belong."

Only a few of the characters in *"The Hairy Ape"* have names. Most are representative types or members of groups. In the stage directions, O'Neill writes that, except for slight differentiations in size and colora-

Scene 3 of *"The Hairy Ape"* as performed at the Kamerny Theatre, Moscow, in the late 1920s. Depicted is the crucial moment when Mildred first sees Yank and calls him a "hairy ape." Directed by Alexander Tairov. (Courtesy Hoblitzelle Theatre Library, Harry Ransom Humanities Research Center, University of Texas at Austin.)

tion, the stokers are all alike. Overall, O'Neill seems to suggest that all human beings in the modern, industrialized world have been distorted—the workers having been reduced to the level of animals, the rich having become useless puppets. These conceptions are embodied in speech and appearance. In Scene 4, almost all the speeches are described as having a "brazen metallic quality as if [the characters'] throats were phonograph horns," and much of what Yank and others say in this scene is greeted with "a chorus of hard, barking laughter." In the scene set on Fifth Avenue, the characters speak in "toneless, simpering voices," and they are masked and dressed to make them look like puppets. In comments on the appropriate performance style for the play, O'Neill suggests that, beginning with Scene 4, everyone that Yank encounters, "including the symbolic gorilla," should wear masks. Yank is set off from the other characters because he is the only one who recognizes the need to seek a coherent relationship between himself and his environment. In his search, he meets no one who understands his need, but O'Neill seems to have hoped that Yank's plight would illuminate for the audience the nature of modern existence.

"The Hairy Ape" is representative of both the outlook and the techniques of expressionism. The episodic structure and distorted visual elements are typical of the movement, as is Yank's longing for fulfillment, with its suggestion that society be changed so the individual can achieve a sense of belonging.

By the time *"The Hairy Ape"* was written, the modernist temperament was dominant in all the arts. Yet, many persons still believed in absolute values and considered much of twentieth-century thought and art misguided or dangerous. The two points of view (and others) coexisted because standards and values (both in life and art) had become so fragmented that tolerance of alternative truths, moralities, and artistic conventions had become the norm rather than the exception. In this atmosphere, the varieties of theatrical experience had multiplied and would continue to do so.

From Epic Theatre
to Absurdism

9

By the 1920s, modernism dominated the arts both in Europe and America. But this outlook was by no means unopposed. The mass audience still preferred the types of entertainment that had been popular before modernism appeared, and as film was increasingly able to meet the demand, this audience drifted away from the theatre. The shift was accelerated by the introduction of sound, which, combined with a major economic depression throughout the 1930s, increased the appeal of film and its low ticket prices. Between 1929 and 1939 approximately two-thirds of all live-entertainment theatres in the United States closed. Consequently, live theatre was left increasingly to affluent and (actual or would-be) sophisticated patrons.

In the United States, new theatrical movements were welcomed first (and often only) by the "art" or "little" theatres. Broadway audiences were not so tolerant of innovation. The peak of experimentation on Broadway seems to have been reached in the early 1920s with Arthur Hopkins' production of an "expressionistic" *Macbeth,* the set for which was an arrangement of Gothic arches that leaned ever more precariously as the action proceeded. Three large masks, symbols of the Witches or Fate, hung above the stage throughout. (See the illustration on page 211.) The unreceptiveness of the audience to this production is sometimes said to have made Broadway producers avoid stylistic extremes thereafter and adhere rather closely to a modified (or simplified) realism, much less detailed than nineteenth-century realism but still basically representational, though carefully designed to reflect the artistic qualities and practical demands of the particular play. Modified realism dominated the Broadway theatre from the early 1920s until the 1950s.

The innovations that become most influential seldom begin in mainstream theatres. Thus, while modified realism dominated the established theatres of both America and Europe during the 1920s, other modes

Design by Robert Edmond Jones for Arthur Hopkins' production of Shakespeare's *Macbeth* on Broadway in the early 1920s. The banquet scene. Note the three masks suspended above the stage. (Courtesy Theatre Arts Books, New York.)

continued to appear. Many made little impact, but a few were eventually to exert significant influence. Among these, one of the most important was epic theatre.

Epic Theatre

Epic theatre developed in Germany during the 1920s in the wake of expressionism. It is associated above all with Bertolt Brecht (1898–1956), who shared the expressionists' desire to transform society but thought their methods vague and impractical. At first, Brecht's ideas also lacked focus, but around 1926 he embraced Marxism and its belief that values are determined by the prevailing economic system. Thereafter, he sought to make audiences evaluate the socioeconomic implications of what they saw in the theatre; he was convinced that if this was done effectively, audiences would perceive the need to alter their society and would work to bring about appropriate changes. He was also convinced that his goals could not be reached in the kind of theatre then dominant—one that sought to evoke an empathetic response so overwhelming that the spectators suspended their critical powers and let themselves be carried along passively by the performance. In such a theatre, according to Brecht, all the problems raised are resolved at the end of the play, and there is no demand that the audience members relate what they have seen to the real world. Brecht wished to alter the audience's relationship to the production by encouraging it to watch actively and critically.

As a means to his goal, Brecht arrived at the concept of "the alienation effect" *(verfremdungseffekt)*—distancing the audience from the stage events so it can view them critically. To achieve alienation, Brecht adopted many conventions not then in use but which, through Brecht's influence, have since become common. First, he reminded the audience that it was in a theatre by calling attention to the medium. Lighting instruments were left unmasked; scenery was fragmentary (sufficient to indicate place but not full-stage sets); musicians were sometimes placed on stage instead of in the orchestra pit; captions, maps, or other images were projected onto screens; objects were flown in from above on deliberately visible ropes. Actors often stepped out of the scene to sing or talk directly to the audience. Brecht sometimes cautioned his actors to present a character rather than become the character (as Stanislavsky supposedly wished). To achieve distance from their roles, the actors were advised by Brecht in some rehearsals to speak of their characters in the third person. For example, an actor might verbalize a character's action in "He crosses the stage and says . . . ." Such conventions marked a conscious break with past practice, in which the goal typically had been to make the audience suspend its awareness of being in a theatre. Brecht did not see the theatre as a place to escape one's problems but as a place where one was led to recognize real problems and the need to solve them outside the theatre. He did not want audiences vicariously to watch fictional characters solve fictional problems in the theatre.

Brecht also sought to achieve alienation with subjects removed (either in time or place) from the audience. According to Brecht, most historical drama treats its subjects in contemporary terms, thereby creating the impression that things have always been the same and therefore are unchangeable. Rather than using this approach, Brecht sought to make the differences between past and present readily apparent, so the audience could see that the world has changed and therefore is changeable.

Brecht further sought alienation through his handling of the various theatrical elements. He opposed the notion (which had been championed by Wagner and embraced by most of his successors) that the most effective theatrical production is a synthesis of all the arts, each

Next-to-last scene of Brecht's *Mother Courage* as performed at the Berliner Ensemble, 1949. (Courtesy Kai-Dib Films International.)

part reinforcing the others in a fully unified work. Brecht called this practice redundant and wasteful, since each element is seeking to duplicate in its own way what is being done by all the others. He advocated instead that each element make its own comment. The disparity among elements would then arouse alienation by making the audience assess the varying comments. For example, Brecht's songs often set cynical or disillusioned lyrics to lighthearted tunes; the disparity supposedly made the listener more critically aware of the song's implications.

Brecht also adopted a number of structural devices to create alienation. Rather than have one scene flow smoothly into another, he wished, as he put it, to call attention to the knots tying the scenes together. Therefore, he used captions (projected on screens), songs, or similar devices to emphasize breaks in the action. Captions also stated the action of the scene to follow in order to undercut attention to story or suspense and direct it to the social implications of the events. These conventions may suggest that Brecht was heavy-handedly didactic, but he also understood the need for theatre to be entertaining. His stories have numerous complications and reversals and are leavened with songs and other devices intended to capture and hold attention. In fact, Brecht the story-

The original production of *The Threepenny Opera*, Berlin, 1928. Act III, Scene 7, Peachum's "Song of the Insufficiency of Human Endeavor." Directed by Erich Engel. Designed by Caspar Neher. (Courtesy Theatermuseum, Munich.)

teller so often subverts Brecht the propagandist that many theatregoers remain totally oblivious of his goals. The audience may also be confused by Brecht's emphasis on alienation, since his statements may suggest that he wishes the audience to be distanced from the events continuously. In actuality, Brecht engages the audience empathetically and then interrupts empathy through some device (such as a song) that creates the distance needed to evaluate what has been experienced during the empathetic moments. Thus, there is a continuing alternation of empathy and esthetic distance (much like that created through the alternation of episodes and choral odes in Greek drama).

Brecht called his theatre *epic* because he thought it had more in common with epic poetry (with its alternation of dialogue and narration and its easy shifts in time and place) than with the dramatic traditions that had long been typical. Brecht wrote many plays, including *The Threepenny Opera*, *Mother Courage and Her Children*, and *The Caucasian Chalk Circle*. Let us look at *The Good Woman of Setzuan* as an example of Brecht's drama.

The Good Woman of Setzuan

The Good Woman of Setzuan, written between 1938 and 1940 and first performed in 1943, is a parable distanced by setting it in China. The epic nature of the play is established by the prologue, in which narration and dialogue are mingled and in which time and place are telescoped. The prologue also demonstrates the irony that permeates the piece, since Wong assures the Gods that everyone is waiting to receive them— only to see them have to obtain lodgings from a prostitute. In addition, the prologue establishes the basic situation: the Gods find the good person for whom they have been searching—Shen Te—and enjoin her to remain good. At the same time, they refuse to be concerned about how such a difficult assignment is to be carried out—they "never meddle with economics." Herein lies the basic conflict, for to Brecht economic factors are the very ones that stand in the way of goodness. Thus, Brecht implies that the solution to human problems is not to be sought in divine injunctions.

The Good Woman of Setzuan alternates short and long scenes. The short scenes serve two main purposes: to break up, and to comment on, the action. Both contribute to Brecht's aim of forcing the audience to think by giving clues about the significance of what is shown and by providing time in which to reflect.

The long scenes are devoted to the conflict between good and evil as seen in the two aspects of the "good woman." Her better self is shown in the person of Shen Te, while her materialistic self is embodied in Shui Ta. She assumes the disguise of Shui Ta whenever her goodness has brought her to the edge of destruction. At first, the impersonation is for brief periods, but as the play progresses, she must become Shui Ta for longer periods. Brecht uses this device to show the progressive deterioration of morality under capitalism. The play ends in a stalemate, for the Gods leave Shen Te with the same message as in the prologue, "Be good." She is still no nearer to knowing how this is to be accomplished, and they are still unconcerned over such practical matters.

Brecht makes no attempt to create the illusion of reality. For example, when Wong says he will find a place for the Gods to spend the night, he suggests the attempt, although the various houses are not represented onstage; the action is outlined, but many details are omitted. This approach allows Brecht to telescope events and to eliminate transitions, as can be seen clearly in the scene during which Shen Te meets Yang Sun and falls in love. There has been no preparation for this complication, and it is as if a storyteller had said, "One day, when Shen Te was walking in the park, she saw a young man trying to hang himself."

Brecht's *The Good Woman of Setzuan*. The screen (upper center) is used for captions and for photographs relating the events to contemporary conditions. Directed by Francis Hodge. Designed by John Rothgeb. (Courtesy Department of Drama, University of Texas.)

Brecht's structural techniques are explained in part by his belief that scenes should be clearly separated as part of the alienation process. They are further explained by his insistence that it should be possible to express the basic social content of each scene in one sentence and that all parts of a scene should be clearly related to this statement.

Brecht considerably oversimplifies characters, for he is principally concerned with social relationships. He is not interested in total personalities or the inner lives of his characters. Instead of names, the majority of speakers in *The Good Woman of Setzuan* have been given social designations such as Wife, Grandfather, and Policeman. Their desires are also stated in terms of social action: Shen Te wishes to treat all persons honorably, to make it possible for Yang Sun to become a pilot, to provide proper food for children, and so on. Thus, Brecht's characterizations are confined principally to social attitudes. He did not intend to portray well-rounded individuals but to interpret social forces. The action does not exist to display character; rather, character demonstrates social action. The only character who rises to the level of moral decision is Shen

Te, and the plot progresses in large part through the series of choices she makes and which show the dilemma of humanity under existing economic conditions.

Brecht's career was interrupted in 1933, when the Nazis came to power. While in exile from Germany, he spent several years in the United States before returning to Germany, where in 1949 he founded the Berliner Ensemble, devoted primarily to producing his own plays in the style he thought appropriate to them. By the time Brecht died in 1956, the Berliner Ensemble had been recognized as one of the world's great theatre companies, and Brecht's ideas were influencing staging almost everywhere. Today, many of the most widely accepted conventions (notably those acknowledging the theatrical medium—no front curtain to hide the stage, fragmentary scenery, unmasked lighting instruments, etc.) derive in large part from Brecht.

The Living Newspaper

One of the forms most obviously related to Brecht's epic theatre is the Living Newspaper, which grew out of the Federal Theatre project in the United States. During the economic depression of the 1930s, the United States government authorized a Federal Theatre as part of its Works Progress Administration programs, designed to relieve unemployment. Between 1935 and 1939, the Federal Theatre had units in various parts of the country, although it was most active in New York. It is best remembered for the Living Newspaper, which aimed at achieving in the theatre something similar to the printed newspaper. In actuality, it was more closely related to the documentary film, for each play treated a single problem. The most famous examples are *One Third of a Nation* (on slum housing), *Triple-A Plowed Under* (on the farm program), and *Power* (on public utilities and flood control). The plays alternate scenes illustrating social conditions with narrative sequences. Statistical tables, still photographs, and motion pictures were projected on screens; amplified voices, music, and sound effects were used freely. The plays were written by many authors in collaboration and took a definite point of view (in favor of social reform and corrective legislation). This political and social bias eventually led to the discontinuance of the Federal Theatre, for in 1939 Congress refused to appropriate funds to continue it. It had been the United States government's first financial support of the theatre.

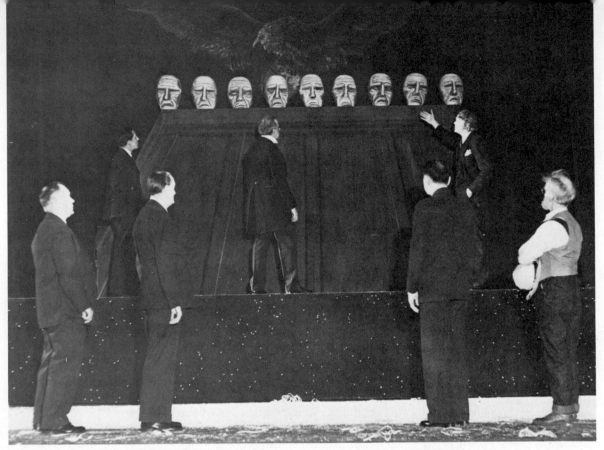

Power, a "living newspaper" presented by the Federal Theatre Project. This scene shows an argument before the U.S. Supreme Court over the constitutionality of the Tennessee Valley Authority. (Courtesy Performing Arts Research Center, The New York Public Library at Lincoln Center.)

Stanislavsky and The Actors Studio

If Brecht's theories seem to be reflected in the work of the Federal Theatre, Stanislavsky's are clearly evident in American acting from the 1930s onward. Americans became aware of Stanislavsky in the early 1920s, when the Moscow Art Theatre toured the United States. Following that visit, some of Stanislavsky's former students founded the American Laboratory Theatre in New York, where they taught his approach to acting. But the upsurge in Stanislavsky's influence owed most to the Group Theatre, founded in 1931 by ex-students of the American Laboratory Theatre and modeled on the Moscow Art Theatre. For the next

The Group Theatre production of Clifford Odets' *Awake and Sing*, 1935.
(Vandamm Collection, Performing Arts Research Center, The New York
Public Library at Lincoln Center.)

ten years, it was probably the most respected theatre in the United States.
Among its members were Lee Strasberg, Harold Clurman, Elia Kazan,
Cheryl Crawford, Stella Adler, Robert Lewis, Lee J. Cobb, and Morris
Carnovsky—the directors, actors, teachers, and producers who would do
most to promote Stanislavsky's system in America.

In 1947, Lewis, Kazan, and Crawford founded The Actors Studio to
provide selected actors an ongoing opportunity to apply Stanislavsky's
system. Strasberg soon became the Studio's director and major teacher.
Awareness of the Studio's work grew quickly after Marlon Brando, a
Studio actor, captured the public's imagination with his portrayal of the
inarticulate, uneducated, and assertive Stanley Kowalski in Tennessee
Williams' *A Streetcar Named Desire* (1947), directed by Kazan. A serious
characterization using substandard speech, untidy dress, and boorish
behavior was extremely unusual at that time, for while low-comedy or
ethnic characters often used such means, serious actors did not. Brando's
impact was enormous. It not only affected acting style but also contrib-

Tennessee Williams' *A Streetcar Named Desire,* 1947. At right, Marlon Brando as Stanley; center, Jessica Tandy as Blanche. Directed by Elia Kazan, setting by Jo Mielziner. (Photo by Eileen Darby.)

uted greatly to the influence of The Actors Studio and the Stanislavsky system in America.

This reputation was further enhanced by Kazan's productions, on which he usually collaborated with the designer Jo Mielziner. Kazan's staging of the plays of Tennessee Williams and Arthur Miller (the two major dramatists of the time) established the production style that dominated the American theatre from the late 1940s until the 1960s. It combined earthy realism in acting and directing with simplified, skeletal settings. It was a style especially suited to the realistic mode then being practiced (in-depth psychological exploration of character, which demanded fluidity of time and place). Let us look more closely at an example.

Death of a Salesman

Death of a Salesman (1949) by Arthur Miller (1915–   ) dramatizes a fundamental conflict in the American consciousness: its tendency to measure success in material terms even as this consciousness upholds love as a major value; as a result, it often mingles these goals, so that approval is withheld from those who have not succeeded materially. Miller has embodied this conflict in Willy Loman's obsessive desire to succeed and his confusion of success with worthiness to be loved.

Willy wants to be liked and admired, and it is his perplexity over the gulf between his accomplishment and his ideal that precipitates the play's action. Because to Willy material success seems so necessary, he believes that his sons cannot love him if he is not successful. He has also conditioned his sons to believe that they do not deserve respect unless they are successful on his terms. Only when Willy understands that Biff loves him even though both are failures, does Willy achieve a degree of insight. Miller has used two characters to represent the poles between which Willy is pulled. Uncle Ben (Willy's brother) epitomizes material success, while Linda (Willy's wife) represents love given unconditionally.

The present action occurs during a twenty-four-hour period (with the exception of the funeral), but the scenes from the past range over twenty years. Past and present flow together as Willy tries to find the answers to his questions: Where did I go wrong? What is the secret of success?

The only unusual structural feature of *Death of a Salesman* is the *flashback* technique, for otherwise the play is organized conventionally in terms of exposition, preparation, complications, climax, obligatory scene, and resolution. Each flashback is carefully introduced by wandering talk, offstage voices, sound effects, music, or some similar cue. Most productions of the play have also used changes in lighting to lead the audience from the present to the past. The flashbacks are carefully engineered so that each reveals only a small part of the past. The outline gradually emerges, remaining incomplete until the climactic moment. In *Death of a Salesman*, psychological realism has replaced external realism, and a greater freedom in dramatic structure has resulted.

By far the most important character in *Death of a Salesman* is Willy Loman. Now sixty-three years old, he is on the verge of a physical and psychological breakdown. All his life he has lied to himself and others out of a desire to believe that he is a success. Recent developments, however, have forced him to see that actually he is a failure, although he cannot see where he has taken the wrong path.

Uncle Ben, who personifies success, in many ways is merely an extension of Willy's personality. He has gone into the jungle and come out rich; thus, he gives a romantic aura to success. Ben also implies that success is bound up with the "law of the jungle," with shady deals and quick-wittedness. Willy, however, wants to triumph on his own terms—as a salesman liked by everybody. Therefore, he can never completely accept Ben's advice, just as he can never give up Ben's ideal. This division is at the root of Willy's character and is seen even in his death,

Miller's *Death of a Salesman* with George C. Scott in the role of Willy. (Inge Morath/Magnum.)

which is a final attempt to achieve material gain and the gratitude of his family simultaneously.

Biff is thirty-four years old but still adolescent in his attitudes. He is irresponsible, a wanderer, and incapable of happiness because of the sense of guilt aroused in him by Willy. From Willy he learned early that the way to success is through lying, stealing, and making powerful acquaintances. But the lure of success has been short-circuited in Biff by his disillusionment with Willy, dating from the discovery of his father's unfaithfulness to his mother. Consequently, Biff rebels against success, flouts authority, and tries to punish his father. Biff has his admirable side, nevertheless, for he has a sense of moral responsibility that his brother, Happy, is totally lacking. It is Biff who finally makes his father see the truth as they both come to understand that love is a gift freely bestowed rather than something earned through material success.

Linda understands from the beginning what Willy and Biff learn during the play: love has no conditions. Because she loves so unconditionally, she cannot understand why Willy commits suicide or why the boys have turned out as they have. Success holds no magic for her.

Happy has inherited the worst of Willy's traits without the saving possibility of love. He is entirely selfish and unfeeling; lying and cheating are integral parts of his nature. He is a materialist and sensualist beyond redemption, but devoid of Ben's vision and strength.

Charley and Bernard have succeeded where Willy and Biff have failed; thus, their principal function in the play is to serve as contrasts. Charley's unconscious commitment to *human* above *material* factors is the key to his happiness, just as the reverse is the key to Willy's failure.

In constructing his characters, Miller concentrated upon sociological and psychological attitudes. His success in creating convincing figures is indicated by the general tendency of audiences to see in the play a reflection of American society.

Miller's ideas about staging *Death of a Salesman* are clearly indicated in the script. Sound is used effectively throughout. Music helps to set the mood and to mark transitions to flashback scenes. Ben has his own special music, played each time he appears; honky-tonk music accompanies Willy's scenes with the Other Woman; music helps to set the locale of the restaurant. The method by which Willy commits suicide is made clear only through the offstage sound of a car driving away.

The continuous presence of the house helps to establish the convention that the flashbacks are fragments of the past and to make clear the simultaneity of the past and the present in Willy's mind. The fragmentary and schematic setting specified by Miller is entirely in keeping with the dramatic techniques, through which the surface is cut away to reveal more clearly the inner reality. *Death of a Salesman* is an excellent example of the modified realism that prevailed in the postwar period.

Artaud and the Theatre of Cruelty

While theatre between the two world wars was varied, most of the best-known dramatists and theatre practitioners concentrated on psychological or social relationships. Like many of his contemporaries, Bertolt Brecht wished to alter socioeconomic conditions that stood in the way of a better life; this goal became increasingly popular during the years of the depression, when economic woes affected most of the world's population. But during these years, another strain of theatre focused on quite different forces, especially those buried deep within the unconscious mind. The most influential exponent of this strain was Antonin Artaud (1896–1948), whose views, like those of Brecht, were not immediately accepted but, again like Brecht's, would become major influences after his death.

Artaud for a time was a member of the surrealist movement, which flourished during the 1920s. Surrealism emphasized one aspect of Freud's teachings: the importance of the subconscious. According to the surrealists, the significant truths are those deeply buried in the psyche and continually suppressed by the conscious mind. To reveal these "truths," then, the conscious mind must be subverted. The surrealists promoted dreams, automatic writing, and stream of consciousness as paths through which images, ideas, and experiences buried in the subconscious could escape the conscious mind's control and surface so that the insights they offered could be experienced. Surrealism made its greatest impact in painting, especially that of Salvador Dali, in which familiar objects are juxtaposed or used in unfamiliar ways, becoming visual metaphors (by establishing relationships not previously recognized) that bring new perceptions. Artaud eventually broke with the surrealists, but his experience with them is important, as was his work on a number of surrealist films.

Artaud's major ideas were expressed in a series of essays collected in *The Theatre and Its Double* (1938). According to Artaud, the theatre in the Western world has been restricted to a very narrow range of human experience, primarily the psychological problems of individuals or the social problems of groups. To Artaud, the most important determinants of human experience are buried in the unconscious, and because they remain buried and unconfronted, they lead to divisions within the person (and between people) and ultimately to hatred, violence, and disaster. He believed that the right kind of theatre could free people from these destructive impulses. As he put it, "The theatre has been created to drain abscesses collectively."

Artaud was certain that his goals could not be reached through appeals to the rational mind (Brecht's approach), since the conscious mind has been conditioned to sublimate the very things that need to be examined. Thus, he argued, it is necessary to subvert the audience's defenses. Artaud sometimes referred to his as a "theatre of cruelty," not because it was physically cruel but because it forced the audience, against its wishes, to confront itself. Because he considered the conventions of the established theatre to be tools of the conscious mind, he proposed to replace them with a "new language of the theatre." He thought that the proscenium-arch theatre created a barrier between performers and spectators, and so he proposed replacing it with a large, undivided space such as would be found in barns, factories, airplane hangars, and warehouses. He wished to have acting areas located in corners, overhead on catwalks, and around the walls so as to place the audience in the midst of the action.

Artaud also wished to do away with scenery altogether and let symbolic costumes or properties suffice. In lighting, he called for a "vibrating, shredded" effect with pulsating changes (comparable to present-day strobe lighting). In sound, he favored great variety, ranging in volume from a whisper to a factory at peak production; he also advocated using the human voice not primarily for speech but for yelps, cries, and varied emotional and atmospheric effects. He considered these innovative conventions means for bypassing the conscious mind. As he put it, "Whereas most people remain impervious to a subtle discourse . . . they cannot resist effects of physical surprise, the dynamism of cries and violent movements, visual explosions, the aggregate of tetanizing effects called up on cue and used to act in a direct manner on the physical sensitivity of the spectators." These new conventions were to be coupled with stories of mythical proportions and implications. The ultimate purpose was to break down the audience's defenses, drag to the surface unconsciously suppressed feelings, and force the audience to face and deal with those things that, if unacknowledged, create hatred and violence.

Artaud's theories were to become major influences on the theatre, especially during the 1960s, when demands were at a peak that society face those forces that had created injustice, repressive social conventions, and wars.

Absurdism

At the heart of Artaud's vision lay a rejection of those conscious standards that had hardened into Western social and artistic conventions. Thus, his attempt to counter accepted practices was another manifestation of the modernist temperament. But his was merely one among many attacks on traditional notions of truth.

The concept of absolute (or verifiable) truth was questioned by Luigi Pirandello (1867–1936), one of the most important of twentieth-century dramatists, in such plays as *Right You Are (If You Think You Are); Six Characters in Search of an Author;* and *Henry IV*. In all of these plays, the dramatic action turns on a question of fact that cannot be resolved because the characters each have their own versions of events in which they have been participants. Thus, Pirandello raises doubt about the possibility of determining truth through direct observation. He concludes that "truth" is personal, subjective, relative, and ever-changing.

During and following World War II, a group of philosophers and dramatists, the existentialists, adopted a more radical version of Pirandello's views. Jean-Paul Sartre (1905–1980), the best-known existentialist, denied the existence of God, the validity of fixed standards of conduct, and the possibility of verifying moral codes. He concluded that since none of the institutions (church, state, society) from which we have taken our standards can prove the necessity of those standards, human beings are "condemned to be free" (that is, deprived of absolute standards, people are condemned to choose individually the values by which they each will live). He further insisted that unquestioning conformity to values established by others is immoral, whereas choosing (and living by) one's own values defines oneself as a moral being. Sartre's views were persuasive because they came at a time when many Nazis were seeking to escape punishment for war crimes by arguing that they were merely abiding by the laws or carrying out the policies of their government. The crucial question was: Which takes precedence, law and policy (no matter how perverted) or individual moral values? Many Nazis were convicted on the premise that the individual should refuse to obey unjust or inhuman (even if legal) demands. This conclusion, which reflects Sartre's, has undergirded the civil disobedience so common since the 1950s in the civil rights movement, demonstrations against the Vietnam war, and other protests against society's injustices.

Sartre was echoed by Albert Camus (1913–1960), whose description of the human condition as "absurd" supplied the label (absurdist) by which a subsequent group of dramatists would be known. Camus concluded that our situation is absurd because our longing for clarity and certainty is met with, and forever thwarted by, the irrationality of the universe into which we have been thrown; we can neither rid ourselves of the desire for order nor overcome the irrationality that stands in the way of order. The only recourse is to choose one's own standards and live by them. Both Sartre and Camus wrote plays that are traditional in structure (the protagonist is faced with a problem, pursues it through a set of complications to a point of crisis, and makes a choice that permits a clear resolution) even though their messages are not.

The absurdists, who emerged in France around 1950, accepted the views of Sartre and Camus about the human condition, but unlike those two writers, they saw no way out, for in such a universe, rational and meaningful choices were impossibilities. Thus, to the absurdists, truth consisted of chaos and lack of order, logic, or certainty. Their plays embodied this vision in a structure that abandoned the logic of cause-and-effect relationships for associational patterns reflecting the illogic of the human situation.

The most important of the absurdist playwrights is Samuel Beckett

Samuel Beckett's *Waiting for Godot* in its first American production, 1956. The actors are Bert Lahr and E. G. Marshall. Directed by Alan Schneider. (Photo by Elliott Erwitt/Magnum Photos, Inc.)

(1906–   ), whose *Waiting for Godot* (1952) first gained international recognition for absurdism. This play, in which two tramps improvise diversions while they wait for Godot (who never arrives), is now one of the best-known plays of the twentieth century. As a group, Beckett's plays suggest the impossibility of certainty about anything. Let us examine one of his plays, both as representative of his work and of absurdist drama.

Happy Days

The story of *Happy Days* (1961) is very simple, almost nonexistent. In the first act, Winnie, a middle-aged woman embedded up to her waist in a mound of earth, passes time by following a daily routine, recalling the past, and attempting to communicate occasionally with her husband,

Willie, who for the most part remains silent and unseen. The second act follows the same pattern. But now Winnie is embedded up to her neck; unable to turn her head, she is uncertain whether Willie is still alive. She has been forced to adapt herself to an altered routine, but she remains cheerful and brave. At the end of the play, Willie crawls up the mound to Winnie, and in joy she sings a song from *The Merry Widow*. There are no complications, crises, or resolutions in the traditional sense. Rather, themes are introduced and developed.

One major theme is the isolation and loneliness of human beings. It is embodied partially in the setting: a mound of earth beyond which one sees an "unbroken plain and sky receding to meet in far distance." It is even more fully embodied in Winnie's entrapment, which throws her back on her own resources, for she can never be certain whether she is communicating with the only other human being within earshot. The setting and Winnie's entrapment create a visual metaphor for the human predicament. As in others of his plays, in *Happy Days* Beckett shows human beings isolated in a symbolic wasteland, cut off from all but the most minimal human contact, passing the time as best they can while waiting doggedly or hoping desperately for something that will give meaning to the moment or to life itself.

The play also suggests that human beings organize their days around routines to convince themselves that they are in control of their lives. That human beings are conditioned to live by routine is reinforced by the bell that awakens Winnie to start her day or whenever she dozes off.

Another theme is the ability of human beings to endure and to consider their lives normal and happy, despite all evidence to the contrary. Winnie never questions why she is buried in the mound, nor does she wonder at her isolation. She apparently accepts her lot as something to be questioned no more than existence itself. Throughout the play, she remains determinedly cheerful, finding something to wonder at in the smallest occurrence and speaking often of her blessings and of the things that will make this another "happy day." Only occasionally does she show a momentary flash of sadness.

The role of Winnie makes great demands on an actress, since she alone must hold the interest of the audience. Unable to move about the stage, the actress must rely on small gestures and stage business; the skillful handling of pauses, volume, tempo, and rhythm; and other means to achieve the variety and intensity normally sought through a much larger range of possibilities. Willie, though essential to the action, has very little to do in sight of the audience. Nevertheless, he must perform with precision if he is to reinforce Winnie's efforts.

In his plays, Beckett has tended increasingly to reduce the scope of action and means to those absolutely essential for projecting his vision.

Irene Worth as Winnie in Beckett's *Happy Days* at the New York Shakespeare
Festival's Public Theatre in 1979. Directed by Andrei Serban. (Photo by
George E. Joseph.)

Many of his late plays have only one character. Because of his methods, audiences and critics have often puzzled over Beckett's intentions. He has said that his plays formulate what he is trying to convey as clearly as he can. Their form, structure, and mood cannot be separated from their meaning. They explore a state of being rather than show a developing action. Perhaps more than those of any other dramatist, Beckett's plays embody the absurdist vision and methods.

In many ways, absurdism extended the relativist view as far as it could go, since it implied that we have no way of proving or disproving the validity of any position. Whereas Brecht suggested that, by examining and weighing arguments, we can arrive at rational conclusions about the changes needed to make the world more just, Beckett suggested that the very notion of rational choice is a delusion. That works embodying such polar visions were often presented in the same theatre for the same audience indicates how varied theatrical experiences had become by 1960.

The American Musical

As the preceding discussion indicates, much drama written between the two world wars depicted a rather grim view of the human condition. But this vision was by no means universally accepted, especially in the musical, which, with its optimistic outlook and visual and aural appeals, was by far the most popular theatrical fare, especially in the United States.

Music has played an important role in theatrical performance in every period. The choral passages of Greek drama were sung and danced; the Italians developed wholly sung opera; and Shakespeare introduced songs into his plays. Even when plays did not use music, some kind of musical entertainment was included on the program. Every theatre had an orchestra that was exploited in various ways at each performance. The eighteenth century introduced a number of popular musical forms—among them ballad opera and comic opera—and the nineteenth century used music to underscore melodrama's action (a convention inherited by film).

During the late nineteenth century, musical comedy began to be recognized as a distinct type. It usually emphasized the romantic appeal of faraway places or exotic situations; the stories were primarily excuses for songs and ensemble choral numbers, often sung and danced by beautiful young women. A major change came around World War I, when ballroom dancing and ragtime music, both then in vogue, were introduced into musicals; with them came more familiar characters and surroundings. Nevertheless, story remained relatively unimportant, serving principally to motivate spectacular settings, songs, dances, and beautiful chorus girls. Not until the late 1920s—in such musicals as *Show Boat*—did story and psychological motivation begin to be important. The new status of the form was recognized in 1931 when for the first time a musical—George Gershwin's *Of Thee I Sing*—won the Pulitzer Prize as the best drama of the year.

By the 1940s, the musical, according to many critics, had become distinctively American and America's most significant contribution to theatre. *Oklahoma* (1943), by Richard Rodgers and Oscar Hammerstein, is often cited as the first work in which music, story, dance (by Agnes DeMille), and visual elements were fully integrated so that all contributed significantly to the dramatic action. Rodgers and Hammerstein solidified this approach in such pieces as *Carousel* (1945), *South Pacific* (1949), and *The King and I* (1951). Their lead was followed by several other composers and authors. Among the most successful post-World-War-II musicals were: *Brigadoon* (1947) and *My Fair Lady* (1956) by Alan Jay Lerner and Frederick Loewe; *Guys and Dolls* (1950) by Frank Loesser; *West Side Story* (1957) by Leonard Bernstein and Arthur Laurents; *Funny Girl* (1964) by Jule Styne; *Hello, Dolly* (1964) and *Mame* (1966) by Jerry Herman; *Cabaret* (1966) by John Kander; and *Sweet Charity* (1966) by Sy Coleman.

After 1968, the musical underwent other changes. The crucial production was *Hair* (1968), with its rock music, barely discernible story, single setting, "hippie" clothing, strobe lighting, and highly amplified sound. This was also the first Broadway production to include nudity and obscene language. A number of pieces using the rock-music idiom followed, among the most successful being *Godspell* (1974) by Stephen Schwartz. Although the older form of musical continued sporadically in such works as *Annie* (1977) by Charles Strouse and *La Cage aux Folles* (1983) by Jerry Herman, after 1970 the musical seemed to lack any clear direction. By far the most successful writer/composer was Stephen Sondheim, who experimented with various approaches: *Company* (1970) had no chorus and used the principal performers in the song and dance sequences; *Pacific Overtures* (1976) borrowed conventions from the Japanese theatre; *Sweeney Todd* (1979) was based on a nineteenth-century melodrama but was operatic in its use of music throughout; and *Sunday in the Park with George* (1983) took its inspiration from a painting by Georges Seurat. All of Sondheim's musicals offered ironic views of human behavior and social values, and avoided the happy endings associated with earlier musicals. Michael Bennett's *A Chorus Line* (1975) was also innovative in its use of the chorus as the principal character and in

Michael Bennett's musical *Chorus Line,* the longest-running production in Broadway's history.' (Photo by Martha Swope.)

its presentational style. Nevertheless, it is often said that the American musical appears to have lost its vitality. Ironically, several of the most popular musicals of the 1970s and 1980s (*Jesus Christ, Superstar; Evita;* and *Cats*—all by Andrew Lloyd-Webber—and *Les Miserables*) were imports from England.

Although one cannot foresee the future of the musical, it seems safe to predict that it will continue to be popular, since its appeals and advantages are so numerous. Its musical and choreographic elements are sources of considerable pleasure in their own right, while certain of its conventions facilitate storytelling. For example, the song lyrics contribute to clarity through their direct statements of emotional response and intention (much as soliloquies and asides did in earlier drama). Under the influence of realism, most spoken drama abandoned such directness, but the musical has continued to use it. Music, through such conventions as the reprise (the repetition of a musical phrase or fragments of lyrics), can also link or recall events separated in time. Furthermore, music assists in condensing time, as when a song or musical passage is used to show quickly a progression of events that in actuality occur over a long period. For example, in *My Fair Lady*, the speech lessons that transform Eliza from a flower seller to a duchess are condensed into one song, "The Rain in Spain." Music additionally establishes mood and builds expectation. Even before the action begins, an overture establishes the general mood of the work to follow, and thereafter music helps to establish the mood and emotional tone of the individual scenes.

Rex Harrison and Julie Andrews in *My Fair Lady* by Lerner and Loewe.
(Courtesy Theatre and Music Collection, Museum of the City of New York.)

A musical usually provides considerable visual stimulation. Scenic, costume, and lighting designers typically are offered wide scope for their talents in musical productions. There is usually considerable variety in time and place and a large cast (often with much doubling). Dance also typically plays a large role, commenting on the action and forwarding the story much as the songs do. Considering all of these appeals, it is not surprising that the musical has long been among the most popular of theatrical experiences. It is also not surprising that audiences have found in the musical an antidote to the dark vision of humanity offered by much twentieth-century drama.

The Contemporary Theatre Experience

10

The contemporary theatre is highly diversified, in large part because of post-World-War-II developments that brought significant innovations especially after 1960. Two of these involved decentralization and subsidization.

Decentralization and Subsidization

By the end of World War II, the live theatre in America was confined primarily to New York and to touring productions that originated in New York. Similarly, in England, the theatre was largely restricted to London, and in France, to Paris. Each of these countries wished to decentralize its theatre by having companies scattered geographically rather than concentrated in one large city. Implementing this goal required money, and the needed financial support came from subsidies.

Subsidization is as old as the theatre. It began with the Greeks and remained the primary means of supporting performances until the Renaissance, when the theatre became essentially a commercial venture. Even thereafter, the king of France provided at least some financial support to all the companies in Paris during the seventeenth century; and it was by his decree that a national theatre—the Comédie Française—was created in 1680. The world's first national theatre, it has continued to the present day and throughout its 300-year history has received governmental subsidies. Seeking to emulate France, then, the Scandinavian countries, Russia, and most of the small German states (Germany was not united until 1870) founded state-subsidized theatres in the eighteenth century. Most of those theatres still survive and are so geographically dispersed throughout northern and eastern Europe that the countries in those areas were not faced, as France was following World War II, with the need to decentralize their theatres.

The Germanic and Scandinavian countries had come to consider state or municipal funding for the arts a cultural responsibility equal to that required for education. (Each of these countries also has privately owned and operated theatres run much like Broadway theatres are in America; they lie outside the pattern discussed here.) While these governments do not underwrite all of a theatre's expenses, they own the theatre buildings and subsidize approximately eighty percent of the theatre's operating expenses. Thus, only about twenty percent of a company's budget comes from box-office receipts, making it possible to keep ticket prices relatively low. The companies usually offer seasons of representative plays from the past in combination with new plays. The theatre staffs (including directors, designers, and actors) are employed on renewable contracts, complete with pension plans and other benefits comparable to those for workers in industry and government. These are the companies and practices that theatre workers in England and America looked to as models.

At the end of World War II, France had four state theatres like those in Germany, but all were located in Paris. In 1947, in an effort to decentralize French theatre, the government began to establish dramatic centers in a number of outlying towns. Subsequently, it helped to finance several "cultural centers" for various arts activities. By 1980, there were eighteen dramatic centers and about fifteen cultural centers, all receiving financial subsidies from the central government.

England, unlike most European countries, had never awarded government subsidies, on the premise that theatre is a business that must be self-supporting. But during World War II, the government began to allocate funds to underwrite performances intended to build the morale of factory workers and military personnel. When the war ended, financial support for the arts was continued, and the Arts Council was created to decide which organizations should receive funds. Government involvement increased after 1948, when Parliament authorized local authorities to devote a percentage of their revenues to the arts. More than fifty cities and towns in Great Britain now subsidize theatres.

Equally important, Parliament authorized the formation of a National Theatre, which, after numerous delays, was inaugurated in 1963 under the direction of Sir Laurence Olivier, one of England's foremost actors. In 1976, the National Theatre moved into its newly completed facilities, the most elaborate in England, with three performance spaces (a thrust-stage theatre, a proscenium-arch theatre, and a flexible theatre). Its varied repertory and overall excellence have made it a major force in world theatre.

Although it does not have the title, the Royal Shakespeare Company is often looked upon as England's second national theatre. Its origins

Stage and auditorium of the Olivier Theatre, one of three theatres in the National Theatre complex, London. (Photo Donald Mill. Courtesy National Theatre.)

can be traced back to the 1870s, when the Shakespeare Memorial Theatre in Stratford became the home of an annual summer festival of Shakespeare's plays. Over the years, this festival grew, until by the 1950s it was presenting plays for about seven months each year. After Peter Hall became its director in 1960, it was given a new charter and name—the Royal Shakespeare Company (RSC). Hall leased a theatre in London as a second base, and therefter the company performed year-round in a diversified repertory that featured Shakespeare but also included some of the most innovative non-Shakespearean productions of the time. Peter Brook, one of the world's finest directors, was associated with the RSC and staged a number of its best-known and most influential productions, among them *Marat/Sade* (which critics labeled an example of Artaud's "theatre of cruelty" and which called public attention to Artaud's ideas for the first time in England and America) and *A Midsummer Night's Dream* (which utilized circus and acrobatic techniques). Since 1968, when Hall left, the RSC has been headed by Trevor Nunn, who, in addition to directing Shakespeare's plays, has come to be known for his staging of musicals (among them *Cats* and *Les Miserables*). In 1982, the RSC moved into elaborate new facilities in London, the Barbican Theatre, while retaining its headquarters in Stratford. The RSC ranks among the world's best companies and is the recognized leader in Shakespearean performance. Like the National Theatre, it owes much to government subsidy. (See the color photos following page 338.)

A third English group, the English Stage Company (ESC), founded in 1956, made its mark by assisting new playwrights. It is considered to have intiated a "renaissance" in English playwriting with John Osborne's *Look Back in Anger* (1956). Prior to this production, the English theatre was devoted primarily to revivals or innocuous, "proper" dramas. Osborne's play, an attack on the English class system and traditional values, was a slap in the face of "respectability." It brought a new audience into the theatre and inaugurated a new school of writers (the "angry young men"). Within a very brief time, the tone of English theatre shifted as the speech and attitudes of disaffected groups brought new vigor to the stage. The ESC, with its willingness to give unknown dramatists a hearing, must be given much of the credit for conditions that have produced an unusual number of outstanding English playwrights since the 1950s.

Off Broadway and Off-Off Broadway

The conviction that theatre must be entirely self-supporting persisted longer in the United States than anywhere else. The government had financed the Federal Theatre during the 1930s, but not because it valued theatre: the project was one among many designed to reduce unemployment. After the Federal Theatre came to an end in 1939, no further government assistance was forthcoming until the mid-1960s. Nevertheless, following World War II, a number of nongovernmental groups sought means to decentralize the theatre.

The first important development began in New York City around 1950. Believing that financial conditions forced Broadway producers to cater almost exclusively to mass audiences, theatrical groups found out-of-the-way buildings where low production costs permitted them to offer short runs of plays not likely to appeal to Broadway audiences. This was the beginning of Off Broadway. Most groups, working in buildings never intended for theatrical purposes, were forced to experiment with spatial arrangements unlike those in Broadway's proscenium houses. Thus, they contributed to the retreat from the picture-frame stage that had long been underway. Off Broadway companies played to small audiences, since theatres holding 200 or more persons had to adhere to fire and safety provisions more stringent than the companies would have been able to meet. Thus, Off Broadway also contributed to the preference for intimate theatres, which (partially owing to television, a medium that became available nationwide around 1950) has steadily increased since World War II.

Off Broadway proved so attractive that about fifty groups performed there during the 1950s. Of these, the most enduring has been the Circle in the Square, which won critical acceptance for Off Broadway when in 1952 it achieved resounding success with Tennessee Williams' *Summer and Smoke*, a failure on Broadway. This company continues to be a major force in Off Broadway theatre.

By the 1960s, Off Broadway had become so successful that theatrical unions insisted on stricter working conditions and higher wages. As a result, production costs rose until the advantages originally offered by Off Broadway largely disappeared. This prompted the development of Off-Off Broadway—in still more out-of-the-way spaces where unions were largely ignored (though most unions eventually approved a special Off-Off Broadway contract with conditions less restrictive than those in Off Broadway contracts). Off-Off Broadway has continued to be the most flexible and diverse venue for productions in New York. As many as 150 groups often are active at the same time.

Of the early Off-Off Broadway groups, the most important was the LaMama organization, founded in 1961 by Ellen Stewart. LaMama provided a place free from restrictions (except those imposed by limited funds) where dramatists could see their plays performed. By 1970, LaMama was presenting more plays each season than all the Broadway theatres combined. Although these plays varied enormously, many were determinedly innovative, defying and altering accepted notions of dramatic effectiveness. This free-ranging experimentation in playwriting also extended to directorial techniques. Tom O'Horgan was the most successful of LaMama's directors. He subsequently directed *Hair*, *Lenny*, and *Jesus Christ, Superstar* on Broadway, using the approach he had perfected at LaMama, which seemingly owed much to Artaud: extensive use of nonverbal vocal sound, extremes in the amplification of sound, highly varied lighting (including strobe), oversized effigies or symbolic stage properties, and the "physicalization" of almost every moment. His productions were colorful and uninhibited. When LaMama toured abroad, it seemed so innovative that it was invited to establish branches in various countries. Its influence, therefore, was not merely American but international.

By 1970, the distinctions between Off Broadway and Off-Off Broadway were so eroded that they were often indistinguishable. (They are differentiated primarily by the type of union contracts under which they operate.) A few of these organizations have been especially important.

Lenny, a musical by Julian Barry based on the experiences of the nightclub comedian Lenny Bruce (especially the controversies created by his comic routines and his personal lifestyle). Note the 15-foot puppets representing popular culture figures, the musicians dressed as bandaged accident victims, the judge (Bruce spent much time in court defending himself against charges of public obscenity), and Bruce's family. Other scenes showed a stained glass window made of bagels and a Mount Rushmore with the faces of Eisenhower, Kennedy, Johnson, and Nixon. Scenery by Robin Wagner, costumes by Randy Barcello. Directed by Tom O'Horgan. (Photo by Martha Swope.)

The Circle Repertory Company has produced most of Lanford Wilson's plays as well as new works by a number of other playwrights. The Manhattan Theatre Club and the American Place Theatre have also been especially helpful to playwrights. But the most influential of these organizations is the New York Shakespeare Festival Theatre, headed by Joseph Papp. After a modest beginning in the 1950s, Papp persuaded municipal authorities to let him stage plays free of charge in Central Park. This program became so popular that in 1962 the city built the Delacorte Theatre there. In 1967, Papp acquired the former Astor Library on the edge of Greenwich Village and transformed it into the Public Theatre with five performance spaces. Not only does this or-

The Delacorte Theatre in Central Park, New York, built for the New York Shakespeare Festival under the direction of Joseph Papp. The production is Shakespeare's *King John*. Setting by Douglas Schmidt. At the top, apartment houses beyond the park. (Photo by George E. Joseph.)

ganization maintain a heavy production schedule, composed of Shakespeare's plays, revivals, and new plays, it also provides performance space for many other companies. Several of its productions, most notably *A Chorus Line* (the longest running production in Broadway's history), have moved to Broadway. Papp is probably the most influential figure in New York's theatre today.

Regional Theatres

While Off Broadway and Off-Off Broadway were diversifying New York's theatre, decentralization was underway elsewhere. During the

1950s, a few companies—in Washington, Houston, San Francisco, and elsewhere—struggled to survive and ultimately received a major boost from the Ford Foundation, which in 1959 made large grants to several companies that had succeeded in winning local support. Thus, the major impetus for decentralization in America came from private rather than governmental subsidy. Decentralization received another boost in 1963 with the opening of the Guthrie Theatre in Minneapolis. Tyrone Guthrie, then one of the world's foremost directors, had selected Minneapolis over established theatre centers as the site for his company, and funds had been raised locally to construct a new building for it. The publicity surrounding this theatre seems to have aroused considerable interest (or envy) in other cities. Something approaching a boom in the construction of new arts centers followed. Today, almost every major city in the United States has such a complex.

Such changed treatment of the arts, however, probably owes most to the legislation that in 1965 established the National Endowment for the Arts. Like Britain's Arts Council, the NEA dispenses federally appropriated funds to arts groups throughout the United States. The federal government also encouraged states to establish their own arts councils, and in turn the states encouraged cities and communities to form such councils. Today, federal, state, and numerous local governments appropriate funds to subsidize the arts. The sums are not large, but they mark a major change in American attitudes toward the arts.

Tax laws have also encouraged corporations and foundations to make grants to arts organizations. Such grants and subsidies made it feasible for resident theatres to be established throughout the country. The companies are linked through the Theatre Communications Group (TCG), which was created in 1961 with funds supplied by the Ford Foundation. TCG serves as a centralized source of information for about 200 non-profit, professional theatres and provides a forum where common problems can be discussed and solutions sought.

The existence of so many theatres may make theatrical conditions appear more stable than they are. Few of these theatres could exist without grants from governments, corporations, or foundations. Unlike European theatres, for which ongoing support is assured, American theatres receive grants for periods ranging from one to five years. They cannot be sure that the grants will be renewed, and they must devote much of their time to developing grant proposals and soliciting support. Unable to make long-range plans, they must be constantly prepared to alter their programs if requested support is not forthcoming. Continued existence cannot be taken for granted. Nevertheless, it is subsidization that has made possible the decentralization of the American theatre.

Most regional theatres offer a season of plays that intermingle revivals of classics with new works. They do not seek long runs and can afford to take greater chances than Broadway does. Therefore, they have become very attractive to playwrights who wish to avoid reshaping their plays to fit the demands of Broadway producers. Several (among them the Actors Theatre of Louisville and the Yale Repertory Theatre) now offer festivals of new plays each year. Such developments have altered the character of Broadway. Formerly the primary producer of new plays in America, Broadway now seldom produces new works but instead chooses among those that have been successful in regional, Off Broadway, Off-Off Broadway, or British theatres.

Ethnic Theatre

After 1960, the American theatre became more diversified in still other ways, including concern for various ethnic groups that had been ignored or treated stereotypically in mainstream drama. This trend reflected a recognition that the "melting pot" view of America had not worked for certain subgroups, especially those whose distinctive skin color or ethnic features (Black, Asian, American Indian, and some Hispanics) had made it impossible for them to be absorbed into the mainstream.

Since the largest of these groups was black, it is not surprising that black theatre would eventually be more extensive than that of any other group. Among the first black playwrights to win critical acclaim was Lorraine Hansberry (1930–1965), with *A Raisin in the Sun* (1959) and *The Sign in Sidney Brustein's Window* (1964). Since the first of these developed most of the themes that would be significant in subsequent black drama, let us look at it more closely.

A Raisin in the Sun

A Raisin in the Sun was the first play by a black woman to be presented on Broadway, where it won the New York Drama Critics Circle Award. In many respects, *A Raisin in the Sun* is traditional, since, like many American dramas, it focuses on the family unit and its dreams. Its straightforward story is developed through a clear cause-and-effect sequence of exposition, complications, climactic reversal, and dénouement. It is divided into three acts, all of which take place in the same setting. Its style is realistic, with a generous sprinkling of humor in a primarily serious plot.

A Raisin in the Sun tells the story of the Younger family: Lena, or Mama, a dignified woman in her sixties; Beneatha, her twenty-year-old daughter, who hopes to become a doctor; Walter, Lena's thirty-five-year-old son, a chauffeur; Ruth, Walter's wife, who does domestic work for white women; and Travis, the ten-year-old son of Walter and Ruth. All live together on the South Side of Chicago in a cramped two-bedroom apartment. There is only one small window for light and air, and the bathroom is shared by all the families on the floor. Though the space is cramped and the furnishings worn, the apartment is clean and neat; thus, the setting reflects its occupants, who may be poor but are not without pride.

The opening scene of the play introduces the family as it anticipates the arrival of a check of $10,000, the life insurance of the deceased father. To the family the money represents a chance to realize its dreams, the most crucial of which are Beneatha's desire to attend medical school and Walter's to become a businessman. In the second scene, the money arrives, but by that time friction is beginning to tear the family apart. The opposition of Mama and Ruth to Walter's plan to invest in a liquor store alienates him so fully that Ruth, upon discovering that she is pregnant, makes an appointment to have an illegal abortion.

In Act II, Scene 1, Mama, in an attempt to bring her family together, makes a down payment of $3500 on a house that can accommodate everyone comfortably. But it seems certain that trouble lies ahead because the house is located in an all-white neighborhood. Nevertheless, everyone except Walter is overjoyed, for the house will permit the family to escape its present environment.

Not until a few weeks later (in Act II, Scene 2), when the family is packing to move, does Mama come to understand Walter's deep need to be recognized as a man capable of making his own decisions. As a result, she designates him head of the family and gives him the remaining money, with the stipulation that $3000 be put aside for Beneatha's medical education. As the scene closes, Walter, overjoyed, is envisioning his future as an executive.

Act II, Scene 3, brings the play's major reversal. Karl Lindner, a white representative of the neighborhood into which the Youngers plan to move, arrives to tell the family of resentment against them and to offer them a sum substantially higher than they have paid for the house. They indignantly refuse. Then Walter learns that one of his prospective business partners has absconded with all the remaining money, including that intended for Beneatha's education. The act ends in despair and recrimination.

At the opening of Act III, Beneatha is cynical and ready to abandon her dreams. The family is reconciled to remaining in the apartment. But

The original production of Hansberry's *A Raisin in the Sun*. The actors are
Claudia McNeil, Sidney Poitier, and Diana Sands. Directed by Lloyd Richards.
(Photo by Joseph Abeles. Courtesy Performing Arts Research Center, The
New York Public Library at Lincoln Center.)

Walter slips out and calls Lindner, intending to sell the new house and
play the role of "polite darky" for a white-dominated world. When his
plan is revealed, the family is horrified. Lindner arrives just as the moving van does (no one has canceled it), but Walter, forced by Mama to
talk to Lindner with Travis present, cannot bring himself to go through
with his plan. Recovering his pride, he tells Lindner that the family wants
no trouble but insists on moving into its new home. As the play ends,
the move is underway. Thus, although the family has realized few of its
dreams, it has grown in understanding, dignity, and unity.

Many features place *A Raisin in the Sun* firmly within the American
tradition, but others set it apart. Perhaps most significantly, all of the
characters except Lindner are black, and their experiences introduce
almost every major theme that would be developed extensively by later
black playwrights.

The play's title is taken from a work by Langston Hughes, *Montage of a Dream Deferred:* "What happens to a dream deferred? / Does it dry up / Like a raisin in the sun?" Almost everything that happens in the play is related to this concept of the "dream deferred." We learn that Mama and her husband were part of the "great migration" during the early twentieth century, when blacks moved north in search of better conditions. But Walter and Beneatha are more concerned about what remains to be done than about what has been accomplished. Of the two, Walter is the more embittered, for as chauffeur to a rich white man, he daily sees wealth that lies beyond his reach. Consequently, he all too eagerly leaps at the chance to acquire his own business as the first step toward riches, which he considers the key to happiness. Beneatha, on the other hand, wants to become a doctor so she can ease human suffering, although it is injustice that ultimately bothers her. In one sense, then, Walter represents the selfish and materialistic approach and Beneatha the altruistic and idealistic approach to realizing the dream deferred.

A closely related issue is integration versus separation of the races. This theme is dramatized in part through Beneatha's two suitors—the rich American student George Murchison and the Nigerian student Jo-

Mama and Walter in *A Raisin in the Sun,* as performed at the Goodman Theatre, Chicago, in 1983–84 to commemorate the play's twenty-fifth anniversary. Directed by Thomas Bullard. (Photo by Lascher. Courtesy Goodman Theatre.)

seph Asagai. George is interested only in maintaining the security his family has achieved, and he is completely unconcerned about the injustices suffered by other members of his race. Joseph, on the other hand, arouses Beneatha's interest in her African heritage, questions the way she dresses (he calls her straightened hair "mutilated" and he brings her a Nigerian robe), and asks her to return to Africa with him. Above all, in the final act Joseph counters Beneatha's disillusionment by arguing the necessity of living one's dream despite suffering and disappointment.

The theme of integration and separation is also dramatized in the purchase of the house, but the response of whites makes it part of a still larger theme—the exploitation of blacks by whites who still deny blacks full civil rights. Walter's desperation stems in part from his awareness of how many more opportunities are open to white men of his age, and Mama's purchase of the house in a white neighborhood comes about only because "them houses they put up for colored in them areas way out all seem to cost twice as much as other houses." Although there is little direct denunciation of whites (even Lindner is treated objectively), a contrast is continuously implied between exploited blacks and exploiting (or uncomprehending) whites.

Another theme concerns growth and maturity. It is reflected in part by Walter's sense of being denied his manhood both by his mother and by the jobs open to him. The theme is also developed through the repeatedly expressed longing for sunlight and garden space and most forcefully by Mama's spindly plant, which she nurtures in the feeble light of the window, just as she has nurtured her family's spirit through all vicissitudes. As the play ends, after everyone has left the apartment, Mama returns for her plant. This final moment implies that neither the plant nor the family will "dry up like a raisin in the sun," but will thrive and grow. The deferred dream still has not been fully realized, but another step has been taken toward its fulfillment.

Although *A Raisin in the Sun* deals specifically with black life, it is universal in its appeal. Whatever one's race, one can sympathize with the dreams, disappointments, and triumphs of the Younger family. Without bitterness, the play makes clear the injustices done to blacks; and while it offers few solutions, it shows the human consequences of the problems. Its enduring strength is indicated by the numerous productions of the play on its twenty-fifth anniversary in 1984.

Black playwrights and producing organizations have multiplied since *A Raisin in the Sun* was first produced. Many of the plays and musicals seen on Broadway in recent seasons have been by black authors or have featured black performers. Among the most effective of these has been August Wilson's *Fences* (Pulitzer Prize, 1987), starring James Earl Jones. In addition, black companies are now found throughout the country.

August Wilson's *Fences* at the Yale Repertory Theatre, 1984–85. Directed by Lloyd Richards. (Photo by William B. Carter. Courtesy Yale Repertory Theatre.)

Of these groups, the most important has been the Negro Ensemble Company, which during the past twenty years has produced some of the finest plays seen in New York, among them Charles Fuller's Pulitzer Prize-winning *A Soldier's Play*.

Although it is the most extensively developed, black theatre is only one example of the use of theatre to reflect the life of minorities in America. Others who have developed their own plays and theatres include various ethnic groups (among them Hispanic-Americans, Asian-Americans, and Native Americans), women, and homosexuals.

The Living Theatre

During the 1960s, the Living Theatre, more than any other organization, epitomized rebellion against established authority in all its aspects:

values, behavior, language, dress, theatrical conventions. Founded in New York in 1946 by Judith Malina and Julian Beck (1925–1985), it was originally devoted to poetic drama but during the 1950s was influenced increasingly by Brecht, Artaud, and anarchist theory. In 1963, charged with failure to pay taxes, it was forced to cease performing; from 1964 to 1968, the group toured Europe, gaining a large and devoted following, especially among disaffected young people. In 1968, it returned to the United States with the repertory it had created during its exile. The most characteristic of the Living Theatre's pieces was *Paradise Now,* which began with actors circulating among the spectators and denouncing strictures on freedom. Thereafter, both spectators and actors roamed the auditorium and stage indiscriminately; many removed all of their clothing. The performance continued for four or five hours, with scenes proceeding simultaneously throughout the theatre. Actors elicited opposition from spectators and then overrode it, often by shouting obscenities or even spitting on opponents; at the end, the company sought to move the audience into the streets to continue the revolution begun in the theatre. Its aggressive behavior, combined with its anarchistic politics, won the Living Theatre enormous notoriety and called attention forcefully to several changes in theatrical conventions.

Among these changes, two of the most important were the introduction of obscene language and nudity. While obscene language and simulated nudity were common features of early Greek comedy and late Roman mimes, neither had been considered acceptable in legitimate theatrical performances since the fall of Rome. But during the 1960s, the rebellion against accepted rules that had begun with the civil rights movement gradually passed over into other areas, until almost every regulation or standard was challenged. Demonstrations, then common, usually involved public violations of some rule or law considered unjust or unwarranted. Continued assaults on the conventions of polite behavior, and the inability of authorities to prevent violations, won acceptance (or tolerance) of behavior previously considered unacceptable.

Nudity and obscenity first came to Broadway in 1968 in *Hair,* an engaging musical that promoted tolerance of alternative lifestyles. In contrast, the Living Theatre abused (and made clear their intention of destroying the society represented by) the middle-class spectators who had paid to see their performances. Rather than being entertained, such spectators were subjected to physical and political intimidation. Why, then, did audiences attend? Novelty and notoriety probably attracted many, while others probably came out of sympathy for the group's political goals and defiance of authority, while still others probably applauded the group's use of the theatre for purposes other than diver-

Paradise Now as conceived and performed by the Living Theatre. This scene is from the third of the eight "rungs" through which the action progressed. (Photo by Ken McLaren. Courtesy World of Culture, Ltd.)

sionary entertainment. By 1970, however, the group had lost most of its following. Still, many things it had promoted remained, and by the 1970s, though the limits of permissibility were somewhat vague, almost any subject, behavior, or manner of speaking was potentially acceptable for theatrical use.

Although the most radical, the Living Theatre was by no means the only group that sought to change society through theatre. The Bread and Puppet Theatre (founded in 1961) used both actors and giant puppets to enact parables (often based on the Bible) to denounce war and the futility of materialism. Beginning in 1966, the San Francisco Mime Theatre performed satirical pieces promoting civil rights, equality for women, and various other causes. El Teatro Campesino (founded in 1965 by Luis Valdez) originally used skits to support grape pickers during a strike in California, then went on to perform plays encouraging pride in the heritage and accomplishments of Mexican-Americans.

Grotowski

All of these groups had extremely limited resources. Most never controlled a theatre and performed wherever they could. They were what Jerzy Grotowski, director of the Polish Laboratory Theatre in Wroclaw, Poland, called "poor theatres." Grotowski made his a poor theatre, not out of necessity but out of conviction. He believed that most contemporary theatres had gone astray by depending on the technological devices of other media, especially movies and television. Rather than a technologically rich theatre, then, he sought to create one in which everything not absolutely necessary had been eliminated. He hoped in this way to rediscover the essence of theatre. Eventually, he concluded that only two elements are essential: the actor and the audience.

Because of the actor's centrality, Grotowski devoted much of his attention to actor training. He coupled intensive physical exercises with training designed to remove psychological barriers, and sought to develop the voice as an instrument capable of exceeding all normal demands. Ultimately, he wished actors to surpass so completely the spectators' own capabilities as to arouse a sense of magic. In performance, actors were permitted to use only those costumes and makeup that were essential to the action; they were not allowed to change costumes merely in order to indicate a change in role or psychological condition; properties were minimal; there was no scenery in the usual sense; any music had to be produced by the actors themselves. In other words, the performers, deprived of all nonessential and technological aids, had to depend entirely on their own resources.

Grotowski worked in a space that was completely rearranged for each production. At first, he tried to involve the audience directly in the action, but he concluded that this only made spectators self-conscious. He then concentrated on creating spatial relationships among spectators and actors that would permit them to interact unself-consciously. For example, in *Doctor Faustus* the action supposedly occurs during a banquet on the night the Devil is to claim Faustus' soul. The audience, seated at long tables on or around which the action occurs, was asked merely to respond as people might at such a function. For *The Constant Prince*, the theatre was arranged so that all the spectators looked down into an arena or hospital teaching theatre, where psychic surgery is taking place. (See the illustration on page 252.)

Grotowski viewed the theatre as the modern equivalent of a tribal ceremony. He searched in scripts for ritualistic archetypal patterns independent of time and place and then developed them (often completely

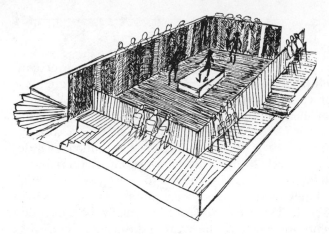

Arrangement of the performance space for Grotowski's staging of *The Constant Prince*. (Copyright 1968 Jerzy Grotowski and Odin Teatrets Forlag. Courtesy H. Martin Berg.)

changing the original script) so as to make both actors and audience confront themselves. Thus, his goals resembled Artaud's, though his means differed markedly. After 1970, Grotowski moved away from theatre into other explorations.

During the 1960s, Grotowski became a major influence on theatre in Europe and America. His company performed widely, and he did workshops for various other theatres and for some of the world's best directors. His influence was further disseminated through his book *Towards a Poor Theatre* (1968). Although few others attempted to restrict resources so severely as he did, many groups adapted his appoach to staging and actor-training.

The Open Theatre

The Open Theatre (1963–1974), based in New York and headed by Joseph Chaikin, was also a "poor" theatre. Like Grotowski, Chaikin concentrated on the things he considered essential to theatre. But his work was grounded in contemporary theories of role-playing and theatre games (based on the work of Viola Spolin). Above all, he was concerned with "transformation"—that is, a constantly shifting reality in which the same performer assumes and discards roles or identities as the context changes. Thus, reality was treated not as fixed but as ever-changing. The implications were that, because reality is not absolute, we can reshape ourselves into the kind of people we would like to be. The Open Theatre's scripts, which sought to reveal the fundamental moral and social patterns buried beneath troubling contemporary events or preoccupations, usually evolved in its workshops in close collaboration with its playwrights. Through improvisations, the actors explored the potentials of situations and characters; the playwright then chose and shaped the discoveries that seemed most effective. The Open Theatre's most successful collaborations were with Jean-Claude van Itallie in *The Serpent* and Megan Terry in *Viet Rock*. Such collective creation was a distinctive feature of several theatres during the 1960s and 1970s.

Environmental Theatre

In 1968, Richard Schechner, after examining various contemporary practices, including those of the "poor" theatres, sought to describe the conventions of a new approach to performance that he labeled "environmental theatre." Some of these conventions affect the performance space. Schechner writes: "The event can take place either in a totally transformed space or in a 'found' space." In other words, space may be adapted until it is appropriate to the action, or a suitable space not requiring alteration may be found (for example, a production depicting war as a game might be performed in an unaltered gymnasium or playground). "All the space is used for performance; all the space is used for the audience." That is, how the space can be used is entirely flexible; any part may be used by performers or spectators, or they may be intermingled.

Other conventions relate to what is performed. "A text need be neither the starting point nor the goal of a production. There may be no text at all." This means that, unlike traditional performances (which seek to embody a pre-existing dramatic text), in environmental theatre performance takes precedence over text and may be entirely improvisational, thereby leaving no text behind once the performance ends. Additionally, during a performance, "focus is flexible and variable." This means that a production need not be shaped by the assumption (typical of traditional theatre) that all spectators must be able to see the same thing at the same time. Instead, there may be a number of scenes going on simultaneously in various parts of the space; each spectator is then free to choose which he or she will watch. Taken together, these attributes indicate a blending of categories long treated as distinct: theatrical space and nontheatrical space; performer and spectator; stage and auditorium; text and performance; sequentiality and simultaneity. Thus, environmental theatre challenged notions long considered essential parts of the theatrical experience. It did not eliminate the traditional views, but it did suggest how easy it is to confuse the theatre's essence with its prevailing conventions.

The Performance Group's production of Brecht's *Mother Courage*. Note the audience-performer relationship. (Courtesy Richard Schechner and the Performance Group.)

Multimedia, Happenings, and Performance Art

Even as the "poor" theatres were restricting their means, other theatres were emphasizing the very elements (electronic and spectacular) that the poor theatres were seeking to eliminate. Living as we do in what is often called "the electronic age," it seems inevitable that the theatre would exploit electronic devices. Marshall McLuhan argues that, as electronic media have replaced the printed page as our primary mode of communication, we have become increasingly adept at processing multiple and concurrent stimuli (for example, we watch events going on halfway around the world as we carry on conversations in our living rooms). Thus, he concludes, we no longer require that visual messages be received in orderly sequence or that there be only one focal point at a time.

Electronic media have also affected the theatre by creating the need to make place as transformable as it is in film and television. One result has been to cut down on the amount and specificity of built scenic elements (because of the time required to shift numerous, heavy units). Another has been to encourage experimentation with "multimedia"— combinations of elements from several media. The major multimedia experimentation has been done by the Czech designer Josef Svoboda. Around 1958, Svoboda began work on two projects—*Polyekran* (multiple screen) and *Laterna Magika*. Polyekran used filmed images entirely but sought to overcome the "visual paralysis" of a single screen by hanging screens of differing sizes at various distances from the audience, projecting different images on each, and changing the images at varying time intervals—thus creating a dynamic visual field and giving the audience a choice of images to watch. Laterna Magika used motion pictures in combination with live actors. Often the performers in the film and on the stage were the same, and at times a live performer seemed to emerge from the screen.

In 1959, Svoboda began to incorporate elements from these experiments into stagings of regular drama. He also experimented with movable scenic units and platforms in an attempt to make the stage instantly transformable both in configuration and visual appearance. Some of his productions also used closed-circuit television, with scenes performed in a studio miles from the theatre projected on screens hung above a stage on which live scenes were under way. Closed-circuit television was also used to overcome one drawback of live theatre by projecting close-up images of the actors' faces on screens during moments of crisis. Such experiments by Svoboda and others popularized a number of practices: using projected still pictures on multiple screens as a scenic background; interjecting filmed sequences into the dramatic action; varying the volume, direction, or quality of stereophonic sound; using closed-circuit television in multiple ways.

These developments are related to others stimulated by dissatisfaction among visual artists with restrictions imposed by the media in which they worked (for example, the two-dimensional and static qualities of

Josef Svoboda's designs for an adaptation of Maxim Gorky's novel *The Last Ones* at the Prague National Theatre. Note the different scenes of live actors and a projected image of the character seen at extreme right. Directed by Alfred Radok. (Photo copyright by Jaromír Svoboda.)

painting). They sought to overcome the restrictions by gluing three-dimensional objects to paintings, attaching motors to sculptures to make them move, using light to alter the appearance of objects, and so on. Out of such experiments eventually came *happenings*, pioneered by the painter Allan Kaprow, who created his first happening in 1959. For this event, a gallery was divided into three compartments, in each of which were several types of visual art and a number of persons performing assigned tasks repeatedly, while images were projected on various surfaces and as taped music and sound effects were played. All those who attended were expected to carry out instructions handed them as they entered. Subsequent happenings varied considerably, but most had common characteristics with implications for theatrical performance: (1) Happenings were multimedia events that broke down the barriers between the arts and mingled elements from several. (2) Happenings shifted emphasis away from creating a product to participation in a process. (3) Because there was no single focus, emphasis shifted from the artist's intention to the participants' awareness; each participant, as partial creator of the event, was free to get from it whatever he could; no single "correct" interpretation of the artwork was possible or sought. (4) Happenings did much to undermine professionalism and disciplined technique, since anyone could participate and there was no right or wrong way of doing anything.

Perhaps because they were so anarchistic, happenings soon passed out of vogue. But the artistic impulse that had prompted them remained and resurfaced in *performance art,* which differed from happenings in at least three important ways: Performance art usually makes clear distinctions (1) between performer and spectator and (2) between performance space and audience space, and (3) it is usually carefully structured and performed. Typically, it does not tell a story, although there may be spoken passages, vocal sound, and musical accompaniment. It juxtaposes images and actions (often precisely arranged and controlled) that have multiple implications (even definite meanings) for the artist; nevertheless, the spectators are left free to make whatever associations and find whatever patterns are most meaningful to them. The major creators of performance art have come from the visual arts, dance, or music; they have been attracted to performance art in part because it disregards boundaries among the arts, thereby greatly expanding their means of expression. Theatre people have tended to find performance art less attractive, perhaps because theatre has always used elements from various other arts and because performance art tends to de-emphasize story/text and to use performers not as actors but as objects to be manipulated spatially. Among current performance artists, two of the most admired are Martha Clarke and Meredith Monk.

Postmodernism

The ideas and practices of environmental theatre and performance art contributed significantly to what is now called *postmodernism,* an imprecise label but one that suggests major changes in modernism. Most of these changes are symptomatic of the breakdown of clear-cut differentiations. With modernism, the crucial battles had involved absolute versus relative standards and values. The triumph of relativism, as we have seen, meant that artists did not all have to work in the same style, but each could choose the one that seemed most appropriate. In the theatre, directors came to consider each production a problem requiring its own stylistic solution. In addition, numerous new styles (symbolism, expressionism, surrealism, etc.) enlarged the available choices. Nevertheless, once a stylistic choice was made, the director sought to shape every aspect of a production to fit that mode. In other words, under modernism, once a mode was chosen from among the multitude of possibilities, it imposed a set of demands and expectations comparable to those of an absolutist vision. Thus, realism, expressionism, epic theatre, and the other styles each had their own conventions and rules. Under modernism, then, categories, though numerous, were clearly differentiated.

Postmodernism collapsed categories by ignoring the differentiations. This did not occur overnight, nor are all categories always collapsed, for within individual postmodernist works some categories may be collapsed while others remain quite distinct. Taken as a whole, art is still more nearly modernist than postmodernist. Nevertheless, postmodernist trends have accelerated since the 1960s. We have already considered some manifestations: collapsing the boundaries between the arts, as in performance art and multimedia; breaking down the barriers between spectator and performance space, as in environmental theatre; removing distinctions between audience and performers, as in happenings. Another sign is the blurring of distinctions between dramatic forms, as in absurdist and much other contemporary drama. Still another is the mingling of elements from disparate styles, periods, or cultures. Postmodernist architecture is recognizable in large part by its combination within single buildings of varied styles and forms from the past. Similarly, several directors have utilized conventions borrowed from several cultures. Since the early 1970s, Peter Brook has been exploring the theatrical conventions of cultures in an attempt to arrive at a "theatre language" that will bridge cultural and language barriers.

Many aspects of postmodernism come together in the theatre pieces of Robert Wilson, among them *A Letter to Queen Victoria* (1974), *Einstein on the Beach* (1976), and *CIVIL warS* (1983–84). In these pieces, Wilson borrows from several media, cultures, and historical periods. They are essentially visual pieces (though there is much music and sound) in which juxtaposed visual images appear, disappear, reappear, grow, diminish, metamorphose. The connections among these images are not always readily apparent. Time is an important element; typically, it is slowed until movement becomes almost imperceptible, permitting every detail to be experienced; different elements within a scene may progress at different tempos. While some of Wilson's pieces include spoken portions, they do not have scripts in the traditional sense. Text and performance cannot be separated (as they can be with a traditional play script). Most of the pieces are very long, from four to twelve hours; one lasted seven continuous days and nights. *CIVIL warS,* intended for the Olympic Arts Festival in Los Angeles in 1984, was created in segments, one each in West Germany, the Netherlands, Italy, France, and the

Robert Wilson's *CIVIL warS*. The tall figure at right is Abraham Lincoln. At left, an owl, and at stage level, King Lear. From a performance at the American Repertory Theatre (Cambridge, MA). Design and lighting by Robert Wilson with Tom Kamm and Jennifer Tipton. (Photo by Richard Feldman.)

United States. It included such disparate historical figures as Abraham Lincoln, Karl Marx, Frederick the Great, Voltaire, and a Hopi Indian tribe, as well as wholly invented present-day characters. It was intended to reflect all types of conflicts (public and private) that interfere with human relationships. Utilizing twelve languages, it was not meant for an audience from a single culture.

According to Wilson, there is in his pieces nothing to understand, only things to experience, out of which the spectators each construct their own associations and meanings. Many spectators have been infuriated or bored by the length and lack of clear-cut intention in Wilson's pieces, but a large number of critics consider him the most innovative and significant force in today's theatre.

Trends in Directing

Postmodernism has influenced directing in several ways, perhaps most significantly by altering attitudes about the director's relationship to the playwright and the script. Under modernism, it was usually assumed that the director's task was to translate the playwright's script faithfully from page to stage. This assumption incorporated another: that the director can determine a playwright's true intentions through a meticulous analysis of the script. Postmodernists, on the other hand, argue that there can be no single "correct" interpretation of a text because words do not convey precisely the same meanings to everyone. Furthermore, once a work is finished, its creator's statements about its meanings have no more authority than anyone else's, since it is the text and not its author that elicits the responses and interpretations. Such arguments free a director to interpret a script as he or she thinks appropriate even if this interpretation is at odds with the playwright's. They also encourage directors to discover new implications in well-known plays. In fact, since the 1960s, directors have often been judged by the novelty (sometimes more than by the aptness) of their interpretations. Some directors have argued that a number of classics have come to be so revered that we can see them with a fresh eye only in radical (even shocking) reinterpretations.

Peter Sellars' production of Handel's *Orlando*, an eighteenth-century opera, with the action relocated to the Space Age and several characters transformed into astronauts. (Photograph by Richard Feldman.)

Most radical reinterpretations have involved plays by authors long dead. But in the 1980s, certain directorial decisions have elicited strong objections from living authors. Samuel Beckett threatened to withdraw his *Endgame* from production at the American Repertory Theatre in Cambridge, Massachusetts, because the director, JoAnne Akalaitis, had relocated the action in a derelict subway station and made one of the leading characters black. In another instance, Arthur Miller threatened to sue the Wooster Group, a New York company directed by Elizabeth LeCompte, to prevent its use, in a piece called *L.S.D.*, of portions of *The Crucible* to illuminate contemporary attitudes about LSD by juxtaposing them against attitudes about witchcraft in colonial New England as shown in Miller's play. The Wooster Group had previously incorporated portions of Thornton Wilder's *Our Town* into a piece called *Route 1 & 9*, where they were juxtaposed with a black vaudeville routine and a pornographic film. The group's idea was to comment on Wilder's idyllic view of America in which ethnic groups and sex are ignored, as are the industrial wastelands though which run the two highways that give the piece its title.

Beckett's *Endgame* as directed by JoAnne Akalaitis. Setting the play in an abandoned subway station and using a black actor made Beckett threaten to withdraw the play from production. (Photo by Richard Feldman.)

These productions raise important questions. Can playwrights protect their work from distortions? Are directors justified in reshaping (even radically altering) a playwright's script to suit their own vision even if it distorts the playwright's intentions? What are the implications of demanding that directors adhere to playwrights' notions about how their works should be staged? Should the playwright's preferences be honored even after audience tastes and staging conventions have changed? What is the place of the script in performance (does it guide everything else, or is it as malleable as acting, scenery, lighting, etc.)? What is the role of the director (principal creative artist, as in film, or servant of the script)? None of these questions can be answered definitively, but recent trends have created heated debate about them.

Contemporary Playwrights

Like the other theatre arts, playwriting has contributed to postmodernism. Absurdist dramatists, among them Beckett, did so by choosing as their primary theme the inconclusiveness of all interpretations of human experience. The Open Theatre, the Wooster Group, Robert Wilson, and performance artists also contributed to it by breaking down many of the distinctions between playwriting and performance. No doubt others have contributed in still other ways. Nevertheless, many playwrights, perhaps because they work in relative isolation and because most still produce scripts in the traditional sense, have continued the modernist traditions. Only a few of today's dramatists can be discussed here.

Among English playwrights, some of the most admired are Bond, Pinter, Stoppard, Shaffer, and Hare. Edward Bond has long been one of England's most controversial playwrights because of such plays as *Saved* (1965), in which a baby is stoned to death onstage. Largely because of the battles fought over his plays, Parliament abolished censorship in 1968. All of Bond's plays, which include *Lear, Bingo,* and *War Plays,* depict a world in which the absence of love and compassion have bred a callousness so complete that violence is considered normal.

Harold Pinter is often considered England's greatest living dramatist. His plays, which include *The Birthday Party, The Homecoming,* and *Old Times,* share common characteristics: all the events could occur in real life (sometimes the situations and dialogue suggest naturalism); nevertheless, they create a sense of ambiguity and menace, primarily because the motivations of the characters are never clarified. Pinter believes that people use speech to conceal more than to reveal their attitudes and feelings. Thus, pauses and silence are essential to his plays, because during them the unspoken subtext is glimpsed.

Edward Bond's *Saved* at the English Stage Company (London) in 1965. During this scene, the baby in the carriage is stoned to death. (Photo by Zoe Dominic.)

Tom Stoppard won recognition first with *Rosencrantz and Guildenstern Are Dead* (1967), a play reminiscent of Beckett's, focusing on two minor characters from *Hamlet* who sense that important events are going on around them but who die without ever understanding the action of which they have been an insignificant part. In subsequent plays, among them *The Real Inspector Hound, Jumpers, Travesties,* and *The Real Thing,* Stoppard has continued his highly theatricalized comments on the nature of reality.

Peter Shaffer has been extremely successful on the stage and in films with *Equus* and *Amadeus,* in both of which a competent professional must cope with a character whose strength comes from sources beyond the reach of rationality; both envious and repelled, the professional is forced to reassess his own being but with no satisfying results.

David Hare began his career in the "fringe" theatres (comparable to Off-Off Broadway) that sprang up in England following the abolition of censorship in 1968. His early plays, such as *Slag,* focus on the deprivations and emptiness of working-class life. His later plays, among them *Plenty* and *A Map of the World,* concern ineffectual intellectuals. Hare's literate, often witty plays depict a severely flawed world seemingly beyond repair.

Among America's dramatists, some of the most admired are Wilson, Mamet, and Rabe.

Lanford Wilson began his career in the Off-Off Broadway theatre. He has written an extremely large number of plays, among them *Balm in Gilead, Hot L Baltimore, Talley's Folly* (Pulitzer Prize, 1980), *The Fifth of July,* and *Angels Fall.* The story line in these plays is minimal; the focus is on character relationships and the eventual revelation of hidden feelings, disappointments, and hopes. Wilson's compassionate treatment of the misfits and rejects of society marks him as one of the most humane of contemporary playwrights.

David Rabe wrote most of his early plays in response to the Vietnam War. *The Basic Training of Pavlo Hummel, Sticks and Bones,* and *Streamers* all show the price exacted by violence and war, which embody the rejection of other more humanizing impulses. His recent *Hurlyburly,* set in Hollywood, treats characters who apparently are indifferent to the casual cruelties they inflict on each other. The moral void suggested by this

Rabe's *Streamers* performed at Lincoln Center, New York. Directed by Mike Nichols. (Photo by Martha Swope.)

play probably reflects Rabe's perception of contemporary American society.

David Mamet, who began his career in Chicago, has written a number of plays, among them *American Buffalo* and *Glengarry Glen Ross* (Pulitzer Prize, 1984), about the debasement and distortion of human beings by the materialistic goals of American society as epitomized in its business dealings. Others of his plays, among them *Sexual Perversity in Chicago*, treat the inability of people to make personal commitments and establish satisfying relationships.

Since the 1960s, women playwrights have gained greatly increased acceptance. Among the most successful have been Norman, Henley, and Churchill. Marsha Norman has written primarily about loss of belief in self and others. *Getting Out* concerns the problems of a woman leaving prison, while *Traveler in the Dark* treats a surgeon's despair about his life. Norman's most successful play, *'night, Mother* (Pulitzer Prize, 1983), shows a woman preparing for and ultimately committing suicide. Beth Henley, in such plays as *Crimes of the Heart* (Pulitzer Prize, 1981), *The Miss Firecracker Contest,* and *The Lucky Spot,* has written primarily about complex, often bizarre relationships in small Southern towns. Caryl Churchill, an English playwright, has written primarily about the effect

Beth Henley's *Crimes of the Heart* at the Alley Theatre, Houston, 1984. From left to right, Meg, Lenny, and Babe. (Courtesy Alley Theatre.)

of socioeconomic forces on human relationships. *Top Girls* contrasts famous women of the past (who recall the price they paid for asserting themselves in a male-dominated world) with a group of present-day women (still trapped in a male world). *Fen* shows female farmworkers seeking to cope with low wages and unsatisfying lives. Her most popular play has been *Cloud 9*, which with great humor explores how stereotyping social forces determine the sexual roles people adopt.

Of all contemporary playwrights, Sam Shepard has been among the most prolific and provocative. He began his writing career in 1964 in the Off-Off Broadway theatre, and for many years thereafter he turned out a large number of plays, among them *Chicago*, *Mad Dog Blue*, and *The Tooth of Crime*, without revising the scripts because he considered it dishonest to change what he had originally written. In the mid-1970s, he altered this view and since then has written his most successful plays, including *Curse of the Starving Class*, *Buried Child* (Pulitzer Prize, 1979), *True West*, and *A Lie of the Mind*. Although there is much variety in Shepard's work, a number of motifs recur: attempts to escape or deny the past; the cowboy and the West as basic American myths; the family as a battleground; and characters caught between empty dreams and an insubstantial reality. Let us look at one of his plays as an example of contemporary drama.

Fool for Love

Fool for Love was first performed in 1983 at the Magic Theatre in San Francisco under Shepard's own direction. This production was subsequently moved to New York, where it ran for several months to high critical praise. The play has also been performed by several regional professional companies, and made into a film.

Fool for Love is a compact play. The action, involving only four characters, takes place in a single room and, according to Shepard, "is to be performed relentlessly without a break." The basic outline is simple: Eddie returns to May after an unexplained absence, swears that he loves her and will never leave again, and then, after a brief stay, slips away without warning. It is this pattern—apparently endlessly repetitive—that the play explores. It is the pattern not only of Eddie's and May's relationship but also that of their father and his wives—a compulsive, seemingly uncontrollable attraction, so intense and overpowering that it cannot long be endured, leading to unannounced departures, long absences, and unpredictable returns. In *Fool for Love*, this pattern is embedded in a gradually revealed and somewhat sensational story of multiple families (the Old Man's) and incest (Eddie's and May's as half-brother and half-sister, products of the Old Man's double life).

While the story told in *Fool for Love* is clear, the implications are complex. As in most of Shepard's plays, in *Fool for Love* many of the implications are grounded in myths about America, especially those relating to the West and the cowboy. The myth of almost unlimited American space has encouraged the idea that problems can best be dealt with by leaving them behind and moving on to another place. It also implies the dream of fulfillment in some new, still-unexplored location. While this myth has its positive side, it can also suggest rootlessness, temporariness, and the substitution of fantasies about future possibilities for facing present realities. All of these are suggested by *Fool for Love*. The motel room in which the action is set is a visual embodiment of rootlessness. Furthermore, all of May's possessions apparently can be thrown into one suitcase, and Eddie's are kept in his truck.

The cowboy in many ways sums up the myth of the West, but Eddie is a rodeo cowboy, completely divorced from the land. In several of his plays (including this one), Shepard suggests that the West depicted in American myth no longer exists (perhaps never did), but that it remains

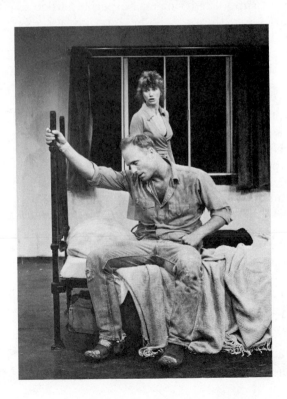

Sam Shepard's *Fool for Love* at the Circle Repertory Company, New York, 1983. Ed Harris as Eddie; Kathy Whitton Baker as May. Directed by Sam Shepard. (Photo by Gerry Goodstein.)

Fool for Love **267**

a potent fantasy. The failure to distinguish between fantasy and reality undergirds much of *Fool for Love*. Fantasies about love have afflicted both the Old Man and Eddie: both have believed that their women will wait happily at home while they themselves go away without warning and return when ready; ultimately, the Old Man chose fantasy over reality, since dealing with real women became more than he could handle. Early in the play, the Old Man asks Eddie to look at an invisible picture of a woman he identifies as Barbara Mandrell: "That's realism. I am actually married to Barbara Mandrell in my mind." And at the end of the play, he says of the same invisible picture: "That's the woman of my dreams. . . . And she's mine. She's all mine. Forever." This fantasy creature makes no demands and has no expectations.

Shepard probably may wish to suggest that true love makes no demands, since when he published *Fool for Love*, he preceded the text with the following quotation: "The proper response of love is to accept it. There is nothing to *do*." But the characters in *Fool for Love* cannot merely accept love; they demand it, and they feel cheated if they believe what is owed them is given to another. May threatens violence to both Eddie and the Countess; the unseen Countess vents her rage through violence; and Eddie projects an aura of suppressed violence, especially when a potential rival appears. Throughout the play, Eddie and May also express frustration, guilt, and resentment at their own inability to fulfill others' expectations, and it is implied that the Old Man finally gave up both his families because of the same feelings. The only time he leaves his chair is upon hearing that Eddie's mother committed suicide when she found out about his double life. Love, then, makes fools of those who wish to own and control loved ones. It becomes a sadomasochistic game that no one wins. It is simultaneously obsessive and destructive. The one character who deviates from this pattern is Martin, who seems indifferent to, perhaps incapable of, love. He is an island of calmness and sanity, though an uninteresting one.

That Shepard is not attempting to write a wholly realistic play is indicated in several ways. The Old Man is both present and absent. He is a visual reminder of the ongoing pattern the play examines, both observer and participant, one who has deliberately embraced fantasy because it is safe, though in doing so he has cut himself off from those he supposedly loves. Furthermore, the incestuous relationship of May and Eddie is symbolic as well as actual; their compulsions are a form of inbreeding that perpetuates a pattern.

Shepard also treats the setting as partially symbolic. He insists that the walls and doors should be wired so that contact with them will reverberate throughout the theatre. This sound becomes a type of punctuation and emphasis. The walls are also treated as more than mere walls.

During the early part of the play, May and Eddie hug the walls, sometimes clinging to them as if for protection, at other times treating them as boundaries that they simultaneously seek to maintain and wish to break. Thus, sound and setting are at times projections of the characters' frustrated desires.

Overall, both the realism and symbolism in *Fool for Love* are important only as they support or reflect the underlying pattern. The failure to resolve the action is an indication that the pattern will continue, that, in fact, it may be inherent in human nature and not merely an attribute of these particular characters in this particular situation.

Epilogue

In the preceding chapters, we have looked at several varieties of theatrical experience. All of these are important, but they are not exhaustive. Several others from the theatre's long past might have been selected, and as time goes by, those with which we are now familiar will give way to new ones. We can only speculate about what the future will hold, since accurate prediction requires the ability to foresee the course of events. Nevertheless, we can be reasonably sure that change will occur, and we should not oppose change, since the theatre can be vital only if it remains a significant reflection of the society within which it exists.

Part III

THEATRICAL PRODUCTION

As we have seen, theatrical conventions and practices vary widely from one period to another and from one society to another. So far, however, we have been looking at the theatre retrospectively and primarily from the viewpoint of the audience in an attempt to understand how theatrical experiences vary. We need now to examine how the theatre functions today.

What follows, then, is an account of the purposes, principles, materials, and working methods of each of the theatre arts—that is, the varied processes involved in the creation of a production. The principal focus is on typical procedures, although important variations are noted. Among the topics explored are: types of theatrical spaces and how they influence production; the elements and principles of design used in all the theatre arts; and the work of producers, directors, actors, and designers (scenery, costume, and lighting). Taken altogether, these topics provide an overview of theatrical production today.

Theatrical Space and Production Design

11

Since the essence of theatre lies in the interaction of performers and audience assembled in the same place at the same time, the physical space in which a performance occurs is an important element in the theatrical experience. Like other elements, the theatrical space can be organized in several ways, each with its own potentialities and limitations.

The Influence of Theatrical Space

The nature of the theatrical space influences both audience response and how production elements are used. First, the degree of formality acts as an influence. An elaborate theatre building with carpeted lobbies and auditorium, fixed comfortable seating, and complex equipment creates a different set of expectations than does a theatrical space improvised in a warehouse, where the audience sits on the floor, wooden platforms, or folding chairs, and in which the equipment is minimal. The former suggests refinement, permanence (including continuity with the past), and extensive resources; it may lead to expectations of sophisticated design, skilled acting, and polished productions. The latter suggests roughness, temporariness (perhaps a deliberate break with tradition), and make-do resources; it may lead to expectations of experimentation and the need for imagination to supply what can only be suggested. Similarly, an indoor theatre usually seems less festive than an outdoor theatre.

Second, the size of the theatrical space exerts an influence. Very large spaces make it difficult for all members of the audience to see and hear all that the performers are doing or saying; small details are apt to be lost; consequently, stage business may be simplified or exaggerated, and spectacle may be given increased emphasis. More intimate spaces permit subtlety in the use of voice, gesture, and facial expression; precision of detail in dress and properties can be conveyed. Intimate spaces are now generally preferred over large ones, in part because close-ups and sound tracks in television and film have conditioned audiences to expect readily visible and audible detail. The influence of size on the total theatrical experience accounts for many of the differences among theatres of the past and present. For example, a Greek theatre holding 15,000 persons demanded conventions quite different from those used in today's theatres intended for a few hundred persons.

Third, the arrangement (or configuration) of theatrical space is an important influence. Not only does it define the physical relationship of the performer and the audience, it also determines how production elements can be handled. There are four basic physical arrangements: (1) The acting area may be placed at one end of the space, with all the spectators facing it; this has long been the most common arrangement, the picture-frame stage. (2) The acting area may be surrounded on two or three sides by the audience; this is the arrangement used with a thrust or open stage. (3) The acting area may be completely surrounded by the audience; this is the configuration used with the arena stage (or theatre-in-the-round). And (4) the relationship of performer to audience may be flexible and variable. Spectators and actors may be intermingled in multiple playing and seating areas; the arrangement may change from one production to another or even during the same performance. The place of performance may shift, as when scenes are played continuously or at various sites along a route of procession (as in medieval theatre or in some contemporary street theatre); there may even be a different audience for each scene or at each site, although the basic configuration of the theatrical space may not have changed.

Overall, then, theatrical space creates an environment that influences the theatrical experience. Let us look more closely at the typical configurations and their influences.

The Proscenium-Arch Theatre

Probably the most familiar type of theatre is still one with a raised stage framed by a proscenium arch, although other types have become increasingly common. In the proscenium theatre, all audience seating faces the stage; all the seats may be on the same level (though usually with the floor raked upward toward the rear to ensure a view of the stage), or there may be one or more balconies. In the proscenium

Proscenium-arch theatre at Pennsylvania State University. It includes an elevator to raise or lower a segment of floor at the front of the stage; when level with the stage floor, this segment becomes acting space; when level with the auditorium floor, it may be used for audience seating; when lowered below auditorium level, it serves as an orchestra pit. The auditorium is steeply ranked to ensure good sightlines. (Courtesy Pennsylvania State University Theatre.)

theatre, the stage is designed to be seen from the front only. This affects the director's use of actors in creating stage pictures, of movement, gesture, and business; and of devices to achieve emphasis and subordination. It also affects the actors' bodily positions, their use of voice and speech, and all other aspects of their performance. Since the stage action is oriented in one direction, the designer may utilize three sides of the stage for the scenery, entrances, and exits. The scenery may be as tall as the designer wishes, and may consist of few or many units. There is only one basic restriction: the view of the audience must not be blocked.

The lighting designer need be concerned with giving three-dimensionality to actors and objects only as dimension is perceived from the auditorium.

The proscenium stage is usually equipped with a curtain that may be used to conceal or reveal the playing space (although nowadays the front curtain is used infrequently). The stage ordinarily is rigged so that drapes or scenic pieces can be hoisted into the space above the stage or lowered to stage level; there is usually offstage space on either side to permit the shifting and storage of scenery. There also may be other machinery for shifting scenery, such as hydraulic lifts (on which portions of the stage are mounted, thus permitting them to be lowered or raised—in other words, elevator stages), or turntables (which permit portions of the stage to be revolved—in other words, revolving stages). Such complex machinery is not common because of its cost.

In the proscenium theatre, the action and scenery are usually farther removed from the audience than in other types of theatres. There may be an orchestra pit or forestage between the first row of seats and the acting area. Since scenery and costumes typically are not viewed at close range, they may be less precisely detailed than in other situations.

The Thrust Stage

In a theatre with a thrust stage, the seats are usually arranged around three (or occasionally two) sides of a raised platform. The thrust stage brings the audience and performers into a more intimate relationship than in the proscenium theatre, since a greater proportion of the spectators are closer to the action than is possible in a proscenium theatre of the same size. Since it is usually seen from three sides, the acting area is a more three-dimensional space than the proscenium stage; therefore, the director, actors, and designers must seek to project in three directions simultaneously rather than one.

The thrust stage discourages realistic spectacle of the type made possible by the picture-frame stage. Its use of scenery must be restricted. Tall units must be kept to the rear of the platform so as not to interfere with sightlines. Although some thrust stages are backed by an area equipped with features typical of a proscenium stage, extensive use of scenic effects there tends to divide audience attention between the action on the forestage and scenic or lighting effects on a rear stage. Most thrust theatres make no provision for flying scenery, drops, or curtains above the main platform, although lighting instruments are mounted in recesses in the ceiling above the stage. As a rule, furniture, properties,

Thrust stage at the Guthrie Theatre, Minneapolis. Built in 1963 and designed by Tyrone Guthrie and Tanya Moiseiwitsch, the theatre seats 1441 persons with no one more than 52 feet from the center of the stage. (Photograph by Robert Ashley Wilson. Courtesy Guthrie Theatre.)

and scenic units are shifted by hand. Some furniture or properties may be set on wagons (platforms on wheels) and moved on and off the stage from the rear of the platform. A few thrust stages have some portions mounted on hydraulic lifts, and there may be several traps in the stage floor. But all onstage units must remain simple so as not to interfere with audience sightlines.

The Arena Stage

The typical arena theatre has no stage as such (that is, there is no raised platform). Rather, an open space is left at floor level in the middle of the auditorium. In some arena theatres, the floor of the performance area can be raised or lowered in segments so as to provide variety in levels or to differentiate locales. The seating is usually a bleacherlike arrangement on four sides of the acting area. In many theatres of this type, the seats are not permanently installed, and the configuration may be varied at will.

The arena theatre provides a three-dimensional playing area. Therefore, the director, actors, and designers must be concerned with expressiveness from every angle. The costumed actors, lighting, furniture, and properties are much more important than scenery. The scene designer may use a few open structures, such as trellises and pavilions, through which the audience can see, but ordinarily must depend on furniture and properties. Provision is seldom made for flying scenery, although a few architectural pieces are sometimes suspended overhead. Occasionally, multileveled settings are used, but they must be constructed so that the audience can see the action on all levels clearly. Screens for projections are sometimes hung at various spots over the acting area, over the audience, or around the walls (the same image may be projected on different screens simultaneously so that all members of the audience can see it), but as a rule the set designer must suggest locale, period, mood, and style with a few touches.

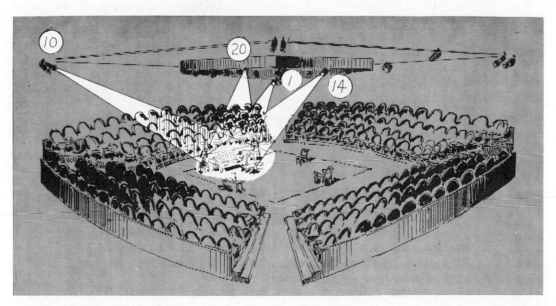

Arena stage, showing the audience-actor relationship, use of scenery, and mounting positions for lighting instruments. (Parker, Smith and Wolf, *Scene Design and Stage Lighting*, 5th ed. Courtesy Holt, Rinehart and Winston.)

Since there is no curtain, all changes are made in full view of the audience or in the dark. As a rule, all shifting is done by hand. Many arena theatres have passageways running under the seating and opening onto the acting area. These serve as exits and entrances for actors and as ways of getting scenic units or properties on and off the stage. Most arena stages are relatively small. Thus, they are usually intimate in feeling but make special demands on staging, since all elements are viewed and must communicate from every angle.

Flexible Space

In modern times, the intermingling of performers and audience has occurred primarily only since the 1960s. This arrangement usually requires a large open space without fixed seating or stage. Thus, the areas used by the performers or by the audience can be varied from one production to the next or even during the course of a single performance. In this type of arrangement, different scenes are often performed at various places within the space simultaneously. Therefore, unlike most theatrical performances, which aim to have all members of the audience see and hear the same things at the same time, the intermingled arrangement may use multiple focus. Thus, some spectators may be watching one scene while others are watching another, or spectators may be able to choose which scenes they will watch, moving about in the space in order to see the scene that has attracted their attention. Sometimes the spectators participate in the action and are asked by the performers to move about or to assist with some task. In other instances, the distinctions between performers and spectators remain clear and the space each group occupies remains distinct; in still others, the entire space becomes both acting area and spectator space.

Such theatres normally do not utilize scenery, but there may be posters, banners, or a few props. The actors often wear casual street clothes; and lighting is often minimal. The emphasis is on the immediacy of the experience or breaking down the barriers between audience and performer.

Beginning in the 1960s, there was a movement to reject theatre buildings altogether. Some argued that, like museums and concert halls, theatres tend to discourage all except a cultural elite. These innovators sought instead to take performances into parks, streets, coffeehouses, and other places where theatrically unsophisticated spectators might discover the theatre. Instead of a building, they advocated the use of "found" space—either adapting a production to fit into existing areas or altering existing areas to fit the needs of productions. The variations were numerous, but they all involved one or more of the four basic theatrical types. Still, the experiments with performance spaces remind us that theatre does not require a permanent structure built especially for it.

Auxiliary Spaces

In addition to the performance space, theatre buildings usually have auxiliary spaces. Several of these are intended primarily to serve the audience—box office, lobby, rest rooms, corridors, exits, and refreshment stands. Others are spaces for theatrical personnel.

The amount of work space provided in theatres varies widely. A well-designed, self-contained theatre (one that has facilities for preparing productions as well as performing them) will include the following: a scene construction shop (with space to store equipment and materials), painting facilities, an area for assembling scenery, sufficient offstage space for storing and shifting scenery during performances, and permanent storage space for scenery not in use; a property room near the stage, and another area for the permanent storage of furniture and bulky props; a costume shop; laundry, dyeing, cleaning, and pressing facilities, and an area for permanent storage of costumes; a work space for lighting personnel, a storage area for lighting equipment, a room to house the lightboard, and a lighting booth for the controlboard operator during performances (ideally with full view of the stage); a number of large rehearsal rooms; a number of dressing rooms, each with makeup facilities (unless a separate makeup room is provided); adequate showers and rest rooms for the actors and crews, and an area (the *green room*) where all the actors and crew members can assemble to receive instructions or relax; space to house sound equipment and from which to operate it; and adequate office space.

Using the Theatrical Space

Normally, in planning a production, little is done to shape the audience and its space. Most directors accept that the audience space of the theatre in which they will be working is fixed—as is the case in the majority of theatres. While directors must take into account the auditorium's size, shape, sightlines, acoustical properties, and the physical relationship it creates between audience and performers, they tend to view these factors as given and unchangeable circumstances. Directors may try to predict what the makeup of the audience will be and how it is apt to respond, but for the most part they conceive of the audience members as reactors who come to see a product created for them. Still, some theatrical spaces are designed so their overall configuration and audience-actor relationship can be altered from one production to another. In these instances, directors may shape the audience space as they consider best for their production.

Jerzy Grotowski made audiences an integral part of his production concept. For each production, he had a specific number of spectators in mind (never more than one hundred), and he would permit no more than that number to attend. He also sought to make the audience participate in the action unconsciously. In his production of *Doctor Faustus*, Grotowski organized the space like a banqueting hall. The audience, treated as friends invited to share Faustus' last meal before his soul is claimed by the Devil, sat at the tables, while the action took place on, under, and around the tables. The German director Peter Stein has staged a number of productions in film studios or gutted and rearranged theatrical spaces. In his production of Ibsen's *Peer Gynt*, all of the seats in a conventional proscenium-arch theatre were removed to clear the floor space for the dramatic action. New bleacher-style seating was erected along the sides, leaving an area some 70 feet long on which scenic units, representing the various locales of the action, were erected. The actors moved from one location to another much as in a medieval outdoor theatre. Stein's *Peer Gynt* required two full evenings to perform. (See p. 54.) The Living Theatre often encouraged the audience and actors to use the same space indiscriminately, thereby forcing some spectators to become unwilling participants in the action.

But these are atypical approaches. Normally, the director lets others (through publicity, news releases, and other means) attract as large an audience as possible for the space being used for the production.

Production Design

Each production has an overall design, made up of many parts. As we have seen, the size of the theatrical space and the spatial relationship of audience and spectators affect how the director, actors, and designers conceive the total design and the means each may use to realize the design for the audience. (How each theatre artist works will be discussed in subsequent chapters.)

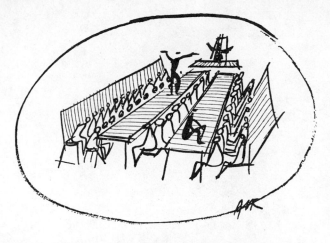

Grotowski's arrangement of space for *Doctor Faustus*. The dark figures are performers, the lighter figures spectators. Faustus is seated at the smaller table at top. (Copyright 1968 by Jerzy Grotowski and Odin Teatrets Forlag. Courtesy H. Martin Berg.)

The total theatrical design addresses only two of the spectators' five senses: hearing and sight. Hearing is addressed primarily through the sound of the actors' voices and sometimes through music or sound effects; therefore, a large proportion of the director's and actors' work is devoted to conveying relationships, motivations, emotions, ideas, and meaning through the skillful handling of dialogue. Perhaps even more effort goes into the elements directed to sight. Although we normally think of visual design only in terms of scenery, costumes, and lighting, directors and actors also are concerned with visual design. How the actors are grouped on stage, how much space they use, and how they relate to the setting, costumes, and properties create visual compositions that communicate quite apart from the spoken dialogue. Thus, almost all theatre artists should be concerned with the elements and principles of design. Although in discussion these elements and principles may sound abstract, they are manifested concretely (either effectively or ineffectively) in every aspect and in every moment of a theatrical performance. One of the challenges of production arises from the need to coordinate individually designed parts (acting, scenery, costumes, lighting) so as to create a harmonious whole.

The Elements of Visual Design

All visual design uses the same basic elements—*line, shape, space, color, texture,* and *ornament.*

Line defines boundaries and thereby permits us to perceive shape and

Setting by Ruddi Barch for Goethe's *Iphigenia in Tauris*. Note the use of curved lines and the repetition of forms to create a strong focal point suggesting a vortex or "black hole." (Courtesy German Information Center.)

form. There are two basic kinds of line—straight and curved—but these may be combined to form zigzags, scallops, and other variations. The dominant lines of the performance space (with the scenery in place but without performers) are horizontal (the floor and any overhead masking) and vertical (the upright scenic units). This basic pattern may be varied by the addition of furniture, ramps, steps, and platforms. In performance, other lines are created through movement and by the placement of the actors in relation to each other and to the scenic elements. The costumes worn by the actors have their own lines created by the silhouette of garments and by darts, seams, ornamentation and other features that result in visible lines.

Line is often said to evoke identifiable responses: straight lines connote stability; curved lines, grace; zigzags, confusion. In scenery, two lines that move farther apart as they rise vertically may generate a feeling of openness, whereas lines that come closer together may create a sense of oppression. Thus, line is important in creating mood and atmosphere as well as in defining shape.

Shape and *space* are closely related and are frequently treated together as a single element—*mass*. While line has only direction or length, mass involves three dimensions. It identifies shape (square, round, oblong) and space (height, width, and thickness).

The stage may be thought of as a hollow cube that can be organized or altered in a variety of ways. Scenery may outline or limit the space. So may light or the actors' movement. Like line, shape and space may be used to affect audience response. An effect of compression may be achieved through the use of thick, horizontal forms overhead (such as a low ceiling with thick beams), while a sense of openness and grace may be achieved with narrow, vertical, and pointed forms (such as thin tall columns and high Gothic arches). Mass is also reflected in the overall shape of costumes and furniture, the space they occupy, and in the way a director groups or isolates actors. Perhaps the most effective means of revealing, concealing, or altering apparent mass is lighting, which through its direction and intensity can create or eliminate those contrasts that let us perceive shape and dimension.

Color may be described in terms of three basic properties: *hue, saturation* or *intensity,* and *value. Hue* is the name of the color (red, green, blue, etc.). *Saturation* or *intensity* refers to the relative purity of a color (its freedom from its complementary hue or "grayness"). *Value* is the lightness or darkness of a color—its relation to white or black. A color that is light in value is usually called a *tint,* while one dark in value is called a *shade.*

Colors are classified as *primary, secondary,* or *intermediate.* The *primary* colors are those that cannot be created by mixing other colors, but from which all other colors are derived. The primary colors in pigment are yellow, red, and blue. The *secondary* colors—orange, violet, and green— are created from equal mixtures of two primary colors. The *intermediate* colors are mixtures of a primary with a secondary color. Colors may be arranged around a wheel to indicate their relationships. Those opposite each other on the wheel are called complementary, those next to each other, analogous. Colors may further be described as warm or cool. Red,

COLOR WHEEL

Diagram showing the arrangement of colors around a wheel.

orange, and yellow are warm; green, blue, and violet are cool. Almost any combination of colors may be used if saturation, proportion, and value are properly controlled.

Mood and atmosphere depend much on color. Many people believe that light, warm colors are more likely to evoke a comic response than are dark, cool colors. Some color combinations are considered garish, others sophisticated. Designers, therefore, may use color to create the appropriate mood and atmosphere and to establish the tastes of the characters who inhabit the settings or wear the costumes. Color can also point up the relationship among characters through the colors of their garments. Color can be used to make some characters stand out and others fade into the background. As with mass, lighting is one of the most important means of controlling color, since it can enhance, distort, or reduce apparent color in scenery, costumes, makeup, and all the other elements.

Texture may help to elicit the desired response through its smoothness, roughness, shininess, softness, or graininess. Some plays seem to demand rough textures, others smooth. Such qualities as sleaziness, fragility, or richness depend much on the textures (actual or simulated) of settings, costumes, and (by analogy) acting.

Ornament includes the pictures hung on walls, decorative motifs, wallpaper patterns, moldings, and similar details in settings. It is one of the chief means for achieving distinctiveness. In costume, ornament includes ruffles, buttons, fringe, and lace. Ornament can be used to indicate taste or the lack of it. Too much ornamentation or too many kinds.of ornamentation may indicate lack of restraint or impart a sense of clutter. Accessories, such as canes, swords, purses, and jewelry, may also be considered ornaments. In acting, gesture and stage business (the amount and complexity, relative simplicity, or fussiness) serve much the same function as ornament in visual design.

The Principles of Visual Design

In applying the elements of design, certain artistic principles must be used if the results are to be effective. The principles of design are *harmony, variety, balance, proportion, emphasis,* and *rhythm.*

Harmony creates the impression of unity. All of the parts of each setting or costume should be harmonious, and the various settings and costumes should be related so that all are clearly parts of a whole. If monotony is to be avoided, however, *variety* is needed. Similarly, the director seeks both harmony and variety through the choice of actors and through use of movement and gesture.

Balance is the sense of stability that results from the distribution of the parts that make up the total picture. There are three basic types of balance. Perhaps the most common is axial, which is achieved by the apparent equal distribution of weight on either side of a central axis. This type is especially pertinent to the proscenium stage, which may be thought of as a fulcrum (or seesaw) with the point of balance at the center. Axial balance is achieved if the elements placed on each side of the central line appear equal in weight. Apparent visual weight is not the same as actual weight, since a large light-colored object may appear to weigh no more than a small dark-colored object, and a small object near the outer edge may balance a large object near the center. A second type of balance, radial, is especially important on arena and thrust stages because they are viewed from several angles. Radial balance is organization that radiates in every direction from a central point. A third kind of balance is usually called occult. It is especially pertinent to flexible and variable staging, in which there may be no readily discernible axis or center. Occult balance results from the relationship among unlike objects and of mass to space.

Balance, especially axial, may also be thought of as symmetrical or asymmetrical. Symmetrical balance means that if an object or space is divided down the middle, each side mirrors the other. Most costumes (especially before ornaments or accessories are added) are symmetrical. Complete symmetry in a stage setting creates a sense of formality and order, whereas asymmetry, which depends on irregularity, may create a sense of informality or casualness. In performance, the stage picture is constantly shifting because of the movement of the actors, so directors must be especially aware of balance and how it is affected by what they are doing.

Proportion involves the relationship between the parts of an object and the parts that make up the total picture: the scale of each element in relation to all the others; the relationship among shapes; and the division of the space (for example, the length of a dress bodice in relation to the skirt). Proportion can create the impression of stability or instability, of grace or awkwardness. Furniture that is too large in proportion to the size of a room may give a cramped feeling; furniture that is too small may create a sense of meagerness. Our perception of beauty or ugliness depends in large part on the proportion of parts. In costume, the manipulation of proportion can do much to change an actor's appearance.

All designs need a focal point, or center of *emphasis*. Directors are constantly seeking to focus attention on what they consider most important and to subordinate the things of lesser concern. A well-

Josef Svoboda's design for *Oedipus the King*. Note the strong emphasis on horizontal lines. The repetition of line creates rhythm through progression; it also creates unity, within which variety is achieved by interrupting the lines with platform spaces at left and upper right. The setting also creates a feeling of solidity and mass through proportion. This production was staged at the Prague National Theatre in Czechoslovakia. (Courtesy Kai-Dib Films International.)

composed scene or design will direct attention to the most important point immediately and then to the subordinate parts. Emphasis may be achieved in several ways, among them line, mass, color, texture, ornamentation, contrast, and movement. The setting may make one area of the stage more emphatic than others; a costume may use emphasis to draw attention to an actor's good points and away from defects; and movement within an otherwise still picture will always attract the eye.

Rhythm is the factor that leads the eye easily and smoothly from one part of a design to another. All the elements of design may be used for rhythmic purposes. Lines and shapes may be repeated; the size of objects or the amount of movement may be changed gradually so as to give a sense of progression; gradations in hue, saturation, and value may lead the eye from one point to another; changes or repetitions in texture and ornament may give a sense of flow and movement; and the movement of the actors may increase or diminish in tempo.

Sound in Design

Not only visual appearance but also sound is an essential part of the total production design. Sound in the theatre may be divided into three basic categories: vocal, musical, and sound effects. Of these, the sound of the actors' voices is usually the most important, for it is through what the characters say and how they say it that we assess situations, motivations, and responses. Voice may also be used to sing or to create a variety of sounds that do not involve words. Music may be a necessary feature in a theatrical production, as in musicals, or it may be incidental, as optional additions to establish mood or to enliven an occasion. Sound effects may be realistic (doorbells, alarm clocks, breaking glass, thunder, etc.) or wholly abstract (sounds with no recognizable origin, used to punctuate the action of a nonrealistic play or to underscore a theme or establish a mood).

Sound has a number of controllable properties: *pitch, volume, direction, duration,* and *quality.* The same sound may be produced on pitches that range through several octaves. In the theatre, pitch is probably most important as it relates to the speaking or singing voice, but even a doorbell and other sound effects have pitch. Thus, it is possible to choose voices and other sounds for pitches that create the desired effects. Volume is the relative loudness of sound. Any sound can be produced at any volume, and the volume can be controlled either through the natural capacity of the instrument (the human voice, trumpet, etc.) or through electronic means. In the theatre, it is often necessary to lower the volume of some sounds and increase the volume of others so as to achieve the desired balance. For example, the audience may need to understand what characters are saying, even though they are speaking against the noise of a passing train. In large theatres, it is often difficult for actors to make themselves heard clearly even when there are no competing sounds; in such instances, amplification may be required.

Sound also has direction. With well-designed and skillfully operated equipment, it is possible to make sound appear to begin at any place in the theatre and move from one point to another. For example, the sound of a car may become barely audible from one side of the stage, seem to approach, pass behind the set, and then pass out of hearing on the other side. Or directional sound may make an airplane seemingly pass directly over the audience.

Sound has duration—it can be prolonged or shortened. Many decisions about duration also involve proper timing. For example, in a storm scene, someone must decide when thunder is to begin, how long it is to continue, when it is to reach its peak, and when it is to die away.

Sound has quality. Thunder is recognized in part by its rumbling, echoing quality, just as an alarm clock may be by its shrill quality or a gunshot by its explosive quality. In the speaking or singing voice, quality is especially important. Shrill, harsh vocal qualities seem out of keeping with admirable characters, because the unpleasantness of the voice contradicts the pleasant traits.

All of the controllable properties of sound may be varied in relation to each other and in accordance with the demands of a production. Like the visual elements, they, too, need to be shaped in terms of unity, variety, proportion, balance, emphasis, and rhythm.

The Integrated Production Design

Although each visual and aural element, considered in isolation, has characteristics capable of evoking a limited range of typical responses, in actuality elements are seldom wholly separated from others. In theatrical production, all appear simultaneously, and their relationships change continually as the action develops in time and through the movement and speech of the actors. Furthermore, how each is shaped depends on the theatrical space in which the performance occurs. Thus, the implications of individual elements are modified by the total theatrical context. A production is a composite of messages projected by a collection of visual and aural elements. The director, actors, and designers shape the elements according to their vision, trusting that in performance the production will elicit the responses they seek. But the possibilities are so numerous (as to how the elements can be shaped, how skillfully they will be shaped and coordinated, and how spectators will respond to the shaping) that the results can seldom be foreseen.

In the chapters that follow, the roles and working methods of each theatre artist will be examined.

Producing and Directing

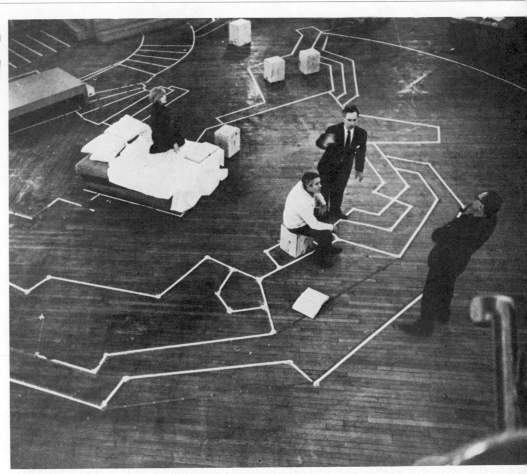

Although directors have ultimate responsibility for the artistic aspects of productions, they usually depend on others to provide the resources (money, space, and personnel) required for production. These essential financial and managerial tasks fall to producers, who may not make artistic decisions directly, but nevertheless influence such matters indirectly by their willingness or unwillingness (or sometimes ability or inability) to grant the requests of the director and other artists. Producers are often accused of placing commercial success above artistic integrity, but if someone did not carry out the producer's functions, productions would never reach the stage.

The Producer

Although almost all producers have the same basic responsibilities, the specific conditions that govern their work vary considerably from one type of organization to another. The producer's responsibilities are most clearly defined in the Broadway theatre. Nowadays, producers of Broadway shows most usually are organizations, a group of individuals, or consortia who raise the necessary capital and carry out the other functions of a producer in return for payment for these services and a very large percentage of any profit. Because production costs on Broadway are so great, often running into millions of dollars, and success is so unpredictable, producers usually seek financial backing from many persons or groups. They usually approach prospective investors with a proposed budget (covering expenses up to opening night) and a statement about how profits will be divided. Sometimes it takes months, even years, to raise the money needed for a production. Each production is usually capitalized as a corporation or partnership so as to limit the financial liability of investors.

After the necessary capital has been raised, the producers negotiate contracts with all the persons who will be involved. This can be difficult, especially since some eleven different unions may be involved—those representing dramatists; directors and choreographers; actors; musicians; stagehands; wardrobe attendants; press agents and managers; treasurers; ushers and doorkeepers; porters and cleaners; and engineers. Producers must also rent space for auditions and rehearsals, lease a theatre for performances, and make sure the production is publicized and tickets sold. They are responsible for the payroll, keeping financial records, and making reports to investors at specified intervals. Occasionally, productions return very large profits, but most never recover the original investment because the weekly running costs consume most of the income from ticket sales. The producers are also responsible for closing a show at the end of its run. Given all the problems and risks, it seems remarkable that anyone produces on Broadway.

The producer's responsibilities are not so clearly defined in other situations. Most professional resident companies are ongoing organizations that present a number of plays each year. Therefore, they often own a theatre, or else perform in one owned by a municipality or arts organization or in one leased for an extended period; they are more concerned with financing an ongoing organization than with a single production (although each production has its own budget within the theatre's total budget). In most companies of this type, responsibility is divided between an artistic director, who is concerned primarily with staging, and a managing director, who is concerned with finances and marketing. Both are usually involved in raising money, establishing policy, and choosing the repertory. There is also a board of directors, which must be consulted about certain problems and which may assist in raising funds. Since such groups cannot support their activities entirely from box-office receipts, much time is spent pursuing grants or soliciting contributions. As not-for-profit organizations, they are eligible for grants from foundations, the National Endowment for the Arts, state and local arts councils, and private donors. Although this form of organization distributes the producer's responsibilities somewhat differently than is the norm on Broadway, it delegates most of them to the managing director.

In community theatres, the organization is usually the producer, although many of the responsibilities are carried out by volunteers under the supervision of the organization's officers and board of directors. Some of the duties may be delegated to an individual (president or treasurer) or to a production committee. Most community theatres hire only a director and a designer-technician, since the purpose of such organizations is to provide an outlet for the talents of persons for whom theatre is an avocation.

In educational theatre, the producer's functions may be divided among several persons. Usually, the performance space is owned by the school, and most of the supervisory work is done by persons who are on the payroll in other capacities. The chairman of the department or the Director of Theatre may have responsibilities that combine those of the artistic and managing directors of a resident company. Some theatre programs have a paid business manager, who is responsible for keeping accounts, making purchases, running the box office, and handling publicity. In many small schools, the director of each play may have to assume many of the producer's functions.

Regardless of the type of organization, then, the basic tasks are much the same, though who performs them and the procedures may vary. In all cases, financial support must be provided, contractual arrangements made, space and personnel provided, publicity for productions disseminated, tickets sold, and bills paid. The producer is concerned with the business of show business.

The producer is also often involved in choosing the scripts to be produced. On Broadway, it is the producer who selects the play. Often the director and designers are not even contacted until after this fundamental choice has been made, although increasingly producers bring productions (in part or in their entirety) to Broadway that have been successful in regional theatres, Off Broadway, or abroad (principally London).

Most permanent organizations present a season composed of several plays covering a range of periods. In choosing a season of plays, the group may take into consideration (1) the need for varied types of plays; (2) the requirements of each play (size of cast; scenic, costume, and lighting demands); (3) total cost in relation to the organization's budget and projected income; and (4) tastes of local audiences and probable box-office appeal. Therefore, during the play-selection process, input and advice may be sought from a number of sources.

Professional organizations deal directly with living authors or their agents in negotiating arrangements to produce plays. Amateur production rights are usually handled by play agencies, such as Samuel French and Dramatists Play Service. A play under copyright (which continues for the lifetime of the author plus sixty years) may not be performed without written permission (usually in the form of a contract) from the copyright owners or their authorized agent. Such contracts require that royalties be paid for each performance. Older plays may not require payment if their copyrights have expired, but recent translations of older plays may be copyrighted even if the copyright for the play in its original language has expired.

Once the play is selected and production contracts signed, the process of play production begins.

The Director

Just as the producer is concerned with the financial aspects, the director is responsible for the artistic aspects of production. Ordinarily, the director (1) decides upon the interpretation to be given the script and the production concept that will shape the staging; (2) casts the actors; (3) works with the designers; (4) rehearses the actors; and (5) integrates all the elements into a finished production.

Understanding the Script   The starting point for most productions is a script. Therefore, the director needs to understand as thoroughly as possible the play to be staged. There is no standard way of studying a script (one way has been described in Chapter 3). Most directors begin by reading through the play several times so as to become familiar with its overall qualities. They may note the pattern of preparation, complications, crisis, and resolution. Some directors then divide a play into short segments (units or beats) and examine each in terms of the characters' motivations within that segment and the function of the segment in relation to those that precede and follow it and in the play as a whole. They usually discover the "through line" of action (or "spine") that holds the entire play together, and they seek to determine the overall intention of the play—its basic themes, point of view, and implications for meaning. The director also studies all the characters so as to understand their individual functions in the play and the demands they will make on the actors who play the roles. The director notes everything involving scenery, costumes, and lighting so as to be able to work intelligently with the designers. Through such study, the director becomes aware of the potentials and pitfalls of the script and of the opportunities and difficulties they pose for the production.

In order to understand the script thoroughly, directors may need to go to a number of other sources. They usually seek information about the author's life and read the playwright's other works in an effort to understand more fully the concerns that have shaped the play. They may also need to explore the period or environment depicted in the play. They may wish to read what critics have written about the play or what reviewers have said about previous productions. They may ex-

Explorations of socioeconomic and cultural forces of the Elizabethan era in preparation for producing one of Shakespeare's plays led West Berlin's Schaubühne am Halleschen Ufer to create a two-evening dramatic presentation, *Shakespeare's Memory,* out of its researches. Shown here, inside the skeletal framework of an Elizabethan ship, is a recreation (using model ships) of the Spanish Armada. (Photo by Ruth Walz. Courtesy German Information Center.)

amine still other written sources and anything else that will increase their understanding of the script and the context out of which it came.

If the script is new, the director may work directly with the playwright. This can simplify the director's task, since many questions about the script can be answered by its author, but it may also complicate the director's work if what the playwright says he or she intended is not clearly embodied in the script. In the latter case, the director may suggest (even demand) revisions, although most contracts specify that the playwright cannot be required to alter the script. Fortunately, most dramatists welcome the insights offered by the director and the rehearsal process, and they frequently revise the script right up to opening night.

If the script was originally in a language other than English, the problem of understanding may be complicated by translation. The director usually examines all the available translations and assesses their relative effectiveness. If none is satisfactory, the director may have another made. Plays from the past pose comparable problems because they frequently include obsolete phrases, outmoded social customs, or unfamiliar ideas. Sometimes the dramatic or theatrical conventions that shaped a play are barriers to presentation. The chorus in Greek tragedy almost always creates difficulties for the modern director, as do plays from other cultures (for example, Noh drama). The director must assess whether these difficulties can be overcome in a production intended for a present-day audience and, if so, how.

Approaches to Directing Once the director understands the script, the next step involves how to approach its staging. A number of different approaches have become common. One stems from the belief that the director is an interpretive artist who serves the playwright by transferring the script as faithfully as possible from page to stage. Directors who accept this notion of their function usually retain the time and place specified in the script, and follow (though not necessarily slavishly) the playwright's prescriptions about staging. A second approach stems from a view of directors as translators whose goal is to capture the spirit of the playwright's script, although to do this they may have to depart from the playwright's suggestions. Just as a word-for-word, literal translation of a literary piece from one language to another may distort the spirit of the original, an overzealously faithful production may fail to project a play's essential qualities, especially if the play is from the past and the theatre's conventions have changed considerably since the script was written.

This second approach is probably now the most common, although how it is applied varies widely from one director to another and even from one production to another. Directors using this approach usually search for a metaphor, dominant idea, or set of conventions that will convey a *directorial* (or *production*) *concept*. One director has shaped a production of *Hamlet* around the metaphor of the world as a prison; to reflect this metaphor, the setting was composed of cell-like cubicles in which various scenes were played. Perhaps a more common practice is to base a production on a simile rather than a metaphor (that is, to suggest that the action in a play is like that in another time and place). For example, one production of *Macbeth* relocated the action in a Latin-American country prone to military coups, and *Troilus and Cressida* (which is set during the Trojan War) has been relocated in America during the Civil War.

Peter Brook shaped his widely admired production of *A Midsummer Night's Dream* around a central motif: the potentials and dangers of love. The fantasy scenes became dreamlike demonstrations to Theseus and Hippolyta, who are about to be married, of the effects of misunderstandings between lovers and about love. To underscore these connections, Brook used the actors cast as Theseus and Hippolyta to play Oberon and Titania (their parallels in the fantasy world). Most earlier productions of the play had exploited the opportunities for visual spectacle offered by Theseus' court and the enchanted forest. Brook used the same set throughout—a white box (with front and top removed), totally devoid of decoration. Thus, the stage was treated not as a place to re-create visually the locales indicated in Shakespeare's script, but as a space where its fundamental human relationships could be isolated and examined. Most earlier productions had also emphasized the magical aspects of the fairy world, and had sought to make Puck's flying convincingly real. For the fairy magic, Brook substituted stage and circus magic: trapezes were used for the flying scenes, and characters on the trapezes performed such tricks of stage magic as keeping plates spinning on sticks. Bottom, rather than being transformed into an ass, became a clown. Thus, the magic was translated from fairyland into a context more familiar, though no less magical, to a modern audience. Despite all his visual substitutions, Brook altered none of the lines. His goal was to make audiences consider the implications of certain human relationships rather than concentrate on the spectacle and fantasy. (See the illustration in the collection of color prints following page 338.)

Ariane Mnouchkine, working with the Théâtre du Soleil in Paris, has used conventions borrowed from Japanese theatre in several produc-

Ariane Mnouchkine's production of Shakespeare's *Richard II* at the Théâtre du Soleil, Paris, in which Japanese and Western Conventions are intermingled. For another illustration of this production, see the color photographs following page 338. (Photo by Martine Franck/Magnum.)

tions of Shakespeare's history plays. She believes that Western audiences understand Japanese conventions in a very general sense but that the conventions are still so strange that they call attention to themselves; thus, she uses them to create discernible patterns that illuminate the repetitive, almost-ritualized power struggles that make up the action in these history plays.

Other variations on this second approach could be cited, but all would be based on the assumption that, though the script's dialogue should be respected and retained, its significance can best be conveyed to a present-day audience through devices that, though they depart from the playwright's instructions, convey the script's intentions by revealing the fundamental patterns that lie hidden beneath the surface detail. While this approach can be extremely effective, it can, if ineptly applied, distort the script or diffuse attention and become more confusing than revealing.

A third approach to directing places far less emphasis on the script. It sees directors as those who, though they may begin with the script, are free to reshape it as they see fit. Although this approach is less common than those already discussed, it has been increasingly accepted since the 1960s. The Polish director Jerzy Grotowski often began with well-known scripts, uncovered what he considered to be basic (archetypal) patterns of human behavior in them, and then reshaped the scripts, often radically, with the intention of provoking audiences into self-recognition and self-examination. One of his best-known and most radical reshapings of a play involved Wyspianski's *Akropolis* (1904), one of Poland's most revered classics, set in the royal palace at Cracow (the Polish equivalent of the Athenian Acropolis) on the Feast of the Resurrection. During the action, the walls' tapestries come to life and enact what amounts to a history of Western civilization, at the end of which the resurrected Christ leads all the figures in a procession that sets out to liberate Europe from its past errors. Grotowski saw the play as treating hopes and fantasies that had been totally destroyed by World War II and the Nazi concentration camps. Therefore, he almost completely reshaped the play from a statement about the possibility of redemption to a statement about "the cemetery of our civilization." He set it in the extermination camp at Auschwitz. All the characters are prisoners who, during the course of the play, build cremation ovens and occasionally in their nightmares perform scenes based, in a distorted way, on those in Wyspianski's play. At the end, they march into the ovens they have built, following a lifeless figure representing Christ. In such an approach, the director's vision overrides the playwright's, and the original script becomes merely material to be shaped (just as acting, lighting, scenery, and costumes are). This approach to directing reflects that of film, where the director is usually considered the principal creative force (the *auteur*).

Still another approach to directing virtually eliminates the playwright (or at least the distinctions between writer and director). In Robert Wilson's theatre pieces, the written scripts are so short and convey so little information that they are wholly inadequate as bases for productions by others. These pieces can properly be said to exist only in the performances staged by Wilson. Similarly, performance artists usually conceive their pieces as performances rather than as scripts, and only they can stage their works.

Regardless of the approach, directors have to work with others in

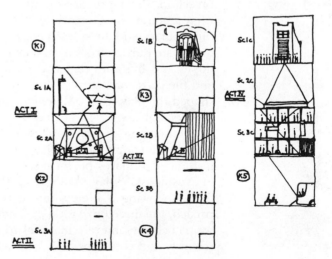

Robert Wilson's storyboard outline of the four acts of his opera, *Einstein on the Beach*. (Courtesy Byrd Hoffman Foundation.)

Wilson elaborates his basic storyboard outline in a number of sketches (in this instance, eight to ten) for each scene. The sketch here is for Act I, Scene 2A of *Einstein on the Beach*. (Photo by Geoffrey Clements. Reprinted with the permission of the Byrd Hoffman Foundation.)

transforming their vision into reality, since at least some production tasks must be delegated to others. The discussion that follows will undoubtedly make directing seem far more rational and precise than it is. In actuality, though most directors begin with a reasonably clear idea of what they wish to accomplish, they also make discoveries (through interactions with designers and actors as well as through new insights into the script) that alter their initial plans. Thus, like Christopher Columbus, where directors ultimately arrive may be different from (and more rewarding than) their original destination. But such discoveries are unpredictable, and consequently we must content ourselves with a look at some typical working procedures used by directors.

The Director and the Designers   Some directors serve as their own designers, but that is not usual. Since designing and constructing the visual elements is a lengthy process, the director meets as early as pos-

Act, I, Scene 2A of *Einstein on the Beach* in performance as staged by Robert Wilson. Note the costume (pants, shirt, and suspenders), which was worn by practically all of characters throughout the opera and thus served as one unifying motif. (Photo by Babette Mangolte. Reprinted with the permission of the Byrd Hoffman Foundation.)

sible with the designers to discuss the play and the production concept. The concept may even evolve out of such discussions. However arrived at, the production's focus should be clear to the designers if they are not to work at cross-purposes with the director and each other and if they are to contribute significantly to the production. The director also needs to be clear about any specific demands he or she may have: the shape of the set; the need for multiple levels; the floor plan; placement of doors; specific mood lighting; projected images; garments with specific features; etc.

After the initial meetings, the designers must be allowed time to conceive designs and make sketches. At subsequent meetings, designs are considered and revisions requested until director and designers are mutually satisfied. Before designs are approved, a number of questions should be asked. Do they adequately project the production concept? Do they fit the play's action, mood, theme, and style? Are they functional? Do the designs for each aspect (scenery, costumes, lighting) complement and support those for the other aspects? If changes must occur during performance, will the proposed costumes, scenery, and lighting permit changes without undue delays? Consideration of such questions during the planning stages can avoid costly last-minute changes.

After the designs are approved, there may be regular conferences, but each artist works more or less independently until the final rehearsals. Meantime, the director's prime task becomes casting and rehearsing the actors.

Casting   In casting, various methods are used. One is the open tryout, which permits all those interested to apply. (In some educational theatres, tryouts are open only to theatre majors, and in some community theatres, only members are eligible. In professional theatres, a certain amount of time may be devoted to open tryouts, though only members of Actors Equity may be considered.) If the applicants are numerous, some may be eliminated on the basis of résumés or interviews. Even those granted auditions usually have only a short time (two minutes is typical) in which to demonstrate their suitability. Under such circumstances, choices may be made on the basis of personal or physical attributes rather than proven ability. Many large professional organizations have casting directors who sift through résumés or conduct initial auditions, on the basis of which likely candidates are selected for more lengthy auditions. Open tryouts, then, are usually preliminary to closed or invitational auditions, during which candidates are permitted considerably more opportunity to demonstrate their suitability to the roles.

The procedures used during tryouts vary. Sometimes actors are asked to prepare two short, contrasting audition scenes unrelated to the play being cast. Sometimes actors are able to study the script in advance and to read a passage from it as an audition piece. The director may ask actors to read material they have not previously seen, then give explanations and ask the actor to read the same material again with these instructions in mind. In this way, the director seeks to judge the actor's flexibility and quickness in assimilating suggestions. Some directors use improvisations to test imagination, inventiveness, and physical agility.

Many factors determine final casting. Some roles demand specific physical characteristics (such as being fatter or taller than others), accent, or vocal quality. The director must consider the emotional range of each role and the potential of actors to achieve this range. Characters often need to be paired or contrasted (in romantic situations, for example), and casting must reflect this. The director must also look at the cast as a whole and how the actors will look and work together. After weighing all the factors, the director eventually chooses the actors who seem most capable of embodying the qualities he or she is seeking.

Working with the Actors   After casting is completed, the director seeks to mesh actors with roles so as to bring the script to life on the stage. The director explains the production concept, supervises rehearsals, reacts to characterizations and stage business, and makes suggestions for improvements. But a director is not a dictator. Actors bring their own insights, many of which may be novel and provocative. Thus, directors should be willing to discuss ideas and be sufficiently flexible to adopt those that improve their initial plans.

The director attempts to create an atmosphere free from unnecessary tensions in which the actors may explore and develop their roles. The director needs to be tactful and understanding, since each actor has unique problems and favorite working methods. Some actors take criticism gracefully in the presence of others, but some become argumentative or are so deeply embarrassed they find it difficult to continue.

Because actors cannot see their own performances from the point of view of the audience, the director must perform this service for them, assess the probable effects, and work with them to alter, correct or intensify characterizations. An effective director is a sensitive listener and observer, a critic, disciplinarian, teacher, and friend.

The Director's Means

The director's means include the entire resources of the theatre: the script; the voice, speech, physical appearance, movement, and psychological and mental capacities of the actors; the stage space, scenery, and properties; costumes and makeup; electronic equipment, lighting, and sound. Since each of these elements is discussed elsewhere in this book, the focus here is on the director's work with the actors: the stage picture; movement, gesture, and stage business; voice and speech.

The Stage Picture   Each moment of a performance may be thought of as a picture that transmits messages to the audience quite apart from speech and movement. Therefore, the director needs to control the visual design of a scene moment by moment, not for the sake of creating beautiful pictures but as visualizations of situation, emotions, and character relationships. (In actuality, these pictures operate in conjunction with the actors' lines and movements, but if left to chance, they can easily contradict what is said by sending the wrong messages.) In composing the stage picture, the director uses various devices to emphasize what should stand out and to subordinate other parts of the picture.

These devices will be described first as they relate to the picture-frame stage and later as they are modified for other types of stages.

One of the most important controls over emphasis and subordination is the *bodily positions* of the actors, for—all other factors being equal—the actor facing the audience most fully will be the most emphatic. (Bodily positions are explained more fully in Chapter 13.) A second source of emphasis is *height,* since, if other factors are equal, the most elevated character will be the most emphatic. To vary height, the director may have characters stand, sit, kneel, lie down, or mount steps or platforms. A third means of controlling emphasis is through the use of *stage areas.* Since centerstage and downstage are the most emphatic areas in the proscenium theatre, the director may control emphasis by the placement of actors within the stage space. (How the proscenium stage may be divided into areas is illustrated in the diagram shown below.) The use of stage areas is closely related to a fourth means of controlling emphasis: *spatial relationships* among the characters, as, for example, when a single character on one side of the stage is given emphasis by massing a group of actors on the other side. This example also illustrates a fifth means—*contrast.* Emphasis may also be created through *visual focus*—as when all those on the stage look at the same person or object, thereby creating the equivalent of a pointing finger. Still other ways of gaining emphasis include *costume* (a brilliantly colored garment amid drab clothing), *lighting* (a spotlighted area), and *scenery* (placing a character in a doorway or against a piece of furniture to strengthen the visual line). Seldom do directors depend on a single source of emphasis. Several are often used simultaneously, especially when emphasis needs to be divided among several characters, each requiring differing degrees of emphasis.

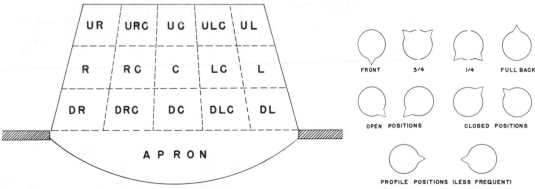

Stage areas (at left) and bodily positions (at right).

When one moves from the proscenium to the thrust stage (which is viewed from three sides) or the arena (which is viewed from four sides), some of the devices that are most effective on the proscenium stage are no longer very useful. For example, bodily position becomes relatively meaningless, since actors facing one part of the audience may have their backs turned to another. Similarly, stage area loses much of its effectiveness. But most of the other devices still apply. Nevertheless, in thrust and arena theatres it is difficult to compose stage pictures that are expressive from every angle, and they need to be recomposed frequently from different angles so that no part of the audience is neglected.

How the devices for achieving emphasis are used depends greatly on the stage setting. The placement of doors and furniture encourages some compositional patterns and impedes others. The absence of furniture in settings for many period plays (for example, *Oedipus the King* and most of the scenes in *Hamlet*) rules out the detailed routine of daily life that is typical in such modern plays as *The Wild Duck*. Picturization is also affected by the type of play (for example, visual devices appropriate to *The Servant of Two Masters* might be out of keeping with *"The Hairy Ape"*).

Some directors consider picturization and composition legacies of a time when the picture-frame stage was the only type in use, and they argue that its conventions have been invalidated by more recent stage forms. Others believe that concern for picturization leads to a self-conscious or unnatural positioning of actors on stage. Still others argue that if the actors understand the dramatic situation, they will instinctively group themselves properly. The most serious challenge to the concept of picturization has been posed by flexible (or variable) stages, since in them several scenes may proceed simultaneously in various parts of a space shared by audience and performers. This use of theatrical space rejects the traditional view that each moment of a performance should have a major focal point to which every spectator's attention is directed and which should be visible and audible to every member of the audience. But the flexible theatre's primary break with past practice is in its use of multiple focal points. The individual simultaneous scenes still create pictures, whether planned or not.

Most objections to deliberate picturization concern the possibility that compositions will draw attention to themselves and distract attention from more important elements. No doubt poorly conceived or inappropriate composition may have this effect. But one cannot deny that the visual pictures that continually form, dissolve, and transform as the audience watches are a major component of any production. Therefore, although there can be much controversy over how this element is to be approached, it cannot be ignored.

Movement, Gesture, and Business   So far, the stage picture has been treated as static, but in performance the dominant impression is one of movement—flow, change, and development. Consequently, movement is among the director's most powerful means of expression.

Movement can be divided into three main types: *from place to place, gesture,* and *business.* Each type may be dictated by the script or may be invented by the director or the actors. Many movements (such as entering, exiting, dancing, or lighting lamps) may be specified in stage directions or dialogue. On the other hand, many older plays include no stage directions, and all movement must be deduced. Since a completely static stage picture soon becomes boring, the director usually makes considerable use of physical action. In doing so, the director takes cues from the script, so that movement seems motivated rather than aimless. Character relationships and emotional connotations are among the most common motivators of movement—love, anger, and eagerness normally

Jean Genet's *The Blacks,* staged in a film studio in West Berlin by Peter Stein. Note how the lines in the diamond-shaped area (bottom) create a secondary focus on the ritual figures at its center. Note also that the floor texture of this area repeats that of the back wall, and that the composition in this scene places primary focus on the map of Africa. (Photo by Ruth Walz. Courtesy German Information Center.)

make persons move toward each other, whereas disgust, fear, and reluctance separate them. Thus, movement illustrates inner feelings.

Movement serves many functions. First, it *gives emphasis* because it catches the eye and directs attention to the strongest movement. Second, it *characterizes.* An elderly person normally uses fewer and slower movements than a young person, just as a nervous or angry person moves differently than does a casual or relaxed person. Third, movement *clarifies situation.* Highly emotional scenes normally demand more movement (and more rapid and sharply defined movement) than do quiet moments. Fourth, movement may be used to *build scenes to a climax,* for *contrast,* and for *tempo.* The amount and size of movement may be gradually increased to create a sense of growing confusion or conflict or of development and change. Contrast in movement from one scene to another can point up differences in mood, tempo, and situation, as well as provide variety. Fifth, movement may be *indicative of dramatic type.* The movement of *Oedipus the King* is more stately and formal than that of *Raisin in the Sun.* Some plays that depart from realism, such as *"The Hairy Ape,"* deliberately distort or stylize movement.

Much stage movement does not involve movement from place to place. *Gesture, facial expression,* and *bodily attitude,* which together create what is usually called *body language,* are of special importance for achieving subtlety and clarity.

Gesture normally involves only the hands and arms, but at times the torso, head, feet, or legs may be used gesturally. Gesture is especially important as a subtle means of gaining emphasis, since a gesture by an actor who is about to speak is usually sufficient to shift attention to that actor at just the right moment. Gesture is indicative of basic psychological traits. For example, a great many spontaneous gestures suggest an uninhibited, outgoing personality, whereas few and awkward gestures suggest the opposite.

Bodily attitude—stiffly upright, slumping, relaxed, and so on—is an especially useful means for displaying emotional states and for indicating immediate reactions. So is facial expression, which, though it is not always visible in a large auditorium, is a supplementary aid in projecting response.

Another kind of movement, *stage business,* involves detailed actions such as filling and smoking a pipe, arranging flowers, wrapping packages, eating and drinking, dueling, etc. Such business is frequently prescribed by the script, but it may also be invented by the director or actors to clarify action or enrich characterization. It needs to be carefully timed to make appropriate points and to be coordinated with dialogue to avoid distracting attention from important lines or action.

In recent years, several nontraditional uses of movement, gesture, and

Ibsen's *Rosmersholm* at the Trinity Repertory Company. This unusually complex setting, including three levels, several rooms, stairways, and an exterior view, provides almost limitless opportunity for movement, composition, and emphasis. Note the realistic stage business both on the middle and upper levels. Directed by Adrian Hall, production design by Eugene Lee. (Photo by Robert Emerson. Courtesy Trinity Repertory Company.)

business have become common. Actors may writhe on the floor in tangled masses, crawl about the set, and climb onto various structures. Movement in general has become more uninhibited, and the range of acceptable movement has been considerably extended.

Voice and Speech   The director's means also include the voice and speech of the actors. Just as innovative movement has become important, so too has nonverbal vocal sound. Directors now frequently use voice to create dissonances, modulations ranging from the loudest to the softest, cries, yelps, and so on. Nevertheless, the director is still most commonly concerned with voice as a medium for language or song. (Since voice and speech are more fully the actor's concern, they are discussed at greater length in Chapter 13.) Still, the director needs to understand voice and speech thoroughly in order to use them effectively and to coach actors intelligently.

In using voice and speech, the director must make sure the dialogue is both audible and understandable, that there is variety, and (most important) that voice and speech enhance characterization, situation, and meaning. As with movement, voice and speech may be used to build scenes (or the entire play) to a climax.

Thus, the director's means are varied. Although they have been discussed separately here, they are applied simultaneously in the theatre, first one and then another being given primacy. Through such continuous adjustments, the director seeks to achieve clarity in motivation, action, and meaning, in addition to creating that underlying and indefinable sense of excitement that characterizes theatrical performance at its best.

Rehearsing the Play

Rehearsals can seldom be held under conditions approximating those of performance. As a rule, the scenery, costumes, lighting, and properties are not available until the final days, and the rehearsal space is seldom the stage on which the play will be presented. Therefore, the director and actors must rely heavily on imagination during rehearsals.

The typical rehearsal space is a large room (at least as large as the stage) on the floor of which the ground plan of the set is outlined with tape or paint. (See illustration on page 291.) If there is more than one set, each is indicated with different colors. Chairs, tables, and improvised doors and levels help the actors become familiar with the setting. Temporary properties that approximate those to be used in performance also are necessary if there is complex stage business, such as serving a meal or fighting a duel. Similarly, rehearsal garments may be needed for plays in which unusual headdresses, hooped skirts or trains, and other unfamiliar features or accessories appear.

In order to plan rehearsals adequately, the director needs to know how much time will be allotted. In the nonprofessional theatre, actors are usually available only in the evenings for three or four hours and for a period of four to eight weeks. In the professional theatre, a rehearsal period of three or four weeks is typical with actors available for approximately eight hours each day. A group that evolves its own scripts may require months to ready a performance. Whatever the particular situation, the director ascertains the approximate number of hours avail-

Peter Weiss' *Marat/Sade* as directed by Peter Brook for the Royal Shakespeare Company. This production was greeted as a major example of Artaud's "theatre of cruelty." The actors are Patrick Magee, Glenda Jackson, and Ian Richardson. (Jessie Alexander/Nancy Palmer.)

able for rehearsals and then plans a schedule that uses the time to maximum advantage. Since all problems cannot be worked on simultaneously, the director breaks down the schedule into phases and objectives.

Before beginning rehearsals on the actual script, some directors devote time to group activities (such as improvisations and theatre games) intended to familiarize the actors with each other, break down inhibitions and encourage trust, and prepare the actors for the work ahead.

The first phase of rehearsals is usually devoted to reading and discussing the script. The amount of time devoted to textual study varies from director to director, with the complexity of the script, and with the experience of the cast. During this period, the director tries to see that all the actors have a basic understanding of their roles and how they

A reading rehearsal of Thomas Babe's *Taken in Marriage* at the New York Shakespeare Festival's Public Theatre. In the background, the playwright and Joseph Papp, the director and producer. At right, Shirley Knight and Meryl Streep. (Photo by Jack Mitchell.)

function within the action. The director may explain the production concept and clarify the main objectives toward which everyone will be working.

The next phase is usually devoted to *blocking* (establishing each actor's movements from place to place and position at each moment). For example, an actor might be directed to enter up center, cross slowly to the sofa down left, and stand facing front. At this time, the director is concerned only with the gross patterns of movement; subtleties and refinements come later. When the blocking for one unit is clear, the director moves on to the next, repeating the process until the entire play is blocked. The process as described here is far more orderly than in most actual blocking rehearsals. Many directors consider all blocking to be tentative, and they adjust it often as rehearsals proceed. Others believe that blocking should evolve out of character relationships and the actors' sense of their roles—a collaborative process among actors and director, and often a slow one. Regardless of how blocking is achieved, eventually it must be set so as not to be a constant source of distraction and misunderstanding.

The next phase is usually devoted to lines. The director normally specifies for each act the date by which the actors should know their lines. As with blocking, there is disagreement about the best time to learn lines (early versus after the actor is thoroughly familiar with the role), although it is generally acknowledged that it is difficult for performers to achieve subtlety or to build scenes properly if they must continually consult their scripts.

Once the actors have mastered their basic movement patterns and lines, the director can proceed to the next phase—detailed work on characterization, line readings, business, transitions, progression and build, variety, and ensemble playing. Much of this phase may be spent exploring motivations or clarifying relationships. If the actors have difficulties, the director may ask them to do improvisations designed to stimulate those responses he or she is seeking and which can then be adapted to the scripted situation. During this phase, directors may go over the same scene repeatedly so as to achieve proper timing or build, just as they may adjust the pacing of scenes for the sake of variety.

With musicals, the director's task becomes especially complex during this and later phases of rehearsals. For musicals, a choreographer normally creates and rehearses the dances separately, just as the musical director rehearses the singers and chorus separately (normally with only piano accompaniment). The director must eventually integrate songs and dances into the whole and devise the transitions that lead smoothly from spoken lines into song and from stage movement into dance.

The final phase of rehearsals is devoted to integrating all of the elements of production. For the first time, the actors are able to rehearse in their costumes and makeup and with the scenery, lighting, and sound (including, in musicals, the full orchestra) that will be used in performance. Frequently, this is also the first time that the actors have rehearsed in the actual performance space. Many adjustments generally have to be made during these final rehearsals. It is usual to have at least one technical rehearsal to work out problems with lighting levels and cues, costume and scene changes, sound, music, and properties. Typically, there are then two or three dress rehearsals that seek to approximate as nearly as possible the conditions of performance. During these rehearsals, difficulties are noted and attempts are made to correct them before the next rehearsal. Some directors invite a number of people to the dress rehearsals to get indications of probable audience response and to prepare the performers for a larger audience. In the professional theatre, preview performances function as a series of additional dress rehearsals, after each of which changes are made. The alterations are then tried out on other audiences until the play opens. (Critics are expected to wait for the official opening before reviewing the production.)

When the play opens, the director's job is considered to be complete, although many directors come back at intervals to revitalize performances. By opening night there is a *production promptbook*, in which have been recorded the blocking, stage business, lighting cues, sound cues, and everything that is required to run the show as the director intended.

The Director's Assistants   In fulfilling all these functions, the director usually has several assistants, among which the most important are the rehearsal secretary, assistant director, and stage manager.

The *rehearsal secretary* takes notes from the director during rehearsals about points to discuss with the actors, designers, or technicians. The secretary may also post notices and keep everyone informed of things they need to know. The *assistant director* performs whatever tasks are assigned by the director: attending conferences, serving as liaison with designers, coaching actors, or rehearsing scenes. The *stage manager* is responsible for running the show at each performance and, during the rehearsal period, for compiling the promptbook, which becomes the blueprint for performances. In the professional theatre, the stage manager may organize and run auditions and, after the show opens, may rehearse the actors if it is considered necessary. The stage manager is the director's surrogate during performances, seeking to see that everything functions as the director intended.

Looking at the Director's Work

Nowadays, not only are approaches to directing varied, so too are the scripts (ranging from the Greeks to the present, and from tragedy to comedy to indeterminate forms) and the theatrical conventions (ranging through the whole history of Western theatre and borrowing liberally from other cultures). Therefore, when we attend the theatre, our experiences may also be varied: we may find ourselves confronted with the commonplace and boring, the exotic and puzzling, the novel and exciting, or some combination of these. Such variety often makes it difficult to respond intelligently. Consequently, here is a list of questions that may help the theatregoer assess the director's contributions.

1. Was there an identifiable production concept, unifying metaphor, or interpretational approach? If so, what was it and how was it manifested in the production? to what effect?
2. How closely did the production adhere to the playwright's script? (In the script, where and when does the action take place? Did the production alter time, place, or other aspects of the script? If so, how? to what effect? If not, how did this production make—or fail to make—the script's action understandable or relevant to its audience?)
3. Did the production make use of any unusual conventions? If so, which? with what effect?
4. In what type of performance space was the production staged? How was the production affected by the space? with what gain or loss?
5. How did the visual elements (scenery, costumes, lighting) support (or fail to support) the production concept? Were they coordinated? Did the director make specific use of any of them? with what effect?
6. How did sounds (the actors' voices, special effects, music) support (or fail to support) the production concept? Were they audible, understandable, properly balanced?
7. How did casting influence the production?
8. Was the action clear? Did it build climactically? Was there appropriate variety in mood and tempo?
9. Were all the elements of the production compatible and coordinated? If not, what seemed out of place or inadequately integrated with the rest? with what effect?
10. Overall, did the production achieve its apparent goals? If not, where did it fall short? with what overall results?

Other questions could be posed, but many of them will arise as other areas of production are examined in the chapters that follow.

Acting

13

Of all theatre workers, the actor most nearly personifies the stage for the general public. In fact, the actor is the only theatre artist the audience normally sees. The actor's function is to give concrete embodiment to characters that otherwise exist only in the written word and the imagination. It is through what the actors say and do and how they interact with each other and their surroundings that a play's action develops. Though the script may provide the blueprint, the designers the visual context, and the director the overall focus, it is the living presence of the actor that is most essential to the theatrical experience.

Actors are among the few artists (along with dancers and singers) whose basic means of expression cannot be separated from themselves; they must create a role with their individual body and voice and out of their individual psychological and intellectual endowments. The director, designers, and playwright can sit in an auditorium and see their work, but stage actors can never completely separate themselves from what they create. Even a film of a performance is insufficient because it violates the essence of stage acting: the simultaneity of creation, performance, and audience response. In films, scenes are almost always shot out of sequence, the entire filming process often requiring several months; the actors usually have only a vague notion of how the scenes fit together, and typically they do not see their work in sequence until the film is released months later. Even then, the performance they (and the public) see has been given much of its shape by the film's editor. Furthermore, audience response can in no way alter or influence what is shown on the screen. All of this does not make the screen actor's job less difficult than the stage actor's, but it does make it different. Stage actors play scenes in the order specified by the script and complete the entire play at each performance. Thus, they must be constantly aware of how the story develops and see that the tensions build and relax properly. They have been prepared for these tasks by many rehearsals with a director whose critical advice and editing may have shaped the total production, but it is the actors who must recreate the performance each night—and each time for a new audience, whose immediate feedback continuously influences that evening's performance.

In many ways, acting is an extension of everyday human behavior. Most persons speak, move, and interact with others. They also play many "roles" as they adjust to the demands of changing contexts: home, business, school, recreation, and so on. Perhaps not surprisingly, then, it is not always easy to distinguish acting talent from personality traits or to convince would-be actors that rigorous training is necessary. Nevertheless, acting is an art, and the ability to use behavior expressively in the theatre differs from the ability to function adequately in daily life. The actor's development involves three basic ingredients—innate ability (a special talent for acting), training, and practice (or experience). Talent is perhaps most essential, but it is not enough in itself; it must be nurtured and developed through extensive training and application in actual productions.

The Actor's Training and Means

Probably no aspect of theatre training has undergone so much change in the past twenty-five years as acting. Until the 1960s, the tendency was to break the training process into parts and to pursue each part independently (movement, voice, psychological preparation, etc.). In the 1960s, acting teachers began to advocate more unified approaches. Most took their cues from Gestalt psychology (which argues that processes operate as wholes rather than as sums of parts) and sought to integrate processes that previously had been approached separately. The overall result has been greater concern for the interrelationship of various processes, but typically each process is still singled out for special emphasis at some point (or on a continuing basis) during training. This is probably inevitable, since, though we may recognize the ultimate importance of the whole, we cannot be concerned with everything simultaneously. Therefore, we choose parts for special attention, presumably without forgetting the whole. Thus, in training actors, old and new approaches are often intertwined.

Body, Voice, and Inner Impulse As the actor's primary means of communicating, the body and voice need to be flexible, disciplined, and expressive. Flexibility is needed so the actor can express physically or vocally a wide range of attitudes, traits, emotions, and situations. But flexibility alone is not sufficient; actors must also be able to control body and voice at will, and such control comes only through understanding, practice, and discipline.

One of the actor's primary problems is to understand how the body and voice function. Most actors begin by learning how the human body and voice operate in a general, physiological sense, then proceed to explore how their own body and voice actually are functioning. If actors can discover what their normal body alignment is, how their center of balance functions, how they are breathing, what their patterns of tension are, and so on, they should then be able to work toward gaining effective control over their physical and vocal instruments. The initial goal is to eliminate inhibiting tensions so the performer can move freely and ef-

Marlon Brando (Stanley) and Jessica Tandy (Blanche) in Tennessee Williams' *A Streetcar Named Desire*. Directed by Elia Kazan. (Courtesy Theatre and Music Collection, Museum of the City of New York.)

fortlessly and achieve a resonant, flexible voice; the ultimate goal is control over both body and voice for expressive use in performance.

Since the body and voice are integral parts of a total system and are consequently affected by psychological forces, it is difficult to achieve freedom and expressiveness without some concern for the psychological processes that create tensions and blocks. Perhaps the most popular means of dealing with these has been through improvisational theatre games designed to break down inhibitions and build self-confidence and trust in fellow actors. Other exercises have been borrowed from a variety of Oriental sources, as well as more familiar Western sources. Almost all treat inner impulse, body, and voice as interrelated processes, and thus work on any one of these helps the others. The ultimate goal is to produce actors who are sensitive, skilled, and expressive.

In addition to overall mastery of body and voice, actors usually seek more specialized training in dancing, fencing, singing, and other skills that increase their ability to play a wide range of roles.

Observation and Imagination   Actors must also be concerned about their powers of observation and imagination. Since human beings learn about each other in large part through observation, actors need to develop the habit of watching other people (for example, the dominant behavioral patterns of various personality types or age groups). While the results may not be directly transferable to the stage, they can be drawn on in creating believable characterizations.

Actors must also develop imagination in order to "feel their way" into the lives of others and into fictional situations. They are sometimes counseled to develop "emotion memory"—recalling how they felt in certain types of situations—as a resource for building psychologically convincing characterizations.

Control and Discipline   No matter how well actors have mastered the foundation skills, they are unlikely to use these skills effectively onstage unless they have also learned to control, shape, and integrate them as demanded by the script and the director. Control is usually achieved only through daily practice and disciplined effort over a long period.

One mark of control and discipline is *concentration*—the ability to immerse oneself in the situation and to shut out all distractions. In performance, some actors, through overfamiliarity with the script, may seem little more than automatons, whereas truly effective actors create the illusion that this is the first time they have experienced these situations, no matter how often they have performed the roles. To create such an illusion, actors must concentrate on what is developing around them—not in a general way but on specific words, gestures, and movements—and must respond in the appropriate key and at the appropriate moment. This requires that actors immerse themselves in the "here and now" of the stage action.

Stage Conventions   Centuries of experience have convinced actors that some ways of doing things onstage are more effective than others, and many routine tasks have been reduced to a set of conventions that actors are expected to know. Directors take for granted that actors are familiar with these conventions, and therefore give many instructions in a kind of stage shorthand based on them.

Discipline and control are especially important in extremely demanding roles, such as Othello, seen here just before he kills Desdemona. The actor is Brewster Mason in a production by the Royal Shakespeare Company. (Courtesy British Tourist Authority.)

One of the most basic conventions is the division of the stage into areas, which facilitates giving directions. *Upstage* (a term dating from the time when the stage actually did slope upward toward the back) means toward the rear of the stage, just as *downstage* means toward the front; *right* and *left* refer to the actor's right or left when facing the auditorium. The stage floor may also be spoken of as though it were divided into squares, each with its own designation: *up right, up center, up left, down right, down center, down left.* (See the diagram on page 305.) The actor is also expected to be familiar with body positions. *Full front* means facing the audience; *one-quarter* indicates a quarter-turn away from the audience; *one-half* or *profile* means turned 90 degrees away from the audience; *three-quarter* designates a 135-degree turn away from the audience; and *full* means turned completely away from the audience. (See the chart on page 305.)

Other terminology may supplement designations of area and bodily position. *Open up* means to turn slightly more toward the audience; *turn in* means to turn toward the center of the stage; *turn out* means to turn toward the side of the stage. Two actors are sometimes told to *share a scene,* meaning that both should play in the one-quarter or profile position so they are equally visible to the audience. To *give stage* means that one actor gives the dominant stage position to another by facing away from the audience more than the other actor. In most scenes, emphasis shifts frequently from one character to another, and the actors may constantly be giving and taking the stage according to who needs to be most emphatic at a specific moment. To *focus* means to look at or turn toward a person or object so as to direct attention there. Actors may also be told to *dress the stage* (that is, move so as to balance the stage picture). Experienced actors make such movements almost automatically and without being obtrusive.

Some devices are commonly used to emphasize or subordinate stage business. A letter that is to be important later may need to be *planted* in an earlier scene. To make sure it is noticed, the actor may hesitate, start to put it one place, then select the final spot. Conversely, some actions need to be masked from the audience. Eating, for example, must be faked to a large degree, since actors can seldom eat the actual food or the amount indicated in the script. Scenes of violence (such as stabbings, shootings, and fistfights) must also be faked. To be convincing, they require careful planning and timing.

In whatever they do, actors normally strive to be graceful, since gracefulness is usually unobtrusive, whereas awkwardness is distracting. Similarly, movement should be precise and clear, since imprecision suggests vagueness and indefiniteness. (Awkwardness and impreciseness can, of course, be used to good dramatic effect if they are deliberate.) Actors

Shakespeare's *As You Like It*, performed at the National Theatre, London, with an all-male cast (as the original production was). At left, Rosalind (disguised as a boy); at center, Celia; at right, Orlando. Such casting creates special problems for the actors if the production is to be received favorably by modern audiences (as this production was). Overhead, the forest is suggested by a patterned plexiglass panel. (Photo by Dominic Photography.)

also need to be familiar with all aspects of theatrical production, since the more they know about scenery, costumes, and lighting, the better they will be able to use these elements to their own advantage.

From Training to Performing

Prior to the twentieth century, would-be actors usually learned on the job. First, they had to be accepted into a company as "utility" actors—roughly equivalent to apprentices. They then played supernumerary roles in a great variety of plays and observed the established actors closely. Thus, training was essentially a mixture of observation and trial-and-error. After a few years, the young actors discovered the types of roles to which they seemed best suited and settled into that "line of business," usually for the rest of their careers. But in the late nineteenth century, when resident companies were driven out of existence by touring productions (cast in New York with experienced actors), would-be actors were deprived of their traditional training ground. Although some acting schools had existed before this time, the demise of the resident companies was the principal spur to the founding of actor-training programs in the United States. Eventually, actor training gained a foothold in colleges and universities, which are now the principal trainers of actors, although there are still some private actor-training studios, especially in large cities.

Most training programs stage productions to provide students opportunities to apply what they are taught. Thus, these programs retain some features of the earlier apprentice system, although in schools the learners often play major roles that in resident companies were assigned to experienced professionals. Both old and new systems represent attempts to stimulate and integrate the three major foundations of artistic skill—talent, training, and practice.

Although would-be actors may complete training programs and receive degrees or certificates, there are no exams or boards, such as there are for lawyers or doctors, to certify an actor's readiness to practice the profession. Certification, such as it is, comes from being cast in professional productions. The decision to become a professional actor takes considerable courage, for the number of aspirants greatly exceeds the available jobs. Although there are now more acting jobs in the nation's resident companies than in New York's theatres, the majority of theatre companies still hold auditions and do much of their casting in New York. Thus, though it is possible to be an actor and live in one of the many cities that support professional companies, aspiring stage actors tend to gravitate to New York, just as aspiring film and television actors gravitate to Los Angeles. Chicago and a few other cities have managed to remain largely independent of both New York and Los Angeles.

Regardless of where actors live or wish to work, they all have the problem of being cast. To work in the professional theatre, an actor must be a member of Actors Equity Association, the actors' union. But less than one quarter of Equity's members are ever employed at the same time, and only a small percentage make a living from acting. For most actors the chances of being cast are improved if they have an agent, whose job it is to help them get employment and whose own income depends on the clients' success, since the agent receives ten percent of their earnings. But, though the odds against success are great, large numbers of young people persist, and enough are sufficiently successful to keep others trying.

Most of the procedures involved in casting have been discussed in Chapter 12. So, let us assume that the actor has been cast and is now ready to work on a role.

Creating a Role

Each time actors undertake a new role, they are faced with a number of tasks. Among these perhaps the most basic is to understand the role. (One approach to analyzing script and role is described in Chapter 3.) It is helpful to look at the role in relation to levels of characterization: What does the script reveal about the character's physical appearance, age, and conditions of health; profession, social class, economic status, family background, standing in the community; basic attitudes, likes, dislikes, general emotional makeup; ways of meeting crises and conflicts? Which of the character's traits are most important to the dramatic action? Such inquiries form a broad base for further inquiries.

The actor should next define as clearly as possible what the character wants (dominant motivation) and what the character is willing to do to get it (the ethical framework within which the character operates). Together, these are usually the most important indicators of character. But they are still overviews. In preparing the role, the actor needs to examine how the character's major goal (the "spine" of the role) is manifested in each unit (or beat) and how it changes and evolves. This will help the actor find the focus of each unit, just as examining individual units in relation to the whole play will show how the characterization must build and grow.

The actor may next examine how the role relates to all the others in the play. What does the character think of each of the others? How does the character present himself to each? What do each of the others think of the character? How does each of these variations affect the action?

The actor needs to understand the script's themes, implied meanings, and overall significance. This demands not only attention to observable relationships among characters and ideas but also sensitivity to subtext—the emotional undercurrents and unexpressed motivations and attitudes that add complexity.

The actors also need to examine their roles in relation to the director's concept. They may wish to talk with the director about their reactions to the concept and how it affects their roles; some may even try to persuade the director to alter the production concept. Ultimately, however, the actors must make their roles fit whatever concept is used to shape the production.

Psychological and Emotional Preparation   In addition to understanding the script and how a role fits into the total concept, the actors must be able to project themselves imaginatively into the world of the play,

Glenda Jackson in the emotionally demanding role of Charlotte Corday in *Marat/Sade*. (Photo Jessie Alexander/ Nancy Palmer.)

the specific situations, and their individual character's feelings and motivations. An actor who has difficulty doing this may need to experiment with ways of inducing empathic involvement. One method, borrowed from Stanislavsky, is to employ emotion memory. Another is to search out persons similar to the character and find out more about their situations. For example, an actor playing a hospital worker may come to understand the character's attitudes and frustrations more fully by spending time in a hospital participating in or observing what goes on there. Perhaps the most typical method is the use of improvisations and theatre games to explore, in collaboration with other actors, multiple feelings about, and responses to, situations similar to those in the script. Such explorations may occur several times during the preparation or rehearsal process.

Movement, Gesture, and Business As a rule, blocking is done in an early phase of rehearsals. The director either may indicate where each character is to be at each moment or may, at least initially, let the actors position themselves and move about as their responses impel them. Actors should feel comfortable with their blocking and movement; if they do not, they should tell the director. Most disagreements can be settled by discussing the character's motivations, relationship to other characters in the scene, and the function of the text unit.

Even though the director may specify much of the movement, the actor still must fill in many details—the character's walk, posture, bodily attitudes, and gestures. (For a discussion of movement and its purposes, see Chapter 12.) In shaping physical characterization, actors may find it helpful to approach it in three steps. First, the actors need to make sure that they have taken into consideration the physical attributes required by the action and any changes that occur during the play. Second, they may wish to assess which of a character's physical traits need to be dominant in any given unit. It is sometimes helpful to think of a play as though it had no dialogue, in which case the actors would have to convey through visual means the situation, motivations, and emotional re-

Movement and stage business are crucial parts of the scene in which Tartuffe seeks to seduce Elmire while her husband, Orgon, is hidden under the table. In this Yale Repertory Theatre production, the actors are (from top to bottom) Austin Pendleton, Frances Conroy, and Jerome Dempsey. Directed by Walton Jones. (Photo by William B. Carter. Courtesy Yale Repertory Theatre.)

sponses. This approach, if followed fully, would probably lead to an overabundance of movement (and overacting), but using it in the preparatory stages can stimulate the actors' imaginations and provide them with a number of possibilities from among which they can choose. Third, without violating the limits established by the script, role, and production concept, the actors should work for distinctiveness so as to avoid clichés. A physical characterization can be judged by its appropriateness, clarity, expressiveness, and distinctiveness.

Vocal Characterization   Although actors cannot radically change their dominant vocal traits during a rehearsal period, they may, if they have well-trained voices, modify their vocal patterns considerably for purposes of characterization. The variable factors in voice are *pitch, volume,* and *quality,* each of which may be used to achieve many different effects. (For a discussion of these aspects of sound, see Chapter 11.) In some contemporary productions, the voice is used to create dissonances, harmonies, or rhythmical effects for mood purposes or as a type of nonverbal gesture. More typically, the voice is used as a medium for speech that evokes or defines emotions, ideas, or situations.

The variable factors of speech are *articulation, pronunciation, duration, inflection,* and *projection* (or audibility). *Articulation* involves the production of sounds, while *pronunciation* involves the selection and combination of sounds. A person may articulate sounds clearly but mispronounce words, just as a person may know how to pronounce a word but articulate sounds so imprecisely as to be unintelligible. The well-trained actor should be able to speak clearly or to alter articulation and pronunciation as needed to suit character and situation. Among the most memorable features of Marlon Brando's roles in *A Streetcar Named Desire* and *The Godfather* were his vocal characterizations, achieved through control over articulation, pronunciation, and quality.

Duration refers to the length of time assigned to any sound, *inflection* to rising and falling pitch. Both duration and inflection are used to stress some syllables and subordinate others. Without stress, words may be unrecognizable. (Try, for example, shifting stress from the first to the second syllable of "probably.") Duration also refers to the number of words spoken per minute. Slowness can create the impression of laziness, old age, or weakness, whereas a rapid rate may suggest tension or vivacity. *Inflection* (change in pitch) is one of the principal indicators of meaning. Surprise, disgust, indifference, and other reactions may be indicated by tone of voice, and the alteration of inflection can often completely change the meaning of a line. Duration and inflection also play key roles in dialects (or regional "accents"). Acting coaches often counsel those working on a Southern accent, for example, to end sentences on a rising inflection and to prolong the final sounds.

In performance, actors should be both *audible* (which depends on *projection* or volume) and *intelligible* (which depends primarily on articulation and pronunciation), since the audience needs both to hear and to understand what the characters are saying. Actors must also be concerned with *variety* (which depends on how all the variable aspects of voice and speech are handled). Nothing is more deadening than all lines delivered at the same pace and intensity. Variety usually comes easily if the actor clearly understands situation and motivations, since any change in thought or feeling motivates changes in volume, pitch, or quality, as well as in the variable factors of speech.

Memorization and Line Readings A task that every actor faces is memorization. In this process, it is usually helpful to memorize speeches and movements simultaneously, since they reinforce each other. Furthermore, because blocking is done in relation to specific speeches, this conjunction ultimately becomes fused in the memory.

Dietrich Strebel's *Body Language Composition* on the experimental stage of the State Opera, Munich. This production made no use of spoken language or music. The only sounds were breathing, rustling, stamping, and scraping. (Photo by Anne Kirchbach. Courtesy German Information Center.)

Memorization is aided by a few simple procedures. Since it is impossible to memorize everything at once, the script should be broken into units and mastered one unit at a time. In each, the actors must ultimately not only learn their own lines but also be familiar with the lines of others in the scene. In addition, actors must memorize *cues* (the words or actions of others that immediately precede and trigger their lines) as thoroughly as they memorize their own lines. Before seeking to memorize specific lines, it is helpful to study the sequence of ideas or shifts in emotion and tone—the overall development of the unit. Familiarity with sequence, along with a thorough understanding of the meaning and purpose of each line in a unit, are the greatest aids to memorization. (The actual process of memorization requires going over the lines many times, usually while someone else keeps an eye on the script—as a check on accuracy as well as to provide the appropriate cues.)

Once the actors know their lines well enough not to need the script as a crutch, they usually need to do considerable fine tuning to mesh their understanding of the lines and their use of the controllable factors of voice and speech. They need to make sure that speeches, especially long ones, build properly, that their line readings create a sense of spontaneity and conviction, and that the readings are appropriate to character, emotion, and situation.

Refining the Role   The foundation work—understanding the role; psychological and emotional preparation; movement, gesture, and business; vocal characterization; memorization—proceeds simultaneously with rehearsals, some of it in isolation, much of it with the director and other actors. In these early phases, different approaches to a scene or aspects of character may be tried and abandoned. But, eventually, the major decisions are made, the movement and vocal patterns become reasonably clear, and the lines have been committed to memory. There follows a period of refining and perfecting the role and integrating it into the whole.

This phase is difficult to describe specifically, since it varies with the actor, the role, and the production. Typically, much of the time is spent on deepening one's understanding of motivations and relationships. Work on complex business, precise timing and pacing, and variety is also common during this phase. Additionally, actors must be concerned about progression and build in their roles.

No single role (except in those rare plays with one character) is complete in itself. It is sometimes said that performing in a play is not merely acting but reacting. The director usually works to achieve the sense of give-and-take, cooperation, and mutual support that characterizes *ensem-*

Scene 1 of O'Neill's *"The Hairy Ape"* as performed at the Wilma Theatre, Philadelphia, 1985. Yank threatens Paddy. Directed by Blanka Zizka. (Photo Stan Sadowski. Courtesy Wilma Theatre.)

ble playing. The goal is a seamless whole rather than a series of separate performances. This goal can be reached only if all actors are willing to subordinate themselves to the demands of the production. Ensemble playing depends much on the actors' awareness of each other's strengths and weaknesses, where they will get support, and where they need to compensate for another's inadequacy.

Dress Rehearsals and Performance   Not until dress rehearsals are actors usually able to work with all properties, settings, costumes, makeup, and stage lighting. Frequently, this is also the first time they have been able to work on the stage that will be used in performances. Thus, this may be a time of considerable stress.

Of special importance to actors are their costumes, since they affect not only appearance but also movement and gesture. Actors should find out everything they can about their costumes in advance of dress rehearsals—which movements a garment enhances or restricts, its possibilities for use in stage business, and so on. If stage garments are significantly different from clothing they are used to, actors should have been provided with suitable rehearsal garments from the beginning. Actors should also give considerable thought to their makeup before the dress-rehearsal period begins. They should know what effects they wish to create and how to achieve them. They should also have rehearsed with reasonable facsimiles of the properties they will use in performances.

Performance is the ultimate goal. The better prepared the actors are, the more confident they will feel on opening night, although it is a rare actor who does not experience some stage fright—which, because it increases alertness, may be turned to advantage. Some actors feel a letdown after opening night and must guard against diminished effectiveness. This is a special danger in long runs. The best guards against such letdowns are concentration and reminders that each performance is the first for this particular audience. Ultimately, performance offers the actor one of the best opportunities for learning, since the ability to affect or control an audience's responses is a major test of acting skill.

Looking at the Actor's Work

When we attend the theatre, our attention is focused primarily on the characters, for it is through them that the action develops. But what the actors who play the characters do and say is based on the dramatist's script, just as the interpretation and production concept are decided by the director. What the actors wear is determined by the costume designer; the stage environment is created by the scenic designer; and much of the mood and visual emphasis is provided by the lighting designer. In such a cooperative venture, it is not easy to isolate the actors' contributions. Perhaps that is as it should be, since the director's goal is to create a unified whole rather than a collection of easily distinguishable parts. Nevertheless, even if we cannot determine precisely what is to be attributed to each production element, we often make the attempt. Here are some questions that may help us assess the actors' performances and estimate their contributions to the production:

1. Were the roles appropriately cast? (Were actors and roles adequately meshed? Were some actors inadequate to their roles? In what ways? How did this affect the other roles and the action of the play? Were some actors especially effective? If so, how and with what effect?)

2. Was the production concept evident in the acting? If so, in what ways? with what results?
3. In what type of space did the performance take place? How did this affect the actors' tasks? with what results?
4. Were the actors audible? understandable? Were the vocal characterizations suited to the roles? Were there actors whose voices notably enhanced or detracted from their performances? in what ways?
5. Were the physical characterizations suited to the roles? Were there actors whose movement or gestures notably enhanced or detracted from their performances? in what ways?
6. Were the characters' psychological attributes and motivations clear? Were some actors especially effective or ineffective in projecting these aspects of characterization? If so, how and with what effect?
7. Were the relationships among the characters clear? Were some actors especially effective or ineffective in clarifying relationships? If so, how and with what effect?
8. Were any special skills (such as dancing, singing, fencing, playing a musical instrument) required of any of the actors? If so, how effectively were the demands met? with what effect on the production?
9. Did the actors make any special use of costume, scenery, properties, or lighting? If so, in what ways and with what effect?
10. How extensively was movement and stage business used? Did they have distinctive qualities? If so, what was the result?
11. Did the actors achieve a sense of "the first time"? Did they work together effectively as an ensemble? If so, with what effect? If not, what interfered? with what result?
12. Overall, were the themes and implications of the play clear? Was the clarity or lack of it attributable to the acting? (script? directing? visual design? total production?)

Most of these questions cannot be answered precisely, not only because some of the needed information may not be available but also because, even if the information were available, responses would be at least partially subjective. Thus, conclusions about each question are apt to vary widely. Nevertheless, trying to answer the questions as they relate to specific productions or performances will focus attention on the processes and results of acting and will encourage detailed attention to actors' performances.

Scenic Design

14

T he scene designer is concerned with the organization and appearance of the acting space. The designer defines and characterizes the space, arranges it to facilitate the movement of the actors, and uses it to reinforce the production concept.

The Designer's Skills

Scene designers need a variety of skills, many of them pertinent to other arts, especially architecture, painting, interior design, and acting. Like architects, scene designers conceive and build structures for use by human beings. Although scene designers do not design entire buildings, as an architect does, they nevertheless sculpt space and, like the architect, must be concerned with its function, size, organization, construction and visual appearance. Also like the architect, they must be able to communicate their ideas to others through sketches, scale models, and construction drawings that indicate how each element is built and how it will look when completed.

Scene designers, in some aspects of their work, use skills similar to the painter's. For example, one of the designer's primary ways of communicating with the director and other designers is through sketches and drawings. During preliminary discussions of a production, designers usually make numerous sketches to demonstrate possible solutions to design problems; then, before these designs can be given final approval, they must be rendered in perspective and in color. For final designs, watercolors are the scene designer's most common medium, but pastels and other color media are sometimes used. In addition to making sketches showing entire settings, designers also make painters' elevations—scale drawings of each piece of scenery showing how it is to be

The musical *Cats*. The details of the setting are scaled to suggest a cat's view of the world. Note, for example, the auto license plate in the background. The costumes emphasize the individuality of each cat. Production designed by John Napier; wigs by Paul Huntley. Directed by Trevor Nunn. (Photo by Martha Swope.)

The Book of Job, a play by Orlin Corey adapted from the Bible. The costumes and makeup by Irene Corey are based on mosaics and stained glass windows. (Dennis Stock/Magnum.)

The musical *42nd Street* uses the lights of theatre marquees, bright costumes, and vigorous dancing to suggest the glamor of Broadway. (Photo by Martha Swope.)

Peter Weiss' *Marat/Sade* as directed by Peter Brook for the Royal Shakespeare Company. Stark, angular forms and subdued colors are used to create the insane asylum in which the action takes place. (Photo by Dennis Stock/Magnum.)

Act I finale of *Sunday in the Park With George*, a musical by Stephen Sondheim and James Lapine. This scene recreates Georges Seurat's painting, *A Sunday Afternoon on the Island of La Grande Jatte*. Scenery by Tony Straiges; lighting by Richard Nelson; costumes by Patricia Zipprodt and Ann Hould-Ward. (Photo by Martha Swope.)

Shakespeare's *A Midsummer Night's Dream* at the Guthrie Theatre. Design by Beni Montresor. Directed by Liviu Ciulei. (Courtesy Guthrie Theatre.)

Shakespeare's *A Midsummer Night's Dream* as performed by the Royal Shakespeare Company under the direction of Peter Brook. Titania's bower is represented by the ostrich feather bed. Bottom, instead of being transformed into an ass, is given a clown's nose. Note the trapezes used for flying characters and the undecorated white walls of the set, designed by Sally Jacobs. (Photo by Max Waldman/ Magnum.)

Shakespeare's *A Midsummer Night's Dream* at the American Repertory Theatre. Directed by Alvin Epstein, with music from Henry Purcell's *The Fairy Queen*. (Photo by Richard Feldman.)

Shakespeare's *Richard II* as performed by the Théâtre du Soleil (Paris), under the direction of Ariane Mnouchkine. This production combines Elizabethan (note the neck ruffs) and Japanese costumes and acting conventions. (Photo by Martine Franck/Magnum.)

Alcestis as staged by Robert Wilson at the American Repertory Theatre. The text includes a prologue by the contemporary German dramatist, Heinar Mueller, and a Japanese Kyogen play, in addition to Euripides' text. Setting by Wilson and Tom Kamm, lighting by Wilson and Jennifer Tipton. (Photo by Richard Feldman.)

painted and the painting techniques to be used. Designers sometimes must paint (or supervise others who paint) the scenery they have designed.

In other aspects of their work, scene designers use the skills of an interior decorator, since many sets are incomplete without furniture, rugs, drapes, pictures, and decorative details. In creating appropriate interiors, designers also need some of the actor's skills, since they must understand the characters who inhabit the spaces and whose tastes dictate the choice of furnishings and decorative features.

Additionally, scene designers need to be well grounded in art history (including architecture, crafts, and decorative arts), since in creating settings, designers must be familiar with architectural styles and the history of decorative motifs, furniture, and bric-a-brac. Such details not only reflect a specific period or place but also indicate the economic status and tastes of the characters. Similarly, designers need to know stage history so they may (when appropriate) draw on the theatrical conventions of other times, places, or cultures to connect the play with its original context or to enhance the production concept.

Scene designers must understand scenic construction techniques (since they must specify how each part of their settings are to be built) and scenic painting (since they must specify the color of each visible surface and the painting techniques to be used). Designers should also be familiar with new materials and technologies and their potential for design purposes. Plastics, styrofoam, and laser projections, for example, have opened up new possibilities and stimulated innovative designs.

The Functions of Stage Design

Scenic design serves many functions. It *defines the performance space* by establishing distinctions between onstage and offstage. Through the use of flats, drapes, platforms, and other means, designers delineate the areas that will be used for the dramatic action. Designers may employ a great deal of masking so that persons or objects outside a clearly marked area cannot be seen by the audience; or they may use virtually no masking and thereby acknowledge that the place of the action is a stage that continues into the wings as far as the audience can see. In arena and thrust theatres, the audience seating arrangement may outline the acting space. In a variable space, acting space and audience space may be intermingled.

Scene design *creates a floor plan* that provides multiple opportunities for movement, composition, character interaction, and stage business.

The location of exits and entrances, the placement (or absence) of furniture, the presence or absence of steps, levels, and platforms—all the elements of the setting and their arrangement—are among the greatest influences on blocking, picturization, and movement. A setting can be organized in a great number of different ways; arranging it to maximum advantage for a specific production requires careful and cooperative planning by designer and director.

Scene design visually *characterizes the acting space.* How it does so depends much on the production concept. If the concept demands that locales be represented realistically, the designer will probably select architectural details, furniture, and decorations that clearly indicate a specific period and locale. For example, the designer might create a setting for *The Wild Duck* that suggests a room in a Norwegian house around 1880. Another production concept might demand fragmentary settings with only enough pieces to establish the general character of the locale. Still another concept might rely largely on visual motifs and theatrical conventions from the era when the play was written. A setting for *Tartuffe,* for example, might use decorative motifs and a wing-and-drop setting reflecting the age of Louis XIV. Or, as has become increasingly common, the concept may demand that the time and place of the action be altered (such as *Hamlet* being translated to an American Mafia context).

Another way of characterizing the space is to treat it as flexible and nonspecific. This is common for plays with actions divided into many scenes and set in many places. To represent each place realistically would require a large number of sets as well as a great deal of time to change them, thereby interrupting the continuity, rhythm, and flow of the action. On the other hand, to play all the scenes on the flat floor of an undecorated stage would be monotonous. A common solution is an arrangement of platforms, steps, and ramps that breaks up the stage space, provides several acting areas that can be used all together or isolated singly through lighting, and that can be localized as needed through the addition of a few well-chosen properties, pieces of furniture, banners, images projected on screens, or through other means.

Scene design may *make a strong interpretational statement.* The setting for Beckett's *Happy Days* sums up visually the human condition as depicted in the play: an individual isolated, trapped, forced to make the best of her lot. For a play about war, the game of chess has been used as a metaphor—with the stage floor laid out in black and white squares, and the characters costumed to suggest chess pieces. The settings for *"The Hairy Ape"* incorporate images of human beings caged and dehumanized.

Scene design *creates mood and atmosphere.* Robert Edmond Jones' setting for *Macbeth* creates a powerful mood of foreboding and fatedness as the

Setting by Santo Loquasto for Chekhov's *The Cherry Orchard*. Usually, this final act is staged in a fully enclosed realistic interior, but here the wall of the house is indicated only by the chest at center. The entire stage (from front to back) is covered by a white carpet. The cherry trees, normally only glimpsed during the production, become the dominant visual element throughout the action. Directed by Andrei Serban. (Photo by George E. Joseph.)

masks of the witches brood over the stage throughout and as the Gothic arches lean ever more precariously. On the other hand, Ezio Frigerio's settings for *The Servant of Two Masters* create a sense of carefree improvisation through details painted on cloths suspended like shower curtains on visible rods and with slits for entrances.

Scene design is only one *part of a total design*, which includes costumes, lighting, acting and all the other elements of a production. Thus, it needs to evolve in consultation with those who are responsible for the other parts of the whole. It is not, as a painting is, complete in itself; it cannot be judged entirely by appearance, for not only should it look appropriate, it should also function appropriately.

Working Plans and Procedures

Scene designers, like other theatre artists, usually begin their preparations by familiarizing themselves with the play. Initially, they seek to understand the script as a total structure—its action, characters, themes, language, meaning—since what they design may be affected by all of these and since the scenery needs to reflect or enhance all of these. As designers continue their study of the script, they focus increasingly on clues about scenic demands and visual style. During this process, they accumulate information of various sorts: the number of locales; the types of locales (prison, living room, park, etc.); the space required by the action in each scene; the arrangement (location of entrances and exits, placement of furniture, need for steps and levels, etc.) required by the action in each scene; the period, geographical place, and socioeconomic conditions; and any other factors that influence the scenery.

Designers may also utilize information from sources other than the script. They may wish to know about the manners and customs, decorative motifs, architectural styles, furnishings, and favorite color schemes in use during the period of the play's action. They may wish to understand more fully the political and social context out of which the play came. They may explore the staging conventions for which the play was originally written. And they may undertake various other explorations. Although they may not incorporate all that they learn into their designs, their imaginations may be stimulated by the fuller understanding they have gained of the script and its context.

Before they make sketches and plans (and perhaps before they have begun to study the script and its context), scene designers meet with the director and other designers to discuss the play and the production concept. The director may use an initial meeting to elicit ideas from the designers and may ask them to participate in formulating a production concept. Many directors explain the production concept they have already arrived at, although they may still be open to suggestions and may be willing to make alterations in the concept. However it evolves, a concept (or interpretational focus) is needed as a guide for the designers' work. In addition to the concept, other information should also be made available to the designers before they begin work. They need to know if the director has any special demands (location of entrances and exits; specific floor plan; space for dances or fight scenes, etc.). They need to know what the budget for scenery will be, what space will be used for performances, what equipment and personnel will be available. Understanding the limits within which they must work—the script, the production concept, the performance space, and the budget—the designers are ready to proceed.

There is no standard way of moving through the design process. Most designers make numerous preliminary sketches, many of them very tentative, as a means of thinking through possibilities. Some make a scale model of the empty performance space and try out different arrangements of scenic pieces within the space. Some think in terms of design elements—the kind of line, mass, color, or texture needed to capture

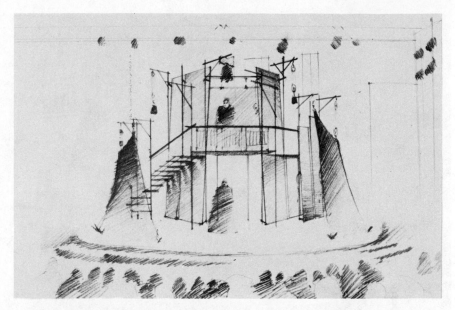

Designer's preliminary sketch for Shakespeare's *Richard III* at the Colorado Shakespeare Festival. Design by Robert Schmidt. (Courtesy Mr. Schmidt.)

the dominant qualities of the dramatic action or the production concept. However they work, designers eventually arrive at proposed designs to present at a conference with the director and the other designers. Some proposals may be abandoned and others may need to be reworked. (Design decisions involve not only how the settings function as acting spaces, but also how they relate to costume and lighting designs and the total "look" of the production.) Through a process of reaction and revision, tentative agreement is finally reached, but before the designs are given final approval, they must be rendered as perspective, color sketches that indicate how the sets will look on stage when lighted. Scene designers must also supply floor plans (drawn to scale) that show the layout of each set on the stage. Designers may also be asked to construct three-dimensional scale models that show in miniature how each set will look when completed. (It is not unusual for directors to require either the color sketch or the scale model rather than both, but in many situations both are expected.)

After the designs have been approved, the next step is to make working drawings. The number and type of drawings needed vary from one type of organization to another. For example, in a permanent company that maintains a stock of scenic units, it may be unnecessary to make working drawings of every flat and platform, since they are not to be

Model of the setting for *Richard III*. (Courtesy Robert Schmidt.)

The setting for *Richard III* in use. The character Richard III is seen at center. Directed by Jack Clay. (Courtesy Colorado Shakespeare Festival.)

built but merely pulled from stock. In the Broadway theatre, every piece is usually built new by union workers who insist on having precise drawings for every detail. Thus, the director may have to provide some or all of the following, in addition to perspective sketches, floor plans, and scale models: (1) rear elevations, which indicate the type of construction, materials, and methods to be used in assembling each unit; (2) front elevations, which show each unit in two dimensions from the front, with indications of such features as molding, baseboards, and platforms; (3) side elevations, which show units in profile and indicate the thickness and shape of each unit; (4) detailed individual drawings, which show the methods by which such units as platforms, steps, trees, columns, and similar objects are to be built; and (5) painters' elevations, which show the color of the base coat and any overpainting to be used on each unit. With the exception of the perspective sketches, all of the plans are drawn to scale so that the exact size of any object may be determined. In addition to the drawings listed above, designers may also need to provide special plans showing how the scenery is to be shifted and how it is to be stored during the show when it is not on stage.

Once the plans are completed, the construction phase can begin. While designers may not be directly involved in building the scenery, they must approve all work to ensure that it conforms to the original specifications.

Basic Scenic Elements

A combination of rising costs, changing tastes, improved materials, and new equipment since World War II has steadily diminished concern for full-stage, realistic settings. Although complete box sets are still seen occasionally, they are far less common than they used to be. The majority of settings today are composed of a few set pieces and stage properties or of steps and levels. In other words, settings tend to be fragmentary and evocative rather than completely representational; many are wholly abstract. Furthermore, since the 1960s, innovative approaches have been encouraged by new materials and unconventional construction techniques. Nevertheless, traditional stagecraft practices still play a major role in most settings, since the built pieces (though fewer in number than formerly) are usually constructed according to time-tested procedures.

Designers utilize two basic kinds of built units: standing (those that rest on the floor or on other parts of the set) and hanging (those suspended from above). Let us look briefly at each type.

Standing Units   The basic standing unit is the *flat* (a wooden frame over which canvas or muslin is stretched). Flats of almost any width or height could be made, but experience has shown that as they become larger, they become more unstable. Therefore, the height of flats usually ranges from 8 to 16 feet, and the width from 1 to 6 feet. Perhaps the most common unit is the *plain flat*—one without an opening. Other types of flats include the *door flat* (with an opening into which a door frame may be set), *window flat, fireplace flat,* and *arch flat* (with an opening shaped like one of the basic types of arches: Roman, Gothic, etc.). There are many variations on these basic units. Flats may be constructed with slanting sides or with edges (either top or sides) shaped to simulate trees, rocks, distant mountains, ruined arches, etc., but most have smooth edges so they may be hinged together to create larger units, such as the walls of a box set or pieces used to suggest a larger structure.

Other standing units include *door frames* (with or without *doors*), *window frames* (usually with some type of *window*), *fireplace* units, *rocks, mounds, tree trunks,* and *columns.* Among the most common units in both interiors and exteriors and in both representational and abstract settings are *platforms, steps,* and *ramps.* How these units are constructed is beyond the scope of this book; the processes are described fully in books on scenic practices.

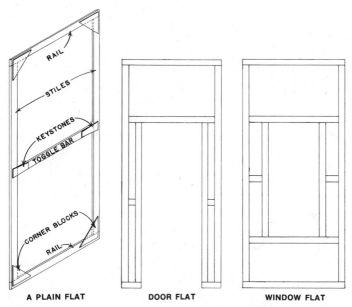

Types of flats: plain flat, door flat, window flat.

Hanging Units Hanging units include *borders, drops, draperies, cyclo-ramas,* and *screens* (for projections). The *border,* a short curtain or piece of painted canvas, is the most common overhead masking for both interior and exterior scenes. Borders are hung parallel to the front of the stage and in a series from front to back. They may be of black cloth or painted and shaped to represent the beams of a ceiling, foliage, or some other visual element. (Arena and thrust stages often do not use borders; instead, the area above the stage is painted black and is sometimes divided into boxlike compartments within which lighting instruments may be mounted. On no type of stage is overhead masking now considered to be of great importance.)

Drops are used to enclose settings at the back and as surfaces on which scenes can be painted. A drop is made by sewing together enough lengths of canvas to create an area of the desired size. Most typically, the cloth is attached to a wooden or metal batten at the top to support it and to another at the bottom to keep it stretched and free from wrinkles. Occasionally, it is framed on all four sides. A drop may also have portions cut out so that another drop or object is visible behind it, thereby creating apparent depth and distance.

Draperies may be hung parallel to the proscenium on either side of the stage in a series from front to back in order to mask the sides of the stage in the manner of wings. They may be of any color. Black draperies are sometimes used to surround the acting area or to create an enclosing void for a fragmentary setting. Draperies may also be made of canvas or muslin; they may be dyed, or they may have scenes (such as a forest or a distant city) painted on them and be hung in folds to create stylized backgrounds. *Scrim,* a specialized curtain made of gauze, appears opaque when lighted only from the front but is transparent when lighted from behind. It can be hung in folds or stretched tightly. It may be used initially as a background for a scene and then become transparent to show another scene behind the first one; or it may be used for the appearance and disappearance of ghosts and apparitions; it can also create the effect of seeing a scene through a fog or mist.

A *cyclorama* is any arrangement of curtains or other materials that surrounds the stage area on three sides. It may be composed of draperies or may be a plaster dome, but typically it is a continuous, tightly stretched curtain suspended on a U-shaped pipe that curves around the back and sides of the stage. It is usually neutral or gray, so its apparent color may be changed through lighting. It is used to represent the sky, to give the effect of infinite space, and to allow the maximum use of stage space without the need for numerous masking pieces. It is also used as a surface for projections (such as moving storm clouds or abstract, symbolic patterns).

Screens have become typical scenic units since the 1960s, when the incorporation of projected still or moving pictures began to be common. Screens may be used alone or in conjunction with other screens. They may rest on the floor, but usually they are flown. Some may be relatively near the audience, others far upstage; they may be rigged so they can be raised, lowered, or moved laterally during a performance; they may be of any shape or size and may be made from almost any material—wide-mesh netting, transluscent plastic, textured cloth, and so on. Some of these surfaces blur images, some give texture, some permit images to bleed through onto other surfaces; on some screens, images can be projected only from the front, on others, only from the rear. Screens can be used for projected still or moving images, for scenes fixed on film, or for portions of live performances transmitted to the screens by way of closed-circuit television. Thus, the range of possibilities is extremely wide, although many options require technology more advanced than is available in many theatres.

Most hanging units are more useful for proscenium stages than for thrust or arena stages, where hanging pieces can easily interfere with sightlines. Nevertheless, fragments of architecture or other objects may be suspended above a thrust or arena stage to suggest what is not shown.

Ming Cho Lee's setting for *Death of a Salesman* at the Arena Stage (Washington, D.C.). Note how the outline of the roof overhead and the turned posts create a sense of place and period. (Courtesy Arena Stage.)

For example, for *Death of a Salesman* at the Arena Stage in Washington, the designer Ming Cho Lee hung architectural fragments overhead to create a sense of place (see illustration on page 346).

Innovative Materials and Methods   During the past two decades, experiments with nontraditional materials have been numerous. Metal pipes have been welded together to create intricate towers and structures of various kinds. Fiberglass (treated with chemicals to make it pliable) has been molded into rocks, mounds, and other shapes and then allowed to harden, thereby creating lightweight pieces capable of supporting heavy loads. Such material as Styrofoam has been incised to create the three-dimensional form of molding, bricks, and carvings, or it has been sculpted to create figurines and other properties formerly difficult to construct. Vacuform molds, with which one can duplicate in plastic almost any shape (including armor, swords, or small scenic units), have also become common. Thus, traditional and innovative stagecraft coexist and supplement each other.

A setting for Shakespeare's *A Midsummer Night's Dream* made of structural steel, plexiglass and Mylar surfaces. Design by John Jensen. (Courtesy Guthrie Theatre.)

The basic units discussed here are the building blocks with which designers usually work. They must decide which pieces are needed for the settings they have designed, and they must supply the working drawings for construction or indicate which pieces in existing stock are to be used. For pieces using unusual materials or construction methods, designers need to supply detailed drawings and instructions.

Assembling Scenery

Once the units are constructed, they are ready to be assembled to create a setting. Some pieces may be more or less complete as built, but others need to be combined with, or attached to, other units to complete a section of the setting. How the pieces are assembled depends in part on whether the scenery must be transported from one place to another and whether it must be shifted during performances. Sometimes, scenery is built in the performance space, but that is unusual. Permanent companies often build scenery in shops adjoining the stage, but for Broad-

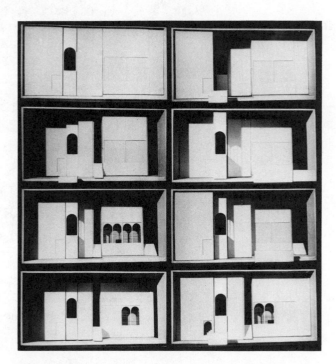

A model of settings for Shakespeare's *Romeo and Juliet*. A number of units are assembled and reassembled to create various locales. Design by Josef Svoboda. (Photo by Jaromír Svoboda.)

One scene from the production of *Romeo and Juliet*. (Photo by Jaromír Svoboda.)

way productions, the scenery is built in scenic studios far removed from the theatres in which the performances will occur. Touring companies carry their scenery with them from city to city by plane or truck. How scenery is assembled is also determined in part by shifting demands. Once erected, one-set shows may never have to be moved until the production closes. Such sets can be assembled differently from those that must be taken down and put up quickly. Another determinant is the method used to shift those sets that must be changed. For example, sets that are to be shifted manually may need to be put together in smaller units than those mounted on movable platforms. Thus, several factors influence how a set will be assembled.

The typical methods of assembling scenery include *hinging, permanent joining,* and *lashing.* One of the most common assemblages is made by joining two or more flats to create a wall. This is usually done with hinges attached to the front edges of the adjoining flats, so that a fully assembled unit of some length can be folded for moving and storage. The hinges and cracks between flats are covered with strips of muslin (*dutchmen*), and the entire assembled unit is then painted to hide the hinging. Braces are attached to the back of each assembled unit to hold it rigid when it is in use (that is, to keep it from folding at the hinged points); when the unit must be taken down, the braces are removed and the unit is folded. Hinges may also be used to hold units together temporarily. For example, loose-pin hinges (with pins that may be removed so the two halves of the hinge come apart) are sometimes used to hold platforms or step units firmly in place and to facilitate rapid disassembly when they must be moved.

Permanent joining is done with screws, bolts, nails, or by welding. This kind of assembly is used for heavy units that do not need to be shifted, or for those that are shifted by means that do not require the units to be taken apart. Because of its greater stability, permanent joining is used whenever possible.

Lashing is a method of joining scenic units temporarily with lines or ropes drawn around cleats attached to the back of units. It allows settings to be assembled and dismantled rapidly during performance.

Scenery is assembled in stages. The first two stages usually occur in the scene shop. First, the building-block units (flats, door frames, doors, steps, platforms, etc.) are constructed (or brought from storage). Second, these basic units are combined into the somewhat larger units (the wall of a room, a door frame and door, a stairway, etc.). When this step has been completed, the units are painted. Then they are transported to the stage on which they will be used, and there they are assembled into complete sets.

Painting Scenery

Scenic studios (or paint shops) usually stock dry *pigment* in a wide range of colors that may be combined to obtain paint of any desired hue, saturation, or value. The dry pigment is then combined with a *binder*— a liquid solution that makes the pigment adhere to a surface after it dries. The most common binder is a glue-and-water solution, but others may also be used. Scenic studios may also stock and use ready-mixed paints (such as those used for home interiors) and aniline dyes (which impart color to cloth without making it opaque and without creating a surface that will crack when folded).

Newly constructed flats are usually treated with a solution of glue and pigment to stretch and seal the cloth. This process, called *sizing*, may be done before the flat is joined to others. Once the larger units are assembled, they may be given a *priming coat* of paint, which creates a relatively uniform surface on which to apply the paint to follow. The priming coat is usually mixed from cheap pigments to keep down costs.

Next, the *base coat* is applied. The result should be a uniform color of

Painting the snow-scene backdrop for the ballet, *The Nutcracker*. The designer, John Rothgeb, is also the scene painter. (Courtesy Mr. Rothgeb and the Austin Ballet.)

smooth texture. The final step usually involves some modification of the base coat through *overpainting,* which simulates textures (such as plaster, brick, or wood) or condition (peeling, mildewing, uneven fading, etc.), or which softens a surface that would otherwise appear unnaturally flat. Overpainting may also be used to shade the upper portions of settings so as to decrease their prominence, to emphasize the shape and form of objects by giving emphasis to corners or curves, or to counterfeit three-dimensional details such as molding, paneling, bark, or mortar.

Scene painting makes use of a variety of techniques. The prime and base coats normally employ *flat painting* (intended to give an even surface) done with a large brush or a spray gun. Since overpainting adds texture, shading, or details, it requires colors different from the base coat. The degree of contrast depends on the purpose. For example, the texture of relatively smooth plaster may be achieved by *spattering* (that is, flicking small drops of paint from a brush onto the base coat) with one color that is slightly lighter and a second that is slightly darker than the base coat, thus creating the effect of raised and receding surfaces. Rough plaster may be simulated through *rolling,* which involves a rolled-up piece of burlap or other rough-textured cloth dipped in paint and rolled over the base coat in irregular patterns. Other common painting techniques include *sponging* (dipping a natural sponge in paint and patting it on the surface of the base coat) and *scumbling* (simultaneous application and blending of more than one shade of paint on the same surface to give a mottled effect, simulating foliage or walls on which the paint is faded, mildewed, or crumbled). The appropriate painting techniques are specified by the designer on the painters' elevations. The designer must also approve the finished job.

Assembling and Shifting Scenery Onstage

After the scenery is painted, it is transported to the stage on which it will be used. In resident and university theatres, this may merely mean moving scenery from one part of the building to another. In the Broadway theatre, it means moving the scenery by truck from a scenic studio to the theatre.

How scenery is assembled on stage depends on the method of shifting employed. A single setting may be set up permanently; multiple settings may need to be planned so the individual units can be assembled quickly and quietly, moved easily, and stored economically. Several different methods are used in shifting scenery, the most common being *manually, by flying, on wagons, on elevators,* and *on revolving stages.*

The simplest method (in the sense that no stage machinery is required) is to change all the elements *manually.* Using this method, each part of a set is moved by one or more stagehands to some prearranged storage space offstage, and the elements of a new setting are brought onstage and assembled. Parts of almost every setting must be moved manually, even when the major shifting is done by other means. Since manual shifting can be used on any stage, however simple or complex, a designer can always rely on it, though a large crew may be required to do it efficiently. Its drawbacks are relative slowness and the need to break the setting into small units.

Another common method of shifting is *flying.* Using this method, scenic elements are suspended above the stage and raised or lowered as needed. Flying is normally reserved for drops, curtains, borders, cycloramas, screens for projections, ceilings, and small units composed of flats. Flying beyond the most elementary requires a *counterweight system* composed of battens, lines, and pulleys. For such a system, a *gridiron* (a network of steel girders at the top of the stage house) serves as the weight-bearing structure. From the gridiron *steel battens* are suspended (parallel to the front of the stage and at intervals from front to back) on *wire lines,* which run upward from the battens to the gridiron, pass over *pulleys,* and continue to one side of the stage house, where they pass over another set of pulleys and turn downward; these lines are then attached to the top of *cradles* (or frames), into which are placed *weights* in the amount needed to balance whatever is being flown. *Ropes* attached to the bottom of the cradles run downward to the *flyrail,* where they can be tied off securely when not in use and from which the entire counterweight system can be operated by stagehands. With an adequate counterweight system, a single stagehand can easily raise and lower scenic elements of any size and weight. Some recent flying systems use electrically controlled winches without counterweights, permitting battens to be rigged at various angles rather than always parallel to the front of the stage.

Another common device for shifting scenery is the *wagon* (a platform on casters). The larger the wagon, the more scenery it can accommodate, but many stages do not have wing space sufficient to store or maneuver large wagons. Some stages have permanently installed tracks that guide wagons on- and offstage with precision, but such a system has little flexibility. Wagons can be used singly, in pairs or groups, or in combination with other shifting devices. The primary advantage of the wagon is that it permits heavy or complex scenic pieces to be shifted far more efficiently than by hand.

Another device for shifting scenery, the *revolving stage,* is far less common in America than in Europe and Japan, perhaps because of the expense involved. In theatres with permanently installed revolving stages, a circle of the stage floor (normally larger in diameter than the proscenium opening) is mounted on a central supporting pivot that can be turned by electric motors. Theatres sometimes use one or more temporary revolving stages, which are made by mounting a low circular platform on casters and attaching it at its center to the stage floor. Such temporary stages can be mounted almost anywhere in the acting space. The revolving stage is used primarily to hold two or more settings simultaneously; the individual sets are placed so that each faces the circumference of the circle. To shift scenery, the stage is revolved until the desired setting faces the audience. Settings may be changed on the backstage part while another is in use on stage. Complex arrangements of steps and platforms may also be erected on revolving stages; different views and playing areas are then revealed by turning the stage.

Still another shifting device, the *elevator stage,* raises and lowers segments of the stage vertically. In some theatres, portions of the stage may be lowered to the basement, where scenery is mounted and then raised to stage level. In other theatres, the stage is divided into several sections, each mounted on its own lift that can be raised, lowered, or tilted; the sections can then be used in combinations that create platforms, ramps, or a variety of levels without the need of building and shifting such units in the usual way. Theatres in which the stage proper is fixed may have a lift that raises and lowers the orchestra pit, so that it can be set below stage level for musicians, raised to the auditorium level and used for audience seating, or raised to stage level for use as a forestage.

Seldom is a single method of shifting used exclusively. But designers must know what methods are available to them and which is to be used with each unit that must be moved.

Set Decoration and Properties

Even after the sets are assembled onstage, they are incomplete without set decoration (which includes furniture) and properties. These elements, though part of the design, are not structural parts of the setting.

Set decoration and properties include such items as banners, coats-of-arms, tapestries, draperies, thrones, desks, tables, pictures, and books—anything that completes the setting. Properties may be subdivided into *set props* and *hand props.* The former is a property that is either attached to the setting or functions as a part of the design. The latter is used by the actor in stage business. The designer is always responsible for the selection of set props and may also choose the hand props, although more frequently hand props are considered the director's responsibility because of their intimate connection with the acting. Responsibility for obtaining both types may be assigned to a property master and crew. The appropriate pieces may be bought, made, rented, or borrowed.

Setting for John Osborne's *The Entertainer* at the Guthrie Theatre. The action, in which the decline of a music-hall entertainer parallels the decline of the British Empire, takes place on a stage and in the entertainer's living room. This setting, by Ming Cho Lee, is partially realistic and partially symbolic; the realistic furniture is seen against a lion (symbol of the British Empire) and Britannia (dressed as a music-hall showgirl). (Courtesy Guthrie Theater.)

Regardless of how they are obtained, set decoration and properties are necessary to complete the design.

Technical Rehearsals, Dress Rehearsals, and Performances

When the settings are complete, they must still be integrated into the production. Typically, this is accomplished through one or more technical rehearsals and one or more dress rehearsals. A technical rehearsal, as the term suggests, is devoted primarily to making certain that all the "technical" elements—scenery (including scene shifts), costumes (including changes), makeup, lighting (including light levels and cues), sound (including all settings and cues), and properties (including business involving properties)—are available and are functioning as they should both in terms of the action and the production concept. A technical rehearsal focuses attention on elements other than acting (although all or portions of scenes are performed), so that the various designers and technicians can see if the elements for which they are responsible are functioning properly both separately and as parts of the whole. A technical rehearsal seeks to uncover any difficulties and permit them to be corrected so that dress rehearsals can proceed as nearly like performances as possible. In complex productions, more than one technical rehearsal may be needed in order to make certain that any necessary adjustments have been made. As for scenery, it is very difficult to make major changes at this late point.

Since dress rehearsals approximate performances, they offer opportunities to see the settings as the audience will. The designer must be available for consultation and changes until the play has opened. On opening night, responsibility for the scenery passes to the stage manager and the stage crews.

The Designers' Assistants and Coworkers

Scene designers are aided by a number of persons. In the professional theatre, designers must be members of the United Scenic Artists Union, and they are usually assisted by members of this or other unions. Well-established designers often employ one or more assistants who make working drawings, search for furniture and properties, act as liaison between the designer and the scenic studios—anything the designer may request.

In the nonprofessional theatre, the *technical director* is likely to perform many of these functions. In many theatres, however, the technical director's job is quite independent of the designer's and of equal status. When a permanent organization produces several shows a year, the designer's job may be divided into its artistic and practical aspects. A designer may then conceive the designs, and the technical director may be responsible for building, assembling, and painting them. The technical director may also purchase all materials, supervise the scene shops, and be responsible for the crews that run the shows.

The scenery is built, assembled, and painted in a scene shop (or another work space that fills that function). In the professional theatre, all persons involved usually must be union members. In other types of organizations, this work is done by assigned or volunteer helpers under the supervision of the designer, technical director, or shop foreman.

When the scenery is delivered to the stage for rigging and shifting, scenery and property crews take over. In the professional theatre, again, all such persons must be union members. A master carpenter travels with a show on tour and makes sure the scenery is kept in good condition. In the nonprofessional theatre, scenery and props are usually handled by volunteer or assigned crews, but in all types of theatres, the heads of stage crews operate under the supervision of the stage manager. Their duties include the efficient movement and accurate placement of scenery and properties during the performance and the upkeep of units during the run of the show.

The designer's assistants frequently go unnoticed by the public, since little is done to draw attention to them. Often, and especially in the professional theatre, their names do not appear in the programs. Nevertheless, they are indispensable members of the overall production team, since without them the scenery would not be built and painted and could not function efficiently or be shifted during performances.

Looking at the Scene Designer's Work

The range of scenic design in today's theatre is great. It may be realistic or abstract. It may incorporate or intermingle elements from almost any period, style, culture, or set of conventions. So much variety, seemingly almost endless, can be confusing. The questions that follow seek to focus attention on certain crucial aspects of scenic design as an aid to understanding more clearly the designer's part in the performance, no matter the situation or mode in which the designer works:

1. In what type of space was the production staged? What opportunities did the space offer? How did the designer take advantage (or fail to take advantage) of them? What limitations did the space impose? How did the designer overcome (or fail to overcome) the limitations?
2. Did the scenery define the performance space? If so, in what ways and through what means? If not, with what effect?
3. How did the floor plan affect the action? Were there multiple levels? If so, how did they relate to each other, and how were they used? Were there specific entrances and exits? If so, how did their placement affect the action? Did the arrangement of furniture (or other elements) enhance or inhibit action? How did the overall arrangement affect movement and pictorial composition?
4. Of what sort of units was the setting composed? What standing units were used? hanging? other? Was the setting realistic? fragmentary? abstract? What was the overall effect?
5. Were sets (or any parts) changed during the performance? If so, by what means? How long did the changes take? How did the changes affect the mood, tension, and tempo?
6. What characteristics did the scenery embody? What did it convey about the characters? socioeconomic conditions? period? locale? How did it affect the play's tone? mood and atmosphere?
7. Were there any unusual scenic features? projected images? highly distinctive effects? If so, what was the result?
8. How did the scenery relate to the costumes and lighting? Did they enhance and complement each other? If so, how? If not, in what ways? with what results?
9. Did the setting suggest any specific interpretation of the play? If so, what interpretation? How did the setting convey this interpretation? If it did not, what was the result?
10. Overall, how did the scenery contribute (or fail to contribute) to the total production? What would have been lost if the scenery had been taken away?

The relevance of each question may vary according to the particular production and setting. Furthermore, there can be no absolute answers to many of the questions because responses to them are inevitably subjective, at least to some degree. But so are most responses to art of whatever kind. Nevertheless, formulating answers to the questions that have been posed force us to go beyond our usual cursory reaction to scenery and examine it and its function in production more specifically and critically.

Costume Design and Makeup

15

The costume designer is concerned primarily with the visual appearance of characters. Whereas the scene designer characterizes the stage environment within which the action develops, the costume designer characterizes the persons who function within that environment. Thus, the work of the scene and costume designers interacts and needs to be coordinated carefully.

The Costume Designer's Skills

Costume designers need a variety of skills, many of which are pertinent to other professions, such as fashion designer, visual artist, tailor, seamstress, social and cultural historian, and actor. Like the fashion designer, the costume designer creates garments for particular types of persons to wear for particular occasions or purposes. In creating garments, both types of designers keep in mind social and economic class, gender, activity, climate, and season, as well as stylistic qualities. But unlike fashion designers, costume designers must work within given circumstances established by the script, director, performance space and budget, and thus the restraints under which costume designers work differ from those imposed on fashion designers. Furthermore, costume designers must be able to project themselves into any period and create garments, not merely for present-day circumstances, but for those of other eras.

Since they communicate their ideas to others through sketches, costume designers must develop skills like those of the visual artist. They use a multitude of sketches to indicate their preliminary ideas about individual costumes and the overall look of the production. This facilitates discussion of the costumes, their relationship to the other visual elements, and their appropriateness to character, dramatic action, and production concept. Costume designers must also be able to render their final designs in color—most frequently watercolor, but sometimes pastel or another color medium.

Although costume designers are not always involved in the actual construction of the garments they have designed, they should know how the clothes will be cut and sewn. Thus, they need to see the garments as tailors and seamstresses would. Costume sketches should indicate how garments are shaped, the location of seams, darts, and other features that create visible lines and affect cut and fit. Such information is essential to making patterns from which the garments are constructed. Since costume designers also specify the material to be used in making each garment, they need to be thoroughly familiar with various fibers (cotton, wool, rayon, polyester, silk, etc.) and the characteristics of each. Such information permits cloth to be chosen for appearance, durability, specific use, cost, and other pertinent factors. Designers must also be knowledgeable about weaves, textures, and other qualities of cloth, since all are important in the overall appearance of a costume.

Costume designers must be well grounded in social and cultural history (including the visual arts and theatre), since clothing reflects the mores, standards of beauty, and stylistic preferences of each period and place. Thus, the more designers know about daily life, occupations, class structure, and favorite pastimes of a society, the better prepared they will be to design garments that reflect the status and function of a character within a specific world. Since much of our information about clothing of the past comes from painting and other visual arts, a knowledge of art history is of considerable help. Similarly, many productions today make some use of theatrical conventions in use when the play was written or in other cultures; consequently, theatre history, especially the history of theatrical costuming, may be especially pertinent.

Above all, costumes need to be suited to the characters who wear them. Therefore, costume designers must be able to analyze characters in the same way as actors do, so as to understand each role's significant traits, motivations, feelings, and functions within the dramatic action.

The Functions of Costume Design

Costume design may serve several functions. It may help to establish *time and place*. If the production concept calls for a realistic approach, the costumes may be based on the clothing worn at the time of the dramatic action (fifth century B.C., Shakespeare's lifetime, present-day);

they may indicate a particular country or region (Japan, ancient Rome, southwestern United States); a particular type of place (throne room, battlefield, hospital, farm); or a time of day or occasion (casual morning at home, formal evening dance).

Costumes may establish the *social and economic status* of characters by distinguishing between lower and upper classes, between rich and poor, or between more and less affluent members of the same group. Costume may identify *occupation* (nurse, soldier, policeman) or *lifestyle* (conservative middle-class, fashionable leisure-class, disaffected youth). Costumes usually indicate *gender* (male, female) and may reflect *age* (by adhering to stereotypical notions of what is appropriate to each age group). Costumes may also reflect a character's *atypicality* through dress that departs from the norm. More than settings or lighting, costumes are apt to retain some realistic qualities, probably because they are worn by actors who must be able to move effectively and appropriately in them and because actors tend to draw on real-life behavioral patterns in building their characterizations.

Costumes do not always adhere to realistic standards. Costumes may embody a *metaphor, symbol,* or *allegorical concept.* For example, the medieval play *Everyman* shows the title character summoned to his grave by a character called Death; Everyman then tries unsuccessfully to persuade several of his companions (Beauty, Strength, and Goods among them) to accompany him. Thus, the costumes need to capture the essence of each character as indicated by its name. On the other hand, a production of *Hamlet* based on the metaphor of the world as prison may embody this perception in more subtle and varied ways.

Costumes may reflect *mood and atmosphere.* Winnie's neat and somewhat refined costume in *Happy Days* (see the illustrations on pages 40 and 229) contrasts sharply with her entrapped state and reinforces her determined cheerfulness. Costumes may help to establish a particular

Shakespeare's *Cymbeline* at the Stratford (Ontario) Festival, 1986. The action of this play occurs in Rome and in Roman Britain around the first century B.C. The principal characters are kings, nobles, and aristocrats. In this production, the action is relocated to the twentieth century, but the costumes still identify the characters as belonging to the upper classes. The major characters here are Iachimo (seated) and Posthumus (standing right). Costumes by Daphne Dare. Directed by Robin Phillips. (Photo by Robert C. Ragsdale. Courtesy Stratford Shakespearean Festival Foundation of Canada.)

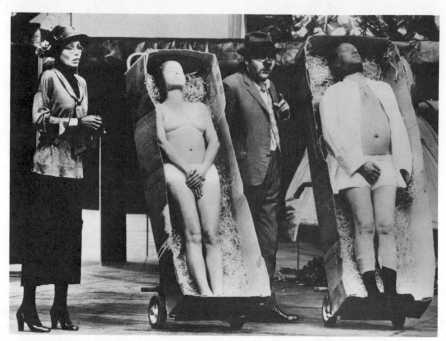

Büchner's *Leonce and Lena* (1836), a comedy about the attempt to escape boredom and find love, reinterpreted here as a contemporary story, with two of the main characters treated like large dolls, carted about and displayed. Note that the faces are covered with protective wrapping. The costume on the woman at left gives her a spinsterish appearance, while the rubber-ball nose on the man at center establishes his clownish disposition. Performed at the Kammerspiele, Munich. Directed by Dieter Stein. (Photo by Rabanus. Courtesy German Information Center.)

style. In *"The Hairy Ape,"* the fashionable people on Fifth Avenue are dressed like marionettes to reinforce their mechanical behavior. Costumes may reflect formalized *conventions,* as they do in commedia dell'arte and Noh theatre.

Costumes may enhance or *impede* movement. Light, flexible, and close-fitting garments (such as leotards) leave the body free, whereas heavy garments (with such features as bustles or trains) slow down and restrict movement. Garments, then, help to determine the amount, type, and overall pattern of movement and stage business.

Costumes can establish or clarify *character relationships.* For example, in Shakespeare's history plays, in which warring factions are significant, members of the same faction can be identified and contrasted with members of rival factions through color scheme. Color can also be used to show a sympathetic or antipathetic relationship among characters in any play. Furthermore, changes of color may be used to indicate an alteration in the relationship among characters.

Costume may establish the relative *importance of characters* in the action. Major characters can be made to stand out from minor ones by manipulating any or all of the elements and principles of design. For example, Hamlet is given emphasis in part through his insistence on wearing black (the color of mourning), while the others are dressed in colors more appropriate to festivities following the wedding of Gertrude and Claudius.

Costume may underline the *development of the dramatic action* through costume changes. A movement from happiness to sorrow or alterations in a character's fortunes, age, or sense of well-being may be underscored by changes in what the character wears. Costume may create both *variety and unity,* since characters are not only individuals but are also parts of a whole. Thus, while each costume may be distinctive in some way, each must fit the total visual look of the production.

Costume can alter an actor's *appearance.* By manipulating line and proportion, the costumer may make a plump actor appear more slender

The use of costume to establish stereotypes. The figure at left is a psychiatrist, while the figure seeking an interview is dressed as a schoolboy to indicate his acceptance of his subordinate role. From *The Managed Mind* as performed at the Hamburg Schauspielhaus. (Courtesy German Information Center.)

or a thin actor stouter. Boots may disguise an actor's thin legs; color and ornament can draw attention to an actor's good features and away from weaker ones. Contrarily, costume can be used to make a handsome actor plain or misshapen. And, in many children's plays, actors may be transformed into animals, trees, or fantastic creatures.

Beginning in the 1960s, some groups questioned the need for stage costume at all. Such groups tended to wear the same casual clothing in performance as they did in rehearsal or on the street. Since 1968, nudity has also been used in some productions. But both casual clothing and nudity are variations on stage costuming, since both merely extend concepts about what is effective and dramatically appropriate.

Working Plans and Procedures

Costume designers, like other theatre artists, usually begin their preparations by becoming thoroughly familiar with the script in its totality—action, character, themes, language, and spectacle—since the costumes must function within, and be appropriate to, the total piece. Subsequently, designers may concentrate on factors specifically related to costuming: the number of characters; the specific nature of each character (gender, age, occupation, socioeconomic status, likes and dislikes, goals and motivations, ethical qualities); the function of each character in each scene and in the play as a whole; the relationships among the characters; times, places, and occasions that influence costume choices; indications of changes in costume; developments in the action or changes in the fortunes of characters that might be clarified by costuming; the physical action, stage business, and movement patterns that might affect or be affected by costuming; moods and variations on them that affect costume; form and style as influences on costuming.

Costume designers may need to do considerable additional study. They may need to determine the dress in use at the time of the play's action (characteristic silhouettes, typical textures and materials, dominant colors, ornamental motifs, usual accessories). They may also need to know about the manners and customs of the time in order to understand why or when each garment or accessory was worn or used. They may explore stage costuming conventions in use when the play was written. They may need to undertake a variety of still other explorations, depending upon the production concept to be followed.

Before they make sketches (and perhaps before they undertake detailed research), costume designers meet with the director and other designers to discuss the script and the production concept. The director may already be firmly settled on a production concept, or may wish to get the designers' ideas before reaching a definite decision. However it comes about, a production concept (or interpretational focus) should guide the designers' work. Other information is also needed before a costume designer can proceed effectively; what the budget for costumes will be; the space to be used for performances; the available work space, equipment, and personnel; any special plans or demands the director may have (specific business that will affect costuming; desired costume changes; special treatment of any character, etc.); and any plans of the other designers that will affect costume. It is also helpful (but not always possible) to know which actor will play each role, so that the designs may be adapted to the wearer. All of this information helps to define the limits within which the costume designer must work.

There is no agreed-upon procedure to follow in designing costumes. Since there are usually several characters, and since they appear in many scenes in many different combinations, the designer typically makes numerous tentative sketches and examines them in various combinations to see how they fulfill or fail to fulfill the needs of individual scenes, whether they sufficiently reflect the progress of the dramatic action, and how the costumes fit together as a total group. There is usually a series of design conferences at which the designers show their sketches and explain their proposals. Through a process of reactions and revisions, tentative agreement is eventually reached. Before final approval is given, however, the designs usually must be rendered in color and in a manner that conveys a clear impression of the final product.

The costumer's basic working drawing is a color sketch for each costume (although sometimes the same basic design is used for several characters if they are part of a group—soldiers, for example—or members of a mob in which everyone wears variations on the same clothing). A sketch shows the lines and details of the costume as seen from the most distinctive angle. If there are unusual features, the details are shown in special drawings (usually in the margins of the sketch); and if the front, back and sides of a garment all have distinctive features, it is usual to show the costume from each of these angles. Samples of the materials to be used in making the garment are attached to each drawing. (See the illustration on page 366.)

A costume chart is also needed. This is made by dividing a large sheet of paper into squares. Down the left side, the name of one character (and usually the name of the actor playing the role) is listed in each square. In like manner, each scene (or act) is listed across the top. Thus, there should be one square for each actor in each scene of the play. In the squares, the designer may indicate the costume items (including

Sketch by Paul Reinhardt of a costume for Helen (of Troy) in Euripides'
Orestes. At upper right are swatches of the material to be used in making the
costume. (Courtesy Mr. Reinhardt.)

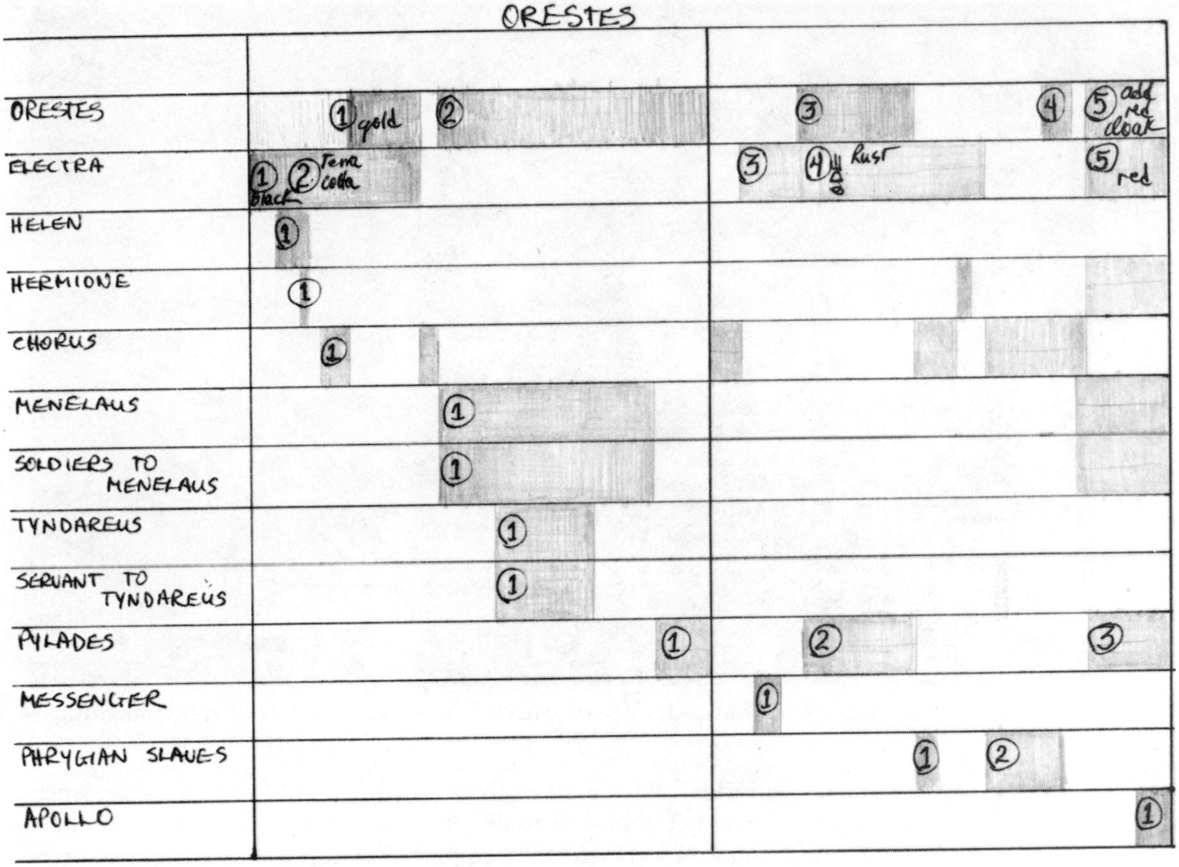

Costume chart for the production of Euripides' *Orestes*. (Courtesy Paul Reinhardt.)

Character	Costumes / Notes
ORESTES	① gold ② ③ ④ ⑤ add red cloak
ELECTRA	① black ② terra cotta ③ ④ rust ⑤ red
HELEN	①
HERMIONE	①
CHORUS	①
MENELAUS	①
SOLDIERS TO MENELAUS	①
TYNDAREUS	①
SERVANT TO TYNDAREUS	①
PYLADES	① ② ③
MESSENGER	①
PHRYGIAN SLAVES	① ②
APOLLO	①

accessories) to be worn in the scene and may attach color samples of each garment. The range of colors and the overall color scheme may then be seen at a glance. The chart can also be used as a guide for dressing the actors and keeping the costumes organized for running the production efficiently. (See the costume chart above.)

Realizing the Designs

Costumes may be borrowed, rented, assembled from an existing wardrobe, or made new. When costumes are borrowed, designers look for garments that fit their needs, but they often must accept clothing that

Scene from Euripides' *Orestes*. Helen is at center. (Courtesy Paul Reinhardt.)

is less than ideal. Borrowed clothing can be altered only slightly, since as a rule its owner expects it to be returned in much the same condition as when taken. Nevertheless, through the imaginative use of accessories and ornamentation, much can be done to alter the appearance of a garment. The practice of borrowing clothing is restricted primarily to nonprofessional theatres and short-run productions.

Costumes from rental houses vary considerably. Some of the larger agencies buy the costumes of a Broadway or road show when it closes and rent these costumes as a unit. Other houses employ staff designers who create costumes for frequently produced plays. In still other cases, costume houses merely assemble a large variety of costumes for each period, and from this stock the most appropriate garments are selected for any given show. When costumes are rented, the costume house assumes many of the designer's functions. The director and costumer may give detailed explanations of their interpretation of the play and request specific colors and kinds of garments, but they ultimately have to accept what is sent. Sometimes a costume agency is located nearby, and the costumes can be selected and approved by the designer or director in person; but rented costumes normally arrive at the theatre only in time for one or two dress rehearsals, and there is seldom time to obtain replacements or do more than make minor changes. The better costume houses provide dependable service, but the work of even these cannot match well-designed garments made with the specific production in mind. Nevertheless, even groups that normally make their own costumes rent some articles (such as military uniforms and men's tailored period suits) that are extremely difficult or costly to construct.

Permanent theatre organizations that make their own costumes usually maintain a wardrobe composed of items from past productions. In this way, a large stock of garments is built up over time. When garments are taken from stock, the play is designed with these in mind. The costumer knows what is available and can choose carefully. Furthermore, existing costumes in the theatre's own wardrobe can be remade or altered to fit new conceptions.

The procedures and working conditions for creating new costumes vary from one kind of organization to another. In the Broadway theatre, the producer contracts with a costume house to make the costumes. The designer must approve the finished products but has little to do with the actual work beyond supervising fittings. The designer does not supply patterns or cutting, stitching, and fitting directions, since the costume house does all this.

In resident and nonprofessional theatres, designers may supervise the construction of their own costumes. If so, they must be skilled in pattern drafting, draping, and fitting. Whether or not they supervise the construction, designers should understand the techniques used to carry out designs so they will know what effects can be accomplished and by what means.

Regardless of who actually makes the costumes, standard procedures are involved. First, accurate measurements must be made of all the actors. (The rehearsal secretary, stage manager, or assistant director usually makes appointments for actors to have measurements taken and, later on, for fittings.) Second, materials must be bought. While the designer specifies materials, precisely the right cloth or color may be difficult to find. The designer or some other authorized person may need to search at length for the specified materials or acceptable substitutes. Next, patterns must be drafted as guides for cutting and shaping the materials. At this point, the technical knowledge of the tailor is of great value. Some costumes can be made more easily through draping than from patterns. For example, Greek garments, which hang from the shoulder in folds and are not fitted to the body, are most easily made by draping the material on a mannequin or a human body. After the patterns are completed, the material is cut and the parts basted together. The first fitting usually takes place before stitching is completed. Each

The costume workshop at the Royal Shakespeare Company, Stratford-on-Avon. (Courtesy British Tourist Authority.)

garment is put on the actor who is to wear it so that the fit and appearance can be checked by the designer. It is easy at this point to make many alterations or changes that would be impossible (or very troublesome) later. Finally, the garment is stitched, and ornamentation and accessories are added. Another fitting is then arranged to assure that the costume looks and functions as planned.

Many costumes, though made new, need to look worn, faded, or tattered. Consequently, they may need to be "distressed" (that is, treated in ways analogous to overpainting in scenery). Garments may be washed a number of times, may be rolled up wrinkled to get a rumpled look, may be sprayed with paint or dye to indicate fading or staining, may have the nap worn off the cloth with brushing in strategic places to indicate wear, or may be subjected to a variety of other processes to produce the desired effect.

The Costume Parade, Dress Rehearsals, and Performances

When the costumes are finished, it is usual to have a *dress parade,* during which each scene of the play is covered in sequence so that the actors may appear in the correct combinations, in the appropriate costumes, and under lights that simulate those to be used in performance. The actors may be asked to perform characteristic portions of each scene to make sure the costumes are properly functional. The dress parade allows those concerned (especially the designer and director) to see and evaluate the costumes without the distractions of a performance. This permits problems to be noted and corrected before dress rehearsals begin. In the Broadway theatre, the dress parade is held at the costume house; in other organizations, it usually occurs onstage. It is normally supervised by the costume designer.

After problems are corrected, the costumes are moved to the dressing rooms in the theatre to be used for the performances. If no dress parade is held, its functions must be accomplished during the technical rehearsal. Dress rehearsals allow the costumes to be seen under conditions as nearly like those of performance as possible. Changes at this time should be few, but any that are necessary need to be made speedily so that the actor is not faced with new details on opening night.

Once dress rehearsals begin, a wardrobe supervisor or costume crew usually assumes responsibility for seeing that costumes are (and remain) in good condition and that each actor is dressed as planned. In the nonprofessional theatre, the costume designer frequently assumes these duties. In most situations, however, the designer's work is considered to be over after opening night.

The Costume Designer's Assistants

The costume designer needs a number of helpers. In the professional theatre, costume designers must be members of the United Scenic Artists Union, and their helpers are usually members of this or other unions. The designer's assistant, usually a younger member of the United Scenic Artists, may make sketches, search out appropriate materials, supervise fittings, act as liaison with the other theatre workers, or take on any other assigned task.

Pattern drafters, drapers, cutters, tailors, stitchers, and fitters make the costumes. In the professional theatre, such workers must be union members. In the nonprofessional theatre, much of this work is done by volunteer or student labor, although frequently a paid staff person supervises the construction and maintains the theatre's wardrobe.

When the costumes are finished, the wardrobe supervisor takes charge and is responsible for seeing that costumes are ready for each performance. The costumes may need to be mended, laundered, cleaned, or pressed. In long-run productions, garments are replaced when they begin to be shabby, so the show will continue to look as the designer intended. During performances, the wardrobe supervisor is directly responsible to the stage manager.

Dressers help actors into and out of costumes. The number of dressers depends on the size of the cast and the number and rapidity of costume changes. Sometimes actors need little or no help, but quick changes and complicated garments may require more than one dresser for a single actor. Dressers should be sufficient in number to keep performances running smoothly and to keep the costumes in good repair and order at all times.

The Costume Designer and the Actor

Costume designers and actors need to cooperate, since each supplements and extends the work of the other. Designers need to consider the strengths and weaknesses of each actor's figure when planning costumes. They also need to keep in mind the movement demanded of the actor. It is difficult for an actress to climb steps in a tight skirt, and an actor who must fence may be seriously endangered by billowing shirt sleeves, although these garments may enhance movement in other situations.

For their part, actors need to make an effort to understand the potentials and limitations of the costumes they will wear. Almost all unfamiliar garments will seem awkward initially, but if actors recognize that the clothes in each period emphasize qualities that were admired at that time and allow movements that were then socially useful, beautiful, or desirable, they may use those qualities more effectively. For example, the sleeves of a man's fashionable coat in the eighteenth century would not allow the arms to hang comfortably at the sides (they had to be bent at the elbows and held away from the body), whereas the modern suit coat is cut so the arms are most comfortable when hanging at the sides (although outward and upward movements are restricted). Both garments reflect attitudes about appropriate male behavior and consequently encourage some movements and inhibit others. If designers un-

Shakespeare's *Titus Andronicus* at the Oregon Shakespearean Festival, 1986. The action of this play is set in late Roman times, when the Romans were at war with the Goths. Using such complex costumes effectively requires actor-designer cooperation. Directed by Pat Patton. Costumes by Jeannie Davidson. (Photo by Hank Kranzler. Courtesy Oregon Shakespearean Festival.)

derstand the relationship between cut and movement, they can help the actors get the feel of the period by making their garments from authentic period costumes.

The designer can also aid the actors by proper attention to shoes. The height of the heel exerts considerable effect on stage movement (a high heel throws the weight forward onto the balls of the feet, while flat shoes shift weight toward the heel). Similarly, undergarments affect movement. Hooped crinoline petticoats, for example, will not allow the same freedom of movement as modern underwear does. Corsets can force the body into certain configurations and thereby inhibit action. If costumes encourage appropriate movement, they can be of enormous help to the actor. For optimum effectiveness, however, the actor and director must be willing to explore the possibilities of garments and allow sufficient time for rehearsal in them.

Makeup

Typically, makeup has been considered the actor's responsibility, and often each actor is presumed capable of achieving any desired effect. This is not always true, however, and it is especially questionable in the nonprofessional theatre. In the latter situation, makeup is sometimes placed under the supervision of the costumer, director, or another skilled person. In the professional theatre, actors are expected to create their own makeup, except when it involves unusual challenges. Because how makeup is handled varies so widely, and because of its intimate connection with the actor's appearance, it is treated here in conjunction with costuming.

Function Makeup can serve several functions. First, makeup *characterizes.* It can indicate age, state of health, and race; within limits, it may suggest profession (outdoors versus indoors), basic attitude (through facial lines that suggest such qualities as grumpiness or cheerfulness), and self-regard (pride, or lack of it, in personal appearance). Makeup aids *expressiveness* by emphasizing facial features and making them more readily visible to the audience. Makeup restores *color and form* that otherwise would be diminished by stage lighting. Makeup is indicative of *performance style.* In realistic plays, it is usually modeled on everyday reality and appearance, whereas in expressionistic plays, it is used to make statements, often by using distorted makeup as indications of distorted ideas or behavior.

The Makeup Plot When the makeup for a production is designed and supervised by one person, it is usually coordinated through a makeup plot (sometimes supplemented by sketches). The plot is a chart that records basic information about the makeup of each character: the base color, liners, eye shadow, and powder; special features, such as a beard or enlarged nose; and changes to be made during the performance. The plot serves both as a guide for applying makeup and as a check on how the makeup of each actor relates to that of all the others. Sometimes a sketch is made of each actor's face to show how the makeup is to be applied.

Types of Makeup Makeup effects may be achieved in two basic ways: through *painting,* and through *added plastic (three-dimensional) pieces.* Painting involves the application of color, highlights, and shadows to the face or other parts of the body. Plastic makeup includes the addition of such items as false noses, warts, beards, and wigs.

Painted makeup may be divided into four subcategories: age groups; straight or character makeup; racial types; and special effects. *Age makeup* is of concern only when actors are to play characters whose age differs significantly from their own. As preparation, makeup artists need to be familiar with the characteristic distinctions among various age groups: typical coloration, highlights, shadows, and lines. Artists should not neglect hands, arms, and other visible parts of the body, since if these are not made up appropriately, they easily destroy the illusion created by facial makeup. A *straight makeup* utilizes the actor's own basic characteristics without altering them significantly. A *character makeup* is one that markedly changes the actor's own appearance. The change may be in age, or it may involve making the actor seem fatter and coarser, more lean and wizened, or it may emphasize some distinctive facial feature (such as a thin, sharp nose or large, soulful eyes). *Racial makeup* emphasizes characteristic skin coloration, eye shapes, hair color and texture, and other traits that differentiate Oriental, Polynesian, Indian,

Genet's *The Blacks*. Note the masks, costumes and makeup, important elements in this play about multiple illusion. Costumes and masks by Patricia Zipprodt. (Photo by Martha Swope.)

Black, Caucasian, or various subgroups. *Special painted effects* include clown makeup, distortions for stylistic reasons, and decorative designs painted on the face as in a tribal ritual. (For an example of a special painted makeup, see the color illustration following page 338.) The number of effects that can be achieved by painting are almost endless.

Nevertheless, significant transformations in an actor's appearance are most easily accomplished with three-dimensional elements. For example, a change in the shape of the nose and the addition of a beard and bushy eyebrows can mask an actor's features more completely than painting can. Prominent cheeks, hanging jowls, a protuberant forehead, fleshy jaws, warts, or large scars may be constructed and applied to change the shape of the face or to give it a grotesque or unsightly appearance. Beards and moustaches may be grown by male actors, but they may also be made with relative ease. The appearance of the actor's hair can be changed significantly through styling and coloring, but wigs may be required for extreme changes or rapid switches. Baldness can be simulated with a "bald wig."

Makeup Materials The materials needed for these and other effects are available from manufacturers and makeup supply houses. Most makeups begin with a *base* (pigment suspended in an oily solution that permits the makeup to be applied easily and prevents it from drying on the skin). Packaged in tubes, base colors are available in a wide range of colors: various shades of pink, tan, yellow, beige, brown, black, and white. Each color may be used as it comes or mixed with others to create still more gradations. The base is applied over the exposed portions of the face, neck, and ears. A fairly wide range of colors is also available in liquid form for application to large surfaces of the body (arms, legs, and torso), if these will be visible on stage.

Used alone, a base color is apt to make the actor's face appear flat and uninteresting. Therefore, lines, highlights, and shadows are applied over the base. For this procedure, *liner* (a thick paste, usually packaged in small tins) is used. It is available in a wide range of colors, among them white, light brown, dark brown, blue, green, red, gray, and black. Like the base colors, liners may be mixed to create subtle gradations. Liner is used for shadows under the eyes, hollows in the cheeks or temples, furrows in the forehead, creases that spread outward and downward from the nose, or for any other highlighting or shadowing needed to emphasize facial characteristics. Red liner may be used for lipstick and rouge.

Beards and moustaches are usually made from *crepe hair,* available in a wide range of colors that may be combined to achieve very convincing effects. To make beards, moustaches, and bushy eyebrows, and to attach them to the face, *liquid adhesive* is required. This is a plastic substance that becomes solid, though retaining its flexibility, when exposed to the air. In creating a beard, liquid adhesive is applied to the face (usually several layers are built up) to create a base on which crepe hair can be attached in layers with still more liquid adhesive. When a beard of the desired shape and size has been completed (including shaping and trimming), the whole structure can be removed in one piece. This reusable beard can be applied for each performance by reattaching it to the face with liquid adhesive.

Nose putty is useful for changing the shape of the nose, chin, cheekbones, or forehead, since it may be shaped and then attached to the face with liquid adhesive. It is not very satisfactory when attached to flexible areas of the face, however, since it is inclined to loosen with movement and fall off. For plastic effects on flexible parts of the face, gauze may be stretched over pieces of cotton and glued to the face with liquid adhesive; these additions are then covered with the same base used on the rest of the face. Liners may be used for shadowing and highlighting to make the additions more realistic.

Hair coloration may be altered with *bleach* or *dye,* but this may be longer lasting than is desirable. A white liquid, frequently called *hair whitener,* may be combed through the hair to gray it, although this seldom is convincing. More realistic graying can be achieved by *oiling* the hair lightly and combing aluminum *metallic powder* through it. *Wigs* have now become so easily available that they often provide the easiest means of altering hair color and style. Wigs in contemporary hair styles are readily available in department stores; period wigs may be rented from costume supply houses or made from the type of hair used on store-window models. Wigs made from anything other than human or plastic hair are seldom satisfactory if a realistic effect is sought. For more stylized wigs, various materials may be used: hemp, crepe hair, yarn, confetti, strips of paper, etc.

Once the actor's makeup is fully applied, the visible painted portions are powdered so as to keep them from appearing greasy or shiny under stage lights. *Powder* comes in the same variety of shades as base paints. It is applied freely and the excess brushed off. When the performance ends, makeup is removed with *cold cream* and *facial tissues.*

Together, costume and makeup aid the actor's transformation into the character, although in productions that do not seek realistic effects, makeup may not be used at all; the performer is said to be "presenting" the character rather than attempting to "be" the character, and consequently there is no need to disguise the actor's own appearance. Nevertheless, makeup should be mastered so that it can be used effectively when it is deemed appropriate.

Looking at Costume and Makeup

The range of costume and makeup in today's theatre is great. Each may be treated realistically and reflect closely what is indicated by the script; or each may deviate markedly from the script's specifications; or each may be largely ignored (with performers wearing their own casual clothing and no makeup). Costumes and makeup may make strong stylistic or interpretational statements, or they may be so unobtrusive as to go practically unnoticed. In all cases, the important issues concern why the specific choices were made and how they affect the production. Here are some questions that may contribute to a fuller understanding of choices and their results in the use of costume and makeup.

1. In what type of space was the production staged? Did it permit close-range viewing of costumes and makeup? Were details easily visible? What was the overall effect of the space on costumes and makeup?

2. Did the costumes reflect a specific period, style, or production concept? If so, which? Did the approach adhere closely to the script? If not, in what ways did it depart from the script? with what effect?

3. Did the costumes and makeup characterize each role by clarifying specific occupation or profession? socioeconomic status? occasion? lifestyle? age of character? taste? psychological traits? If so, through what means? If not, what was the effect of nonspecificity? Were some character traits ignored? if so, which and with what result?

4. Did costumes clarify character relationships? If so, how? with what results? If not, how did they fail to do so? with what results? Did they create appropriate emphasis and subordination? If so, through what means? If not, what prevented them from doing so?

5. Did the costumes enhance or inhibit movement and business? in what ways? with what results?

6. Were the costumes and makeup adapted to the actors? Did they enhance or alter the actor's appearance appropriately in terms of the role? Was the actor's overall physical appearance effective (or ineffective) for the role? In what ways was the effectiveness (or ineffectiveness) attributable to costume and makeup?

7. Were there costume or makeup changes? How did they relate to developments in the dramatic action or alterations in the character's situation or attitudes? Did the changes in costume or

makeup clarify the developments? If so, in what ways? If not, why not?

8. Were there any unusual, unexpected, or highly distinctive costumes or makeup? What features or means served to create these effects? Did the distinctiveness enhance or detract from the overall effect?

9. How did costumes and makeup relate to scenery and lighting? Did they enhance and complement each other? If so, how? If not, in what ways? with what results?

10. Overall, how did costume and makeup contribute (or fail to contribute) to the total production?

The relevance of each of these questions may vary according to the particular production and play. Furthermore, answering some of the questions would be too time-consuming if they had to be pursued for every costume or for the entire cast; for still others, wholly adequate answers may require information available only to those actually involved in the creation of the costumes and makeup. Nevertheless, attempts to answer parts or all of these questions will require us to look closely at costumes and makeup and evaluate their contributions to a theatrical production.

Lighting Design, Sound, and Multimedia

16

Lighting makes the other elements of theatrical production visible. But it does much more, since it plays a major role in creating mood and atmosphere, in emphasizing and subordinating visual elements, and in blending the entire stage picture. It often escapes conscious notice because it is intangible, takes up no space, and is visible only when it strikes a reflecting surface. Consequently, lighting is often ignored unless it is obviously inadequate or obtrusively obvious.

The Lighting Designer's Skills

Lighting designers need a variety of skills, many of them pertinent to other professions, such as electrical or optical engineer, display designer, visual artist, electrician, social and cultural historian, and stage director. Like electrical engineers, lighting designers need to understand physics and electricity, since they work with complex instruments and controlboards operated primarily by electricity. They need to know not only how the equipment works but also the scientific principles involved, so that they can make maximum use of the available resources and avoid misusing them in ways that are both inefficient and dangerous. Like optical engineers, lighting designers need to understand the principles of optics and light, since it is the variable properties of light that they manipulate when they use lamps, lenses, reflectors, color filters, and other equipment. The fuller their understanding of the principles and properties of light, the greater their potential for using light effectively for artistic purposes. Although lighting designers work in a sphere that is much more restricted and specialized than that of electrical or optical engineers, all work from more or less the same base of information.

In the application of their skills, lighting designers' work resembles that of display designers, since both use the intensity, distribution, direction, and color of light to focus attention on important elements, and to blend all of the elements into a whole that creates the appropriate mood. The lighting designer's work is usually more complex than the display designer's, however, because in the theatre one is concerned with a space that is used continuously by live, moving actors, whereas in a display the artist usually lights a fixed picture or one in which movement is created by electronically programmed elements.

Like other theatre designers, lighting designers need skills like those of the visual artist, since they must be able to communicate through sketches. They may demonstrate their preliminary ideas for lighting by making numerous drawings, then render their final designs as finished sketches that place special emphasis on light and shade—gradations in intensity, dominant direction, distribution—as well as color. Lighting designers must also be able to make various scale drawings of the stage and auditorium to show the mounting positions of lighting instruments and the areas they are to light.

Although lighting designers may not do the physical labor required to realize their designs, they must know what has to be done and supply all the information that will be needed by those who actually do the tasks. Consequently, like the stage electrician, designers must know what instruments are available, what each can and cannot do, what types of lamps, electrical cable, connectors, etc. are needed, where instruments are to be mounted and plugged in, and a host of other details. Thus, the designer's practical knowledge must be as extensive as the electrician's, although the designer may not be as skilled at installing and operating the equipment.

Lighting designers should be well grounded in social and cultural history (including the visual and performing arts), since they often must know what role light played in various periods in the past. They need to be aware of what illuminants (candles, oil, torches, gas, etc.) were available in each period, how each was used for lighting, and what qualities of light each generated (so they can recreate or adapt these illuminants for their work as desired). Although nowadays lighting designers normally work entirely with electrical light, they frequently must create the effects of other illuminants. They discover much of this by studying social, cultural, and art history. Designers also need to know the conventions that governed stage lighting in each era of theatre history, in case these are required by a production.

In their work, lighting designers take an approach more nearly resembling that of the director than that of any other theatre artist, since they must keep in mind the entire stage picture and seek to do justice to each aspect while unifying all. Thus, lighting designers must be especially attuned to the overall needs of each scene as it develops moment by moment, since light is the most flexible of all theatrical means, being variable instantaneously and continuously. Therefore, the lighting designer needs to work closely with the director in realizing the production concept.

The Controllable Factors of Light

Whatever their goals, lighting designers can achieve them only by manipulating the four controllable factors of light: *intensity* (or brightness), *distribution, color,* and *movement.*

Intensity depends primarily on the number of lamps used and their wattages. It may be controlled (that is, increased or decreased) in several ways: through the number of instruments focused on the same area or object; through the distance of instruments from what is being lighted (brightness diminishes with distance); through the use of dimmers to decrease or increase brightness; and through the presence or absence of color filters (the intensity of light decreases when it passes through a filter).

The visible spectrum of light is divided into *colors* (red, orange, yellow, green, blue-green, blue, and violet), each of which is distinguishable from the others because it is composed of light waves of a given length. We attribute color to objects because of their capacity to absorb some wavelengths and to reflect others. In stage lighting, color is controlled with filters, which function through the principle of selective transmission (that is, each color filter permits only certain wavelengths to pass through). A blue filter, for example, works by screening out other wavelengths. This process considerably reduces the amount of light that reaches the stage. Color filters also affect our perception of color. For example, if a red object is lighted only with blue light, its apparent color will be magenta. To achieve a desired effect or to avoid unwanted distortions, light from a number of color sources can be mixed. Consequently, lighting designers usually focus multiple instruments on each part of the stage, to ensure control not only over intensity but also over color. Like pigment, light has primary colors from which all others may be derived by mixing them in varying proportions. The primary colors of light are red, blue, and green, which together produce white light. Various tints and shades are produced through mixing colors in differing proportions, saturations, and intensities.

Distribution depends on the direction from which light comes and the way it is spread over the performance space: all light may be directed at one area, or it may be distributed equally or unequally over the entire stage. Direction is determined by the position of a light source in relation to the area being lighted. Instruments may be mounted almost anywhere in the theatre: in the auditorium, above the stage, on the floor, on vertical or horizontal pipes, or on stands. These variations permit frontlighting, backlighting, downlighting, uplighting, or crosslighting, each separately or in various combinations.

Movement refers to perceptible alterations in any or all of the controllable factors. The principal device for creating movement is the controlboard. By using it, some lamps may be brightened and others dimmed to control intensity, color, or distribution. Movement allows light to change moment by moment in accordance with shifting moods and the development of the dramatic action. This ability to move and change continuously makes lighting the most flexible of the production elements.

The Functions of Stage Lighting

By manipulating all the controllable factors at their disposal, lighting designers achieve the various purposes or functions of stage lighting. First and most basically, light creates *visibility*. Quite apart from artistic considerations, a minimal level of intensity is essential if the performance is to be seen. Second, lighting aids *composition*. By directing the eye to the most important elements, it creates emphasis and subordination. On the proscenium stage, the acting (or foreground) areas are usually more brightly lighted than the background, just as the level of intensity at stage level (where the action takes place) is usually greater than on the upper parts of the setting (which are of secondary concern).

Third, lighting affects perception of *dimensionality* (mass and form). A three-dimensional structure will appear flat if all its surfaces are evenly lighted, whereas its shape will be revealed or emphasized by light that varies markedly from one surface to another. Thus, by manipulating direction (backlighting, downlighting, frontlighting, or crosslighting), intensity (degrees of brightness), and color, the lighting designer can define or alter apparent shape and dimension. This ability to influence perception of mass and form is among the lighting designer's most potent means of creating mood, atmosphere, and stylistic qualities.

Fourth, lighting enhances *mood and atmosphere*. Bright, warm light is associated with gaiety and well-being, cool light with somberness. Glar-

In this photograph, backlighting is used to emphasize the shape and dimension of the table and chairs, while front and sidelighting are used to illuminate the faces of the characters. The light reflected by smoke is used to create a strong atmospheric effect and to give added emphasis to the character at center. *Self and I* at the Dusseldorf Schauspielhaus. (Photo by Lore Bermbach. Courtesy German Information Center.)

ing white light may create a sense of starkness or clinical probing and low-intensity lighting with many areas of shadow may create an atmosphere of mystery or threat. It is impossible to specify precisely the effect of each use of lighting, since our response is determined by the total context and not merely by the lighting.

Fifth, lighting may help to establish *style*. If the goal is realism, the lighting may seek to establish the source of the light (sun, moon, lamps, firelight) and let the source motivate intensity, direction, distribution of light and shadow, color, and movement. Light may reflect the time of day, weather conditions, or season of the year, and it may suggest the play's period through the lighting fixtures used on stage. If the goal is not realism, the source of the light and how it is handled may be more arbitrary. Visible light sources may be used to distribute light evenly over the entire stage, thus establishing the performance space itself (rather than some fictional locale) as the place of the dramatic action. For an expressionistic play, light from very low or sharp angles may be used to distort facial features, or saturated colors may be used to indicate the dominant emotion.

Sixth, lighting may *underscore* the development of the dramatic action by reflecting the dominant feeling of each scene and the changes in mood from one scene to the next (for example, from sunny cheerfulness to despair or regret). Light may also underscore the rhythmical patterns of scenes and changes in rhythm from one scene to another. Seventh, lighting *supports the production concept* through a combination of the other functions.

Although it serves many functions, lighting is among the most abstract of theatrical means. It works primarily through suggestion and association rather than through concrete references (as scenery, lighting, and acting tend to do). Consequently, if lighting is in proper harmony with the other production elements, the audience may not be consciously aware ot it.

The Lighting Designer's Working Procedures

Like other theatre artists, the lighting designers usually begin by studying the script—its action, characters, themes, language, spectacle, mood. After gaining a sense of the whole, they may proceed to specific indications of lighting: time of day; sources of light (lamps, sunlight, etc.); changes during scenes (growing darkness, lamps being turned on); variations required for different parts of the stage (distinctions between indoor and outdoor in a divided setting, some areas lighted by lamps and other areas in relative shadow); the direction of light (moonlight through a window, light from an overhead fixture); color of light; and special effects (lightning, firelight). Lighting designers also need to note carefully the dominant mood of each scene, which characters are most important in each scene, and other factors that will affect the lighting designs.

Lighting designers may need to do additional research. They may need to know what lighting fixtures were typical during the period of the action, the quality of light produced by each, and how each was used. In productions that make use of stage conventions, designers may need to familiarize themselves with the stage lighting practices of a particular era. In productions that make use of a specific style, designers may need to study carefully the characteristic features of that style. They may need to undertake a variety of other explorations, depending upon the production concept to be followed.

Before they make sketches (and perhaps before they undertake any detailed research), lighting designers meet with the director and the other designers to discuss the script and production concept. The director may already have firm ideas about the production concept to be used, or may wish to discuss several possibilities with the designers and get their input before reaching a final decision. Whatever the process, an interpretational approach must be settled on before the designers can work effectively. Lighting designers must be sensitive to the ideas of the scene and costume designers, since the work of each influences the others so strongly. Lighting designers also need to be aware of any specific demands of the director (such as the need to isolate areas through lighting, scenes requiring projections, specific atmospheric effects, etc.). In addition, lighting designers need to know what performance space will be used, what the budget for lighting is, what equipment and personnel will be available, and how much working time will be available to install and focus lighting instruments and equipment. With all of these given circumstances in mind, the lighting designer is ready to begin.

There is no standard approach to the design of lighting. Lighting designers are in a position somewhat different from that of other theatre artists, since lighting is seen only as it is reflected by the actors, costumes, setting, and performance space. Thus, what they light is created by others, and frequently lighting designers must adjust their work to enhance that of others rather than proceeding as they would desire. They can make general plans, but until the floor plan and setting are agreed upon, lighting designers cannot make firm decisions about the placement and direction of lighting instruments, and until the movement pattern of each actor is established, they cannot know precisely how the light needs to be distributed. Lighting design, therefore, seldom becomes as firmly fixed as other design elements do during the planning stages.

Like the other designers, lighting designers should be able to convey their ideas through sketches that show how the stage will look when lighted. Often, the sketches place special emphasis on mood and atmosphere or on light and shadow. The number and type of sketches required depend upon the complexity and variety of the lighting to be used. In the nonprofessional theatre, lighting designers sometimes do not make any sketches but instead work entirely from a general agreement (reached by the production team of director and designers) about the qualities to be sought in the lighting. The specific design is then worked out fully only when the lighting instruments are hung and focused. Whether general or specific, a plan must be approved before the lighting designer can proceed.

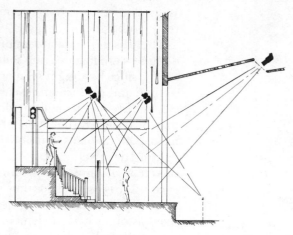

A lighting designer's sketch of a realistic interior without a ceiling. At right, a vertical section plot for lighting the set. (Parker, Smith, and Wolf, *Scene Design and Stage Lighting*, 5th ed. Courtesy Holt, Rinehart and Winston.)

The Light Plot and Instrument Schedule

If the sketches of lighting designers sometimes lack specificity, the same cannot be said of their two primary working plans: light plots and instrument schedules.

Light plots may be divided into two types: floor plans and vertical sections. The floor-plan plot is drawn to scale and shows, as seen from above, the layout of the stage, the setting, and the auditorium; on this plot are indicated the type, size, and position of each instrument and the area it will light. The section plot, also drawn to scale, shows the

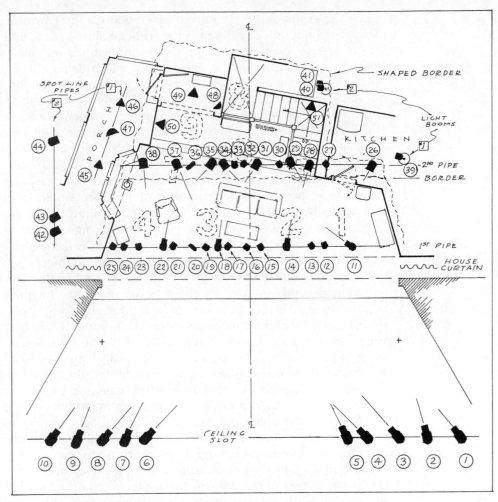

Floor-plan light plot for the realistic interior without ceiling. (Parker, Smith, and Wolf. Courtesy Holt, Rinehart and Winston.)

vertical arrangement of the stage, scenery, and auditorium, and the type, size, and position of each instrument and the area it will light. Together, these plots show the horizontal and vertical distribution of the light sources. It is usual to make a separate light plot for each setting and then a composite plot that shows all of the settings simultaneously in order to see how the lighting for each scene relates to that of all the others. This facilitates the use of the same instruments in multiple scenes. Overall, then, light plots specify with considerable precision what instruments are to be used and where each is to be mounted.

The Light Plot and Instrument Schedule 389

Light plots must also take into consideration the three principal types of stage lighting: specific illumination, general illumination, and special effects. *Specific illumination* is light that is confined to a very limited area. It is used principally for the acting areas, which demand the greatest emphasis and often require much variety in intensity, color, and distribution. The principal source of specific illumination is the spotlight, which emits a concentrated beam that can be confined to a limited area. But because a single spotlight can illuminate only a small segment of the stage, the total acting space is usually divided for purposes of lighting, into several smaller areas, typically six or more. Each area is then lighted separately. At least one spotlight is focused on each area from each side so as to strike it at an angle of 45 degrees both horizontally and vertically. Nowadays, several instruments (mounted at varying levels and angles) are usually focused on each area. The lighting for each area should overlap into adjacent areas so as to avoid distracting differences in brightness and darkness as actors move about the stage.

Where instruments are mounted in order to achieve the desired distribution depends in part on the type of stage. In the proscenium theatre, forward acting areas cannot be lighted effectively from behind the arch, and therefore some instruments are mounted in the auditorium—in ceiling apertures, in vertical apertures at the sides, or on the front of the balcony. Upstage areas are normally lighted by instruments hung back of the proscenium—on the light bridge just behind the opening, on vertical pipes at either side of the stage, on pipe battens suspended over the stage at intervals from front to back, on stands, or on the floor. In the arena theatre, all instruments are usually mounted above the acting area and audience, or on vertical pipes located where they will not interfere with sightlines. Since performances are viewed from four sides, the acting areas must be lit from all directions. On the thrust stage, most of the instruments are mounted over the platform or in the audience areas, but there may be a space behind the main platform where others are hung. Since the action is normally seen from two or three sides, lighting on thrust stages is usually a compromise between lighting used for the proscenium and that for the arena stages. In flexible or variable performance spaces, lighting may be nothing more than normal auditorium illumination, often no more than is required for visibility. If more selective lighting is used, the instruments may be mounted almost anywhere in the performance space.

General illumination, as the name suggests, spreads over a much larger area than specific illumination. The former is most fully exploited on the proscenium stage, where it serves three basic functions: to light all of the background elements (cyclorama, ground rows, drops) not illuminated by spotlights; to blend acting areas together and provide a smooth transition from the high intensity of the acting areas to the lower intensity of the background; and to enhance or modify the color of settings and costumes. General illumination is provided primarily by striplights and floodlights. Although general illumination cannot be confined to small areas, its direction can be partially controlled. Footlights point upward and backward from the floor. Borderlights are hung above the acting area and are pointed downward or tilted in one direction. Other striplights may be placed on the floor to light ground rows or cycloramas. Floodlights may be suspended on battens above the stage, mounted on vertical stands, or placed on the floor. On the arena stage, general illumination plays a minor role, since usually there is no background to light and the specific illumination covers the entire acting space. On the thrust stage, general lighting may play a somewhat larger role, especially if there is a stage house. In flexible or variable spaces, all of the lighting may be general.

Special effects are out-of-the-ordinary demands—among them projections, fires and firelogs, rainbows, fog and smoke, bright rays of light (to simulate sunlight or moonlight), explosions, lightning, strobe lights, and "black" light (ultraviolet light used to pick out specially treated substances on a dark stage).

In making light plots, each type of light (specific, general, and special effects) is considered separately and then as a part of the total unit. All lights must be indicated on the plots.

After the light plots are completed, an *instrument schedule* is made. This is a chart that lists separately each lighting instrument with its specifications (type, wattage, lens, reflector, lamp, and any other pertinent information), mounting position, color filter, area lighted by it, circuit into which it is plugged, and dimmer to which it is connected. The schedule summarizes in tabular form all the technical information needed for acquiring and setting up lighting instruments. (See the illustration on page 392.)

Lighting Instruments, Accessories, and Controlboards

The lighting designer's materials may be divided into three basic categories: lighting instruments, accessories, and controlboards. Designers must be thoroughly familiar with the characteristics of each type of instrument, accessory, and controlboard as a basis for making the light plots and instrument schedules that constitute the plans for realizing their lighting designs. Most resident and nonprofessional theatres own

No.	INSTRUMENT	LOCATION	PURPOSE	LAMP	COLOR	REMARKS
1	8" ELLIPS'L SPOTLIGHT	CEILING-L	AREA 2 L	750 T12	R 02	
2	8" " "	"	" 1 L	" "	R 02	
3	8" " "	"	" 3 L	" "	R 02	
4	8" " "	"	" 4 L	" "	R 02	
5	8" " "	"	SPECIAL	" "	R 02	SOFA
6	8" " "	CEILING-R	AREA 1 R	" "	R 60	
7	8" " "	"	SPECIAL	" "	R 60	SOFA
8	8" " "	"	AREA 2 R	" "	R 60	
9	8" " "	"	" 4 R	" "	R 60	
10	8" " "	"	" 3 R	" "	R 60	
11	6" ELLIPS'L SPOTLIGHT	1ST PIPE	AREA 9 L	500 T12	R 02	
12	6" FRESNEL SPOTLIGHT	"	" 5 L	500 T20	R 02	
13	6" " "	"	" 6 L	" "	R 02	
14	6" ELLIPS'L SPOTLIGHT	"	SPECIAL	500 T12	02	STAIR & LANDING
15	6" FRESNEL SPOTLIGHT	"	AREA 9 L	500 T20	R 02	
16	6" " "	"	" 7 L	" "	R 02	
17	6" " "	"	" 5 R	" "	R 60	
18	6" ELLIPS'L SPOTLIGHT	"	SPECIAL	500 T12	R 02	UPPER LANDING
19	6" FRESNEL SPOTLIGHT	"	"	" "	R 02	WINDOW SEAT
20	3½" ELLIPS'L SPOTLIGHT	"	"	300w TH-L	R 60	FRAME ON TROPHY
21	6" FRESNEL SPOTLIGHT	"	AREA 6 R	500 T20	R 60	
22	6" ELLIPS'L SPOTLIGHT	"	SPECIAL	500 T12	R 02	AREA 9-FRAME TO ARCH
23	6" FRESNEL SPOTLIGHT	"	"	500 T20	R 02	WINDOW SEAT
24	6" " "	"	AREA 7 R	" "	R 60	
25	6" " "	"	" 9 R	" "	R 60	
26	8" FRESNEL SPOTLIGHT	2ND PIPE	7-L BACK LT.	1000 G40	R 09	MAT OFF SCENERY TOP
27	6" " "	"	STAIR - LEFT	500 T20	R 02	" " " "
28	8" " "	"	2L BACK LT.	1000 G40	R 02	
29	8" " "	"	1R " "	1000 G40	CLEAR	
30	6" " "	"	AREA 8 L	500 T20	R 02	
31	8" " "	"	3L BACK LT.	1000 G40	R 09	
32	6" " "	"	STAIR RIGHT	500 T20	R 60	
33	6" " "	"	AREA 8 R	" "	R 60	
34	8" " "	"	2R BACK LT.	1000 G40	CLEAR	
35	8" " "	"	4L " "	" "	R 09	
36	3½" ELLIPS'L SPOTLIGHT	"	SPECIAL	300w TH-L	CLEAR	FRAME ON TROPHY
37	8" FRESNEL SPOTLIGHT	"	3R BACK LT.	1000 G40	"	
38	8" " "	"	4R " "	1000 G40	CLEAR	
39	6" " "	(4'BOOM #1	KITCHEN LT.	500 T20	"	
40	6" " "	16' " #2.	HALL+UPPER	" "	R 02	
41	6" " "	" "	LANDING	" "	R 02	
42	8" " "	SPOTLINE PIPE #2	STREET LTS.	1000 G40	R 62	
43	8" " "	"	" "	" "	R 62	
44	8" " "	"	" "	" "	R 62	
45	SPECIAL	SPOTLINE PIPE#1	PORCH LIGHT	100 w	CLEAR	
46	"	"	" "	"	"	D.S. FIXTURE IN VIEW
47	14" ELLIPS'L R. FLOOD	"	WINDOW WASH	500 PS	R 02	
48	9" " " "	HALL	WALL WASH	250 G30	R 02	
49	SPECIAL	HALL	CEILING FIXTURE	3/ 40W	CLEAR	
50	"	SR WALL	WALL FIXTURE	2/ 40W	"	
51	"	STAIR	" "	2/ 40W	"	

Instrument schedule for lighting the realistic interior without ceiling shown on page 388. (Parker, Smith, and Wolf. Courtesy Holt, Rinehart and Winston.)

a supply of lighting equipment sufficient to meet the demands of their productions. Furthermore, they typically use buildings that have permanently installed controlboards. Many Broadway theatres, as well as many road theatres, do not have permanent controlboards or lighting equipment. Consequently, when lighting designers plan productions for such theatres, they must list (with exact specifications) every item necessary for the production. This material may be rented or bought. If the production is to tour, the lighting equipment must be transportable and easily installed.

Lighting Instruments   There are several categories of lighting instruments: spotlights, striplights, floodlights, and special lighting equipment.

Spotlights are designed to illuminate restricted areas with a concentrated beam of light. They are the primary source of specific illumination. Most spotlights have a metal housing, lamp socket, reflector, lens, color-frame guide, mounting attachments, and some means of adjusting the focus. Spotlights are normally classified according to wattage, lenses, and reflectors. They range from 100 to several thousand *watts* in size, the most typical being 1000. The *lens* gathers the light from a lamp and bends it into parallel rays to create a concentrated beam. Two types of lenses—*plano-convex* and *Fresnel*—are used in spotlights. The plano-convex lens is flat on one side and convex on the other, it gives a sharp, distinct beam of light. The Fresnel lens is ridged on its convex side (it is composed of concentric rings of differing diameters) and is much thinner than the plano-convex lens; it diffuses the light somewhat to avoid the sharp edges typical with the plano-convex lens. Each spotlight is designed to use a specific type of lens and will not operate efficiently with any other. Lenses are further described in terms of *diameter* and focal length. The most common diameters are 6, 8, 10, and 12 inches. The *focal length* of a lens (also stated in inches or centimeters) indicates the distance that the filament of the lamp should be from the axis of the lens. Each spotlight is designed to use a lens of a specified diameter and focal length.

A *reflector* is placed behind or around the lamp to throw forward light that would otherwise be wasted. Thus, a reflector increases the spotlight's efficiency (the ratio of the amount of light emitted by the source and the amount of light that actually reaches the stage). Reflectors are made of metal and in various shapes, although those used in spotlights are either spherical or ellipsoidal.

Spotlights are usually divided into three categories: *Fresnel, plano-convex,* and *ellipsoidal.* The differences between the Fresnel and plano-convex spotlights result principally from their lenses, since otherwise their basic parts, including a spherical reflector, are similar. The Fresnel is the more popular of the two. The ellipsoidal spotlight may be equipped with a lens of either type; its distinctive qualities are determined by its reflector. (See the diagrams on page 394.) The ellipsoidal spotlight is by far the most efficient type. It is also the most expensive and largest. It is used primarily where the distance between the instru-

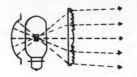

FRESNEL SPOTLIGHT

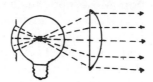

PLANO-CONVEX SPOTLIGHT

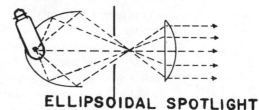

ELLIPSOIDAL SPOTLIGHT

Diagrams showing the relationship among lenses, lamps, and reflectors in three types of spotlights.

ment and the stage is great and where mounting space is not at a premium. Its major use has been to light acting areas from the auditorium.

Most spotlights have other features: *guides to hold color frames* (placed just forward of the lens); a *mounting* (usually a swivel C-clamp that allows the spotlight to be attached firmly to a pipe and be rotated from side to side or up and down); and an *adjustable-focus* device that changes the relationship among the lamp, lens, and reflector.

A less typical but simpler spotlight is also in common use. Known as the *PAR-kan,* it consists of a simple tincanlike housing without a lens but with guides for color frames; it uses a PAR lamp that has a built-in reflecting surface. Because it is relatively inexpensive, the PAR-kan is popular with groups that must operate on a very limited budget or in small theatres.

A *striplight* is a series of lamps set into a narrow rectangular trough. It is used for general illumination. As a rule, each strip is wired with four separate circuits. Every fourth lamp is on the same circuit, and may therefore be controlled together. All the lamps on the same circuit are

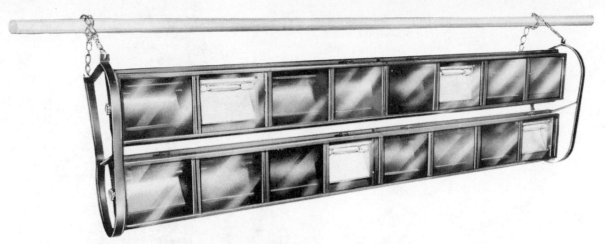

Two striplights mounted in the same frame. Each has four-color circuits and uses 300–500 watt lamps. The two striplights can be adjusted independently of each other. (Courtesy Kliegl Brothers.)

covered with filters of the same color. Thus, each strip can produce four different colors when each circuit is used alone, or it can combine circuits to produce a wide range of additional colors. Consequently, striplights can be used to "tone" (give color to) settings, costumes, and makeup. Striplights vary considerably in length—from those with only three or four lamps to those extending the entire width of the stage. Short lengths are most popular, since they may be used alone or combined with others as needed. They also vary considerably in wattage, using individual lamps ranging from 75 to 500 watts.

Striplights are often subdivided into three categories: *footlights, border-lights,* and *miscellaneous.* Footlights normally are recessed in a slot at the front (or, in thrust stages, around the edges) of the stage. They are used to erase shadows caused by any hats the actors wear or by sharp-angled overhead lighting, to enhance color, and to blend the specific and general illumination. Borderlights are hung from battens above the stage, usually in a series from front to back. They are used more often than any other instrument for blending together the acting areas and for toning the settings and costumes. Miscellaneous striplights may be placed on the floor to light ground rows and drops, and around the base of the cyclorama (as "cyc foots") to create various sky or mood effects. Small strips are often used to light backings for doors and windows.

A *floodlight,* designed to give general illumination, uses a single lamp as its source. It has a housing with a large opening; there is no lens. Most floodlights have either ellipsoidal (the most typical) or parabolic

A 16-inch floodlight, using 300–1000 watt lamps. Note the color-frame guides spaced around the opening. (Courtesy Kliegl Brothers.)

reflectors. Wattage varies from 250 to several thousand, and a frame is provided to hold color filters. Floodlights may be used singly or in combination. They may be suspended above the stage to substitute for borderlights, or, like striplights, they may be placed on the floor to light drops or ground rows, or they may be used to light backings and other scenic units. Floodlights are used most frequently to light the cyclorama (several may be used to achieve smooth, even light over the entire visible surface).

It would be difficult to specify all the special effects that are sometimes required. Perhaps the most common special equipment is the *projector*. For still pictures, 35-millimeter slide projectors are often satisfactory. Since these projectors are not designed for stage use, however, it is usually more satisfactory to use lens projectors bought or rented from lighting supply houses or made by knowledgeable stage technicians. Some projectors are designed for use with moving circular discs on which such images as clouds, waves, rain, smoke, or fire have been painted; a motor revolves the disc past the lens to create the effect of movement. Motion-picture projectors of various types may be used with filmed sequences.

Lightning effects can be produced by bringing into close proximity two carbon sticks, each attached to an electrical terminal; as the current leaps between the two, a bright light, as in welding, produces a realistic lightning effect. For *fireplaces* or *campfires,* prop logs or coals may be constructed and painted appropriately, a lamp placed inside, and light permitted to shine through holes covered with transparent orange, red, and amber material. Flames are sometimes simulated by a revolving multicolored disc in front of a light, or by irregular strips of colored silk, chiffon, or plastic kept in motion by a fan.

These common special effects may be supplemented by anyone with a knowledge of electricity and stage-lighting instruments. Additional equipment is also available from lighting supply houses.

Accessories   Several accessories—lamps, electrical cable and connectors, color frames and color media—are needed. Each instrument is designed to use a particular *lamp.* Similarly, each lamp is designed for specific purposes. Lamps vary according to type of base, filament, wattage, whether gas-filled (and if so, the kind of gas), shape, treatment of the glass, and position in which it should be used (base up or base down). Manufacturers' catalogs give complete details about lamps designed for stage use.

Electrical cable for the stage should be heavily insulated, since it must withstand much wear. It is available in a number of sizes, each designed to carry a maximum electrical load. *Connectors* (plugs) used with electrical cable differ considerably from those in household use. They are made for heavy-duty use, and most can be twisted to lock in place so they cannot be accidentally disconnected during performances.

Almost every lighting instrument is equipped for color filters. Consequently, *color frames* and *color media* are needed. A frame is usually made of metal, with an opening of the same size and shape as that of the instrument with which it is to be used. A number of color media are used in stage lighting. The most ‧common is plastic (with varying names—roscolene, cinemoid, cinabex, mylar), which is available in a wide range of hues, saturations, and intensities. It may be cut to any desired shape or size. Glass is sometimes used with striplights; it is the most durable medium, but is available in only a limited range of colors.

Connecting Panels and Controlboards   No lighting system is complete without some means of control. Instruments and color filters provide the possibilities for control, but before they can be exploited, a *controlboard* is needed. With a board, some instruments can be fully on while

Controlboard located so the operator has an unimpeded view of the stage. (Courtesy Kliegl Brothers.)

others are off or partially dimmed, and colors from several instruments can be mixed. But if a controlboard is to be efficient, a means for connecting each instrument to it must be available. This need is met by a *connecting panel* to which all stage circuits and controlboard dimmers run, thus making it possible to connect any dimmer to any stage outlet.

At its simplest, a controlboard is merely a panel of switches for turning lights on and off. But if control is to be subtle, dimmers are required. Dimmers are of many types, the most common being *resistance, autotransformer,* and *electronic.* Each works on a different principle, but each allows a gradual increase or decrease in the electrical power reaching the lamps so that they may be dimmed or brightened. (It is not within the scope of this book to explain how each type of dimmer works.) The resistance dimmer is now considered to be outmoded, although it continues to be used in some theatres. In theatres with restricted space and budgets, the autotransformer has largely supplanted the resistance dimmer. In those with sufficient space and funds, the most favored type is the electronic dimmer, especially the silicon-controlled rectifier, or SCR.

As the number of dimmers increases, so does the problem of control by an operator. If each dimmer had to be adjusted manually and individually, several persons would be required to operate a large bank of dimmers. To avoid this, all types of dimmerboards are equipped with master controls that allow some or all of the dimmers to be connected so that a single lever can operate all. An efficient controlboard allows dimmers to be connected in almost any combination.

Another problem is the size of a bank of dimmers. Many electronic units are so bulky that they must be installed in some out-of-the-way part of the building and connected with a remote-control console located near the stage. Since neither resistance nor autotransformer dimmers can be operated by remote control efficiently, they must be installed in the stage area. On the other hand, resistance and autotransformer dimmers can easily be put together in "packages" that can be moved readily and thus are useful where portability is a requirement. Although much more bulky than resistance or autotransformer units, packaged SCR dimmers have become increasingly common and will continue to do so as miniaturization of equipment progresses.

The placement of the controlboard console is of considerable importance. The most common locations are at one side of the stage, at the rear of the auditorium, or in a booth built into the face of the balcony. The ideal arrangement permits the operator to see the stage from much the same vantage as the audience.

With some controlboards, dimmers may be preset (that is, the lighting for some or all scenes may be set in advance); then, with a master dimming device, lights for one scene may be faded out and others brought up simultaneously, or changes within a scene may be set on the controlboard beforehand. The ability to preset controls eliminates many mistakes. Consequently, all major manufacturers of controlboards now offer with their SCR systems a computerized "memory bank" capable of storing several hundred cues or preset scenes. The settings for the lighting of an entire show—or for several shows—can be recorded, stored, and called up as desired.

Few aspects of theatrical production have undergone so many changes in the recent past as lighting control, perhaps because it is the one most adaptable to computerization. Lighting designers need to keep abreast of new developments, since detailed knowledge of both the range of equipment and its possible applications is required if the designer is to select wisely and work efficiently.

Curtain of light created by light rays caught in a special aerosol spray of minute, electrostatically charged oil-emulsion droplets that stay suspended in the air for a prolonged period. Part of a design by Josef Svoboda for Wagner's opera, *Tristan and Isolde*. (From *The Scenography of Josef Svoboda*. Copyright © 1971 by Jarka Burian. Reprinted by permission of Wesleyan University Press.)

Setting the Lights, Rehearsals, and Performances

Typically, the performance space is not available for work on lights until a few days prior to technical and dress rehearsals. Regardless of how much time is available, the procedures are reasonably standard. Using the light plots and instrument schedule as guides, technicians mount each instrument and direct it toward the stage area specified in the light plot. The correct color filter is added, then the instrument is plugged into the proper circuit and connected to the designated dimmer. The instruments may be focused tentatively at this time, but the final focusing must wait until the scenery is in place (and sometimes until the technical rehearsal).

Setting and focusing instruments is a time-consuming and sometimes disheartening task, for it is difficult to confine light exactly as desired. Unwanted lines, shadows, and bright areas may appear; and when the same instruments must be used to light more than one scene or setting, an ideal adjustment for one use may not be the best for another. During the process of focusing instruments, the designer usually sits in the auditorium in order to see the stage from the spectator's point of view and relays directions to the lighting crew. This process may go on for hours, sometimes for several days, until the desired results have been achieved.

Cue sheets—indicating the lighting at the beginning of each scene (the dimmer to be used and the intensity setting of each), any changes to be made during the scene, and the cues for the changes—must also be made. If there is a memory bank or other preset device, this information is fed into it. The cue sheets become the basis for controlling the lights during performances.

Lighting is integrated with the other elements for the first time during technical rehearsals. Alterations may be required, and further adjustments may be made during and after dress rehearsals. The lighting designer is often called on to compensate for problems in other aspects of production, since it is easier to adjust lights than to make a new costume or repaint a set at this point in the production process. All changes are made as quickly as possible. After the play opens, responsibility passes to the light crew.

The Lighting Designer's Employment and Assistants

In the professional theatre, lighting designers must be members of the United Scenic Artists union, as must the *assistant designer* (if there is one). The assistant may make sketches and light plots, compile instrument schedules, find the necessary equipment, act as liaison between the lighting designer and the rest of the production staff, and aid in setting up the lights and in compiling the cue sheets.

The *master electrician* or *lighting crew head* works closely with the designer when equipment is being installed and instruments adjusted. After the show opens, the master electrician (or crew head) must see that all materials are properly maintained and must check before each performance to see that everything is in working order. These technicians are directly responsible to the stage manager. In the professional theatre, master electricians must be members of the International Alliance of Theatrical Stage Employees union.

The lighting crew installs, operates, and maintains all lighting equipment and shifts electrical equipment that must be moved during scene changes. The controlboard console operator is of special importance, since this person actually controls the lighting during performances. In the professional theatre, crews must belong to the union (IATSE). In the nonprofessional theatre, crews are usually students or volunteers.

Sound

Like other theatrical elements, sound makes its greatest contributions when it is designed as a unit and carefully integrated with the production as a whole. Because, like lighting, it depends much on electronic means, it is treated here with lighting design. Sound is being increasingly recognized as an area worthy of separate recognition, especially since many theatres now amplify the actors' voices in every production, in addition to using sound effects of a more traditional sort.

Sound may be divided into three categories: *verbal* (the actors' voices), *nonverbal* (music and abstract sound), and *realistic noises* (identifiable with recognizable sources). Since the first category has already been dealt with in the chapters on directing and acting, little need be said about it here.

Sound fulfills two basic functions: it establishes *mood* and serves as *exposition*. For example, music can create an atmosphere of gaiety or somberness, just as abstract hollow noises might suggest mystery or strangeness. Realistic sounds, such as thunder and rain, are often used to set the mood for a murder, while bird sounds may suggest a quiet pastoral scene. Expository sound is usually realistic. Gunshots, crashing dishes, doorbells, telephones, and similar sounds may prepare for onstage action or indicate offstage occurrences. Certain noises are associated with times of the day or year, just as others may place the action in the country or city or near a railroad or river.

Sound may be *live* or *recorded*. Music, if recorded, is handled by the sound crew; if played live, by musicians. Since live sound is created anew at each performance, it may vary considerably from one night to the next. Its major advantage is its adaptability to the variations in performances. In recorded sound, effects are created and then transcribed on tapes or cassettes. Barring human or mechanical error, recorded sound is the same at each performance. A wide variety of effects can be obtained on commercially made tapes, but these are not always appropriate to specific plays. Since most organizations now own taping equipment, they can record their own effects. Such noises as doorbells and telephones, however, can be produced so easily with electrical buzzers that they seldom are taped.

Effective sound requires a sound system of high quality. Some groups must make do with the simplest of tape-recorder/playback units, while others have very elaborate systems. A wholly effective system allows all of the controllable factors of sound—pitch, quality, volume, direction, and duration—to be varied in relation to each other and in accordance with the demands of the production. Complete flexibility in direction, for example, requires a series of amplifiers located at various spots on the stage and in the auditorium so that a sound (such as that of an airplane) can begin on one side, seem to approach, pass overhead, and pass out of hearing on the other side.

A truly efficient sound system will include the following: several tape-recorder/playback units, so that sound may be recorded and then mixed from several tapes played simultaneously; microphones, turntables, and tape/cassette players for recording live sound and musical selections and for use during performances; a high-fidelity speaker system of excellent quality and with considerable versatility, so that sound at any volume can be reproduced faithfully without interference, and so that its direction can be controlled fully; a patch bay, so that sound sources (such as tapes and microphones) can be connected to any outlet; and a control console, so that the entire system can be operated efficiently.

Normally, the only plan for sound is the cue sheet, which indicates each sound, when it begins, how it is to build, and when it is to end. The cue sheet also specifies the method of producing the sound and, where electronic equipment is involved, the desired sound levels. If elaborate and extensive sound equipment is available, it is usual to make a chart similar to an instrument schedule for stage lighting. The chart lists each piece of equipment (with specifications) and indicates its placement, use, and control.

As with other elements, sound must be rehearsed carefully and integrated meticulously with the production as a whole. It must be adjusted relative to the stage, auditorium, and actors' voices to achieve the desired volume, direction, and duration.

Mixed or Multimedia Productions

Since the 1960s, mixed (or multi-) media productions have become common. They may combine elements from a number of media, but characteristically they intermingle live action (which may include dance) with projected still or moving pictures and stereophonic sound and music.

Several factors explain the popularity of multimedia. First, changes in

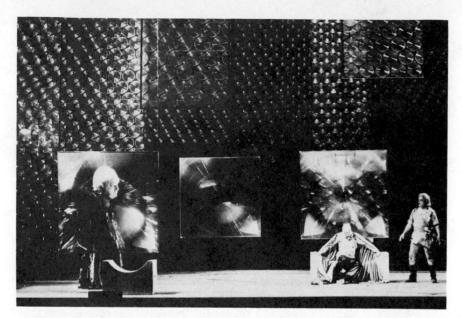

Richard Wagner's *Götterdämmerung* at the Royal Opera, Covent Garden, London. The large lenses are used to magnify features as in a film closeup. At left, an eavesdropping character is given emphasis by the lens. Note the difference in scale between this character and the unmagnified characters at right. The remainder of the setting is composed of similar lenslike surfaces. Design by Josef Svoboda. (From Jarka Burian, *Svoboda: Wagner*. Copyright © 1983 by Jarka Burian. Reprinted by permission of Wesleyan University Press.)

artistic taste and audience perception (probably influenced by film and television) demand that time, place, and focus shift rapidly and without long waits between scenes. Second, playwrights have come to assume that time and place can be altered instantaneously, and they write accordingly. Third, escalating costs have created a demand for means less expensive than full-stage, three-dimensional settings. Fourth, military and space research have brought significant advances in electronics that have been adapted for theatrical use. Fifth, the development of computers has made it possible to program many effects and to control them with great precision. For these and perhaps other reasons, settings of the traditional sort have been largely supplanted by those created with a few built pieces combined with effects created through light and sound. Thus, the stage has become technologically more complex, while stage settings have become more abstract.

A notable feature of multimedia productions has been the liberal use of projected images—often of still pictures, frequently several shown simultaneously on a number of screens. All the images may be fragments

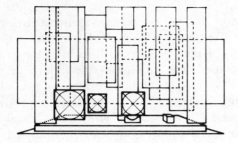

Diagram showing the arrangement of
the lenses and scenic elements for
Götterdämmerung. (From Burian, *Svoboda:
Wagner*. Copyright © 1983 by Jarka Burian.
Reprinted by permission of Wesleyan
University Press.)

of the same picture, or each may be wholly unlike the others. All are usually chosen for their appropriateness to the mood or theme of the piece; some may suggest comparisons between the dramatic events and those of other times and places. For example, a production of Shakespeare's *Troilus and Cressida*—which takes place during the Trojan War— might project images of wars in various periods and places, thereby suggesting the similarity of all wars. Filmed sequences may also be used in various ways. Footage of real events may be used to supply a context for a play's action; or filmed sequences using the play's actors might be interjected to give greater scope to the action; or filmed sequences and live sequences may be coordinated. Closed-circuit television can be used to project onto large screens close-ups of the actors' faces, portions of the action, or even the audience itself. Projections (whatever the type) are often accompanied by stereophonic, directional sound or music.

In these and other ways, multimedia productions have enlarged the range of theatrical means and probably will continue to do so as new technology is developed and adapted to stage use.

Looking at Stage Lighting

Stage lighting is among the most difficult production elements to evaluate, since it usually attracts attention, not to itself, but to the actors, scenery, costumes, or directing. Unless we have difficulty seeing, are distracted by shadows on the actors' faces, are annoyed by glare, or are fascinated by some beautiful or spectacular lighting effect, we probably do not think about the lighting. Yet, light is clearly an essential production element both artistically and for the sake of visibility. Therefore, our understanding of any theatrical production can be enhanced by examining the lighting choices and their effects. Here are some questions that may contribute to a fuller understanding of stage lighting.

1. In what type of space was the production staged (proscenium, arena, thrust, flexible)? How did this affect the use of lighting?
2. How did the lighting relate to that suggested in the script? If it departed from the script, were the changes dictated by the production concept? What overall approach governed the lighting? Did it suggest recognizable sources (sun, moon, lamps, etc.) or a specific time of day, period, or place? If so, how? With what effect? Was the lighting arbitrary? Was it dictated by stylistic or interpretational considerations? If so, what was the result? Were there any unusual lighting effects? Did the lighting call attention to itself at any point? If so, how? with what results?
3. How did lighting affect (or help to create) mood and atmosphere? Did mood and atmosphere change? If so, how? with what results?
4. What was the dominant level of brightness (intensity)? Did it vary from scene to scene? If so, were the variations related to the action?
5. What was the dominant color (or colors) of the light? Did color vary from scene to scene? How did color relate to the action, mood, and overall interpretation? How did it affect scenery and costumes? If color was not used, what was the effect?
6. How was light distributed on the stage (evenly, acting areas/background, some areas isolated by light, etc.)? Did it emphasize (or de-emphasize) shape and mass? Was direction other than frontlighting (downlighting, backlighting, crosslighting) evident? with what effect?
7. Did the lights change? If so, frequently? What motivated the changes? How did the changes enhance (or fail to enhance) the mood, action, or production concept?

8. Were there special effects? If so, which? How were they handled? with what results?

9. How did the lighting enhance or fail to enhance the acting, scenery, costumes, and makeup? Was it adequately unified with all the other elements? Was there sufficient variety? Did lighting underscore the development of the action? Was it used to build climaxes? If so, how?

10. Overall, how did lighting contribute (or fail to contribute) to the production concept and the total production?

The relevance of each of these questions may vary with the particular production and play. Furthermore, some of these questions may not be answerable with any degree of specificity because there is not adequate information or because the lighting cannot be sufficiently isolated from other production elements or the total context. Nevertheless, attempting to answer some or all of these questions can make us look more closely at lighting and lead us to appreciate more fully its contributions to theatrical production.

Afterword

We have now looked at the theatre from several angles: the basic characteristics of theatre as entertainment and as an art form; approaches to evaluating performances; how plays are written and structured; ways in which the theatrical experience has varied in the past and how it continues to change in the present; how each of the theatre arts functions today and how all are meshed to create the performances we see in the theatre. Taken altogether, these explorations provide a solid foundation for a fuller understanding and appreciation of the theatre.

But a foundation is just that—something to build on rather than a finished structure. What one chooses to do with the foundation is as important as the foundation itself. It can be left to decay and be forgotten, or it can be a basis for future growth. Whether your understanding, appreciation, and love of the theatre will continue to develop depends upon whether you attend theatre often and enjoy the experience. Let us hope that what you have learned has stimulated in you an ongoing craving for the theatrical experience.

Appendix
Opportunities to Work
in the Theatre

 **T**here are probably more producing groups in the United States today than ever before. Therefore, the avenues open for theatrical talent are numerous, although a large proportion do not provide a living wage. The professional theatre can absorb relatively few of those who seek employment. Fortunately, there are other rewarding possibilities in community theatre, education, and elsewhere.

Theatre as an Avocation

Most students who receive theatrical training in colleges do not enter the theatre after graduation. To most, theatre is a means for acquiring a liberal education, just as English, philosophy, or history might be. Nevertheless, after graduation, many do continue to participate avocationally in theatre. The opportunities for working in the theatre as an avocation are many, since most theatrical organizations rely upon unpaid personnel. The demand for actors is great, and almost anyone with an interest in scenery, costumes, lighting, properties, makeup, sound, dance, or music can find ample opportunities to express it.

Theatre in Education

Perhaps the largest number of paying theatre jobs are in education. As a rule, theatre workers are employed in schools for two purposes: to teach and to produce plays. Sometimes it is possible to specialize in directing, costuming, lighting, or some other area, but to be assured of

Urashimo Taro, a children's play, written and directed by Coleman Jennings. Costumes by Paul Reinhardt. (Courtesy Department of Drama, University of Texas.)

employment one should be prepared to undertake almost any assignment.

The educational theatre may be divided into levels: *children's theatre*, *secondary-school theatre*, and *college and university theatre*.

Children's Theatre   Children's theatre may operate within three frameworks: professional, community, or educational. Its distinguishing characteristic is its intended audience.

A related area is creative dramatics, although technically it is not a theatrical activity. Children are stimulated to improvise dramatic situations based on stories, historical events, or social situations. Creative dramatics is used to help children feel their way into fictional and real-life situations, to make learning more concrete, to allow children an outlet for their responses and feelings, and to stimulate imagination. Thus, it is an educational and developmental tool rather than a product intended for an audience. Normally, creative dramatics is handled by the classroom teacher, who should have specialized training in its techniques.

Theatre as such is seldom taught in elementary schools. Children are instead offered plays through a variety of channels. The recreation program in most large cities includes children's theatre; many community theatres, high schools, colleges, and universities produce plays for children; and several professional organizations specialize in plays for children.

There is a fairly large demand for persons with some training in children's theatre and creative dramatics. Some colleges and universities employ specialists in these areas; school districts may hire a person who can demonstrate and supervise creative dramatics; some community theatres employ a director whose sole responsibility is the production of children's plays; public recreation programs often employ a specialist in this area. In addition, some professional troupes perform only for child audiences.

Workers in children's theatre need the same basic training required by any other theatre worker. In addition, they should receive some specialized instruction in child and developmental psychology and in the specific techniques of children's theatre.

Secondary School Theatre   Almost every high school in the United States produces one or more plays each year. Still, many do not offer courses in theatre and drama, and plays sometimes are directed by persons with no theatre training at all. On the other hand, some secondary schools have excellent theatre programs.

The teacher in the secondary school should understand the adolescent and usually must be certified to teach subjects other than theatre, such as speech and English.

Undergraduate Colleges and Universities   Most colleges and universities in the United States offer some coursework in theatre. In most cases, theatre courses are included in the liberal arts curriculum, but the production program is extracurricular.

Teachers in a liberal arts college may have a chance to specialize in such areas as directing or design, but often they must teach and supervise several areas of production. Undergraduate programs that offer the BFA degree in theatre usually admit students only after auditions and interviews have established the students' talent and commitment. Since these programs are usually oriented to the professional theatre or additional training at the graduate level, instructors should set high standards through their own work.

Graduate Schools   The graduate school is designed to give specialized training. It requires a staff of experienced specialists, and employment is usually available only to those who have demonstrated considerable ability in specific aspects of the theatre. The graduate school is crucial to the theatre, for most practitioners now receive their basic training in colleges and universities, and graduate schools supply most of the teachers.

University Resident Theatres   Some colleges and universities support resident theatre companies. Many of these companies are made up of students; some mingle students and professionals, and a few are wholly professional. Most typically, each group produces plays of many types and from many periods.

The majority of each company is made up of actors, but a director, a few technicians, and sometimes a designer are usually included. Each year companies belonging to the University/Resident Theatre Association (U/RTA) hold joint auditions for admissions to the companies and/ or to graduate training programs. The number of students from each school who can try out is limited. Companies using only professional actors usually select them through auditions conducted in New York or a few other locations.

The Community Theatre

Almost every town with a population of more than thirty thousand has a community theatre. Many of these theatres are operated entirely by volunteers; others pay the director of each play and may provide a small sum for the designer and other key workers. Most typically, a community theatre employs a full-time director who supervises all productions. The more prosperous groups also have a full-time designer-technician, and some hire a children's theatre director as well.

Because of their purpose, community theatres usually do not hire persons other than in supervisory capacities. The primary function of community theatre—in addition to providing theatrical entertainment for local audiences—is to furnish an outlet for the talents of adult volunteers.

Those who seek employment in the community theatre, therefore, need to be leaders. They should be diplomatic, able to cooperate with diverse personalities, and know a great deal about public relations.

Summer Theatres

Summer theatres are numerous and scattered throughout the country. They usually perform from June until September. There is much variety in summer theatre. Some groups present a different play each week or every two weeks; during the run of a show, one or more additional scripts are usually being rehearsed. Some companies perform a single work for the entire summer. Some specialize in plays by a single author, such as Shakespeare. Some perform only musicals. Still others employ only a nucleus company and import well-known motion-picture, television, or stage actors to play leading roles. Occasionally, summer theatres try out new plays.

There are many kinds of summer companies. Some are entirely professional and hire only professional actors, designers, and directors. Others mingle professionals and nonprofessionals. (Actors Equity classifies companies according to the number of professional actors employed, minimum salaries, and working conditions.) Companies employing professional actors may hire designers and directors who are not union members. Some summer theatres are operated by educational institutions and give college credit for participation.

Many summer theatres have apprenticeship programs. Apprentices may receive room and board and even a small weekly salary; seldom is the pay more than enough for living expenses. Some organizations ask apprentices to pay a fee, but this practice is generally frowned upon.

Most hiring for professional and semiprofessional summer theatres is done in New York and a few large cities. Summer theatres run by colleges may hold auditions on campus. In any case, summer theatre only provides seasonal employment.

Nonprofit Professional Companies

There are now more than 200 nonprofit professional theatres in the United States. Most belong to the Theatre Communications Group (TCG), whose office in New York is a major clearinghouse for information about job openings and opportunities in the theatres affiliated with it. These nonprofit theatres include companies outside of New York as well as many Off Broadway and Off-Off Broadway theatres in New York.

Nonprofit theatres are divided into categories according to their budgets and working conditions. Actors Equity Association controls the contracts for actors throughout the country. It prescribes the percentage of actors in each company who must be Equity members and sets minimum wage scales.

Nonprofit companies obtain their personnel in various ways. Most employ an artistic director and managing director on long-term contracts. Other staff (including designers, technicians, publicity directors, and box-office managers) work on a continuing basis. Such personnel are usually hired on the evidence of portfolios, interviews, recommen-

Patrick Meyers' *K2*, in which the action takes place on the icy face of the world's second highest mountain. The setting, essentially vertical, was made primarily of Styrofoam. Setting by Ming Cho Lee. Lighting by Allen Lee Hughes. (Photo by Martha Swope.)

dations, and demonstrated aptitude or achievement. Actors are frequently hired for a single production, although some may remain on for subsequent shows. Smaller companies, as well as large companies in sizable population centers, may hire many of their actors locally, but most still do most of their hiring on the basis of auditions held in New York. Some companies will audition applicants from colleges and universities, but usually only those who have been carefully screened in advance.

Overall, there are now more persons employed in nonprofit professional companies than in Broadway's theatres.

Broadway

The jobs most difficult to get are those on Broadway, not only because opportunities are few but because of union control. Some of these conditions apply elsewhere than Broadway, but seldom so fully.

Directors   The director is employed by the producer. The director must be a member of the Society of Stage Directors and Choreographers, which has worked out standard contracts to specify the director's rights and working conditions.

Actors   Actors (including dancers and singers) must belong to Actors Equity Association. Performers may be cast without being a member of Equity, but must join before they can be given a contract.

Actors Equity requires producers to devote a minimum number of hours to open interviews or auditions for each show. This screening may be done by an assistant, and few of the applicants may actually be permitted to try out. Many actors obtain auditions through agents, and others are invited by the producer to try out.

Stage Managers   Stage managers must also belong to Actors Equity. Most begin as performers and for extra pay take on the job of assistant stage manager; a large show usually has several assistant stage managers. If they are reliable, they may subsequently be employed as principal stage manager. After the show opens, the stage manager may rehearse the cast as needed. Thus, directing experience may be a considerable asset to the would-be stage manager.

Designers   The designers are employed by the producer. All must belong to the United Scenic Artists Union, the most difficult of all stage unions to gain admission to. Applicants must pay an examination fee and, if they pass the rigorous exam, a sizable initiation fee. This union also controls design in television, films, opera, and ballet. Designers may be admitted to the union as a scenic, costume, or lighting designer, or they may qualify in two or all of these areas. All contracts must meet the union's minimum requirements. Many younger members of the union work as assistants to well-established designers.

Scenery, Costume, Lighting, and Property Crews   Members of the various crews that run shows must belong to the International Alliance of Theatrical Stage Employees. Crews are very carefully separated, so that no one will perform more than one function. This union restricts admission to make sure most of its members will be employed. Acceptance depends as much on knowing the right persons as on training.

Others   Each production must have a company manager and a press agent, who work directly with the producer. The manager aids in letting contracts, arranges for rehearsal space and out-of-town tryouts, and handles the payroll. The press agent is concerned principally with selling the show. Both must be members of the Association of Theatrical Press Agents and Managers.

Any theatrical worker may have an agent, whose job it is to market the client's services. An agent can be crucial in getting a hearing for clients, who might otherwise never be able to display their talents. For these services, an agent is paid a percentage of the client's earnings on each contract negotiated. Agents customarily must be approved by the client's union.

The number of job opportunities in New York is very small in relation to those seeking employment. Usually, fewer than one-fourth of the members of Actors Equity are employed at one time; fewer than twenty-five designers in each of the fields of scenery, costume, and lighting design all the shows seen on Broadway each year; and a few directors direct all the shows. Most work on no more than one show each season.

Many people do their best to discourage would-be professionals from going to New York, but nothing can keep many from doing so. It has become common, nevertheless, for aspirants to look to theatres beyond Broadway, both in and outside New York as alternatives.

Special Employment Opportunities

In addition to the more obvious opportunities discussed, related activities should be mentioned. First, television and motion pictures offer additional opportunities. It has become increasingly common for actors to move from the theatre into television and film. Without these additional possibilities, many professionals would lead a difficult life, indeed. But these supplementary fields have their own unemployment problems, and they merely relieve some of the pressures.

Second, some industrial and commercial firms stage special shows to publicize their products. Frequently, these productions are lavish, and some tour major cities. These shows normally play for invited audiences only; they pay extremely well but provide little further recognition. Most are cast in New York.

Third, the United States Army employs a large number of civilian specialists to stage plays and other entertainment. Many of the positions also offer the opportunity of living and working abroad.

Fourth, many municipal recreation departments employ persons trained in theatre. To be eligible, one must usually have had some training in the field of health, physical education, and recreation.

Fifth, theatre for the aging seems to be emerging as a field. As the average age of retirement is lowered and as life expectancy increases, the potential of this field should expand.

Sixth, theatre by and for the handicapped is a growing field. As awareness has grown of the special problems of the handicapped, theatre has also been adapted to serve the needs of this group.

Seventh, theatrical techniques have been adapted for nontheatrical uses. For example, they are now used therapeutically with emotionally disturbed persons. To work in such a field, sound training in psychology as well as in drama and theatre is needed.

When the variety of theatrical activities—in both the nonprofessional and professional theatre—is considered, the employment opportunities are considerable. There are by no means as many jobs as there are applicants, especially in the professional theatre, but the theatre has never been an easy profession. Still, there is always a demand for talented and dedicated persons, and the future of the theatre depends on these select few.

Bibliography

This bibliography lists some of the many important books on theatre. The divisions correspond to those in the text. All works are in English.

Part One

1

The Nature of Theatre

Brook, Peter. *The Empty Space.* New York: Avon Books, 1969.

Cole, David. *The Theatrical Event: A Mythos, A Vocabulary, A Perspective.* Middletown, CT: Wesleyan University Press, 1975.

Granville-Barker, Harley. *The Uses of Drama.* Princeton, NJ: Princeton University Press, 1945.

Lahr, John, and Price, Jonathan. *Life-show: How to See Theatre in Life and Life in Theatre.* New York: Viking Press, 1973.

Styan, J. L. *Drama, Stage and Audience.* New York: Cambridge University Press, 1975.

Turner, Victor. *From Ritual to Theatre: The Human Seriousness of Play.* New York: Performing Arts Journal Publications, 1982.

Wickham, Glynne. *Drama in a World of Science.* Toronto: University of Toronto Press, 1962.

2

Performance, Audience, and Critic

Cole, David. See under Chapter 1.

Esslin, Martin. *An Anatomy of Drama.* New York: Hill & Wang, 1976.

Kauffmann, Stanley. *Theatre Criticisms.* New York: Performing Arts Journal Publications, 1984.

Lahr, John, and Price, Jonathan. See under Chapter 1.

Littlewood, Samuel R. *The Art of Dramatic Criticism.* London: Pitman, 1952.

Sontag, Susan. *Against Interpretation and Other Essays.* New York: Doubleday & Co., 1966.

Styan, J. L. See under Chapter 1.

3

The Script and the Playwright

Barry, Jackson G. *Dramatic Structure: The Shaping of Experience*. Berkeley: University of California Press, 1970.

Beckerman, Bernard. *Dynamics of Drama: Theory and Method of Analysis*. New York: Alfred A. Knopf, 1970.

Cole, Toby. *Playwrights on Playwriting*. New York: Hill & Wang, 1961.

Grote, David. *Script Analysis*. Belmont, CA: Wadsworth, 1985.

Hayman, Ronald. *How To Read a Play*. New York: Grove Press, 1977.

Heffner, Hubert. *The Nature of Drama*. Boston: Houghton Mifflin, 1959.

Heilman, Robert B. *Tragedy and Melodrama: Versions of Experience*. Seattle: University of Washington Press, 1968.

Kerr, Walter. *Tragedy and Comedy*. New York: Simon & Schuster, 1967.

Olson, Elder. *The Theory of Comedy*. Bloomington: Indiana University Press, 1968.

————. *Tragedy and the Theory of Drama*. Detroit: Wayne State University Press, 1961.

Smiley, Sam. *Playwriting: The Structure of Action*. Englewood Cliffs, NJ: Prentice-Hall, 1971.

Styan, J. L. *The Elements of Drama*. New York: Cambridge University Press, 1960.

Weales, Gerald. *A Play and Its Parts*. New York: Basic Books, 1964.

Part Two

General Works Applicable to Part Two

Brockett, Oscar G. *History of Theatre*, 5th ed. Boston: Allyn & Bacon, 1987.

Carlson, Marvin. *Theories of the Theatre: A Historical and Critical Survey, from the Greeks to the Present*. Ithaca, NY: Cornell University Press, 1984.

Duerr, Edwin. *The Length and Depth of Acting*. New York: Holt, Rinehart and Winston, 1962.

Encyclopedia of World Theater. New York: Charles Scribner's Sons, 1977.

Izenour, George C. *Theatre Design*. New York: McGraw-Hill, 1977.

Laver, James. *Drama: Its Costume and Decor*. London: Studio Publications, 1951.

Leacroft, Richard and Helen. *Theatre and Playhouse: An Illustrated Survey of Theatre Building from Ancient Greece to the Present Day*. London: Methuen & Co., 1984.

McGraw-Hill Encyclopedia of World Drama. 4 vols. New York: McGraw-Hill, 1972.

Nicoll, Allardyce. *World Drama from Aeschylus to Anouilh*, rev. ed. London: George G. Harrap & Co., 1976.

Oenslager, Donald. *Stage Design: Four Centuries of Scenic Invention*. New York: Viking Press, 1975.

Oxford Companion to the Theatre, 4th ed. London: Oxford University Press, 1983.

Southern, Richard. *The Seven Ages of the Theatre*. New York: Hill & Wang, 1961.

4

The Greek and Roman Theatrical Experiences

Arnott, Peter D. *Greek Scenic Conventions in the Fifth Century*, B.C. Oxford: Clarendon Press, 1962.

————. *The Ancient Greek and Roman Theatre*. New York: Random House, 1971.

Beare, William. *The Roman Stage: A Short History of Latin Drama in the Time of the Republic*, 3d ed. London: Methuen & Co., 1963.

Bieber, Margarete. *The History of the Greek and Roman Theater*, 2d ed. Princeton, NJ: Princeton University Press, 1961.

Butler, James H. *The Theatre and Drama of Greece and Rome*. San Francisco: Chandler Publishing Co., 1972.

Deardon, C. W. *The Stage of Aristophanes*. London: Athlone Press, 1976.

Duckworth, George E. *The Nature of Roman Comedy*. Princeton, NJ: Princeton University Press, 1952.

Harsh, Philip W. *A Handbook of Classical Drama*. Stanford, CA: Stanford University Press, 1944.

Hunter, R. L. *The New Comedy of Greece and Rome*. New York: Twayne Publishers, 1985.

Kitto, H. D. F. *Greek Tragedy*, 2d ed. London: Methuen & Co., 1950.

Pickard-Cambridge, A. W. *The Dramatic Festivals of Athens*. 2d ed. rev. by John Gould and D. M. Lewis. Oxford: Clarendon Press, 1968.

Segal, Erich W. *Roman Laughter: The Comedy of Plautus*. Cambridge, MA: Harvard University Press, 1968.

Webster, T. B. L. *Greek Theatre Production*, 2d ed. London: Methuen & Co., 1970.

5

The Theatre Experiences of Medieval England and Japan

Bevington, David. *From Mankind to Marlowe: Growth in Structure in the Popular Drama of Tudor England*. Cambridge, MA: Harvard University Press, 1962.

Chambers, E. K. *The Mediaeval Stage*. 2 vols. Oxford: Clarendon Press, 1903.

Collins, Fletcher. *The Production of Medieval Church Music-Drama*. Charlotte: University of Virginia Press, 1971.

Craik, Thomas W. *Revels History of Drama in English*. Vol. 2: 1500–1576. New York: Barnes & Noble, 1980.

———. *The Tudor Interlude: Stage, Costume, and Acting*. Leicester: University of Leicester Press, 1958.

Inoura, Yoshinobu, and Kawatake, Toshio. *The Traditional Theatre of Japan*. New York: John Weatherhill, 1981.

Keene, Donald. *Bunraku: The Art of the Japanese Puppet Theatre*. Tokyo: Kodansha International, 1965.

———. *No: The Classical Theatre of Japan*. Tokyo: Kodansha International, 1966.

Kolve, V.A. *The Play Called Corpus Christi*. Stanford, CA.: Stanford University Press, 1966.

Komparu, Kunio. *The Noh Theater: Principles and Perspectives*. New York: John Weatherhill, 1983.

Leiter, Samuel L. *The Art of Kabuki: Plays in Performance*. Berkeley: University of California Press, 1979.

Nagler, A. M. *The Medieval Religious Stage: Shapes and Phantoms*. New Haven, CT: Yale University Press, 1976.

Nakamura, Yasuo. *Noh: The Classical Theater*. New York: John Weatherhill, 1971.

Nelson, Alan H. *The Medieval English Stage: Corpus Christi Pageants and Plays*. Chicago: University of Chicago Press, 1974.

Nicoll, Allardyce. *Masks, Mimes and Miracles*. New York: Harcourt Brace Jovanovich, Inc., 1931.

Potter, Robert. *The English Morality Play: Origins, History and Influence of a Dramatic Tradition*. London: Routledge and Kegan Paul, 1975.

Salter, F. M. *Medieval Drama in Chester*. Toronto: University of Toronto Press, 1955.

Wickham, Glynne. *Early English Stages, 1300–1660.* 3 vols. New York: Columbia University Press, 1959–1979.

Williams, Arnold. *The Drama of Medieval England.* East Lansing: Michigan State University Press, 1961.

6

The Theatre Experiences of Elizabethan England and Seventeenth-Century France

Adams, John C. *The Globe Playhouse: Its Design and Equipment,* 2d ed. New York: Barnes & Noble, 1961.

Barroll, J. L., et al. *Revels History of Drama in English.* Vol. 3: 1576–1613. New York: Barnes & Noble, 1975.

Beckerman, Bernard. *Shakespeare at the Globe, 1599–1609.* New York: Macmillan Co., 1962.

Bentley, Gerald E. *The Profession of Dramatist in Shakespeare's Time, 1590–1642.* Princeton, NJ: Princeton University Press, 1971.

————. *The Profession of Player in Shakespeare's Time, 1590–1642.* Princeton, NJ: Princeton University Press, 1984.

Bjurstrom, Per. *Giacomo Torelli and Baroque Stage Design.* Stockholm: Almqvist and Wiksell, 1961.

Harbage, Alfred. *Shakespeare's Audience.* New York: Columbia University Press, 1941.

Hewitt, Barnard (ed.). *The Renaissance Stage: Documents of Serlio, Sabbattini, and Furttenbach.* Coral Gables, FL: University of Miami Press, 1958.

Kernodle, George. *From Art to Theatre: Form and Convention in the Renaissance.* Chicago: University of Chicago Press, 1943.

Lawrenson, T. E. *The French Stage in the XVIIth Century: A Study in the Advent of the Italian Order.* Manchester: Manchester University Press, 1957.

Lough, John. *Paris Theatre Audiences in the Seventeenth and Eighteenth Centuries.* London: Oxford University Press, 1957.

McBride, Robert. *Aspects of 17th-Century French Drama and Thought.* Totowa, NJ: Rowman & Littlefield, 1980.

Nagler, A. M. *Shakespeare's Stage,* enlarged ed. New Haven, CT: Yale University Press, 1981.

Orrell, John. *The Quest for Shakespeare's Globe.* New York: Cambridge University Press, 1983.

Reynolds, George F. *The Staging of Elizabethan Plays at the Red Bull Theatre, 1605–1625.* New York: Modern Language Association, 1940.

Turnell, Martin. *The Classical Moment: Studies in Corneille, Molière and Racine.* New York: New Directions, 1948.

White, John. *The Birth and Rebirth of Pictorial Space,* 2d ed. London: Faber & Faber, 1967.

Wickham, Glynne. See under chapter 5.

Wiley, W. L. *The Early Public Theatre in France.* Cambridge, MA: Harvard University Press, 1960.

Worsthorne, S. T. *Venetian Opera in the 17th Century.* Oxford: Clarendon Press, 1954.

Wright, C. H. C. *French Classicism.* Cambridge, MA: Harvard University Press, 1920.

7
Popular Theatre Experiences: Commedia dell'Arte and Melodrama

Baur-Heinhold, Margarete. *The Baroque Theatre*. New York: McGraw-Hill, 1967.

Birdoff, Harry. *The World's Greatest Hit: "Uncle Tom's Cabin."* New York: S. F. Vanni, 1947.

Bogard, Travis, et al. *Revels History of Drama in English*. Vol. 8: American Drama. New York: Barnes & Noble, 1977.

Booth, Michael R. *English Melodrama*. London: Herbert Jenkins, 1965.

Booth, Michael, et al. *Revels History of Drama in English*. Vol. 6: 1750–1880. New York: Barnes & Noble, 1975.

Cross, Gilbert. *Next Week "East Lynne": Domestic Drama in Performance, 1820–1874*. Lewisburg, PA: Bucknell University Press, 1976.

Donohue, Joseph W. *Theatre in the Age of Kean*. Oxford: Blackwell, 1975.

Duchartre, Pierre L. *The Italian Comedy: The Improvisation, Scenarios, Lives, Attributes, Portraits and Masks of the Illustrious Characters of the Commedia dell'Arte*. Trans. by R. T. Weaver. London: Harrap & Co., 1929.

Goldoni, Carlo. *Memoirs of Carlo Goldoni*. Trans. by John Black. New York: Alfred A. Knopf, 1926.

Gozzi, Carlo. *The Memoirs of Count Carlo Gozzi*. Trans. by J. A. Symonds. 2 vols. London: J. C. Nimmo, 1890.

Joseph, Bertram. *The Tragic Actor*. New York: Theatre Arts Books, 1959.

Lea, Kathleen M. *Italian Popular Comedy: A Study of the Commedia dell'Arte, 1560–1620*. 2 vols. Oxford: Clarendon Press, 1934.

Mammen, Edward W. *The Old Stock Company School of Acting*. Boston: The Public Library, 1945.

Melcher, Edith. *Stage Realism in France from Diderot to Antoine*. Bryn Mawr, PA: Bryn Mawr College, 1928.

Moynet, Jean-Pierre. *French Theatrical Production in the Nineteenth Century*. Binghamton, NY: Max Reinhardt Foundation, 1976.

Nicoll, Allardyce. See under chapter 5.

Odell, G. C. D. *Shakespeare from Betterton to Irving*. 2 vols. New York: Charles Scribner's Sons, 1920.

Oreglia, G. *The Commedia dell'Arte*. New York: Hill & Wang, 1968.

Price, Cecil. *Theatre in the Age of Garrick*. Oxford: Blackwell, 1973.

Quinn, Arthur H. *A History of the American Drama from the Beginning to the Civil War*, 2d ed. New York: Appleton-Century-Crofts, 1943.

———. *A History of the American Drama from the Civil War to the Present Day*, 2d ed. New York: Appleton-Century-Crofts, 1949.

Rowell, George. *The Victorian Theatre*. London: Oxford University Press, 1956.

Schwartz, Isidore A. *The Commedia dell'Arte and Its Influence on French Comedy in the Seventeenth Century*. Paris: H. Samuel, 1933.

Smith, Winifred. *The Commedia dell'Arte*. New York: Columbia University Press, 1912.

Southern, Richard, *Changeable Scenery: Its Origin and Development in the British Theatre*. London: Faber & Faber, 1952.

Vardac, A. N. *Stage to Screen: Theatrical Method from Garrick to Griffith*. Cambridge, MA: Harvard University Press, 1949.

Watson, Ernest B. *Sheridan to Robertson: A Study of the Nineteenth Century London Stage*. Cambridge, MA: Harvard University Press, 1926.

8

The Modernist Temperament

Antoine, André. *Memories of the Théâtre Libre.* Trans. by Marvin Carlson. Coral Gables, FL: University of Miami Press, 1964.

Appia, Adolphe. *The Work of Living Art and Man Is the Measure of All Things.* Coral Gables, FL: University of Miami Press, 1960.

Bablet, Denis. *Edward Gordon Craig.* New York: Theatre Arts Books, 1967.

Bentley, Eric. *The Playwright as Thinker: A Study of Drama in Modern Times.* New York: Reynal & Co., 1946.

Brockett, Oscar G., and Findlay, Robert R. *Century of Innovation: A History of European and American Theatre and Drama since 1870.* Englewood Cliffs, NJ: Prentice-Hall, 1973.

Brustein, Robert. *The Theatre of Revolt: An Approach to Modern Drama.* Boston: Little, Brown and Co., 1964.

Carter, Huntly. *The Theatre of Max Reinhardt.* New York: Benjamin Blom, 1964.

Carter, Lawson A. *Zola and the Theatre.* New Haven, CT: Yale University Press, 1963.

Cornell, Kenneth. *The Symbolist Movement.* New Haven, CT: Yale University Press, 1951.

Craig, Edward Gordon. *On The Art of the Theatre,* 2d ed. Boston: Small, Maynard, 1924.

Garten, H. F. *Modern German Drama.* New York: Essential Books, 1959.

Gorelik, Mordecai. *New Theatres for Old.* New York: Samuel French, 1940.

Koller, Ann Marie. *The Theatre Duke: Georg II of Saxe-Meiningen and the German Stage.* Stanford, CA: Stanford University Press, 1984.

Matlaw, Myron. *Modern World Drama: An Encyclopedia.* New York: E. P. Dutton, 1972.

Patterson, Michael. *The Revolution in German Theatre, 1900–1933.* London: Routledge and Kegan Paul, 1981.

Rischbeiter, Henning. *Art and the Stage in the 20th Century.* Greenwich, CT: New York Graphic Society, 1968.

Roose-Evans, James. *Experimental Theatre: From Stanislavsky to Peter Brook,* new rev. ed. London: Studio Vista, 1984.

Slonim, Marc. *Russian Theatre from the Empire to the Soviets.* Cleveland: World Publishing Co., 1961.

Stein, Jack M. *Richard Wagner and the Synthesis of the Arts.* Detroit: Wayne State University Press, 1960.

Valency, Maurice. *The Flower and the Castle: An Introduction to Modern Drama.* New York: Grosset & Dunlap, 1963.

Volbach, Walther. *Adolphe Appia, Prophet of the Modern Theatre.* Middletown, CT: Wesleyan University Press, 1968.

Waxman, S. M. *Antoine and the Théâtre Libre.* Cambridge, MA: Harvard University Press, 1926.

Willett, John. *Expressionism.* New York: McGraw-Hill, 1970.

9

From Epic Theatre to Absurdism

Artaud, Antonin. *The Theatre and Its Double.* Trans. by Mary C. Richards. New York: Grove Press, 1958.

Brecht, Bertolt. *Brecht on Theatre*. Trans. by John Willett. New York: Hill & Wang, 1965.

Brockett, Oscar G., and Findlay, Robert R. See under Chapter 8.

Brustein, Robert. See under Chapter 8.

Clurman, Harold. *The Fervent Years: The Story of the Group Theatre in the Thirties*. New York: Hill & Wang, 1957.

Davis, Hallie Flanagan. *Arena*. New York: Duell, Sloane and Pearce, 1940.

Downer, Alan S. *Fifty Years of American Drama, 1900–1950*. Chicago: Regnery/ Gateway, 1951.

Esslin, Martin. *The Theatre of the Absurd*, rev. ed. New York: Doubleday & Co., 1969.

Garten, H. F. See under Chapter 8.

Gorelik, Mordecai. See under Chapter 8.

Gottfried, Martin. *Broadway Musicals*. New York: Harry N. Abrams, 1979.

Greene, Naomi. *Antonin Artaud: Poet without Words*. New York: Simon & Schuster, 1970.

Matlaw, Myron. See under Chapter 8.

Patterson, Michael. See under Chapter 8.

Rischbeiter, Henning. See under Chapter 8.

Roose-Evans, James, See under Chapter 8.

Smith, Cecil. *Musical Comedy in America*. New York: Theatre Arts Books, 1950.

Strasberg, Lee. *Strasberg at the Actors Studio*. New York: Viking Press, 1965.

Styan, J. L. *Modern Drama in Theory and Practice*. 3 vols. New York: Cambridge University Press, 1981.

Willett, John. *The Theatre of Bertolt Brecht*. New York: New Directions, 1959.

10

The Contemporary Theatre Experience

Abramson, Doris E. *Negro Playwrights in the American Theatre*. New York: Columbia University Press, 1969.

Ansorge, Peter. *Disrupting the Spectacle: Five Years of Experimental and Fringe Theatre in Britain*. London: Pitman, 1975.

Beauman, Sally. *The Royal Shakespeare Company*. New York: Oxford University Press, 1982.

Berkowitz, Gerald M. *New Broadways: Theatre Across America, 1950–1980*. Totowa, N.J.: Rowman & Littlefield, 1982.

Biner, Pierre. *The Living Theatre*, 2d ed. New York: Horizon Press, 1972.

Boardman, Gerald. *American Musical Comedy: From Adonis to Dreamgirls*. New York: Oxford University Press, 1982.

Brockett, Oscar G., and Findlay, Robert R. See under Chapter 8.

Brook, Peter. See under Chapter 1.

Brustein, Robert. *Revolution as Theatre: Notes on the New Radical Style*. New York: Liveright, 1971.

Burian, Jarka. *The Scenography of Josef Svoboda*. Middletown, CT: Wesleyan University Press, 1971.

Byrd Hoffman Foundation. *Robert Wilson: Theatre of Images*. New York: Byrd Hoffman Foundation, 1984.

Cohn, Ruby. *New American Dramatists, 1960–1980*. New York: Grove Press, 1982.

Cook, Judith. *The National Theatre*. London: George G. Harrop & Co., 1976.

Croyden, Margaret. *Lunatics, Lovers and Poets: The Contemporary Experimental Theatre.* New York: McGraw-Hill, 1974.

Findlater, Richard. *Twenty-five Years of the English Stage Company.* London: Methuen & Co., 1981.

Grotowski, Jerzy. *Towards a Poor Theatre.* New York: Simon & Schuster, 1968.

Hill, Errol (ed.). *The Theatre of Black Americans.* 2 vols. Englewood Cliffs, NJ: Prentice-Hall, 1980.

Hinchliffe, Arnold. *British Theatre, 1950–1970.* Totowa, NJ: Rowman & Littlefield, 1975.

Itzin, Catherine. *Stages in the Revolution: Political Theatre in Britain since 1968.* New York: Methuen & Co., 1981.

Kerensky, Oleg. *The New British Drama: Fourteen Playwrights Since Osborne and Pinter.* New York: Taplinger, 1979.

Kirby, Michael, *Happenings.* New York: E. P. Dutton, 1965.

Kostelanetz, Richard. *The Theatre of Mixed Means.* New York: Dial Press, 1968.

Little, Stuart. *Enter Joseph Papp: In Search of a New American Theatre.* New York: Coward, McCann and Geoghegan, Inc., 1974.

Marowitz, Charles, and Trussler, Simon. *Theatre at Work: Playwrights and Productions in the Modern British Theatre.* New York: Hill & Wang, 1967.

Marranca, Bonnie. *The Theatre of Images* [Robert Wilson, Richard Foreman, Lee Breuer]. New York: Drama Book Specialists, 1977.

Matlaw, Myron. See under Chapter 8.

Neff, Renfreu. *The Living Theatre USA.* Indianapolis: Bobbs-Merrill, 1970.

O'Connor, Garry. *French Theatre Today.* London: Pitman, 1975.

Pasolli, Robert. *A Book on the Open Theatre.* Indianapolis: Bobbs-Merrill, 1970.

Patterson, Michael. *German Theatre Today.* London: Pitman, 1976.

Rischbeiter, Henning. See under Chapter 8.

Roose-Evans, James. See under Chapter 8.

Savran, David. *The Wooster Group.* Ann Arbor, MI: UMI Research Press, 1986.

Shank, Theodore. *American Alternative Theatre.* New York: Grove Press, 1982.

Weales, Gerald. *The Jumping Off Place: American Drama in the 1960s.* New York: Macmillan, 1969.

Ziegler, Joseph. *Regional Theatre: The Revolutionary Stage.* Minneapolis: University of Minnesota Press, 1973.

Part Three

11

Theatrical Space and Production Design

American Theatre Planning Board. *Theatre Check List: A Guide to the Planning and Construction of Proscenium and Open Stage Theatres.* Middletown, CT: Wesleyan University Press, 1969.

Burris-Meyer, Harold, and Cole, Edward C. *Theatres and Auditoriums,* 2d ed. with supplement. Huntington, NY: Robert E. Krieger Publishing Co., 1975.

Cogswell, Margaret (ed.) *The Ideal Theater: Eight Concepts.* New York: American Federation of Arts, 1962.

Green, Peter Arthur. *Design Education: Problem Solving and Visual Experience.* London: Batsford, 1974.

Izenour, George C. *Theatre Design.* New York: McGraw-Hill, 1977.

Jones, Robert E. *The Dramatic Imagination.* New York: Meredith Publishing Co., 1941.

Joseph, Stephen. *New Theatre Forms.* New York: Theatre Arts Books, 1968.

Maier, Manfred. *Basic Principles of Design.* New York: Van Nostrand Reinhold, 1977.

Malcolm, Dorothea C. *Design: Elements and Principles.* Worcester, MA: Davis Publications, 1972.

Mielziner, Jo. *Shapes of Our Theatres.* New York: Clarkson N. Potter, 1970.

Schubert, Hannelore. *Modern Theatre Buildings: Architecture, Stage Design, Lighting.* New York: Praeger Publishers, 1971.

Scott, Robert G. *Design Fundamentals.* New York: McGraw-Hill, 1951.

Sommer, Robert. *Design Awareness.* San Francisco: Rinehart Press, 1972.

12

Producing and Directing

Ball, William. *A Sense of Direction: Some Observations on the Art of Directing.* New York: Drama Book Publishers, 1984.

Benedetti, Robert. *The Director at Work.* Englewood Cliffs, NJ: Prentice-Hall, 1985.

Braun, Edward. *The Director and the Stage: From Naturalism to Grotowski.* New York: Holmes and Meier, 1982.

Brook, Peter. See under Chapter 1.

Clurman, Harold. *On Directing.* New York: Macmillan, 1972.

Cohen, Robert, and Harrop, John. *Creative Play Direction.* Englewood Cliffs, NJ: Prentice-Hall, 1974.

Cole, Toby, and Chinoy, Helen K. (eds.) *Directors on Directing,* rev. ed. Indianapolis: Bobbs-Merrill, 1963.

David, Christopher. *The Producers.* New York: Harper & Row, 1972.

Dean, Alexander. *Fundamentals of Play Directing,* 3d ed., rev. by Lawrence Carra. New York: Holt, Rinehart and Winston, 1974.

Farber, Donald C. *From Option to Opening: A Guide for the Off-Broadway Producer,* rev. 3d ed. New York: Drama Book Publishers, 1977.

————. *Producing on Broadway.* New York: Drama Book Publishers, 1969.

Hodge, Francis. *Play Directing: Analysis, Communication, and Style,* 2d ed. Englewood Cliffs, NJ: Prentice-Hall, 1982.

Langley, Stephen. *Producers on Producing.* New York: Drama Book Publishers, 1976.

————. *Theatre Management in America, Principles and Practice; Producing for Commercial, Stock, Resident, College and Community Theatre.* New York: Drama Book Publishers, 1974.

Newman, Danny. *Subscribe Now!* New York: ACA Books, 1984.

Reiss, Alvin. *The Arts Management Handbook,* rev. ed. New York: Law-Arts Publishers, Inc., 1973.

Shagan, Rena. *The Road Show: A Handbook for Successful Booking and Touring in the Performing Arts.* New York: ACA Books, 1984.

Shaw, George Bernard. *The Art of Rehearsal.* New York: Samuel French, 1928.

Staub, August. *Creating Theatre: The Art of Theatrical Directing.* New York: Harper & Row, 1973.

Wills, J. Robert (ed.). *The Director in a Changing Theatre.* Palo Alto, CA: Mayfield Publishing Co., 1976.

13

Acting

Benedetti, Robert L. *The Actor at Work,* 4th ed. Englewood Cliffs, NJ: Prentice-Hall, 1986.

Berry, Cicely. *Voice and the Actor.* New York: Macmillan, 1974.

Chaikin, Joseph. *The Presence of the Actor: Notes on the Open Theatre, Disguises, Acting and Repression.* New York: Atheneum Publishers, 1972.

Cohen, Robert. *Acting Professionally,* 3d ed. Palo Alto, CA: Mayfield Publishing Co., 1981.

Cole, Toby, and Chinoy, Helen K. (eds.). *Actors on Acting: The Theories, Techniques, and Practices of the Great Actors of All Time as Told in Their Own Words.* New York: Crown Publishers, 1949.

Hagen, Uta. *Respect for Acting.* New York: Macmillan, 1973.

Harrop, John, and Epstein, Sabin. *Acting with Style.* Englewood Cliffs, NJ: Prentice-Hall, 1982.

King, Nancy. *Theatre Movement: The Actor and His Space.* New York: Drama Book Publishers, 1971.

Kuritz, Paul. *Playing: An Introduction to Acting.* Englewood Cliffs, NJ: Prentice-Hall, 1982.

Lessac, Arthur. *The Use and Training of the Human Voice.* New York: Drama Book Publishers, 1967.

Lewis, Robert. *Advice to the Players.* New York: Harper & Row, 1980.

McGaw, Charles J. *Acting Is Believing,* 2d ed. New York: Holt, Rinehart and Winston, 1966.

Machlin, Evangeline. *Speech for the Stage.* New York: Theatre Arts Books, 1966.

Spolin, Viola. *Improvisation for the Theatre.* Evanston, IL: Northwestern University Press, 1963.

Stanislavsky, Constantin. *An Actor Prepares.* Trans. by Elizabeth Reynolds Hapgood. New York: Theatre Arts Books, 1936.

―――. *Building a Character.* Trans. by Elizabeth Reynolds Hapgood. New York: Theatre Arts Books, 1949.

―――. *Creating a Role.* Trans. by Elizabeth Reynolds Hapgood. New York: Theatre Arts Books, 1961.

Turner, J. Clifford. *Voice and Speech in the Theatre,* 3d ed., rev. by Malcolm Morrison. New York: Drama Book Publishers, 1977.

14

Scenic Design

Aronson, Arnold. *American Set Design.* New York: Theatre Communications Group, 1985.

Bablet, Denis. *Stage Design in the Twentieth Century.* New York: Leon Amiel, 1976.

Bay, Howard. *Stage Design.* New York: Drama Book Publishers, 1974.

Bellman, Willard F. *Scenography and Stage Technology: An Introduction.* New York: Harper & Row, 1977.

Burdick, Elizabeth B., et al. (eds.). *Contemporary Stage Design.* Middletown, CT: Wesleyan University Press, 1975.

Burris-Meyer, Harold, and Cole, Edward C. *Scenery for the Theatre,* 2d rev. ed. Boston: Little, Brown and Co., 1972.

Corey, Irene. *The Mask of Reality: An Approach to Design for the Theatre.* Anchorage, KY: Anchorage Press, 1968.

Jones, Robert Edmond. *The Dramatic Imagination.* New York: Meredith Publishing Co., 1941.

Larson, Orville K. (ed.). *Scene Design for Stage and Screen: Readings on the Aesthetics and Methodology of Scene Design for Drama, Opera, Musical Comedy, Ballet, Motion Pictures, Television and Arena Theatre.* East Lansing: Michigan State University Press, 1961.

Mielziner, Jo. *Designing for the Theatre.* New York: Atheneum Publishers, 1965.

Oenslager, Donald. *Scenery Then and Now.* New York: W. W. Norton & Company, 1936.

Parker, W. Oren, Smith, Harvey K, and Wolf, R. Craig. *Scene Design and Stage Lighting,* 5th ed. New York: Holt, Rinehart and Winston, 1985.

Pecktal, Lynn, *Designing and Painting for the Theatre.* New York: Holt, Rinehart and Winston, 1975.

15

Costume Design and Makeup

Anderson, Barbara and Cletus. *Costume Design.* New York: Holt, Rinehart and Winston, 1984.

Barton, Lucy. *Historic Costume for the Stage.* Boston: Baker's Plays, 1935.

Corey, Irene. See under Chapter 14.

Corson, Richard. *Stage Make-up,* 5th ed. Englewood Cliffs, NJ: Prentice-Hall, 1975.

Emery, Joy S. *Stage Costume Techniques.* Englewood Cliffs, NJ: Prentice-Hall, 1981.

Ingham, Rosemary and Covey, Liz. *The Costume Designer's Handbook: A Complete Guide for Amateur and Professional Costume Designers.* Englewood Cliffs, NJ: Prentice-Hall, 1983.

Jones, Robert E. See under Chapter 14.

Motley. *Designing and Making Stage Costumes.* London: Studio Vista, 1964.

Payne, Blanche. *History of Costume from the Ancient Egyptians to the Twentieth Century.* New York: Harper & Row, 1965.

Prisk, Berneice. *Stage Costume Handbook.* New York: Harper & Row, 1966.

Russell, Douglas. *Costume History and Style.* Englewood Cliffs, NJ: Prentice-Hall, 1983.

————. *Stage Costume Design: Theory, Technique and Style,* 2d ed. Englewood Cliffs, NJ: Prentice Hall, 1985.

Smith, C. Ray (ed.). *The Theatre Crafts Book of Make-up, Masks, and Wigs.* Emmaus, PA: Rodale Press, 1974.

16

Lighting Design, Sound, and Multimedia

Bellman, Willard F. *Lighting the Stage: Art and Practice,* 2d ed. San Francisco: Chandler Publishing Co., 1974.

————. *Scenography and Stage Technology.* See under Chapter 14.

Bergman, Gosta M. *Lighting in the Theatre.* Totowa, NJ: Rowman & Littlefield, 1977.

Burian, Jarka. See under Chapter 10.

Collision, David. *Stage Sound.* New York: Drama Book Publishers, 1982.

Jones, Robert E. See under chapter 14.

Jones, Tom Douglas. *The Art of Light and Color.* New York: Van Nostrand Reinhold, 1973.

McCandless, Stanley R. *A Method of Lighting the Stage,* 4th ed. New York: Theatre Arts Books, 1958.

Palmer, Richard H. *The Lighting Art: The Aesthetics of Stage Lighting Design.* Englewood Cliffs, NJ: Prentice-Hall, 1985.

Parker, W. Oren, Smith, Harvey K., and Wolf, R. Craig. See under Chapter 14.

Rosenthal, Jean, and Wertenbaker, Lael. *The Magic of Light.* New York: Theatre Arts Books, 1972.

Warfel, William B., and Klappert, Walter R. *Color Science for Lighting the Stage.* New Haven, CT: Yale University Press, 1981.

Index

STUDENT QUESTIONNAIRE

In preparing the fifth edition of *The Essential Theatre*, we would appreciate your evaluation of the present edition. Please return this questionnaire to the Theatre Editor, College Division, Holt, Rinehart and Winston, 111 Fifth Avenue, New York, NY 10003. Thank you!!

Name _____

School _____

Course title _____

Instructor's name _____

Other required texts _____

1. In comparison to other theatre textbooks, the reading level of *The Essential Theatre* was:

   _____ too difficult   _____ just right

   _____ too easy

2. Did *The Essential Theatre* succeed in clarifying the roles of the various professionals involved in a play production? Can you give us an example or two?

   _____

   _____

   _____

3. Are there any topics covered in your course not covered in *The Essential Theatre?* What topics would you like added to this book?

   _____

   _____

   _____

4. Please rate each chapter on a scale of 1 to 6.

	Liked Least	Liked Best	Not Assigned

PART I. FOUNDATIONS

1. The Nature of Theatre   1   2   3   4   5   6   ____

2. Performance, Audience, and Critic   1   2   3   4   5   6   ____

3. The Script and the Playwright   1   2   3   4   5   6   ____

PART II. VARIETIES OF THEATRICAL EXPERIENCE

4. The Greek and Roman Theatre Experiences   1   2   3   4   5   6   ____

5. The Theatre Experiences of Medieval England and Japan   1   2   3   4   5   6   ____

6. The Theatre Experiences of Elizabethan England and Seventeenth-Century France   1   2   3   4   5   6   ____

7. Popular Theatre Experiences: Commedia dell'Arte and Melodrama   1   2   3   4   5   6   ____

8. The Modernist Temperament   1   2   3   4   5   6   ____

9. From Epic Theatre to Absurdism   1   2   3   4   5   6   ____

10. The Contemporary Theatre Experience   1   2   3   4   5   6   ____

PART III. THEATRICAL PRODUCTION

11. Theatrical Space and Production Design   1   2   3   4   5   6   ____

12. Producing and Directing	1 2 3 4 5 6	_____
13. Acting	1 2 3 4 5 6	_____
14. Scenic Design	1 2 3 4 5 6	_____
15. Costume Design and Makeup	1 2 3 4 5 6	_____
16. Lighting Design, Sound, and Multimedia	1 2 3 4 5 6	_____
Appendix: Opportunities to Work in the Theatre	1 2 3 4 5 6	_____

5. Do any chapters need more explanation, examples, or photos? Which chapters and why? _____

_____

6. Did the end-of-chapter questions help you in analyzing a live play performance? If so, how?

_____

_____

7. Did you read the Appendix? How helpful was it? _____

_____

_____

8. Will you keep this book for your library? _____

9. Please write additional suggestions, criticisms, or comments about *The Essential Theatre?*